For Karen

Robert A Mayers
April 14, 2019

ALSO BY ROBERT A. MAYERS

The Forgotten Revolution—When History Forgets—Critical Places of the American Revolution that have been Neglected by History

The Portrait of an American Family

The War Man—The Story of a Soldier who Fought from Quebec to Yorktown

SEARCHING FOR YANKEE DOODLE

Searching for YANKEE DOODLE

Washington's Soldiers in the American Revolution

ROBERT A. MAYERS

Staunton Virginia

Staunton, Virginia
(888) 521-1789
Visit us on the Internet at:
www.Americanhistorypress.com

First Printing June 2016

Image preparation, cover, and text layout by Gordon Bond Designs
www.GordonBondDesigns.com

Library of Congress Cataloging-in-Publication Data

Names: Mayers, Robert A. (Robert Adrian), 1930- author.
Title: Searching for Yankee Doodle : Washington's soldiers in the American Revolution / Robert A. Mayers.
Other titles: Washington's soldiers in the American Revolution
Description: Staunton, Virginia : American History Press, [2016] | Includes bibliographical references and index.
Identifiers: LCCN 2016025279 | ISBN 9781939995155 (hardcover : alk. paper)
Subjects: LCSH: United States--History--Revolution, 1775-1783--American forces. | United States. Continental Army--Military life. | Soldiers--United States--History--18th century. | United States. Continental Army--History. | United States--Militia--History--18th century.
Classification: LCC E255 .M39 2016 | DDC 973.3--dc23 LC record available at https://lccn.loc.gov/2016025279

Printed in the United States of America on acid-free paper.
This book meets all ANSI standards for archival quality.

DEDICATION

In memory of all American fighting men who followed in the footsteps and shared the traditions of the Yankee Doodles—the "Billy Yanks," "Doughboys," "Grunts," "GIs," and all the common soldiers that took up arms to safeguard our great nation and make possible all that followed—and especially those who did not return, or were shunned when they came home.

Table of Contents

Preface

George Washington's common soldiers—the men of the Continental Army—were mainly responsible for achieving America's independence by winning the Revolutionary War. But who exactly were these participants of the American Revolution, and what inspired them to endure such appalling hardships during this most critical time in American history?

Nearly every adult male in the American colonies played some role in the struggle for independence. Reading their words and tracking their actions day to day brings the soldiers to life, and allows us to experience their emotions. Fortunately, intimate details of these veterans' lives can now be found in archived documents and obscure works located in comprehensive public collections, as well as in sources available on the Internet.

Yet, there are few dedicated studies devoted to unraveling the lives of the "grunts," "doughboys" or "GIs" of our most important war. Various writers have instead concentrated on battles, commanding officers, and regional distinctions of these soldiers. During the more than two centuries that have elapsed since the end of the Revolution, historians have found it a daunting challenge to expose the attitudes and behavior of these valiant warriors. What was lacking was an effort to salvage and bring together information from the pathos of that war.

Historians have offered vastly different opinions concerning the true nature of the most essential element of the War for Independence—the common foot soldier. For most of America's history, little was known about the identity of these men, their motivations for fighting, and how the war affected their lives. A handful of these soldiers were identified by their exploits in battle, but most only appear as another name on lists of thousands of soldiers compiled by each state.

During the two decades following the Revolutionary War, Americans regarded it as a people's war waged by a virtuous citizenry, a conflict in which everyone participated. It was thought that the Continental Army played a peripheral role. At that time the public also feared that a standing army might either usurp power or become a costly burden. As a result, when the war ended, the glorious Continental Army was completely disbanded. Returning veterans were neither honored nor rewarded, and were virtually disregarded.

To this day, the Yankee Doodles still remain elusive figures who appear briefly in military records and then quickly vanish.

Thirty-five years after the war, during a spell of fervent patriotism, and at a rare time of treasury surplus, there was an outpouring of sympathy for the plight of aging soldiers, and they were finally rewarded. In 1818 Congress approved a plan that provided a modest pension for Continental Army veterans. Unfortunately, the nationalistic exuberance of that time had the effect of sanitizing the image of the common soldier, and for more than two hundred years Americans cherished the golden myth of the zealously patriotic citizen-soldier.

This illusion portrayed the fighting men of the Revolution as yeoman farmers and part-time combatants. They responded to immediate threats from British invaders by snatching their muskets from the mantel and joining their neighbors in a rush to defend their homes and families. Afterwards, they returned to plowing their fields and awaiting the next alarm.

While this romanticized stereotype was often true during the first six months of the war at places such as Lexington, Concord and Bunker Hill, it did not accurately depict the common foot soldiers of the Continental Army, the men who continued to fight for all eight years of the war. This deceptive image of Washington's soldiers was only recently challenged. But the new image that emerges is that of a mercenary, motivated by personal economic concerns. Which of these versions is the true Yankee Doodle?

The present work explores and evaluates these diverse conceptions by sketching a fresh portrait of the foot soldiers of the American Revolution. An examination of their motivations, personal lives and experiences before, during, and after the war reveals a compelling story. The Continental Army did indeed allow soldiers the opportunity to combine self-interest with commitment to their country but, in fact, there was a more complex combination of motives which encouraged soldiers to enlist.

Personal details of the lives of the foot soldiers are revealed in original military documents, their service records and personal papers. Diaries and pension applications tell the story in their own words. New insights are gained from the neglected eyewitness accounts of British and German participants. While part-time citizen-soldiers—the militiamen—were the most numerous troops, the focus of this work is on the Continental Army, the standing force of regular full-time soldiers that were the heart of America's armed forces.

There are justifiable reasons why the image of the common soldier of the American Revolution remains obscure in history. Few personal accounts of enlisted soldiers have survived from the American Revolution. Most of their diaries cover only brief time spans. Others are vague, repetitive or questionable as sources of meaningful information. Even though many of these soldiers were literate, few significant journals of common soldiers exist today. I believe a personal quote means more to the reader than all the secondhand information that can be found in archives, rare manuscript collections and academic search engines, so I have sourced these whenever possible.

Oral history must have poured from veterans in the decades that followed the war. Husbands, fathers, sons and brothers, as well as their wives, recounted the greatest adventure of their lives in vivid detail to all who would listen. However, later generations remembered fewer details, and as the years passed most eyewitness narratives were entirely lost and forgotten forever.

Enlistment terms were typically only for a few months during the first year of the war, but were extended to much longer periods after that time. This changed the composition of the entire army considerably over eight years, and remains an obstacle in describing the common soldier.

The men of the Continental Army remained in harm's way for long periods. Food and clothing were insufficient, and their infrequent pay was devalued by rampant inflation. Unsanitary conditions in camps led to raging health epidemics. Soldiers endured harsh corporal punishment for petty infractions, and ambiguous terms of recruitment were used to prolong their enlistments. They were beset by the same fear, homesickness and stress experienced by soldiers of all wars. Post-traumatic stress disorder, battle fatigue, shell shock and other war-related illnesses were not understood or officially recognized.

Of the men under arms in the War for Independence, more than 25,500 either perished in battle, while incarcerated as prisoners, or from various diseases. More than 8,000 others survived serious wounds, and nearly 1,500 simply disappeared. Nearly one out of five soldiers were killed, wounded, or missing in action, which amounts to about one of every three men of the Continental Army. By comparison, the Union Army in the Civil War sustained about 13 percent casualties. While the image of common Revolutionary War soldiers has been difficult to define in the centuries since the war, I hope this work will help us better understand these valiant men and remind us that we will remain forever in their debt.

Posterity! You will never know how much it cost the present generation to preserve your freedom. I hope you will make good use of it.

—John Adams to his wife Abigail Adams, April 26, 1777

Chapter One

Hearts Touched by Fire

The Birth of the Continental Army

What really decided the outcome of the American Revolution? Historians have attributed American success to political influences, geography, logistics, French assistance and British blundering. In the end, though, it was the Continental Army, a force of regular full-time soldiers, which was directly responsible for achieving the nation's independence. The common soldiers of America's standing army did a large amount of the fighting, and in the process they suffered casualty rates between 30 and 40 percent, a comparatively larger number than the average of 13 percent among Union troops during the Civil War. The privates of the Revolutionary War faced a much greater challenge than is commonly believed, and in the process suffered huge wartime losses.

The Continental Army overcame daunting challenges along the way. As the Revolutionary War was drawing to a close, General George Washington confided to trusted colleague Major General Nathanael Greene that he doubted future generations would believe that the British forces had been beaten by the ragged American Army, and not by other circumstances. The Americans were a smaller force, sometimes suffering from starvation, and often clothed in rags. They were rarely paid for their services, and experienced every kind of misery of which humans are capable.

The new nation was created by these men in the ranks. Original military documents and diaries are filled with illustrations of common soldiers whose lives were punctuated by heroism, courage and endurance. Our histories reveal little about these personal deeds, and provide few eyewitness accounts of George Washington's common soldiers. But their pension applications are a unique oral history that was dictated or written without revision. Beginning thirty-five years after the war, they provide many narratives of wartime experiences. Some of the aging veterans, without any proof of service other than their memories, produced literary masterpieces with vivid descriptions of great historic value. Thousands of these pension applications from the eighteenth century are on file at the National Archives, and they provide much of the content of this work.

In the third week of July, 1775, seventy-three eager young men and boys converged in the hamlet of Clarkstown, New York. They had journeyed many miles from the surrounding countryside and from adjoining states in order to enlist in the fledgling Continental Army, which had been created only a month earlier. The majority of recruits who were joining the 10th Company, 3rd New York Regiment of Foot were farmers and laborers in their early twenties. The eldest was Simon Trump, age forty-eight, a German-born carpenter. The youngest, John Conelio, was only ten years old. Several had trades or skills, and others were more educated, such as Robert Frayer, a schoolmaster.[1] Twelve had even been born in other countries.

Since weapons were scarce, some of these potential soldiers brought along their well-worn family muskets, so that they could earn a ten shilling bounty. Ultimately, after only two weeks of perfunctory drilling on the town green with no time to harden into the rigors of army life, this collection of men began trudging north on a forced march covering over three hundred miles. The majority started out barefoot, without weapons or uniforms. This became the colonies' first offensive campaign, the Invasion of Canada.

During the next two months one third of these men would desert, while others would fall sick along the way. In the end, only twenty-seven soldiers from the group that had enlisted in Clarkstown survived to feel their first sting of combat after twelve weeks in the army. On October 9 these fresh soldiers charged through a hail of grapeshot and cannon fire in an assault on a heavily-defended British fort just below Montreal. A few somehow managed to remain alive to storm the walls of Quebec City eleven weeks later, only to fall when they and their fellow survivors were annihilated by a raging snowstorm.

In 1775, the first year of the Revolutionary War, the scene at Clarkstown was witnessed again and again throughout the American colonies. What inspired these men to put their lives on hold in order to join their countrymen and rush into combat? Their chief motivation was the astonishing news of the events which had occurred in Lexington and Concord, Massachusetts, which swiftly reached every rural hamlet throughout the settlements. Americans were amazed that unorganized and untrained New England farmers, called up on short notice, had lined country roads to entrap 1,800 British regulars who had been sent on a punitive expedition to destroy military stores. By the end of April, 1775, this feat had inspired more than 10,000 enthusiastic Patriots to gather outside Boston in a combined effort to besiege the city, the headquarters of the British expeditionary forces in America.

By June, Fort Ticonderoga, a formidable and strategic British bastion on the invasion route to Canada, had fallen without a fight. It was overrun by the Green Mountain Boys, a brash, loosely organized band of Vermont backwoodsmen headed by Ethan Allen. In the same month the British regulars, largely regarded as the best trained and most disciplined army in the world, lost 2,500 men (40 percent of its force) when they fell to gunfire while attempting a massed frontal assault on Breed's Hill, an amazing feat we now recall as the Battle of Bunker Hill.

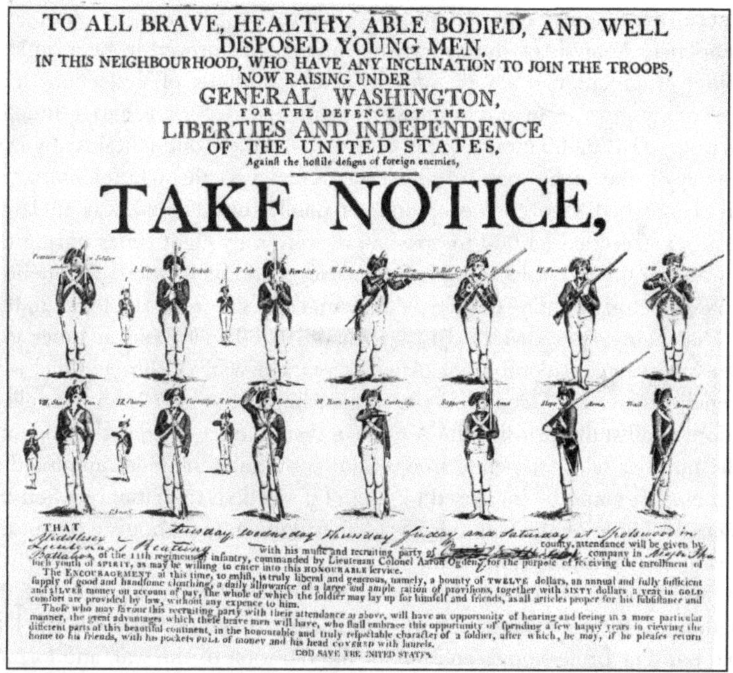

TO ALL BRAVE, HEALTHY, ABLE BODIED, AND WELL DISPOSED YOUNG MEN,
IN THIS NEIGHBOURHOOD, WHO HAVE ANY INCLINATION TO JOIN THE TROOPS, NOW RAISING UNDER
GENERAL WASHINGTON,
FOR THE DEFENCE OF THE
LIBERTIES AND INDEPENDENCE
OF THE UNITED STATES,
Againſt the hoſtile deſigns of foreign enemies,

TAKE NOTICE,

THAT county, attendance will be given by with his muſic and recruiting party of company in of the 11th regiment of infantry, commanded by Lieutenant Colonel Aaron Ogden, for the purpoſe of receiving the enrollment of ſuch youth of SPIRIT, as may be willing to enter into this HONOURABLE ſervice.

The ENCOURAGEMENT at this time, to enliſt, is truly liberal and generous, namely, a bounty of TWELVE dollars, an annual and fully ſufficient ſupply of good and handſome cloathing, a daily allowance of a large and ample ration of proviſions, together with SIXTY dollars a year in GOLD and SILVER money on account of pay, the whole of which the ſoldier may lay up for himſelf and friends, as all articles proper for his ſubſiſtance and comfort are provided by law, without any expence to him.

Thoſe who may favour this recruiting party with their attendance as above, will have an opportunity of hearing and ſeeing in a more particular manner, the great advantages which theſe brave men will have, who ſhall embrace this opportunity of ſpending a few happy years in viewing the different parts of this beautiful continent, in the honourable and truly reſpectable character of a ſoldier, after which, he may, if he pleaſes return home to his friends, with his pockets FULL of money and his head COVERED with laurels.

GOD SAVE THE UNITED STATES.

Benjamin Jones's engraving of a soldier performing the manual exercise, as it appeared in a 1798 edition of Baron von Steuben's *Regulations for the Order and Discipline of the Troops of the United States.* (Courtesy of the American Antiquarian Society)

Throughout the colonies, young men were inspired by these daring accomplishments, and a large part of the population became swept up in a patriotic fervor which later became known as the *rage militaire*. Recruiting efforts were tremendously successful and companies, each averaging sixty men, filled their quotas within a few weeks. Many men brought their own weapons, and in return some received five dollars and an issue of clothing; others did without uniforms or weapons for several weeks. The year 1775 was a glorious time for the cause of independence, but the patriotic fervor was on its way to dying out. Bitter defeats and failures would soon put an end to the earlier optimistic viewpoint, and the once-zealous Patriots, with their short six-month enlistments now expired, headed home.

ADMIRED CAUSE - UNPOPULAR ARMY

There were between two-and-a-half and three million people living in the colonies at the onset of the Revolutionary War. Excluding women, the aged, the young, slaves, pacifist Quakers and Loyalists, an estimated 200,000 to 250,000 men performed some type of military service in support of American independence. Analysis of their surviving military has proved to be a difficult task, since fragmentary data is scattered over hundreds of collections, and contains many short-term and duplicate enlistments. Historians have estimated that as many as 120,000 men actually bore arms in the Continental Army over the course of the eight years of the war.[2] Known as the Continentals, this regular army, which George Washington personally commanded, was not large, and it never exceeded 24,000 troops. There were only eight times during the entire war that the monthly strength figures exceeded 20,000 men. Throughout 1779, Washington's fighting force typically ranged in size from 10,000 to 20,000 men. That figure later dwindled to less than 10,000 men, and at times that number was even considerably less. After six years of war, Washington met with the French Lieutenant General Comte de Rochambeau in 1781 to plan allied operations against the British. The American commander estimated at the time that the number of Continental troops who could take the field amounted to 8,250 men, but could be increased to 10,250 if needed. In actuality, when the final decisive battle of the war, the Siege of Yorktown, was about to begin, the American army numbered less than 5,000 troops.[3]

It has been calculated that less than 15,000 men, a mere 1 percent of the population of the new nation, were longer-term Continental soldiers. This intrepid band of professionals enlisted for the duration of the war, and formed the foundation of the American army. Since they had enlisted for the entire war, they became known as the *War Men*. Although many had not understood the terms of their recruitment, and had therefore anticipated being released earlier, they willingly and loyally continued to soldier on until hostilities were ended.

Washington placed special value on these dedicated professional soldiers, believing that these combat-hardened men exemplified the fighting spirit of the American Revolution. He proudly oversaw them as they developed personal pride and *espirit de corps*, and matured into competent and disciplined soldiers. These War Men often served as non-commissioned officers in the elite units of light infantry that comprised the special forces of the day, and their skills in combat eventually grew to match any fighting force in the world.

When the war ended in 1783 and the troops were disbanding at New Windsor, New York, Washington acknowledged the thousands of War Men who had remained with him during the worst of times. He described them as ". . . those gallant and persevering men who resolved to defend the rights of their invaded country so long as the war should continue. For these are the men who ought to be considered as the pride and boast of the American Army . . . ."[4]

Volunteers became insufficient to fill the ranks as the war slowly ground on. In 1778, the Continental Congress recommended that the states draft men from their local militias for one year's service in the Continental Army. The states then resorted to providing enlistment bounties in the form of land, but this enticement met with limited success. These properties were located in the remote western wilderness, which was known to be populated by hostile Native American tribes. Some states tried to entice with up-front cash bounties, but this attracted some of the more marginal members of society, who frequently deserted or reapplied to collect again elsewhere.

DISPERSE YOU REBELS! - THORNY OBSTACLES FOR A FLEDGLING ARMY

The rebelling colonies that sponsored the Continental Army were both politically and culturally divided. About a third of the American people openly supported an uprising against the mother country, and another third remained openly loyal to Great Britain. The remainder were either neutral, were in disagreement with the objectives of the rebellion. Many changed sides for economic advantage, or had a slippery loyalty based on whether their neighborhood was or was not occupied by opposing forces.

The colonies were without a strong centralized government to unify operations, and had no stable currency for financing a war. Initially they lacked both an army and navy. Since the economy was primarily agricultural, it produced enough food, provisions, forage, wagons, horses, and oxen to support an army, but lacked an adequate transportation system to distribute provisions to a scattered fighting force. The small number of manufacturing facilities that did exist could not produce enough muskets, cannon or supplies to wage war against a superpower. As a result, it quickly became evident that imports would have to provide the bulk of the ordnance, medical supplies, and clothing that the Continental Army would require.

Possibly the greatest challenge for this loose confederation was that the Whig leaders—the people who had inspired the movement for independence and who held positions of leadership—never trusted the army. They feared that a trained professional standing force, filled with men from the lower classes who had no stake in society, would lead to tyranny and eventually become an onerous financial burden when peacetime resumed. The majority of American political leaders persistently clung to the notion of a militia, a band composed of patriotic land-owning citizen-soldiers who would fight locally. As proof of their conviction they offered the impressive record of accomplishments that armed civilians had achieved at Lexington, Concord, Ticonderoga and Bunker Hill. The Whig leadership maintained that a new standing army would attain power as it became an effective fighting force, and would certainly strike back against the government if it were not adequately supported.

Washington appointed Commander-in-Chief (Library of Congress Prints and Photographs Division, Washington, D.C.)

What is surprising is that the army itself did not allow resentment from lack of public support to stand in the way of its valiant performance. The military carried on in spite of the fact that many Americans vociferously professed to be steadfastly committed to a war for independence, but were only willing to provide token economic backing for the effort. Despite these impediments, Washington's small Continental Army remained the mainstay in persisting in the fight for America's freedom.

By the end of 1775 the patriotic fervor of the *rage militaire* had faded away, and voluntary enlistment of dedicated land-owning citizen-soldiers had waned. When the terms of their enlistments expired at the end of the year, many men simply returned to their homes. These early Minutemen, while effective, were not the force that would serve through the difficult years ahead; the Continental Army would take up this role.

As the war became prolonged, the colonies were eventually divided into seven military departments. When Washington, the newly appointed Commander-in-Chief, designated Major General Philip Schuyler as head of a separate army in June, 1775, he designated the command as the Northern

Department. In late February, 1776, Congress formally established two other military departments—the Middle Department included Delaware, Maryland, New Jersey, New York, and Pennsylvania, and the Southern Department embraced the Carolinas, Georgia, and Virginia. Four other departments were ultimately formed before the end of hostilities.

When armed conflict erupted at Lexington and Concord on April 19, 1775, the men who gathered to confront British regulars, and who fired "the shot heard around the world,"[5] were all militiamen. Four days later, the Massachusetts Provincial Congress voted to raise an army of 30,000 men, consisting of twenty-six regiments, to surround the British stronghold of Boston. They requested New Hampshire, Rhode Island and Connecticut to join in this effort, and then combined them to form a volunteer defense force. These New Englanders were then placed under the command of Massachusetts General Artemas Ward. Short enlistment terms were the tradition in the militia, so volunteers for the new army only signed up for the remainder of the year. In late spring the Massachusetts Provincial Congress dispatched Dr. Benjamin Church to Philadelphia to offer control of the combined force of state militias to the Second Continental Congress.

As the Congress convened in May, 1775, news arrived announcing that Ethan Allen and Benedict Arnold had captured Fort Ticonderoga, on the south end of Lake Champlain. Although celebrated as a welcome victory, this had the effect of ending any possibility of a swift reconciliation with Britain, so Congress began to plan for a longer-term conflict. On June 14 it decided to proceed with the formal establishment of an army that represented all thirteen colonies. The 22,000 New England troops and 5,000 New York men who were encamped on the outskirts of Boston were the earliest units absorbed into this new "Continental Army." Ten rifle companies from Pennsylvania, Maryland, and Virginia were the first soldiers recruited for this army from outside New England.

George Washington, as a veteran combat officer of the French and Indian War, shared the premise with other Founding Fathers that an army should be subordinate to civil authority. Washington impressed Congress not only with his military expertise, but with his reputation as an officer of unimpeachable character. On June 16, 1775 John Adams nominated him as Commander-in-Chief. He was unanimously approved "to command all the Continental forces raised or to be raised for the defense of American liberty,"[6] and the next day Washington formally accepted the post. He served throughout the war without any compensation, except reimbursement of his personal expenses. Washington envisioned a force modeled after European armies, an army capable of fighting in open fields with linear tactics, whereby ranks of foot soldiers stood side by side in rigid alignment to maximize their firepower.

THE CONTINENTALS RISE AND DECLINE

As the Clarkstown men of the 3rd New York Regiment headed north for Canada, new recruits from other states streamed into Cambridge, Massachusetts to reinforce the newborn Continental Army as it continued to surround British-occupied Boston. The fresh troops were flabbergasted by the chaos and complete absence of discipline that they encountered upon their arrival. An egalitarian spirit pervaded throughout the encampment, with little regard for rank or discipline. Washington himself described the hastily-cobbled-together army at Cambridge when he took command on July 3, 1775 as "a mixed multitude of people...under very little discipline, order or government."[7]

Aaron Wright was a private in Thompson's Pennsylvania Rifle Battalion. His diary spans the period from June, 1775, to March, 1776, and covers his service at Boston. Wright trekked in from Northumberland, Pennsylvania and made his way to the siege lines in August. He observed that, "The men were sworn to be true and faithful soldiers in the Continental army, under the direction of the Right Honorable Congress. After we chose our officers when on parade, our 1st lieut. came and told us he would be glad if we would excuse him from going, which we refused; but on consideration we concluded it was better to consent; after which he said he would go; but we said, 'You shall not command us, for he whose mind can change in an hour is not fit to command in the field where liberty is contended for.' In the evening we chose a private in his place."[8]

Relying on his experience as a British officer during the French and Indian War, Washington made every effort to create an army modeled after the British image. At the time he wrote, "Discipline is the soul of an army. It makes small numbers formidable; procures success to the weak and esteem to all."[9] He would have to wait until the bitter winter at Valley Forge, over two years later, for the establishment of any significant military order to begin.

Four major generals—Artemas Ward, Charles Lee, Philip Schuyler and Israel Putnam—were appointed. They were joined in July by eight brigadier generals—Seth Pomeroy, Richard Montgomery, David Wooster, William Heath, Joseph Spencer, John Thomas, John Sullivan and Nathanael Greene. The Continental Congress appointed all general officers, most of whom were prominent community leaders and statesmen. Several of these senior officers had previous experience in the British Army, having served as field officers during the French and Indian War, and many American junior officers were also veterans of this conflict. Their combined experience exceeded most of their counterparts in the British Army, where few had ever participated in an actual battle. Selection of these critical leadership positions marked the real birth of the American Continental Army.

By the end of July new arrivals had swelled the army around Boston to 17,000 men.[10] This main force, directly under Washington's command, was primarily made up of New Englanders, although the other colonies began recruitment drives to fill their own troop quotas as assigned by Congress. This awkward array of inexperienced, untested troops and short-term citizen soldiers made up the early Continental Army that encircled Boston during the summer. Over the next four years this diverse throng would develop into an army equal in professionalism to any major European power.

Artemas Ward
(*Harper's Encyclopedia of United States History*, Vol. 10, 1912)

As time approached to make plans for the following year, the duration of the war became more and more uncertain. Washington recommended to Congress that the new army, now comprising at least 20,000 men, be organized into twenty-six infantry regiments. Riflemen and artillery would operate in separate units, and each regiment was to consist of from eight to ten companies. Each company was to include a captain, two lieutenants, an ensign, four sergeants, four corporals, a fifer, a drummer, and seventy-six privates. Each regiment theoretically had a total strength of about 720 officers and men, but in fact few units ever reached this number during the war. The first American officers were selected not for their military experience, but rather for their ability to recruit men from their individual communities. These leaders were usually prominent men of means who were politically-reliable Patriots.

When the short terms of service of New England troops expired toward the end of 1775, General Washington had the unenviable task of trying to whip up enthusiasm for reenlistment. The men who had volunteered during the *rage militaire* had little knowledge of the realities of military life, and had never intended to leave their homes and families for more than a few months. Most had bona fide reasons for wanting to go home, since the greater part of them were farmers whose labor was needed to plant and harvest in order to keep their families from literally starving. The 18th Massachusetts Regiment was a case in point. A poll of the thirty-four active officers was taken on October 28, 1775, to determine who would be willing to serve for another year. Thirteen officers declined to continue, including a colonel and a major, two of the three highest ranking officers in the regiment.[11]

Even Founding Father John Adams was skeptical of building an army with this manpower base. He doubted that most employed men in the colonies could be persuaded to enlist for extended periods, when they could remain home and enjoy a far better quality of life. Adams belittled men of the lower socioeconomic classes, those in bondage, and foreigners. But these very men would soon swell the ranks of the Continental Army, and achieve victory for the cause of independence. On May 16, 1776 Adams, in his autobiography, wrote:

> *But I contended that I knew the number to be obtained in this manner [volunteers] would be very small in New England, from whence almost the whole army was derived. A regiment might possibly be obtained, of the meanest, idlest, most intemperate and worthless, but no more. A regiment was no army to defend this country. We must have tradesmen's sons, and farmers' sons, or we should be without defense, and such men certainly would not enlist during the war, or for long periods, as yet. The service was too new; they had not yet become attached to it by habit. Was it credible that men who could get at home better living, more comfortable lodgings, more than double the wages, in safety, not exposed to the sickness of the camp, would bind themselves during the war? I knew it to be impossible. In the Middle States, where they imported from Ireland and Germany, so many transported convicts and redemptioners, it was possible they might obtain some. Let them try . . . But I warned them against depending on so improbable a resource for the defense of the country.*[12]

Washington was disappointed by the lack of progress of the reorganization, and knew he would soon be confronted by the horror of losing a large part of his army to short-term enlistments. In February, 1776, he wrote to Congress: "To go into an enumeration of all the evils we have experienced in this late great change of the Army . . . would greatly exceed the bounds of a letter . . . . I shall with all due deference, take the freedom to give it as my opinion, that if the Congress have any reason to believe, there will be occasion for Troops another year . . . they would save money, and have infinitely better Troops if they were [to enlist men] for and during the war."[13]

Short-term enlistments nearly caused the Continental Army to collapse in 1776, even after it had become apparent that the British were beginning to send massive forces to quell the nascent American rebellion. Washington's distress with this enlistment predicament soon led Congress to pass the critical reforms necessary for the Continental Army to survive for the longer term. He was authorized to extend enlistments to three years, or for "the length of the war," to avoid another year-end crisis which could have ended the war. In addition, the Continental Congress passed the "Eighty-eight Battalion Resolve," requiring each state to contribute regiments in proportion to its population. This added an additional sixteen regiments to the depleted army. For now, the problem of enlistments had been resolved.

Chapter Two

Into Harm's Way

Filling the Ranks

To swell the ranks of the devitalized American army, leaders found it necessary to offer incentives to try to attract men from the lower socioeconomic classes. Less motivated by the public spirit of liberty, they could be lured into service with promises of bounties and necessities, such as decent food, clothing and pay. The Continental Army reinvented itself with these men in 1776, and a new army emerged, a transformed army that managed to stay in the field for the next eight years.

Volunteers were insufficient to fill the ranks as the war ground onward, and pleas from officers for longer enlistment periods became more urgent. In 1778, the Continental Congress responded by recommending that the states draft men from their own militias for one year's service in the Continental Army. The spirit of this decree was soon violated, however, when implementation allowed affluent individuals to pay substitutes to serve in their place. These replacements included servants and apprentices who were offered as stand-ins for their masters. Draftees also "purchased" petty criminals and the indigent from law officers, and even British deserters and prisoners of war found their way into the Continental Army. Conscription by the states coerced the young, the helpless, and those drawn from the lower levels of society to serve. In the end, this had a positive long-term effect, for it established an effective army of full-time, long-term soldiers who had few other options in life. However, this first national draft was erratically enforced, and after its failure became apparent the states resorted to enlistment bounties.

There were basically two military organizations that comprised the armed forces of the new nation: 1) the Continental Army and state groups, and 2) the militia and levies. The militia performed duties within the state to meet local threats, and generally served for shorter time periods. Militia service was required of all males between 16 and 60, except clergy, college students, slaves, and, often, free blacks. Men were expected to provide their own weapons. "Levies" were units drawn from the militia or recruited directly from the

Recruiting Sergeant at Work (Courtesy of www.Britishbattles.com)

civilian population for special operations, and they were occasionally assigned out of their home state.

The Continental Army, the military force drawn from all the colonies, was administered by the Continental Congress. With no power to tax, Congress relied mainly on the states to raise and financially support their individual Continental Army regiments. States recruited, reinforced and reorganized their regiments and had the responsibility of providing their pay, food, shelter, clothing, arms, and other equipment. States differed in how well they fulfilled these obligations, and constant funding issues often caused living conditions for the Continental troops to be miserable. Each year Congress assigned the states a quota of men, but no state was ever able to raise enough recruits to fill it.

The combined force was often referred to as the *Continental Line*, a name derived from the linear formation that was the usual arrangement of troops on the battlefield. The commander of the Continental troops, General George Washington, had the power to dispatch his regiments anywhere in the country, and for any length of time.

Number of troops furnishedby each state for the Continental Army

New Hampshire	12,947	Masauchusetts	67,907	New Jersey	10,726
Connecticut	31,939	New York	17,781	Maryland	13,912
Pennsylvania	25,678	Delaware	2,386	South Carolina	6,417
Virginia	26,678	North Carolina	7,263		
Georgia	2,679	Rhode Island	5,908	**Total**	**231,771**

A unique organization was established within the Continental Army in May, 1776, when the Continental Congress authorized the formation of a *Flying Camp*. Early that year it became clear that what was needed was a reliable and substantial permanent army, instead of the short-term, haphazardly-organized militia units with their steady turnover of personnel. During the disastrous Canadian Campaign, entire regiments returned home when their short enlistments expired, and this instability continued during the New York and New Jersey campaigns. General George Washington envisioned the Flying Camp as a force of 10,000 militiamen acting as a mobile reserve. This force was to be paid directly by Congress to serve as a backup unit, brought in to strengthen the regular army for short periods of time. Because of logistical problems and the difficulties involved in assembling troops in a timely manner, these strategic detachments never achieved their objective. However, their officers rendered important service throughout the campaigns of Long Island, Trenton, and Princeton. Most of the Flying Camp units, thirteen regiments from Pennsylvania, Maryland and Delaware, were dissolved within a year.[14]

The militia raised by the each state for short intervals was usually assigned duties within the state's borders. Militia troops can be compared to today's National Guard in many ways. They could not be assigned out of their home states for more than three months, were called out only when needed, and then promptly sent home when their mission was completed. They could be called out several times each year, at times for only a few days. Their tasks typically included patrolling coastlines and rivers, as well as protecting military stores and frontier settlements against Native American and Loyalist raids. They were encouraged to harass the enemy whenever possible. On many occasions they joined the Continental Army in major engagements. Some militia regiments eventually became Continental units, and they proved to be an abundant source of recruits for the regular army throughout the duration of the war.

A FLEETING TASTE OF VICTORY

In one of the more heroic feats of the war, Colonel Henry Knox moved sixty tons of captured British artillery to Boston after the victorious American attack on Fort Ticonderoga. Fifty-nine cannon were dragged three hundred miles by teams of oxen pulling sledges through snowbound mountains. When they finally arrived, the guns were placed on Dorchester Heights in one night, and aimed toward British-occupied Boston. This feat greatly contributed to the success of the American siege, and the British abandoned the area on March 17, 1776. They used New York City as their principle headquarters of operations for the duration of the war. The Continental Army, formed from a jumble of militia regiments over a year before independence, had achieved an early victory. Now, the loose confederation of colonies was confronted by a full-scale war that would require an armed force of much greater magnitude and professionalism.

During the Long Island Campaign in August of 1776, there were many men who became worthless as soldiers due to the loss of body parts and subsequent amputations. These disabling injuries occurred with such frequency that Congress authorized the formation of an "Invalid Corps" in 1777. In effect, this was the first American pension plan. Congress decided to grant half-pay to the wounded and disabled, and formed the corps from officers and soldiers who were found capable of doing light duty. A similar concept had been used in Europe for many years, after it was found that incapacitated soldiers could be used effectively to perform non-combat duties.

The "Corps of Invalids" was formed at the Fishkill Supply Depot, a major Continental Army logistical facility located approximately fifteen miles northeast of West Point. Its role was to relieve combat regiments from guard duty, and to support Washington's forthcoming operations against New York City. It provided valuable service at Fishkill, and freed up scarce manpower for Washington to carry south with him, while at the same time preventing a British incursion in response from New York City up the Hudson River. These units continued their work for the reminder of the war, and served in such non-combat roles as guards at garrisons, arsenals and supply depots, and as workers in hospitals. Some officers from the corps were also employed as recruiters.[15]

For the next five years, the Continental and British main armies fought in New York, New Jersey, and Pennsylvania. A few encouraging events occurred during the war that portended the possibility of American success. At Valley Forge, during the winter of 1777-1778, Baron von Steuben, a Prussian officer, volunteered his services to the Continental Army. With his training and discipline the American forces began to make vast improvement. In the summer of 1780, the entire country was elated when a French expeditionary force, commanded by the French nobleman, Jean Baptiste Donatien de Vimeau, Comte de Rochambeau, arrived with 5,500 troops and a squadron of the French Navy to join the American cause.

After the war began, special companies of light infantry had been unofficially formed. These forces provided a skirmishing screen to harass and delay the enemy in advance of the main body of infantry. The units were composed of the most physically-fit men and the best marksmen, and led by the highest qualified officers, all of whom were detached from each regular army regiment. With their high reliance on bayonets to furnish much of their fighting power, they were regarded as the elite troops of the army. This light infantry was employed by General Anthony Wayne when Stony Point was captured in 1779. In 1781, an important event in the organization of the Continental Army occurred when this corps of light infantry was officially organized. In his General Orders, issued on February 1, 1781, Washington called for a light infantry

Hauling guns by ox-teams from Fort Ticonderoga for the Siege of Boston, 1775
(US National Archives Collection)

company to be formed for each regiment. He specified that commanded officers select these troops based upon outstanding behavior and appearance, and that all members be over five feet tall. Colonel Alexander Hamilton led the New York Light Infantry at the crucial assault on redoubt number ten during the Siege of Yorktown later that year.

WAR - WEARINESS

In the later years of the war, the enthusiastic support given to the troops besieging Boston in 1775 became eroded by war-weariness. By the spring of 1781, despite the assistance of French forces, Washington lamented in despair:

> *Instead of having Magazines filled with provisions, we have a scanty pittance scattered here and there in the different States. Instead of having our Arsenals well supplied with Military Stores, they are all poorly provided, and the Workmen all leaving them. Instead of having various articles of Field equipage in readiness to deliver, the Quarter Master General . . . is but now applying to the several States to provide these things for the Troops respectively. Instead of having a regular System of Transportation established upon credit-or funds in the Qr. Masters hands to defray the contingent expenses of it we have neither the one nor the other and all that business, or a great part of it being done by Military Impress, we are daily and hourly oppressing the people-souring their tempers-and alienating their affections.*[16]

The period from the fall of 1777 to the spring of 1780 was the nadir of America's military and political fortunes. With little funding, and a discouraged and weary public, many officers began to resign and desertions became rampant. The hardships of life in the armed forces did not resemble the fantasies of military glory that many soldiers had envisioned.

As support for the war diminished, the once-patriotic civilian population became more estranged from the army, and eventually developed an adversarial attitude toward the beleaguered fighting forces. It took tremendous amounts of state money to maintain the troops, and additional resources to feed, cloth, equip, house, train, transport, and pay them. The resident population also became frustrated by rampant inflation, profiteering, and pilfering by the needy army, at the same time that their families were being disrupted by members serving in the military. Many Patriots lived in areas occupied by the enemy, and others were surrounded by Loyalist neighbors, so harassment on both sides became commonplace.

George Washington had hoped that the victory at Yorktown in 1781 would be the final and decisive battle of the war, but for the next two years the situation in the north continued to remain the same as before this allied victory. The garrison composed of 15,000 British regulars, Hessians, and Loyalist troops continued to occupy New York City and the surrounding area. This powerful force still had the means to strike the deteriorating Continental Army, or alternately mount a naval attack anywhere on the American coast from Rhode Island to the Delaware Capes.

THE TALL VIRGINIAN

The chaos that Washington encountered when he assumed command of the army was so discouraging that he publicly regretted accepting leadership six months later. In November, 1775, he wrote, "Could I have foreseen what I have, and am likely to experience, no consideration upon Earth should have induced me to accept this command."[17]

From the day he arrived in Boston, until the war ended eight years later, George Washington would serve as the struggling Continental Army's main source of strength and encouragement. A man whose commanding presence and charisma always inspired trust and admiration from officers and men, he had incredible courage and determination, and an inherent instinct to keep the American Army one step ahead of complete disintegration. He often exerted a powerful impact on those around him just by being in their presence, and people at all levels of society consistently testified to his greatness.

He was regarded by the common soldier as strong, decent and courageous. Somewhat aloof and with a commanding physical appearance, he inspired respect, admiration and awe in the ranks. The regular soldiers often met him by chance, and a few wrote to him seeking his assistance with their problems. Several even described personal encounters with him while recalling their experiences during the war in later years.

Samuel Downing was a private in the New Hampshire Line, and was one of the last surviving veterans who received a pension. He died in 1867 at the age of 106! He remembered Washington in this way: "Oh! But you never got a smile out of him. He was a nice man. We loved him. They'd sell their lives for him."[18]

Alexander Milliner, born March 14, 1760, drummer boy in Washington's Life Guard and veteran of Battles of White Plains, Brandywine, Saratoga, Monmouth, Yorktown (Photograph courtesy of Barre Publishers)

Alexander Millner was born in 1765, and died in 1864 at age 104. In 1775, he enlisted as a drummer boy at the age of fifteen, and served for four years in Washington's Life Guard.[19] He claimed to be a favorite of the Commander-in-Chief, who patted him on the head and called him his "boy." On one occasion, Washington even gave him a drink out of his own canteen. His recollection of Washington is distinct and vivid: "He was a good man, a beautiful man. He was always pleasant; never changed countenance, but wore the same in defeat and retreat as in victory." He tells this anecdote about Washington: "We were going along one day, slow march, and came to where the boys were jerking stones. 'Halt' came the command. 'Now, boys,' said the General, 'I will show you how to jerk a stone.' He beat 'em all. He smiled, but didn't laugh out."

Millner also remembered Martha Washington, "She was a short, thick woman; very pleasant and kind. She used to visit the hospitals, was kind-hearted, and had a motherly care." Millner was photographed in 1864, the year that he died, with the last of six veterans of that war who were still alive.

The Marquis de Chastellux, a major general in the French expeditionary forces, remembered Washington in his notes, "The strongest characteristic of this respectable man is the perfect harmony which reigns between the physical and moral qualities which compose his personality . . . . It is not my intention to exaggerate. I wish only to express the impression General Washington has left on my mind, the idea of a perfect whole."[20]

At the Battle of Monmouth in June, 1778, where Washington's appearance on the scene prevented a confused and panicked retreat, Lafayette observed that "General Washington seemed to arrest fortune with one glance."[21]

Dr. James Thacher, writing in 1778, portrayed Washington's physical appearance:

> *. . . remarkably tall, full six feet, erect and well proportioned. The strength and proportion of his joints and muscles, appear to be commensurate with the pre-eminent powers of his mind. The serenity of his countenance, and majestic gracefulness of his deportment, impart a strong impression of that dignity and grandeur, which are his peculiar characteristics, and no one can stand in his presence without feeling the ascendancy of his mind, and associating with his countenance the idea of wisdom, philanthropy, magnanimity and patriotism. There is a fine symmetry in the features of his face, indicative of a benign and dignified spirit. His nose is straight, and his eye inclined to blue. He wears his hair in a becoming cue, and from his forehead it is turned back and powdered in a manner which adds to the military air of his appearance. He displays a native gravity, but devoid of all appearance of ostentation.*

In this same year a friend wrote, "General Washington is now in the forty-seventh year of his age; he is a well-made man, rather large boned, and has a tolerably genteel address; his features are manly and bold, his eyes of a bluish cast and very lively; his hair a deep brown, his face rather long and marked with the small-pox; his complexion sunburnt and without much color, and his countenance sensible, composed and thoughtful; there is a remarkable air of dignity about him, with a striking degree of gracefulness."[22]

Washington had few close friends, and at times his quiet strength and dignified reserve could be mistaken for pompousness. He was on a serious mission that allowed very little time for wit. He wrestled with his temper, and sometimes lost. He was a poor public speaker, so he preferred to express himself in writing. When he did speak, he was candid and direct, and he looked people squarely in the eye.[23] When provoked, the "Father of Our Country" could let loose a torrent of curses that would make even hardened soldiers blush. By the end of the war, he had earned more respect than any other military or civilian leader in America, and he deserved it.

NOT WORTH A CONTINENTAL

The Revolution began before any funds were made available to fight an extended war. Except for issuing paper money, Congress had no means to

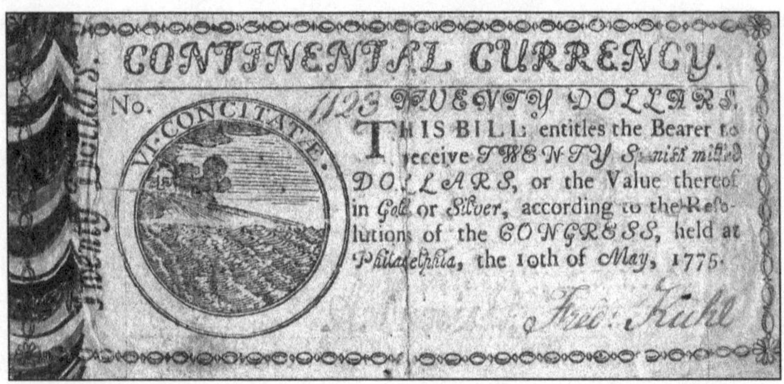

Continental currency

purchase supplies, so that method was used to provide funding for the first five years of the conflict. Before the end of 1776, a total of twenty-five million dollars in paper had been put into circulation. Congress tried to raise additional funds by starting a lottery and selling bonds, but when these methods failed even more paper money was issued.

Continental paper money depreciated rapidly during the course of the war, and prices rose from 50 to 100 percent over those that had been charged in prewar days. Starting in 1779, the financial condition of the new nation went into steep decline. Before the end of that year, forty-two dollars in Continental money did not have the purchasing power of one specie gold coin dollar. The progressive depreciation of the currency eventually spawned the expression "not worth a Continental."[24]

GLIMMERS OF HOPE

The American victory at Yorktown in 1781, the seventh year of the war, renewed the confidence of the Continental Army and inspired it to attain a peak of readiness and professionalism in 1782. When the American troops gathered that year at New Windsor, New York for the last major encampment, they were a well-disciplined force that was proud of its proficiency on both the battlefield and the parade ground. During this gathering, the troops were frequently reviewed by members of Congress and Count Rochambeau and his staff. The French officers congratulated Baron von Steuben for the success of his training, and expressed admiration for the aptitude of the American soldiers.

Baron von Steuben had not inspected the regiments since before the Yorktown campaign, and although nine months had passed he was delighted with their state of readiness. After reviewing a drill by of the 2nd New York Regiment at Pompton, New Jersey in the early months of 1782, he commented, "The regiment is in excellent order, arms and accoutrements are very well attended to and clothing is taken great carefully. Very few men are absent on any duty from the Regiment. The Regiment goes through its exercise very well and performs a variety of maneuvers with exactness and certainty."[25]

General Washington made a special effort to foster this pride by recognizing soldiers that had endured unusual hardships during the duration of the war. He introduced chevrons, awarded for three years of service performed with bravery, fidelity and good conduct. This service stripe, the same color as the facings of the soldier's uniform, was designed to be worn on the arm. An additional stripe could be added for each additional three year term of service. This chevron is known today as the hash mark. At the same time, Washington created the Badge of Military Merit, to be awarded for singular acts of unusual gallantry. In 1932, the United States War Department authorized the Purple Heart Medal for those wounded in action. It also determined that this medal would be considered the official "successor decoration" to the Badge of Military Merit.

A MODEL ARMY FOR WARS THAT FOLLOWED

When the American Revolution began, the American public had the naive conviction that they had superior military skills, and that their idealism alone would secure a victory. This line of reasoning felt that native courage, faith in God, and the skills of frontier riflemen would surely achieve independence. Americans believed that there was no need for a professional military modeled after that of England, France or Prussia. A standing army would lead to oppression because of the financial pressures it could exert against a government. The problem, however, was that the reality of the battlefield quickly forced Washington to create just such an army.

Perhaps George Washington's greatest challenge was to keep the Continental Army together. Its generals were political appointments made by Congress to appease each state, and were often chosen without regard for qualifications or talent. Many high-ranking officers were arrogant men who acted independently, and against his wishes, and were hypersensitive about their seniority. At times they were openly rebellious, and made attempts to usurp his authority by dealing directly with Congress. In most cases, especially with the officers he valued, Washington was able to conciliate and resolve their grievances while maintaining their self-esteem.

The glimmer of hope from the early success at Boston was long remembered by both the military and the American public. Despite the debilitating turnover in personnel throughout the entire war, the Continental Army survived. It was sustained by the loyal, long service of War Men and their reliable career officers. The general aversion to maintaining a standing army would continue throughout the war among the Americans, but they recognized that opposing the professionally-trained British forces required the discipline and organization of an established, stable force. The Continental Army was victorious in the longest war in American history before Vietnam, and overcame physical and political obstacles that appeared insurmountable. The fact that General Washington not only kept the Army together, but also formed it into a hard-hitting professional fighting force, is a tribute to his inspirational direction and wisdom. The Continental Army was the prototype for all the wars that followed, and is the forerunner of the United States Army of today.

Chapter Three

The Golden Myth

Patriotic Farmers and a People's War

For the last two centuries a myth about the identity of the common soldier of the Revolutionary War has persisted in American history. Legend portrays him as a zealously patriotic citizen who abandons his plow, snatches a musket from the hearth, and rushes out on short notice to defend his country's liberty, which is being threatened by tyrannical British rule. Such valiant individuals did make up the 10,000 soldiers, mostly from New England towns, who stood fast on Breed's Hill and successfully besieged Boston in 1775. The majority of them, many of whom were farmers, then followed and fought with George Washington to ultimately achieve independence. After the diabolical Redcoat hordes had been vanquished, these nationalistic yeomen dutifully returned home, but always stood ready to return to the fray if the freedom of their beloved homeland was jeopardized. They expected little reward or fanfare for their service, except gratitude from an appreciative nation. This golden, but quite false, image persists in the minds of many Americans today.

For the first three post-war decades, this notion of the exemplary citizen soldier was not commonly accepted by the American public. Most soldiers returning home in 1783 were not welcomed with cheers of gratitude from an appreciative public, who were eager to bestow honors on them for their service. They arrived penniless, and were quietly absorbed into war-weary communities that were struggling to survive amidst rampant inflation and taxation. The American public not only refused to respect the veterans of the Continental Army; it actually resented these valiant men. The popular belief was that the war had not been won by regular troops recruited from the lower levels of society. Instead, it been a people's war, and victory had been achieved by a combination of the voluntary service of patriotic citizens and by family sacrifices that were shared by the nation.

John Adams introduced this concept of a people's war in 1776 when he proclaimed, "We must all be soldiers."[26] The conviction that the war was an uprising by all patriotic people against tyranny diminished the role of the Continental Army for an entire generation. Even the revered concept of "The Spirit of 76" was redefined to include civilians. The righteousness of an entire nation that suffered great hardship to win independence was eulogized, and for the most part veterans were pushed aside and forgotten.

The recollection of the war as a people's crusade was reinforced by the Americans long-standing distrust of the European model of a standing army. While exemplary leaders such as Washington, Montgomery, Greene and Warren were acknowledged for their deeds, few regular soldiers received any honors or rewards. Citizens in places that were impacted by large-scale military activities during the war were especially resentful of the army. They remembered soldiers as ravenous hoards of hungry men who stole their livestock and tore down barns and fences for firewood. Important sites—major encampments at Jockey Hollow, Morristown, New Jersey and the New Windsor Cantonment in Orange County, New York—languished in obscurity for more than a century while the people living the surrounding countryside remained outraged for many years to come.

VETERANS FINALLY REGOGNIZED

This widespread public image, which marginalized the soldiers of the Continental Army, miraculously changed in 1818, thirty-five years after the war. At that point a surge of nationalism, combined with appeals from disabled and impoverished aging veterans, resulted in the passage of the Revolutionary Pension Act. This law awarded pensions to Continental Army veterans who were "in reduced circumstances," and who had served at least nine months, or until the end of the war. Thousands of old and infirm veterans submitted applications that provided details of their service and current economic situation. Their claims included vivid accounts of their valor during the war, but also told pitiful stories of their present circumstances. This evidence aroused the guilt and compassion of the American public, and soon created a flood of public gratitude. Fortunately, there was a budget surplus at the time, and this eased passage of the act.

It was not until almost 120 years after the war, in 1902, that the first significant study appeared that attempted to divulge the identity of the common soldier of the American Revolution. While Charles K. Bolton's classic study, *The Private Soldier Under Washington,* did make an attempt to explore the social background of the men, it also tended to reinforce the golden myth of the common American soldier as an idealistic landed farmer, a citizen-soldier inspired by patriotism. Various literary works produced in the years that followed confirmed this traditional belief that the American soldiers were patriotic men with a stake in society, i.e., men who owned property and voted.[27]

THE GOLDEN MYTH CHALLENGED

The adored image of the freedom-loving citizen-soldier was so gratifying to Americans that it endured for two hundred years after the war. In the decade that straddled the bicentennial of the nation in 1776, a few academic historians decided to test this notion. Their fresh research suggested that this popular image was not a true representation of the common soldier of the Revolution. They asserted that the loyal citizenry of 1775 who rose up at Lexington, Concord, Ticonderoga and Breed's Hill in the first months of the war were not accurate representatives of the majority of common soldiers. They claimed that the true soldiers were those drawn from the lowest levels of society, men who committed for longer terms of service and formed the standing army that lasted through the dark days of the prolonged conflict. These incompatible images of the enlisted privates of the Revolution deserve further assessment.

In the final months of 1776 volunteerism had all but vanished, and the enthusiastic soldiers who had massed around Boston were being replaced by less fortunate members of society. These land-poor and unskilled young men were recruited without regard for aptitude, character, fitness or skill. But they were urgently needed to make up a European-style army essential to continue the rebellion and achieve final victory. Were they solely motivated by mercenary and personal objectives, or did they truly share the ardor of those that served before them? Was it patriotism, a quest for economic opportunity, or other reasons that drove the American soldiers of the Revolution to triumph over insurmountable odds? Understanding the motives of these recruits will provide a more accurate portrait of the common soldier of the War for Independence.

"THE SPIRIT OF '76" AND "RAGE MILITAIRE"

The initial enthusiasm of the *rage militaire* in early 1775 later evolved into a sentiment known as the "Spirit of '76." This attitude embodied the determination to resist tyranny that swept the country during the war, when impassioned speeches exalting the glory of freedom were heard throughout the colonies. Citizens viewed the current conflict as a test of the faith of a chosen group of people who shared a unique heritage and looked forward to a shining future. Bearing arms for the cause was considered a calling in the eyes of God. Most Americans tended to believe that they were naturally brave, and

Spirit of 1776 by Archibald MacNeal Willard, circa 1875 (Today this large painting hangs in Abbot Hall, Marblehead, Massachusetts)

possessed the innate ability to defend their freedom, regardless of the odds, while the British lacked true motivation. Army recruiters coerced potential enlistees, stating that it was cowardly for men not to sign up to protect their home and families from the predatory aggressors.

The aroused populace assumed that joining a local militia unit and committing to a few months of service would fulfill their patriotic obligation. This part-time service would surely not alter their lifestyle or expose them to the constant life-threatening hazards of battle, and they would remain close to home and family. This was the first brave band of Patriots that surrounded Boston during the early months of 1775, and they created the golden myth of the citizen-soldier.

HOMECOMING AT THE WORST TIME

For many of these soldiers, their patriotic ardor did not endure through the difficult failures of the campaigns in Canada and New York. When short-term enlistments expired after six months or less, individuals and entire regiments headed for home, despite the importance of the times. For some, the novelty had worn off, and the winter was fast approaching. For others, it was a more pragmatic matter—their pay was much lower than which they could earn back home. Others could not adapt to the harsh discipline and regimentation of military life.

A British cartoon from 1775 depicted America as an abyss (US Library of Congress)

In European armies the officer's task to discipline recruits who came from a life of serfdom was not a difficult one. But attempting to control free American citizens, accustomed to acting as they pleased, was a daunting challenge, especially for officers who were new to military life themselves. The volunteer farmers were willing to serve temporarily, but believed they were justified to return home for plowing, harvesting and caring for livestock, tasks that if neglected would cause their families great hardship. They remained in the ranks, but at their own convenience, and only until their absence would disrupt their civilian lives.

As men returned home over the course of the first two years of the war, stories of the deplorable conditions in the military became widely circulated. After the abysmal failure of the campaign to invade Canada, the passion for joining the army subsided, fervent patriotism abated, and the average young American male went to great troubles to avoid serving. At that time, General

Washington was forced to do some swift maneuvering in order to avoid a manpower crisis. These changes entailed a rapid reinvention of the American armed forces.

The crisis created by the shortage of manpower in the Continental Army was apparent in the lack of cohesiveness of the 3rd New York Regiment. These men were the avid Patriots who converged on Clarkstown, New York and other towns in southeastern New York to enlist for five months' service in June and July, 1775, when the *rage militaire* was still in full swing. The contingent was organized in the counties of Ulster, Duchess, Orange, and Suffolk, but also included individuals from Connecticut. Several foreign-born privates were also listed on its muster rolls. The outfit was commanded by Colonel James Clinton, who was eventually promoted to major general, and who later became one of the most prominent leaders of the Continental Army.

Their first destination was Fort Ticonderoga, one hundred miles below the Canadian border. After a four-week forced march they reached the fort, and that served as the staging site for the Canadian Campaign. Once there, the "Yorkers" joined 3,000 New England troops, and all soon discovered that current conditions were chaotic and morale was low. Everyone was inadequately trained, and many were suspicious of their commanding officers. Others were reluctant to work together or to cooperate with units from other states. A muster roll of the 3rd New York's 10th Company on October 3, six weeks after their departure from Clarkstown, shows that out of seventy-three men, only forty-three of the original recruits remained fit for duty. Desertions had begun during the first week of the march, and many men were now sick. Other companies from the southern New York counties experienced a similar fallout rate.

Clinton's regiments left Ticonderoga after only two weeks. They headed north to Canada with only 165 fighters remaining from the original group of 532, all of whose enlistments would expire at the end of the year, a mere two months away. After American forces were victorious in besieging Fort St. Johns in November, they went on to capture Montreal later that month. At that point, it became necessary to consolidate the 3rd Regiment companies, because so few of Clinton's men remained. After that point, the 10th Company disappears from all records. Other than the names of a few New York officers, there is no evidence to prove how many men of the 10th Company continued on the voyage up the St Lawrence River, only to suffer a disastrous defeat at Quebec. At the end of their enlistments most of the survivors left for home, although some were willing to extend their stay until April, 1776. These men remained at the walls of Quebec or at garrisons along the way south. But by mid-1776, less than a year after joining up at Clarkstown, virtually all could be found back in their home counties.

New England troops proved to be even less reliable. General Richard Montgomery, senior field commander on the Canadian Campaign, had reluctantly promised discharges to the Connecticut troops after the much-anticipated fall of Montreal. He considered this the only way to keep the men in the field for a few more weeks. Other New England regiments also threatened to head for home, and demanded concessions in order to remain in the service. With the exception of two hundred men who chose to stay, the entire Connecticut brigade marched away after the capture of Montreal. Most of the other New England troops from Massachusetts and New Hampshire joined the mass exodus as the year 1775 came to a close, although technically their enlistments were not set to expire for another month.

The Death of General Montgomery in the Attack on Quebec, December 31, 1775, by John Trumbull, 1786 (Courtesy of Trumbull Collection)

Montgomery left Montreal on November 28, 1775, for the upcoming Battle of Quebec, with only three hundred New York men and an artillery detachment. Two hundred Connecticut men remained behind to occupy Montreal. This was all that remained from the total campaign strength of 3,000 troops that had departed from Fort Ticonderoga two months earlier. The weakening of the American forces by the exodus of the citizen-soldiers resulted in a devastating defeat at Quebec, where hundreds perished either from exposure to the freezing weather or from smallpox. Throughout the spring of 1776, the now-deflated American forces were forced to retrace their steps as they retreated south.

Major General Philip Schulyer, the commander of the Canadian campaign, complained to Congress about the unprofessional conduct of the Continental soldiers: "They have such an intemperate desire to return home that nothing can equal it. It might not have been expected that men influenced by a sense of liberty would not have required such a promise, and that others to whom it was not immediately intended, would not have taken advantage of it. But all this flows from some unhappy source with the other disorders too prevalent in our troops—a want of subordination and discipline, an evil which may prove fatal to us."[28]

The Canadian Campaign was critical to the fate of the colonies. If it failed, the British might venture south along a route following Lake Champlain and Lake George to the Hudson River Valley, and retake this vital water highway. If successful, the Redcoat drive would virtually divide the colonies in half, thus putting an early end to the American rebellion. Major military setbacks plagued the Continental Army during the first months 1776, as the force retreated south. The final shock to American morale was the forced evacuation of Fort Ticonderoga, which had been captured a year earlier by the Americans under Ethan Allen.

The disastrous Canadian Campaign and the lack of enlistments for the daunting challenges of 1776 convinced Washington that he had to fashion a new version of the Continental Army. To win the war against the British he realized that what was needed was a force of soldiers with long-term enlistments. Troops were required that could be disciplined, and who could withstand both harsh campaigns and the severe conditions of military life. Since upcoming actions were to be local, the front lines would be far away from home. Despite their abundant patriotic motives, this was not a conflict that could be waged with militia-type citizen soldiers

RELUCTANT ACCEPTANCE

A standing army of professional soldiers was regarded as a threat to Congress and the American public. If not supported, both believed that a qualified fighting force would soon turn against the civilian population. They preferred the status quo—armed forces that were composed of state militias of volunteers kept under control by Congress, and called up only when needed. The landed yeomen that made up this force had a stake in the society, and hence did not pose a threat. There would be little chance that these free citizens would make use of their power to destroy their own rights. The nation in general was convinced that the state militias of 1775 were the appropriate model for America's fighting force.

The advocates of this type of military organization could point to the record of successes citizen-soldiers had achieved in the first months of the war. Didn't these landed men, whose voluntary participation epitomized American patriotism, successfully drive the British out of Boston? Would not an army driven by patriotic zeal defending its homeland triumph over an enemy whose recruits were mercenaries drawn from the dregs of society, men indifferent to national interests and disciplined by the lash and fear of their own officers? Civilian suspicion of a standing army grew as an increasing number of American soldiers were recruited from the available pool of underprivileged men who had little interest in the welfare of the society, or any genuine concern about protecting civil liberties.

This mistrust of the army in America persisted though all the years of the war. The new nation, a land rich in resources, fervently displayed patriotic rhetoric, but failed to provide for its freezing and starving soldiers. Curiously, even under these circumstances, the suffering soldiers never developed hostility or bitterness. Little evidence of hatred toward civilians can be found in the writings of soldiers, either during the war or in the years that followed.

Washington faced a severe manpower problem as volunteers began dropping out of the ranks to return home at the end of 1775. He realized he could not rely on temporary soldiers to assure an adequate supply of men available for the army. Congress continued to circumvent the idea of a standing army, but became alarmed when the American forces suffered humiliating defeats as they were driven from New York in 1776. The intimidated legislators finally relented by granted their approval to Washington's proposals for a permanent force that would be sustained by long-term enlistments.

Washington correctly perceived that the best and fastest way to raise an army of sufficient size to carry on the war was to offer financial incentives for enlisting. Starting in June, 1776, recruits for the army were offered a bounty of $20, and were promised a monthly pay of six-and-two-thirds-dollars per month, and clothing for a year. In addition, they were offered one hundred acres of land if they served until the end of the war. In return, the minimum enlistment would be for three years, with an option of signing up for the duration of the war.

With these new enlistment terms now approved, Washington had the opportunity to build a European-type standing army that could form around a core of skilled, long-term professional soldiers. Although chronic manpower shortages would continue to plague him throughout the war, his plan succeeded. An army of men was developed who were willing to serve long periods while enduring the rigors and realities of combat and camp life. These men could withstand a depressing war of recurring defeats, while accepting discipline and enduring threats of disease, starvation and death in combat.

POOR BOYS - THE FLOTSAM OF SOCIETY

During the Revolutionary War, muster rolls listing the name, rank, date of enlistment and status of each soldier were prepared bi-monthly at the company level in order to track the strength of the Continental Army. "Descriptive rosters" are especially valuable to researchers, since they also included age, height, race, civilian occupation, hometown or country of birth. Often a "comments" column provided the soldier's status, such as his present location. Fortunately, a descriptive roster of Captain Johnson's 10th Company, New York 3rd Regiment has survived, and it lists the seventy-three men who enlisted in Clarkstown on August 4, 1775. Similar rosters were also found for the three other companies of the same regiment who served during the same period.[29] Together these documents record the personal data for 289 privates from southern New York counties.

Since this agrarian area of New York had a similar composition to other rural areas of the Northern colonies, this sampling may be considered a reliable gauge of the type of troops that responded from other colonies from that area at the time. An analysis of the men in these units in 1775 challenges the popular myth of the Minuteman citizen-soldiers who dropped their plows to spring into action to defend their kith and kin, the stereotype glorified for two hundred years in Fourth of July speeches.

LIVELIHOODS AND ACTIVITIES

Scrutiny of the occupations of the recruits of the 3rd New York Regiment provides a glimpse into their economic status. A large number, 110 men, were employed in some trade or craft. Their work, with few exceptions, was at the mid-skill level, and consisted of fairly easily-learned talents that required little initial capital. Some were coopers (barrel makers), others were weavers and shoemakers, and a few were carpenters and fullers (wool cleaners). Of the total group, only about a dozen had higher-level skills, such as blacksmith and gunsmith, although they too could have been mid-level employees since there is no indication of whether they were business owners. An almost equal number, 109 men, were landless, unskilled laborers and day workers. Four were schoolmasters, a notoriously low paid profession in that era. The composition of the four companies of the New York 3rd Regiment can be assumed to correspond closely with that of other states.

An analysis of tax and census records in a town in another colony—Peterborough, New Hampshire—beginning in 1775 showed that about 170 men in the town performed military service during the war. Most were poor, and the majority remained privates during their entire length of service; less than a third performed service longer than one year. This group included several men who declared that they resided in other New Hampshire towns at their time of enlistment. But a search in the records of these towns did not disclose any evidence that they ever resided there, an indication that they were most likely drifters. After the war, most of these veterans became landless day laborers. Others included in the Peterborough list were deserters from the British Army, as well as men who had been jailed for indebtedness. Seven soldiers were shown to be legal paupers, and one was described as being mentally deranged.[30]

The origins and careers of 308 privates in the Maryland Continental Line were traced in a study that utilized census returns, tax and pension records. Since they were recruited in 1782, the last year of the war, these men may not be representative of most Continental soldiers, but they too appear to be in direct contrast to the popular image of the common soldier. All were from the lower levels of Maryland's white male society, and included indentured servants, transported convicts, and sons of poor farmers, all of whom may have viewed the Continental Army as their best opportunity for employment. The few who were enumerated as farmers did not have enough land to appear on the local tax lists. In one Baltimore company of 102 men, there were no farmers at all.[31]

Thirty-five years after the war, this pattern held true in Bucks County, Pennsylvania, where most veterans remained landless day laborers, or lower-skilled workers who owned little or no property. Most were men of the lower classes who performed manual labor, such as journeymen, servants, apprentices, minor shopkeepers and craftsmen.

Note here that skill levels varied among craftsmen at that time. At the lower level were such jobs as coopers, weavers, and shoemakers. In Bucks County alone, there were thirty-two shoemakers, and 24 percent of the veterans in this area reported that they were laborers. Farmers, likely the only landed men in the group, formed only 8 percent of the sample population. Eleven percent claimed they did not work or did not have any occupation.
This study supports the conclusion that serving in the Continental Army was largely determined by economic status. The recruits form Bucks County appear to have been destitute men willing to trade their civilian life and liberty for their basic needs—pay, food, and clothing.[32]

John R. Sellers described the common soldiers of the American Revolution from Virginia after the war: "[they were] small-propertied or property less farmers who after the war moved westward to attempt to start another life. The veterans derived few benefits of culture or education and most had never learned to sign their names. Theirs was mostly the hand-to-mouth existence of a tenant farmer or farm laborer and if they wanted something better, the frontier was their best hope of obtaining it. For many the Revolutionary War had offered their first opportunity of employment and immediate cash rewards and migration west, often to their bounty land, was a rare chance for a better life."[33]

Mark E. Lender examined the pension files, muster rolls and tax lists of 710 enlisted men of the New Jersey Brigade. His findings are similar to those of other states. The 2nd Battalion consisted of fifty-three men from Middlesex County. The surviving muster rolls indicate that eight were farmers and eighteen were laborers. The rest were tradesmen, with the exception of one schoolmaster. Lender also concluded that the view of the typical Continental soldier as a farmer-citizen-soldier was flawed, and that the New Jersey troops actually resembled a European army, where a majority of the men regarded financial incentives, such as pay and bounties, as more important than taking up arms to defend their homes or country.[34]

CHALLENGING A REVERED NATIONAL STEREOTYPE

Units such as the 3rd New York, and the Petersborough, New Hampshire recruits, all raised in the first few months of the war at the peak of patriotic fervor, appear to have similar composition to those formed during the remaining seven years of the Revolution. What many historians seen to have overlooked is that the first volunteers, the warriors responding to the *rage militaire* of 1775, also seem to have come from the same lower socio-economic classes. They have almost the identical occupations as the professionals who formed the standing army for the duration of the war. This again refutes the golden myth of the citizen-soldier.

While the social-economic backgrounds of the men may have been similar, their motivation for enlistment shifted over time. Indigent young men who comprised the early volunteers could not have been motivated by substantial financial and land bounty incentives, since these did not exist in the first year of the war. Although the patriotic exuberance of the Spirit of '76 never did return, Yankee Doodle could not be described as a simple mercenary. Contemporary evidence found in original military documents, in combination with a review of the findings of historians, suggests that the American soldier was a composite of the dedicated and idealistic patriot and the economically disadvantaged laborer seeking to improve his quality of life.

Chapter Four

Patriots and Mercenaries

Continental Army soldiers had little to lose. Yet they persevered, often suffering ongoing hardships over extensive periods of time. They continued to fight despite the fact that patriotic fervor had abated, and even after early defeats portended that the war would last for an extended period. Thousands of soldiers perished in battle and from sickness, while others chose to die as prisoners of war rather than switch sides. In 1781, tattered troops who had served over several years time still retained the passion to trudge up to six hundred miles to confront and defeat the enemy at Yorktown, Virginia. Starved, inadequately supplied, and often outnumbered in battle, they rose up time after time despite overpowering odds.

During the desperate days of the miserable winter at Valley Forge in 1777-78, even General Washington himself was baffled by the resilience of his troops: "For some days there has been little less than a famine in the camp. A part of the army has been a week without any kind of flesh and the rest three or four days. Naked and starving as they are, we cannot enough admire the incomparable patience and fidelity of the soldiery, that they have not been ere this excited by their suffering to a general mutiny and dispersion." By the time the Revolutionary War ended four times as many Americans, percentage-wise, had died than in World War II.

Why did these men persevere? The young soldiers of the War for Independence had other options. They would have been eagerly accepted into the British Army at any time during the war and given cash incentives to do so. This option would have provided a more stable and reliable future than that offered by the ragged American forces. The British Army, in turn, would have easily won the war with this added American manpower. In reality, Continental Army deserters rarely joined the enemy, and most choose to return home to continue their lives, albeit at the lowest levels of society.

MIXED MOTIVES

Military service has always attracted young men in search of adventure and glory, and has also provided American men with a rite of passage to manhood.

General George Washington and a committee of Congress at Valley Forge, Winter 1777-78 (Engraving by W. H. Powell, 1866, US National Archives)

Members of the armed forces meet new comrades and travel to new places. They enjoy the prestige and respect of the uniform, and have the satisfaction of doing all this while fulfilling their patriotic duty and getting paid to do so. Revolutionary War soldiers' motivations were no different. Two basic reasons have been proposed as the incentives for these men: patriotic zeal, combined with the desire to gain independence from an oppressive mother country, and the possibility of economic advancement and upward mobility. The desire for a better quality of life does not imply a lack of patriotism. For many, military service was a way to both satisfy personal interests and support the cause of independence at the same time. Camaraderie, *espirit de corps*, and pride in their fighting ability also provided strong drawing-power, especially among men in longer-term service.

At the same time, a study of military records, diaries and other personal documents reveals other motives. Most of the Revolutionary generation of men had lives of repetitive drudgery on the farm or in the workplace. They had a curiosity about the world that surrounded them, since few had traveled beyond the nearest town. Military life instantly provided stimulating adventures, and satisfied their urge for excitement. For instance, surviving accounts show that these soldiers marveled at the mysterious wayside religious shrines and ornate church interiors that they viewed as they marched north into Canada. The customs of the Indians never failed to amaze, and Northerners were astonished by the pervasive slavery in the Southern colonies.

The possibility of meeting new and fascinating friends had great appeal for the raw recruits. New England Yankees came together with men from the Deep South, and served in the same units with German-speaking Dutchmen from Pennsylvania and stunning French foot soldiers in tight-fitting white uniforms with colorful sashes. Despite their regional and cultural differences, they all fought side-by-side.

For some, fear of punishment, rather than patriotism, may have caused them to stay on. Although the official penalty for desertion was death, in fact most deserters were flogged, so many soldiers who ran off returned and accepted the consequences. For many, the army was a convenient opportunity to escape from personal problems; recruits included debtors, petty criminals and even unhappy husbands. Some soldiers, including free blacks and Indians, enlisted because the Continental Army offered the best prospect for their freedom and survival.

The socio-economic background of the privates of the Continental Army was the same as professional European soldiers, but their motives appear to be different. The Redcoat regulars and Hessian jaegers were strictly driven by self-interest, and most of them enlisted for life. For them the army was solely an occupation, and they lacked any burning loyalty to their nation or their rulers. American soldiers were reluctant to become professional soldiers like their foes, and few remained in the army when the war ended. This strongly suggests that their reason for serving could not have been purely mercenary.

THE CASE FOR PATRIOTISM

The women of the colonies displayed unusual support for the army. They were openly willing to sacrifice husbands and sons, and they cheered wildly during parades and other social activities. Single women shunned prospective men who avoided serving. Newspapers reported that mothers who sent several sons off to war stated that they did not want to hear of any deaths except by those facing the enemy. In their view it would be better if all their sons died rather than one return a coward.[35] A group of young girls at a quilting party in the remote country village of Kinderhook, New York, tore the shirt of a Tory man, then "tarred and feathered" him with molasses and weeds.[36] A Hessian soldier who was captured at the Battle of Trenton and taken to Philadelphia described his arrival: "The old women howled dreadfully and wanted to throttle us all. Because we had come to America to rob them of their freedom."[37]

The patriotic women also turned boycotting into an important method of American resistance. They avoided wearing or purchasing clothing made of imported British materials, and wove and spun their own cloth to make clothing for their families and to produce needed clothing and blankets for the

Continental Army. Women also volunteered their homes for the quartering of American soldiers, and supported the Patriot cause through organizations such as the Ladies Association in Philadelphia, who collected funds to assist in the war effort. Martha Washington brought these funds directly to her husband. In 1780, the colonies raised over $300,000 through these female-run organizations.[38]

Proficiency with firearms acquired by frequent hunting added confidence to the fledgling army. Recruits also surmised that their knowledge of the land and its geographic features would be a tremendous asset to operations. They believed that their army would win the war as a superior fighting force, not by being encumbered with awkward maneuvers and mechanical drills of robotic serfs who were the enemy, but by superior marksmanship in familiar terrain. The first call to arms was astonishing. When the British Army marched west from Boston on April 19, 1775, Boston silversmith Paul Revere, and several other couriers on horseback, dashed into the New England countryside to spread the alarm. While church bells chimed, 4,000 citizen-soldiers converged on Concord, Massachusetts, where hundreds of British regulars were planning to destroy a rebel arsenal. Before the day was over, eighty-nine men from twenty-three towns in Massachusetts were killed or wounded. By the next morning, Massachusetts had mustered twelve regiments in the field, and Connecticut soon mobilized a force of 6,000 troops, one-quarter of its military-age men. Within a week, thousands of men from the four New England colonies had formed a siege army outside British-occupied Boston, the army from which the Continental Army was formed.

An address sent from Congress to all inhabitants of the colonies proclaimed that, ". . . our troops are animated by the love of freedom . . . . We confess that they have not the advantages arising from experience and discipline: But the facts have shown, that native courage warmed with patriotism is sufficient to counterbalance those advantages."[39] Patrick Henry's cry of "Give me liberty or give me death!" echoed this sentiment across the land.

GOD WAS A PATRIOT

To provide irrefutable reasoning for enlisting, love of freedom was merged with love of God. Even in the years before the war, preachers and revolutionary orators throughout the colonies had continually ranted that British rule was corrupt and sinful. This message was delivered from the pulpit in every village, and soldiers were constantly reminded of it throughout the entire war by their regimental chaplains. Americans were confident that God would not cause Christian soldiers to be defeated by England, a nation that spread tyranny throughout the world. These satanic British oppressors espoused war and violence, and victory would be assured by driving them out of the land.

The support of every Christian American was needed to defend against this threat to liberty. Those who did not resist, or showed sympathy with the forces of oppression, were in spiritual jeopardy. In a day when religious teachings were trusted to provide explanations for all types of worldly events, these arguments made a profound impression on young men. The evangelical message that brought together political and religious convictions provided a powerful justification for fighting in the Continental Army.

The dominant position of chaplains in the Continental Army helped to combine patriotism with religion. Upon enlisting, chaplains were automatically given the rank of colonel, and were then assigned to individual regiments. While they preached the Word of God, they also encouraged discipline and made every attempt to stir up fighting spirit. One such minister, the Reverend John Gano, served with the New York regiments. While delivering sermons to soldiers who had enlisted for short-term, he taunted them to sign up for the duration by stating that ". . . he could aver of the truth that our Lord and Savior approved of all those who had engaged in His service for the whole warfare." Soldiers who did not attend Gano's services were penalized by being forced to dig out stumps in the woodland surrounding the camp. His zealous sermons sometimes lasted for the entire day.[40]

Chaplain William Rogers delivered a typical message to a brigade of artillery during the campaign against the Iroquois Nations on July 4, 1779. "Let us still under the banners of liberty, and with a Washington for our head go on from conquering to conquer. Our Father trusted and the Lord did deliver them: they cried unto Him and were delivered; even so may it be with us, for the sake of Jesus Christ who came to give freedom to the world. They trusted him and were not confounded."[41]

"SHOW ME THE MONEY"

The Spirit of '76 was marked by endless patriotic celebrations that continued until the signing of the Declaration of Independence. After that time, American society became disenchanted, as support for the war steadily declined and the inspired Patriots faded away. Civilians were tired of contributing to the war effort, and frustrated by their now-worthless money. Both the enemy and the ragged and hungry American soldiers scavenged their homes, and cloth, sugar, tea and liquor were all in short supply. The once-prosperous country with citizens accustomed to living comfortably became exhausted from the upheaval and despair that accompanied the war.

Following the series of devastating defeats throughout New York during 1776, enlistment rates plummeted. Desertions and expirations of short-term enlistments depleted the ranks of the Continental Army, and it began to resemble a European-style military, motivated more by economic and lifestyle incentives than by idealism. It was apparent that patriotic zeal alone could not continue to sustain the army.

George Washington had no illusions about patriotism, and it is difficult to find any evidence of that word in his writings. During the grim days at Valley Forge in 1778, when men were deserting and officers were resigning in droves, he wrote the following to John Banister, a Virginia member of the Continental Congress: "Men may speculate as they will; they may talk of patriotism; they may draw a few examples from ancient story, of great achievements performed by its influence; but whoever builds on them, as a sufficient basis for conducting a long and bloody war, will find themselves deceived in the end."

By the end of 1776, the prevailing stimulus for recruitment shifted abruptly and completely to economic incentives. George Washington brashly announced in the *Virginia Gazette* in January, 1777 that soldiers were to receive one hundred acres of land upon their discharge. And if patriotism and land were not enough, he also granted them "all the plunder they shall take from the enemy."[42]

John Adams too offered a realistic opinion on stimulating enlistments: "I do not mean to exclude altogether the idea of patriotism. I know it exists. But I venture to assert that a great and lasting war can never be supported on this principle alone. It must be aided by a prospect of interest or some reward. For a time it may push men to action, to bear much, to encounter difficulties, but it will not endure unassisted by interest."[43]

Over time, patriotism virtually disappeared as a motive for fighting in the Continental Army. Subsequently, as the demand for manpower intensified, authorities were forced to enhance the monetary and land bounties. Cash bounties in particular were effective during the first few years of the war, but they became less valued as inflation sapped the value of the dollar. Veterans returning from the ill-fated Canadian Campaign related revolting tales of the horrors of battle and the abysmal conditions of life in camp. After that time it was difficult to buy soldiers, and states had no choice but to pass draft bills. While militia service had always had been compulsory, this obligatory service in a national army was a disturbing turn of events in the public mind.

During the bicentennial of the American Revolution, Dr. John R. Sellers, Curator of the Library of Congress, gave this candid view of the demise of the Spirit of '76: ". . . I would refer you to the desertion rate and the apathy of many of these soldiers at critical points of the war. I am not impressed by the patriotic fervor of the privates. I think that they acted overwhelmingly out of self-interest. I do not believe that they really fought with a true understanding of independence. The harangues they got from their chaplains, and the constant lectures, especially on the eve of the winter encampment, about reenlisting tell me that officers had a lot of trouble. I think Washington's chief problem, and chief accomplishment, was to keep an army in the field."[44]

A FARM OF MY OWN

Land was equated with wealth in the eighteenth century, and land bounties were a powerful enticement for poor young men who came from agricultural locales. They were such a meaningful inducement to the men that they surpassed the possibility of suffering severe hardships or even losing their lives. It was considered worth the risk, and those without land dreamed that they might have an opportunity to become independent farmers if they survived the war.

Tragically, few soldiers ever benefited from their land grants, and most of their land warrants ended up in the possession of speculators. Impoverished veterans sold them for a pittance in the decade after the war, when immediate needs outweighed any future advantage. The grants were usually hundreds of miles away, so most required veterans and their families to undergo a perilous trek through the wilderness. Warrants were often lost, and many aging veterans opted out of moving to the land that the federal government had reserved for them.

Many of the western tracts reserved for veterans remained inhabited by Indians, and were held by these hostiles as ancestral tribal territory. The United States regarded these people as having lost the war, since most had allied with the British. Congress simply made the broad assumption that Native lands were within the boundaries of the new nation, and did not recognize any claims from the inhabitants.

States also made various allotments of their territory to veterans. In addition to the one hundred acres provided by Congress, in 1778 North Carolina began offering an additional one hundred acres of land in Cherokee territory. Although Natives were allowed to remain, they could only do so as tenants. After most of the Iroquois were driven off to Canada, New York divided their existing tribal lands and reserved them for veterans' bounty land. This area covered a vast region in the northwest part of the state and was designated as the "Military Tract." It covered the present counties of Cayuga, Cortland, Onondaga and Seneca, and parts of Oswego, Tompkins and Schuyler counties. Twenty-eight towns were created on the tract, and, ironically, Native American words are reflected in current town names in these counties.

Corporal John Allison served during the entire war in the New York Continental Line. He was allotted a one-hundred-acre federal grant, and also received another five hundred acres from the state of New York. The Onondaga tribe of Iroquois, its former occupants, had joined the British cause. They had hoped that the crown troops would protect their land from encroachment by American settlers, but were forced to cede their territory to the United States after the war. They fled north to Canada with their leader, Chief Joseph Brant. For the next seven years, until 1790, the deserted Onondaga land was then assigned and allotted to qualified veterans.

Veteran Allison, who ultimately became a farm laborer in Orange County, New York, sold his bounty rights even before he was assigned his acreage: "On April 16, 1786, John Allison, formerly a Corporal in the 2nd Regiment, sold his land bounty rights to Samuel Coe of Haverstraw for eight pounds."[45] This sum, equivalent to less than twenty dollars today, was in payment for the entire six-hundred-acre portion of his bounty, land that was 140 miles from the veteran's home. Aside from the remoteness of the grant, Allison and other veterans, many of whom were illiterate, had no idea how to proceed with the formalities of applying for the land. When his assignment was finally made formal, he chose not to undertake a trek into the precipitous wilderness with his wife and four children under ten years of age.

At about the same time, Robert Allison, John's cousin, sold his land bounty grant to a man named Joseph Wright. He received three pounds, fourteen shillings for his six hundred acres. Wright and Coe numbered among the many predatory land bounty speculators who traveled from village to village buying land grants from impoverished veterans, in most cases for a pittance.[46]

By late 1779, the Continental dollar had declined in value to only thirteen cents, and states were forced to provide more creative incentives to fill their enlistment quotas. Out of desperation, in 1791 Massachusetts offered anyone agreeing to serve for three years an enlistment bounty of a few dollars in specie and several hundred dollars in paper money, plus a few three-year-old cattle to be delivered when service was completed. Recruits were actually motivated by the promise of being paid with cattle that were not yet born.

ADVENTURE, INDEPENDENCE, PEER PRESSURE AND A BETTER LIFE

The American Army broke all its promises to common soldiers. They were rarely provided with adequate food, shelter or pay, and they endured the unusually harsh corporal punishment that was administered to intimidate them. Their only financial rewards—bounty and pay—were ravaged by the devaluing of the Continental dollar. Yet despite frequent desertions, and three major mutinies, most of them chose to remain in service until their three-year enlistments expired or for the duration of the war.

Convicted felons were offered pardons, along with the option to enlist, as a way to escape flogging or the death penalty. Tories, confronted with the choice of either imprisonment or hanging, were allowed to join the army. Enemy deserters and prisoners were especially valued as recruits, and the mentally handicapped often found their way into the army. In Rhode Island, New Jersey and Maryland, indentured servants were allowed to enlist without their master's approval. In Rhode Island and Massachusetts, hundreds of slaves enlisted and served with distinction.

Joseph Martin, a farm laborer, enlisted twice. In June, 1776, he joined a Connecticut regiment as a private to flee from the drudgery of farm work and to defy his domineering grandparents. Sounding similar to today's youth, he said, "I wanted often to recreate myself, to keep my blood from stagnating." After fighting in the battles at Brooklyn, Harlem and White Plains, he returned home after his first enlistment expired, and vowed he had learned enough about a soldier's life to keep him safely on the farm. But the sixteen-year-old must have grown restless during the winter, because he reenlisted in April, 1777, for the duration of the war.

Peer pressure also motivated Martin. "One of my mates and most familiar associates, who had been out ever since the war commenced, and who had been with me the last campaign, had enlisted for the term of the war in the capacity of sergeant. He had enlisting orders, and was, everytime he saw me, which was often, harassing me with temptations to engage in the service again. At length he so far overcame my resolution as to get me into the scrape again, although it was at the time against my inclination." Martin signed up, but changed his mind the next day, and was allowed to withdraw. A short time later, he was influenced by a cousin-in-law, as well as a cash bounty, to reenlist.

COMRADESHIP AND PRIDE

Joseph Martin was saddened when his friends left town to join the Continental Army in 1776. After being forbidden to enlist by his grandparents, who were also his guardians, he lamented, "I said but little more about 'soldiering' until the troops raised in or near the town in which I resided came to march off to New York; then I felt bitterly again. I accompanied them as far as the town line, and it was hard parting with them then. Many of my young associates were with them, but my mortal part must stay behind."

As in all wars, those sharing constant adversity form fervent bonds of comradeship. Martin described the friendship with his comrades-in-arms: "We had lived together as a family of brothers for several years, setting aside some little family squabbles, like other families, had shared with each other the hardships, dangers and sufferings incident to a soldiers life, had sympathized with each other in trouble and sickness, had assisted in bearing each other burdens, or strove to make them lighter by council and advice, had endeavored to conceal each other's faults, or make them appear in as good a light as they would bear. In short, the soldiery each in his particular circle of acquaintance, were as strict a bond of brotherhood as Masons, and, I believe, as faithful to each other."

The hard core of combat soldiers in the Revolutionary War was composed of the long-service troops, the War Men who had enlisted for the duration. Over time, they developed increased self-confidence and a staunch *espirit de corps* as their expertise in soldiering and proficiency increased. These men were proud of their skills as marksmen, and in their effective use of artillery. They had learned the value of the bayonet charge, and had mastered the fine points of executing linear maneuvers on the battlefield. Above all they had learned to trust and depend on one another. This cohesion created a distinct fighting spirit, especially in smaller company size units, which typically consisted of about thirty men. Comradeship, enthusiasm, and devotion in the light infantry companies of the American Revolution, and in the Special Forces today, can be attributed to training, experience and unit pride. These qualities have always been key attributes of elite military units (think Navy Seals).

As the Continental Army matured, the pattern of desertions showed the influence of *esprit de corps*. After new recruits established bonds of comradeship, they were much less likely to desert. In New York, Maryland and North Carolina, 50 percent of all desertions occurred within the first six months of enlistment.[47] In the New Jersey Continental Line a total of 40 percent of the desertions took place within three months, and 64 percent within six months. The desertion rates in New Jersey decreased over the years, plummeting from 42 percent in 1778 to just 10 percent in 1780.[48] This occurred despite the fact that supplies were steadily dwindling and the buying value of pay was steadily deflating.

The experience and training gained at Valley Forge during the winter of 1777-1778 began to inspire American men to become high-quality soldiers. This transition was begun by the introduction of a set plan of discipline by Baron von Steuben. His relentless efforts in drilling men on the parade ground created a new attitude toward obedience, and provided the momentum for an *espirit de corps* and unit solidarity that continued to accelerate during the remainder of the war. Early victories— especially at Saratoga, Trenton and Princeton—instilled confidence in the men, and fostered professional pride.

When the last permanent encampment of the Continental Army took place at New Windsor, New York in 1782, Washington commented that his men had achieved ". . . the pleasing and honorable task of becoming masters of their profession." In April of that year he was so impressed by the parade of the Connecticut Line that he had the names of each of the 1,427 soldier read aloud, and the proud men continued to perform precision drills as they listened to the roster being called. While there is little evidence of American soldiers aspiring to become career professionals after the war, these War Men found great satisfaction in their competence and endurance.

Henry Brackenidge, a Continental Army chaplain, summed up the soldiers pride and professionalism in a fiery patriotic sermon in 1777: "When the war began we were without this love, and without the skill of war. Now we are sufficiently advanced. It is happy since we must fight the tyrant, that we love to fight him."[49]

Bounties, adventure, escape and camaraderie were all motivations, but patriotism, even when fueled by love of country, freedom and religion, could not alone sustain the level of manpower needed for the war. Economic incentives were required. Unit cohesiveness, professional pride and accomplishment sustained the Continental Army. However, it should not be forgotten that the fate of the American soldier was linked to the success of the new nation. If America lost the war, financial incentives and land bounties, especially valued by impoverished men in an agricultural society, would become worthless. The Continental Army allowed soldiers the opportunity to combine self-interest with commitment to their country.

Chapter Five

Bold, Brash, and Brave

Every American knows that the name *Yankee Doodle* was originally derived from a song. During the Revolutionary War songs often contained satirical and mocking lyrics. The source of the term *Yankee* remains uncertain, but in 1758 British General James Wolfe made the earliest recorded use of the word when referring to the New England soldiers under his command. *Doodle* first appeared in the early seventeenth century, and is thought to be derived from the seventeenth century German word *dödel*, meaning fool or simpleton.

The lyrics of the song "Yankee Doodle" tell the story of a poorly-dressed Yankee simpleton. The tune became so popular with British troops that they played it as they marched to battle on the very first day of the Revolutionary War. American soldiers quickly claimed it as their own, and created dozens of new verses that mocked the British and praised the new Continental Army and its commander, George Washington.

Author Charles K. Bolton, in *The Private Soldier Under Washington*, articulated the myth of the devoted citizen-soldier, an image that had been embraced by the American public for the previous two hundred years. His delightful version of Yankee Doodle vividly portrays a romantic view of Revolutionary War soldiers. But this rarely corresponds to the details of their lives as revealed in their own journals, and the reminiscences of their contemporaries. As Bolton explained, "The Revolutionary rank and file, when their uniforms were fresh, were a picture for the eye, with their cocked hats decked with sprigs of green, their hair white with flour, their fringed hunting shirts, and their leather or brown duck breeches. Many were boys; some at the opening of the war were under sixteen, with the virtues and vices of youth. They were eager for adventure, and every strange sight and custom made its impress upon them."[50]

The personal qualities of Continental troops reappear again and again in diaries and other original sources, all of which provide clues into the persona of the soldiers. Their nature was vastly different from the European soldiers whom they confronted on the battlefield. The egalitarian character of the American soldier stood out in sharp contrast to other eighteenth century troops, and was unprecedented in other armed forces of the day. Since they had been fostered in a culture largely lacking class distinction, and were used to independent thinking, it was difficult for them to take orders, work together or accept regimentation.

Yankee Doodle came from a life of unrestricted freedom, and his preference was to consider those in authority to be his equals. It was normal for him to vocalize his opinions, as had been done for many years in the traditional New England town meetings. He frequently challenged and questioned the decisions of his officers, and insisted that orders be explained and justified, rather than just mindlessly obeyed.

One instance to illustrate this point occurred in October, 1777, when over half of General William Smallwood's Maryland regiment deserted.[51] They left *en masse* in broad daylight, and openly defied their officers as they departed. The men recognized that they faced a superior enemy, and simply choose to head home to harvest crops rather than spend a bitterly cold winter doing nothing around an open campfire. Many of them had come from militia units where their independence had been fueled by actually voting for their officers. In the first year of the war Washington pointed out that American soldiers seemed to be accustomed to such an excess of unbounded freedom that it was difficult for them to accept any degree of subordination. Historian Ray Rapheal commented on the incredible practice of the rank and file militiamen electing their own officers: "Regulars and militiamen battled their superiors continuously over hats and hair, which they wished to wear as they pleased. Continental officers might try to resist these attempts as individual expression, but the hands of militia leaders were tied: if they failed to cede to the wishes of their men, they could be turned out of office. Since militia units in most cases elected their officers, the men in these positions could not be too harsh or arbitrary. Democracy in the army? A new and strange concept indeed."

Connecticut historian Dan Cruson described an election of officers in militia regiments, a practice that began in 1775: "Late afternoons were a time to tend to company business. Among the most important items of business was the election of officers. Noncommissioned officers, corporals and sergeants served as soon as they were elected. Commissioned company officers such as ensigns, lieutenants and captains, once elected, were submitted to the colonial assembly for approval. The election of officers was a critical factor in the development of colonial democratic attitudes, especially those in New England. It also created tremendous independence among the various companies."[52]

In 1775, during the ill-fated invasion of Canada, General Richard Montgomery commented,

'The New England troops are of the worst stuff imaginable. There is an equality among them, that the officers have no authority . . . the privates are all generals but not soldiers." When he ordered an artillery position to move closer to the enemy during the siege of Fort St. Jean, the men believed this move to be too great a risk, so they patently refused to obey the order. The soldiers then went to their officers and persuaded them not to comply.

Montgomery was finally forced to concede, and he ordered the siege to be made from a less advantageous position. He wrote to General Schuyler, his superior, "When I mentioned my intentions, I did not consider that I was at the head of the troops who carry the spirit of freedom into the field, and think for themselves.

Montgomery reported that his men had even called together a sort of town meeting to discuss the maneuvers he proposed.[53] Since the majority of his forces were from Massachusetts, Connecticut, New Hampshire and Vermont, they were accustomed to this participative style of leadership.

Baron von Steuben was also amazed by the autonomy and cavalier attitude of American soldiers. After the war, he wrote to a friend in the Prussian army, "You say to your soldier, Do this, and he doeth it; but I am obliged to say to mine, this is the reason why you ought to do that; and he does it."[54] Throughout the entire war American commanders were concerned about the reluctance of their troops to conform to regimentation. Soldiers even flaunted authority in their appearance. Long hair and distinctive tricorn hats, embellished with cockades, were visual clues intended to remind everyone that they were independent men. The free spirit of the American serviceman has lived on in the wars that followed; even in today's armed forces, orders are rarely given without explaining the purpose of the mission.

It became obvious to many officers early in the war that the boldness of their men more than compensated for their rebellious nature. What the American privates lacked in discipline was balanced by their unusual bravery, stamina and fortitude. Countless instances of resilience appear in accounts of the Revolutionary War. After the battles of Trenton and Princeton, 1,500 Pennsylvania soldiers slept in barns and on the ground in the dead of winter, and only two cases of sickness or death were reported.[55]

Foreign officers were also astounded by the spirit of American soldiers and their ability to survive unremitting hardship. A European army would have disintegrated if it had not been fed, paid or clothed during the dreadful winter at Valley Forge. During that winter General von Steuben was appalled after his initial inspection of Washington's Army, and he noted that no European army would have held together under such deprivation. General Lafayette was brought to tears when he saw starving men with feet and legs that were frozen black with gangrene, which often had to be amputated.

Hundreds of accounts of the behavior of the Continental soldiers in combat attest to their bravery. Colonel Elias Dayton of the 3rd New Jersey Regiment gave this incredible account of casualties and fatalities in two regiments during the battle of Germantown in 1777:

We suffered considerable in advancing, but a party of the enemy had thrown into a large stone house, said to belong to Benj. Chew. At this place fell Capt. McMyer and Ensign Hurley of Col. Ogden's regiment; Capt. Conway, Capt. Morrison, Capt. Baldwin and

Lt. Robinson wounded, of the same regiment, together with about 20 men; Of my regiment Lt. Clark and Ensign Bloomfield were wounded and 18 men killed and wounded; my horse was shot under me at the same place, within about three yards of the corner of the house. I believe every man we had either killed or wounded met his fate full in front as he was advancing. We had one Brigadier General who was shot in the thigh with a cannon ball, of which wound he died three days afterwards. Our good Major Witherspoon was shot dead by a cannon shot in the head as we were advancing through the streets.[56]

American forces lay siege to the Chew house during the Battle of Germantown October 4, 1777, by Christian Schüssele, 1840.

The tenacity of a soldier is often best revealed by his adversaries. Colonel Johann Ewald, a Hessian officer, described such an incident in his diary. In November, 1776, while on patrol with his Jager unit in New Jersey, they captured one of Colonel Daniel Morgan's riflemen. The prisoner was soon being interrogated to try to force him to reveal the locations of American positions. The rifleman refused to answer but, ". . . resolutely declared that he was my prisoner but not my spy. I admired this worthy man." The German commander went on to say, "One should not think that [the American army] can be compared to a motley crowd of farmers." He also saw many Continental soldiers "without shoes, with tattered breeches and uniforms . . . who marched and stood their guard as proudly as the best uniformed soldier in the world."

After peace was declared in 1783, and shortly before Colonel Ewald returned to Germany, he visited a garrison of his former enemy at West Point and wrote this impression of his former enemies: "Although I shuddered at the distress of these men, it filled me with awe for them, for I did not think there was an army in the world which could be maintained as cheaply as the American army . . . . What army could be maintained in this manner? None, certainly, for the whole army would gradually run away. This, too, is a part of

Captain Johann von Ewald (1744-1813), a German military officer (Hessian) from Hesse-Kassel serving with the British Forces in America, by C. A. Jensen (1835), after a drawing by H. J. Aldenrath hanging in Frederiksborg Palace, Denmark

the 'Liberty and Independence' for which these poor fellows had to have their arms and legs smashed."

Five years after he surrendered to the victorious Continental Army at Yorktown, Ewald reminisced, "With what soldiers in the world could one do what was done by these men, who go about nearly naked and in the greatest privation? Deny the disciplined soldiers of Europe what is due them and they will run away in droves, and the general will soon be alone. But from this one can perceive what an enthusiasm—which these poor fellows call 'Liberty.'"[57] What accounted for this individual ruggedness of the American soldier? The environment in the colonies strengthened the fortitude of the American soldier. Early in their lives many had survived in rugged frontier country, and were accustomed to relentless physical dangers and sudden Indian attacks. Before the war, the Virginia Assembly had required every male to bring a weapon to Sunday services, and to join in a drill afterward. The future soldiers had used firearms on a regular basis to hunt for food, and were considered excellent marksmen by their adversaries.

A surgeon at Valley Forge gave us his impression of the private soldier:

> *See the poor Soldier, when in health—with what chearfullness he meets his foes and encounters every hardship—if barefoot—he labours thro' the Mud & Cold with a Song in his mouth extolling War & Washington—if his food be bad—he eats it notwithstanding with seeming content—blesses God for a good Stomach—and whisles*

it into digestion. But harkee Patience—a moment—there comes a Soldier—h-h -is bare feet are seen thro' his worn Shoes—his legs nearly naked from the tatter'd remains of an only pair of stockings—his Breeches not sufficient to cover his Nakedness—his shirt hanging in Strings—his hair dishevell'd—his face meager—his whole appearance pictures a person forsaken & discouraged. He comes, and crys with an air of wretchedness & despair—I am Sick—my feet lame—my legs are sore—my body cover'd with this tormenting Itch—my cloaths are worn out—my Constitution is broken—my former Activity is exhausted by fatigue—my hunger & Cold—I fail fast I shall soon be no more! And all the reward I shall get will be—'Poor Will is dead.'[58]

Corporal John Allison is typical of many Continental soldiers who applied for a pension in 1818. He enlisted in 1775 at age twenty-one, and served in three New York regiments at different times during the entire eight years of the war. Along the way he participated in several major campaigns, battles and encampments. He traveled north for the Canadian Campaign and later further west with Generals Sullivan and Clinton in their efforts to suppress the Iroquois Nations. He suffered through the hard winter of 1778-1779 at Jockey Hollow, and in 1781 he marched five hundred miles to the battle of Yorktown, where he was in the second wave at the storming of Redoubt Number 10, considered by many to be the critical high point of the Revolutionary War.

Allison returned to Haverstraw, New York and resumed his former life as a farmer in 1782. Ten years later, at age forty-six, he sold his fifty-acre acre farm and migrated west with his wife and five children into the Catskill Mountains. Here he cut timber to supply to nearby iron forges. He enlisted again, this time in the Orange County Militia during the War of 1812, when he was fifty-eight years old. When the timber on his land became depleted, he fell into debt and lost his land in a sheriff's sale in 1820. Afterwards he somehow managed to live off of his Army pension of eight dollars a month, and then died penniless in 1828 at the age of seventy-four.[59]

Timothy Murphy, another veteran, was born in the vicinity of the Delaware Water Gap in 1751. Murphy was either indentured or apprenticed to the wealthy Van Campen family, and moved with them to Wyoming County, Pennsylvania, an area exposed to frequent Indian raids. He was of medium height, with a dark complexion and sturdy build. He enlisted in the Continental Army on June 29, 1775 at age twenty-four, in Captain John Lowdon's Company of Northumberland County Riflemen. Aaron Wright, one of Timothy's companions, kept a diary that recorded their adventures.[60] Lowdon's Company marched six hundred miles to join in the Siege of Boston. Murphy then moved to New York with the Continental Army, and fought in the battles of Brooklyn and White Plains, after which he joined in the retreat across New Jersey.

In 1777, Timothy Murphy was selected as one of five hundred hand-picked riflemen to accompany General Daniel Morgan to upstate New York to help stop General John Burgoyne's British Army from invading south from Canada. In the heat of the Battle of Saratoga, the British were being rallied by Brigadier General Simon Fraser. General Benedict Arnold (still on the American side at the time) rode up to General Morgan, pointed at Fraser, and shouted ". . . that man on the gray horse is a host in himself and must be disposed of." Morgan gave the order to his best marksmen, Murphy, to try and take him out. Murphy climbed a nearby tree, found a notch on which to rest his double-barreled rifle, took careful aim at the extreme distance of three hundred yards, and squeezed off a round.

General Fraser tumbled from his horse, shot through the stomach (after being taken from the field he died the next day). Sir Francis Clerke, another British Senior officer who served as General Burgoyne's chief Aide-de-Camp, galloped onto the field to take Fraser's place. Murphy's second shot dropped him. Panic soon spread among the British lines, and the Redcoat defenses collapsed. However, a recent study analyzed the various accounts of the battle to determine the origins and validity of the Murphy legend. After examining the ballistics involved in shooting a round ball bullet at the one-quarter-mile distance attributed to Murphy, it concluded that this feat of marksmanship was impossible.[61]

Murphy survived the cruel winter at Valley Forge. In the early summer, at the Battle of Monmouth, he and three fellow riflemen captured a retreating British general. Morgan's legendary riflemen were then ordered to the Mohawk Valley of New York to help stem the Tory and Native American raids there. Murphy tracked down and killed the notorious Christopher Service and his band of Tory raiders at the Iroquois village of Unadilla in October, 1778.

In 1779 Murphy enlisted in the Albany County Militia. While scouting in the Delaware County, New York forests during the spring of 1780, he was ambushed and taken prisoner by the Natives. He escaped during the night, but not before killing eleven of his captors as they slept. Early in 1781, Murphy reenlisted in the Pennsylvania Line and served under General "Mad Anthony" Wayne. He ended his astonishing military career by fighting at the Battle of Yorktown.

Murphy married twice, and had nine sons and four daughters. He never learned to read or write, but he acquired a number of farms and a grist mill after the war, and became a local political leader. His eventful life ended when he died in 1818 at age sixty-seven from cancer of the neck.[62]

Richard Wallace, another pensioner, was born in Nova Scotia in 1753. He volunteered in 1775 at the age of twenty-two to join the Connecticut Continental Line during the Siege of Boston, and then served as a ranger. As the American forces prepared to assault Fort Ticonderoga in September, 1777, they were blocked by British warships. Wallace was asked by Colonel John Brown to carry a message to the other side of Lake Champlain so the attack could be coordinated with another American assault force. The mission required him to swim across the lake with another soldier in mid-September. Swimming over five miles in the frigid waters of the lake was one of the greatest physical feats of the war. He was age seventy-nine when he described this event in his application for a pension in 1832:

With deep anxiety for the event, we undressed, bound our cloths on our backs, drank a little ginger and water and entered the cold waters of the lake, here about a mile in width. After proceeding a few yards, I was on the point of turning about. The water was so chilling I thought I would never reach the opposite shore, but when I reflected that the lives of many of my countrymen might depend on the success of the effort, I resolved at every hazard to go forward, and if I perished I should die in the best of causes. When we got into the middle of the lake the wind blew and dashed the water onto our bundles and wet them and made them very heavy. And the garter on which I had bound on my bundle swelled and got caught across my throat and choked me. When we had swam about two-thirds across, I found myself almost exhausted and thought I could not proceed further. But at the instant I was about giving up, the Lord seemed to give me new courage and strength and shifting my manner of swimming a little, I went forward and soon discover a tree directly before, about 20 rods from shore. This tree I reached with a struggle and thought I could not have obtained the shore if it had been to gain the world.

Wallace then rescued his companion who was foundering beside him. His mission resulted in an American victory and the capture of five hundred prisoners.[63]

Thomas Craige was born in 1754 and lived in Northampton, Massachusetts in 1776. He persuaded another twelve men to enlist with him. This evidence of his leadership appears to have been the reason he was assigned to recruiting duty, and soon after promoted to sergeant. His regiment joined the main American Army as it was being driven back to White Plains. He displayed almost reckless courage in the midst of the fierce fighting there, and described the action in vivid detail when he applied for a pension in 1833:

General Washington came in the rear, to the right and ordered the men to dig an entrenchment between the road and the place occupied by the two armies, extending right out to the front from the right so as to take the British line lengthwise . . . . The British sent infantry forward, down into the ravine or hollow way, who then turned to the left and came up to storm the entrenchment. The Americans twice repulsed the enemy's infantry back into the hollow. While they were rallying the Highlanders came down, stacked their arms, drew their broadswords and formed to the rear of the infantry. Then they all came up. Our men opened their fire as before, and soon the enemy's infantry opened and the Highlanders marched into our entrenchments, and the Americans retreated down the hill westwardly. After the enemy got into that entrenchment our guns in the redoubts were brought to bear lengthwise of the entrenchment with grape, and the enemy left it pretty soon and did not enter it again, but the cannonade was kept up until after dark.

Next morning the British moved a large column to their left as if they would come round and attempt tom turn our right, and we expected a hot time of it but they did not come within reach of our small arms, for as soon as they came within cannon shot, some large guns placed beyond our right, which I had not before seen, now opened upon the enemy, cut lanes through 'em, and broke them up, and in a short time they marched back.[64]

While the following narratives are not accounts of individual act of bravery, they do provide awe-inspiring descriptions of events of battlefield action.

Samuel Woodruff was born in 1760 in Southington, Connecticut, and served tours in the militia from 1776 through 1779. The climax of his military service was at the Second Battle of Freeman's Farm on October 7, 1777, at Saratoga. Woodruff returned home to Stonington after that American victory, and later moved to Windsor, Connecticut. He wrote the following narrative in 1833 when he applied for a pension. His description of this critical event at Saratoga contains details that can only be described by an eyewitness. However, his narrative, written fifty-six years after the event, appears to be embellished by details of enemy tactics and leadership strategy that could only have been learned afterward.

Woodruff's pension application stated:

. . . that while in his service at Saratoga he was engaged in the battle fought by the hostile armies on the seventh of October . . . about eleven o'clock of the forenoon of that day, the British troops advanced under the command of General Fraser, who led up the grenadiers, drove in our pickets and advanced guards, and made several unsuccessful charges with fixed bayonets upon the line of Continental troops at the American redoubts at Bemis Heights, near the headquarters of General Gates. But meeting a repulse at this point of attack, the grenadiers commenced a slow by orderly retreat, still keeping up a brisk fire. After falling back two or three hundred yards, this part of the hostile army met and joined the main body of the royal troops commanded by Lord Balcarres and General Riedesel.

Here, on a level piece of ground of considerable extent called Freeman's farms, thinly covered with yellow pines, the royal army formed an extensive line with the principle part of their artillery in front. By this time the American line was formed consisting of Continental, state troops and militia. The fire immediately became general through the line with renewed spirit, and nearly the whole force on both sides was brought into the action. General Fraser mounted on a grey horse a little to the right of their center and greatly distinguishing himself by his activity, received a rifle shot through his body (supposed to be from one of Colonel Morgan's sharpshooters), of which he died the next morning at eight o'clock at the Smith house, then the headquarters of general Burgoyne. Soon after the occurrence, the British grenadier reluctantly began to give ground, and their whole line, within a few minutes appeared to be broken. Still they kept up a respectable fire, both of artillery and musketry.

At about this stage in the action, general Arnold, while galloping up and down our line upon a small brown horse which he had that day borrowed from his friend Leonard Chester of Weatherfield, received a musket ball which broke his leg and killed the horse under him. He was at the moment about forty yards distant from the applicant and in fair view.[65]

Edward Elley was born in 1751 in Culpepper County, Virginia and lived there and in Spotsylvania County during his lifetime. He was older and more affluent than his fellow soldiers, so he was able to entertain Lafayette and fifty or sixty of his officers and men when they passed through his plantation on their way to Yorktown. He joined Washington's Army at Williamsburg before that battle, and provided a lively account of the siege at Yorktown. Like other soldiers who kept diaries, he relied heavily on phonetics, so referred to General Cornwallis as "Corn Wallace." He described the battle when he applied for a pension in 1846 at the age of ninety-four:

I was put among the able-bodied men to throwing up bomb batteries, Washington's Grand Battery having been previously finished, and whilst engaged in day and night, we were ordered to squat in the ditch when the enemy fired upon us. And Captain Welsh ordered the men to hurry with the work, else they would not sink deep enough to shelter them from the enemy's cannon by morning. And we who were on the front works were industrious and advanced with the work, and in the morning those behind wanted to crowd up on us when fired upon, but captain Welsh ordered them to keep their place as it was their own fault that they were exposed. And whilst engaged in this work, a cannon ball from the enemy came so near me that the wind of the ball blew my hunting shirt from the bank just by me and another ball came and struck within three feet of us in our work . . . . The works of the battery were thrown up by militia soldier sand whilst they were cutting brush a cannon ball came bounding along on the ground, and a youngster put his heel against it and was thrown into lockjaw and expired in a short time.

I frequently saw General Washington riding around and directing the operations, and after the siege began my place was at the guns in the battery called 'Washington's Grand Battery.' There were in this battery, four twenty-for-pounders, four eighteen-pounders, four twelve-pounders and twelve mortar pieces, and these were fired in platoons, four at a time, four at a time, and the mortars three at a time, making four rounds of mortars in order to keep up a constant fire. And whilst firing, the elevator of the guns got in a violent passion because the men in assistance dodged when fired upon. And General Clinton, coming up at that moment, put things to rights, and I remarked to the men in his hearing, 'Come my brave fellows, stick to your posts and the day will be ours' and for this remark I was very soon rewarded with a good breakfast from the general, which was very acceptable as I had not had a meal in twenty-four hours.[66]

Private Thomas Haines enlisted at Loudon, New Hampshire in 1776 at age eighteen. During the Battle of Saratoga, he was ordered to defend a captured British twelve-pound cannon. He climbed up its carriage and sat astride the barrel. When two British soldiers attempted to retake the cannon, Haines bayoneted one of them, which killed the man instantly. A second soldier thrust his bayonet but Haines knocked his musket to the ground. As the second soldier was attempting to retrieve his weapon, Haines bayoneted him through the head. As he withdrew his bayonet, Haines was shot in the face. The bullet carried away eleven teeth and a portion of his tongue. He fell and remained on the field for two days and nights.

Parties that were collecting and burying the dead had passed by him, and assumed that he was dead. But an officer noticed that his body was not stiff, and showed signs of life. He was taken to a hospital in Albany—miles away—and later to Schenectady, where he remained for thirteen months hovering between life and death. When he finally recovered he rejoined his regiment and served the remainder of his three-year enlistment. He returned home for about a year, but then reenlisted in April, 1781, and served until the end of the war. Haines received a pension and died in Louden in 1847, at age eighty-nine. A paymaster's ledger that contains his service records reads, "Wounded at Bemis Heights [Battle of Saratoga] and rendered unfit for service September 19, 1777."[67]

Continental soldiers were a spirited bunch, and their resilience was hardened by Washington himself, who always set an example of devotion to the cause of independence. He expected his soldiers to measure up to high standards of conduct, and his reputation was that of a harsh disciplinarian. On New Year's Day in 1776, Washington, in his General Orders, announced the beginning of a new army whose foundation must be "subordination and discipline" and that these were "the life and the soul of an army." Without them, the men ". . . would be no better than a commissioned mob."[68] However, a "rabble" would be a more truthful depiction of the army at that time. Few admirable Patriots from any level of society were enlisting, and the Commander-in-Chief would soon have to forge a fighting force from a diverse hoard of young men and children from the lowest levels of American society.

Chapter Six

Strangers, Bad Boys, and Children

Continental Army Soldiers were a horde of men of assorted ages, origins and cultures. In 1775, when seventy-three men enlisted in Johnson's multiethnic and multicultural 10th Company, New York 3rd Regiment, in Clarkstown, New York, thirty-four of the new recruits originated from adjoining states. Kingston, New York, was another central recruiting station, and a fifty-plus mile walk for recruits who came from surrounding upstate New York counties. Many of the men were drifters, since existing tax and census records show little evidence that any had lived in the towns of origin they declared on the muster roll as their home. In western New Jersey, Lieutenant Colonel William Taylor's Battalion had an even greater proportion of men traveling long distances to enlist. Out of 146 new soldiers, 107 came from other counties or states.[69]

Washington realized that native-born Americans would not be enough to fill his ranks, and was well aware that a huge pool of immigrants had poured into the country in the decade prior to the war. Some were destitute—among them English, German and Scots-Irish—and since they had no roots in their newly-chosen society, they found their way into the Continental Army in great numbers. Of the seventy-three men in Captain Johnson's 10th Company, thirty-eight (52 percent) of the recruits were foreigners, while in the New Jersey battalions 22 percent were from other countries.

The war records of the Pennsylvania Continental Line record the place of birth for only 582 of the estimated 15,000 state's troops. However, this small sampling shows that a surprising number of this group, 387 (62 percent), were foreign born. This includes eight-seven men from various provinces of Germany and sixty-four recruits who were born in England. This unusually high number probably reflects the proportion of foreigners in the population of the state as a whole.[70] An analysis of the Maryland Continental Line as it appeared in 1782 shows a similar pattern, with 40 percent of the troops being foreign-born.[71]

Desertion of Hessian soldiers to the American side was frequent because it offered the German men an opportunity to start a new life in America. The soldiers were so impressed by opportunities in the new country that thousands of them never returned to their native land.

After he arrived in New York, Johann Döhla, a private, wrote in his diary, "The American land is good and incomparable land . . . . It is rich and fruitful, well cultivated, and with much grain, especially a great deal of Indian corn; and it has many and beautiful forests of both soft and hardwood trees unknown to us." He praised the freedom of religion in America and related his desire and that of his comrades to learn about life in the colonies. This attitude is repeated in many journals, diaries, and letters written by Hessian soldiers. Many of the men married American women.[72] The German Province of Hesse sent 19,000 of their sons to America. Between casualties and deserters only a little over half of them ever returned home.[73] An estimated one out of every eight men in the Continental Army was of German heritage.

Scots-Irish immigrants were the largest group sought out by recruiters. While most recruiting records do not reveal a place of birth, estimates can be made using a sort of reverse engineering based on the number of Scots-Irish surnames in New England and New York. In regiments from those areas between ten and 20 percent of the Continental Army was made up of these Presbyterian immigrants. Catholic Irishmen did not arrive in American in large numbers until the late 1840s, when the Irish famine took hold.

HOW OLD WERE THEY?

American officers in the War for Independence, as in any war, soon learned that younger men made the best soldiers. They could be bent by discipline more easily, and they were willing to take greater risks than older men. With bodies that were resilient and robust, they could endure exhausting marches and other rigors of life in the field. They were regarded as expendable by society, since they did not have roles of importance in their communities, and their youth made it less likely that they were encumbered with family obligations. Recruiters targeted younger men who had no land, and those who had no commitments to established occupations or businesses. Those who wanted to escape from debt or indenture were especially attractive prospects.

An almost identical pattern of age distribution becomes evident in the few surviving records from that era that provide age data. The average age of the 289 enlisted men in the four companies of the 3rd New York Regiment from southern New York counties who enlisted in the summer of 1775 was twenty-five-and-one-half years. The oldest soldier was Christopher DeWitt, age forty-nine, a laborer from Hanover, New York (now Montgomery Township), located about fifty miles south of Kingston. The youngest was John Conelio, age ten, a laborer from "East Jersey." Six were teenagers, eleven were over age thirty, and three were over age forty.

A rich source of age data, covering about 1,500 enlisted men, can be found in the rolls of the Pennsylvania Continental regiments. This large sampling provides a high degree of accuracy in assessing the ages of the soldiers. At the extreme ends are four boys as young as ten and a man aged seventy-three. Fourteen men were age fifty-four or older. The average age of the soldiers was twenty-five years and five months, with very few older than age thirty. Men who were between eighteen and thirty-two years old comprised over 72 percent of the sampling. This data confirms that the Continental Army was chiefly an assemblage of younger men.

An analysis of the 1818 pension applications of 546 New England soldiers shows that many did not actually know their ages. Age data was listed for 396 members of this group, and the average was twenty-three years. Of that number, almost half were under age twenty-one. A similar study of 419 enlisted men who applied for pensions in Virginia found that 90 percent were less than twenty-five years of age at enlistment, and had a median age of twenty years. Twenty-one soldiers in the group were ages fourteen and fifteen, even though the minimum legal age for service in Virginia was sixteen."[74]

In another Southern state, North Carolina, a descriptive enlistment roster from 1782 shows that thirty-four "planters" from Bladen County had an average age of twenty-five years. Although this was late in the war, it confirms that the average age of recruits did not vary throughout the eight years of the conflict.[75]

Drawn from nine New Jersey towns, the majority of 540 enlisted men of the New Jersey Continental Line were quite young. Over half of them were under twenty-two, and many were teenagers. A smaller number were boys age fourteen and younger.[76]

Here is the age distribution of these New Jersey Soldiers:

Below 18 . . . .57 . . . . .10.5% 33-36 . . . . .38 . . . . . . .7.0%
18-22 . . . . . .238 . . . . .44.1% 37-41 . . . . .33 . . . . . . .6.1%
23-27 . . . . . .101 . . . . .18.7% 41+ . . . . . . .25 . . . . . . .4.6%.
28-32 . . . . . . .48 . . . . .8.9%

America's adversaries also recognized the desirability of youth in their ranks. Hessian infantry Captain Johann Ewald engaged in hand-to-hand combat with Continental troops several times in battles at Coochs Bridge, Brandywine, Monmouth, Bound Brook and the Short Hills. He wrote, "The young people 16 to 18 years of age . . . since they did not yet know the dangers of war, were the ones who attacked best, and upon whom one could rely in critical circumstances. My old soldiers were the first who perceived our situation, and I was forsaken by many of them, but the young lads stood by me in the innocents of their heads, and to them I owed the preservation of myself and my party."[77]

A guide for recruiters issued in England in 1775 expressed a strong preference for young men by stating, "The fire of youth, the fire of emulation, the visions of preferment, even the spirits arising from the novelty and the inexperience of danger, all impel raw soldiers to exertions which veteran soldiers will shun if the can."[78]

Well-known diarist Joseph Plumb Martin was fifteen when he enlisted in Connecticut, artilleryman Jeremiah Levering was about twelve, and hundreds more under the legal age of sixteen served in all branches of service. The men who served under the age of twenty numbered in the thousands.

Ambrose Searl, Secretary to the British fleet commander, provided a description that seems to encapsulate the appearance of the American Army in the eyes of the enemy, as well as civilians. Writing from New York City in 1776, he commented, ". . . their army is the strangest that was ever collected: Old men of 60, boys of 14, and blacks of all ages, and ragged for the most part, compose the motley crew."[79]

CHILD SOLDIERS

When French artillery Lieutenant Clermont-Crèvecoeur first encountered the Continental Army at Philipsburg, New Jersey in July, 1781, he was astonished by the number of "children who could not have been over fourteen."[80] One of them was John Hudson of the 1st New York Regiment. Hudson was age twelve when he enlisted in a militia company; he had joined the 1st New York for the duration of the war. Three months later he was on his way, with dozens of other teen-age boys in his regiment, to the Battle of Yorktown.[81] Historian Charles P. Neimeyer estimates that about 20 percent of the soldiers in the "New York regiments . . . were teen-aged boys."[82]

Child-soldiers of the French Army also headed south with the New York boys. French enlistment records show that there were about half-a-dozen boys aged fifteen and younger in each regiment. They were called *enfants de troupe*. The sons of soldiers could actually enlist at half-pay at the tender age of six. They began their careers as musicians, until they reached age sixteen, at which point they became regular soldiers.[83]

For the American militia draft the minimum legal age was sixteen, but the Continental Army had no legal minimum age. It helps to understand that in the eighteenth century life expectancy was shorter, and men were regarded as mature at a younger age than by today's standards. Men of all ages who were drafted often hired substitutes, or provided a family member to serve in their place. In practice, these replacements, if physically fit, would be accepted regardless of age, so many were boys between the ages of twelve and fifteen. Research from family genealogies, when combined with military and civil records, provides some verifiable clues as to the age of the youngest soldiers.

Young boys were sometimes regarded as mascots by the adult soldiers. Although most of them were listed in muster rolls as regular privates, tradition

The boy is about six or seven years old. He is wearing a uniform, so it appears that he is a combat soldier, not a drummer boy. He is also wearing a Colt Revolver.
(Image taken between 1860 and 1865, courtesy of Morris Gallery of the Cumberland, Nashville, Tennessee)

dictated that they become fifers and drummers. The life of a drummer boy appeared rather glamorous, and boys would even run away from home to enlist. Others may have been the sons or orphans of soldiers from the same unit. The image of a child in battle was considered intensely patriotic by artists, who often depicted them in paintings.

Were child-soldiers victims of adult criminal exploitation? There is little evidence of grieving or remorseful parents in contemporary accounts. These children are most often seen as dutifully serving family economic needs, and joining a benign setting of relatives and friends. Economic necessity often resulted in children joining the army. They were offered in place of fathers or brothers, whose absence would cause hardship because of the loss of their labor. Boys usually passed on their army pay, and any bounties went to their fathers. As an example, at the age of fifteen, Obadiah Benge was shrewdly bartered into the service by his step-father, John Fielder, ". . . as a substitute for one James Green, [and that] his said step-father received from said James Green a horse, bridle and saddle for the same."[84]

University of the Pacific history Professor Caroline Cox found that boy soldiers commonly joined a network of family and friends in the army.[85] Obadiah Benge joined an older brother who was already enlisted. Eleven-year-old Cyrus Allen joined the Continental Army as a servant to his officer father. Elijah Lacey, age fourteen, served as a private soldier in a company of Virginia troops commanded by his much older brother Matthew Lacey. Sixteen-year-old Moses Piper was delighted when his friend, Joshua Davis, who was about age fifteen, enlisted in the same company with him.[86]

Cox sums up what historians deduce about the child-soldiers of the Revolution, a conclusion which lacks any element of pathos: "A broad range of impulses drew boys into the army. Sometimes, it was political idealism, youthful enthusiasm, and a desire for adventure and travel that enticed boys to enlist. Others sought to get away from bad home situations, boring work, or trying masters. Whatever the impulse, it was often put to the service of families' economic needs. As their boys went off to war, families and boys found networks of community to offer them comradeship and familiarity in an alien world."

John Conelio, the ten-year-old from East Jersey, enlisted on August 4, 1775 at Clarkstown, New York in the 3rd New York Regiment. The last evidence of his service appears on a muster roll of his company taken October 3, 1775, at Fort Ticonderoga, where he is listed as a private "On Command at Fort St. Johns."[87] This shows that the child, only two months after enlisting, marched 150 miles to Fort Ticonderoga and then another 180 miles to British-held Fort St. Johns, beyond the Canadian border. On arriving, Conelio's company was immediately thrown into the fierce fighting that took place during the siege of the walled fortress. Enlistments began expiring after the fort fell to the Americans in November, 1775, and the New York regiments began to disintegrate. Few military records were kept during these tumultuous days, and no further documentary evidence of John Conelio can be found for the remaining seven years of the war. Nor is there any evidence of the boy in any type of civil record after the war. He could have perished in the assault at Fort St. Johns or may have continued north with a remnant of New York troops that went on to a tragic defeat at Quebec City. All said, it is likely that he perished at some point during the ill-fated Canadian campaign in the winter of 1775.

Archibald Smithson was born in 1765 in Bush River, Lower Hundred, Harford County, Maryland, the youngest of eleven children. He was age ten when the war broke out. According to information found in land records for the county, he was captured by the British during the New York Campaign of 1776, and imprisoned in New York City along with two other soldiers from his home county. His bad luck probably occurred when the Maryland Brigade was engaged in fierce fighting at White Plains, when many Americans were captured during the retreat north from the city. Alternately, it may have happened when Fort Washington fell in Manhattan, since 2,800 Americans were captured there.

These men were confined to the infamous Sugar House prison in New York City, and on ship hulks in Wallabout Bay, off the shore of Brooklyn. A total of 10,000 American prisoners were kept under inhuman conditions, and many died while in prison from starvation and disease. Somehow Smithson survived his captivity and returned home to Maryland, but despite his suffering and heroism, he does not appear in any Revolutionary War records.[88]

Smithson reenlisted during the War of 1812, as did many aging soldiers in other states. He is listed as a private in the 39th Regiment of Maryland Militia. As a forty-seven-year-old private in the Maryland Militia, the former boy soldier saw action when the British attempted to invade his state. The Redcoats were repulsed by land at North Point and by sea at Fort Mc Henry, where Francis Scott Key wrote the poem that would eventually become "The Star-Spangled Banner." Curiously, Smithson did not apply for a pension. This suggests that he may not have been aware of the law, or was discouraged by the complexity of the process. Many veterans also lost documents over the years that would have proven their enlistment. In the study of 302 soldiers from Maryland who enlisted in 1782, it was found that less than ten applied for pensions.[89] Smithson died in Harford County, Maryland in 1825 at the age of sixty.

Isaac Wheeler, Jr., of Stonington, New London County, Connecticut, was eight years old when he began serving as a fifer. His father, Lieutenant Isaac Wheeler, had enlisted in 1776 in the 5th Connecticut Regiment and brought along Isaac, his eldest son, accompanied by two slaves, Enoch and Caesar. The foursome all joined Colonel Harry Babcock's Regiment at Newport, Rhode Island. A pay record for "wages and bounty" dated April 23, 1776 for Joseph Smith's 8th Company under Colonel David Waterbury, verifies that both father and son were at Newtown, Connecticut on that date. Isaac participated in the Battle of Brandywine, and his regiment went on to fight at the battles of Ridgefield, Connecticut, Newport, Rhode Island and Monmouth. Wheeler died May 11, 1856, in Stonington.[90]

Nathan Futrell was a drummer boy in the North Carolina militia at the remarkably tender age of seven. According to the Futrell family Bible, he was born in Northampton County, North Carolina on September 10, 1773.[91] He likely was in combat at two of the most significant events of the war. In August 1780 his unit was at the battle of Camden, South Carolina where the Americans suffered devastating losses. At the Battle of Guilford Courthouse, North Carolina in March 1781, the militia was the first line of defense. Arranged in a long row behind a fence, they were ordered by Maj. Gen. Nathanael Greene to "fire two volleys and then retreat." As veteran Hessian and British regulars advanced with fixed bayonets they became bogged down in the mud of a freshly-plowed field. British Captain Thomas Saumarez described the action and the effectiveness of the North Carolina troops: "The Royal Welsh Fusiliers had to attack the enemy in front, under every disadvantage, having to march over a field lately ploughed, which was wet and muddy from the rains which had recently fallen. The regiment marched to the attack under a most galling and destructive fire, which it could only return by an occasional volley."[92]

No military records have been found for Nathan Futrell. He died on August 11, 1829. Nathan and his wife Charity were buried on a hill on their farm in Trigg County, Kentucky.[93] A plaque was later placed on their graves by the

A Drummer Boy of the Royal Scotts Dragoons, by George William Joy, 1902

Daughters of the American Revolution. A prominent historical marker on Route 68 near Golden Pond, a ghost town in western Trigg County, Kentucky, reads:

Nathan Futrell was listed as the youngest to serve in the North Carolina Militia. He served as a drummer boy at age seven. (Historical marker off of US 68 in Trigg County, Kentucky)

DRUMMER BOY AT 7. Nathan Futrell, reputed to be the youngest drummer boy in the War of the Revolution, was born, N.C., 1773. Joined N.C. Continental Militia. Married, 1798, came to Ky., 1799. Settled here on Ford's Creek, 1820, where he farmed, set out the first apple orchard, built one of area's first grist mills, was official surveyor. Died, 1829.

George Washington's personal writings reveal much about his impression of his young enlisted soldiers. He was angry when they abandoned the field in retreat, and was appalled when they only enlisted in places where they stood to gain the most bounty money. But, more often than not, he praised them for their courage, loyalty and endurance in conditions that would have broken other armies.

Chapter Seven

Hay Foot-Straw Foot

Recruiting and Training

The most common form of localized communication during the American Revolution was the "broadside." These one-page handbills, quickly printed and posted, had a variety of uses, among them the announcement of recruiting efforts and other breaking military news. Zealous recruiters were strongly incentivized, since they were being paid a fee for each man they enlisted. In New York, they were paid a bounty of one dollar for each soldier. In their eagerness to enrich themselves, many ignored legal constraints, and were less than particular about who they signed up. In the illustration shown, a typical broadside poster of 1777, the restriction that required that recruits be at least sixteen years old and at least five-feet-two inches in height does not appear. As a result, new soldiers were often impressionable younger teenagers and children.

Another recruiting broadside was posted in Philadelphia in 1776. It generously promised that each enlistee would be provided with a uniform and "abundant rations," and would also receive payment of sixty dollars a year in silver and gold. This particular poster concluded on a positive note: ". . . who shall embrace the opportunity of spending a few happy years in viewing the different parts of this continent after which he shall return home to his friends with his pockets full of money and his head covered with laurels."[94] These types of false promises were immediately broken. Obviously the creator of the broadside conveniently ignored the realities of war as he collected his fee.

Recruiting tactics during the Revolutionary War made use of many of the same themes as those used in later wars. Military service would offer the opportunity to travel to new and exciting places, and during these adventures the young soldiers would be showered with praise by a thankful public. They would return home with money and land bounties, and as veterans they would be forever honored by appreciative citizens for their service. These were powerful inducements for impoverished young men who had never traveled beyond neighboring farms.

John Allison was a twenty-one year old laborer on his father's farm. He left his home in Haverstraw, New York to enlist in the Continental Army only two months after the war had begun. John was accompanied by his father, a captain in the Orange County Militia, and his older cousin, who also wanted to join. After traveling two miles to Clarkstown, the nearest large town, they signed up at the hamlet's only tavern, which was owned by John Coe.[95] While John's father very likely served as his role model for becoming a soldier, the gullible country boy must have been impressed by encountering a jovial, smooth talking and impeccably uniformed recruiting officer.

The army recruiter, usually a junior officer selected for his charisma, paraded through town streets to attract attention. There may have been an escort with fifes and drums, or even a full band playing inspiring marches. He usually carried a flag, and gave stirring patriotic speeches in the town square. He rarely mentioned the cause of independence or nationalistic issues, but insisted that the war was all about defending homes and loved ones. The recruiting officer's path usually led to the nearest tavern, where an unlimited supply of free liquor was provided to entice the potential recruits. The wide-eyed farm boys must have been easy pickings under these circumstances.[96]

Like many young men of that time, John Allison came from a large family, in his case a family of seventeen children. In a rural economy children provided the labor, and John no doubt toiled on his father's land with his nine brothers. These young men may also have been hired out to work for other farmers to help pay for family necessities. With few prospects, Allison was typical of farm boys, who saw an opportunity to escape from the repetitive cycle of callous work to an exciting new life that promised steady wages, abundant food and a fine-looking uniform. Since his father was a member of the local militia, he likely created a military culture in the family, and may have encouraged John to enlist. The promise of a bounty of ten shillings for bringing his own musket added to the appeal.[97]

The New York Provincial Congress provided: "Volunteers from the time of their enlistment, to enter into immediate pay, at one shilling and eleven pence per day. They are likewise to be provided with a suit of regimental clothes, a firelock, ammunition, accoutrements, and every other article necessary for the equipment of American soldiers."[98] But the New York Congress did not keep their side of the bargain. The disappointed new soldiers remained in their civilian clothes, and were without weapons, for many weeks. They were not paid until three months later, when one month's pay was reluctantly doled out to quell the rising discontent.

In the town of Milford, Connecticut, Joseph Plumb Martin, envious of his young associates who had marched off to fight, attempted to enlist at age fourteen. At first he was prevented from doing so by his guardian grandparents. After watching his friends depart he wrote, "By and by, they will come swaggering back, thought I, and tell me of their exploits, all their 'hair-breadth 'scapes.' . . . O, that was too much to be borne with by me." He slipped off the next year to enlist at age fifteen for six months in the Connecticut militia. He returned home in December, 1776, for four months, but then reenlisted in the Continental Army. He would not return until the war ended six years later. Martin later described his experiences:

I one evening went off with a full determination to enlist at all hazards. When I arrived at the place of rendezvous I found a number of young men of my acquaintance there; the old bantering began-come, if you will enlist I will, says one, you have long been talking about it, says another-come, now is the time. 'Thinks I to myself,' I will not be laughed into it or out of it, at any rate; I will act my own pleasure after all. But what did I come here for to-night? Why, to enlist; then enlist I will. So seating myself at the table, enlisting orders were immediately presented to me; I took up the pen, loaded it with the fatal charge, made several mimic imitations of writing my name, but took especial care not to touch the paper with the pen until an unlucky wight who was leaning over my shoulder gave my hand a stroke, which caused the pen to make a woeful scratch on the paper. 'O, he has enlisted,' said he, 'he has made his mark, he is fast enough now.' Well, thought I, I may as well go through with the business now as not; so I wrote my name fairly upon the indentures.

And now I was a soldier, in name at least, if not in practice; but I had now to go home, after performing this, my heroic action. How shall I be received there? but the report of my adventure had reached there before I did. In the morning when I first saw my grandparents, I felt considerably of the sheepish order. The old gentleman first accosted me with, 'Well, you are going a soldiering then, are you?' I had nothing to answer; I would much rather he had not asked me the question. I saw that the circumstance hurt him and the old lady too; but it was too late now to repent. The old gentleman proceeded, - 'I suppose you must be fitted out for the expedition, since it is so.- Accordingly, they did 'fit me out' in order, with arms and accouterments, clothing and cake, and cheese in plenty, not forgetting to put my pocket Bible into my knapsack.[99]

Continental Army officers scoured the countryside trying to fill their companies and regiments with volunteers. The Provincial Congress of each colony provided *Instructions for the Inlistment of Men* that were issued to recruiters through company commanders. The list for New York provided these restrictions:[100]

You are not to inlist any man who is not able bodied, healthy and a good marcher: but as men of good appearance have ruptures and venereal complaints, which render them incapable of soldier's duty, you must give attention, that you be not imposed upon and into the opinion of a surgeon, where ther is room for suspicion.

You will have great regard for the moral character, sobriety in particular—let our manners distinguish us from our enemies, as much as the cause we are engaged in.

Those who engage in the defense of their country's liberties shall be enlisted until the last day of December, unless sooner discharged by the Continental Congress.

You shall appoint such men as sergeants and corporals as recommended themselves by their ability, activity and diligence.

Apprentices and servants are not to be signed up without the consent of their masters.

GENERAL WASHINGTON WANTS YOU!

In the autumn of 1776, the debilitated Continental Army was huddled along the shore of the Delaware River. They had lost New York City, and the surviving force of about 10,000 men had been driven across New Jersey in what was later called "The Long March." Due to illness or lack of clothing and weapons, one third of the force was unfit for duty. But the tragic year of 1776 ended well, as every student learns in school. Washington's well-known feat of crossing the river on Christmas night to annihilate the Hessians inspired a nation that was craving for a victory. However, even this astonishing event did not inspire men enough to enlist, and the Continental Army's manpower problem soon became desperate. After the British evacuated the Boston area in March, 1776, the war had shifted from New England to New York. This new theater of action was far from the homes of the New England troops who made up a majority of the American army. Enlistments expired, men returned to their farms, and few new recruits stepped up to replace them.

The smallpox epidemic around Boston was another obstacle. Recruiters were reluctant to sign on men who might be infected with this highly contagious disease. Volunteerism was also reduced by reports of the hardships endured during the Canadian Campaign, and the relatively high wages paid to civilian laborers.

The devastating losses of 1776 called for strong measures. At that time the Continental Army was understaffed by a third to a half. Major General Nathanael Greene wrote to Washington on September 28, 1776: "The Congress has never furnished the men voted by near one half, certainly by above a third. Had we had numbers we need not have retreated from Long Island or New York. But the extent of ground to guard rendered the retreat necessary; otherwise the army would have been ruined by detachments. The enemy never could have driven us from Long Island and New York if our rear had been secured. We must have an army to meet the enemy everywhere; to act offensively as well as defensively. Our soldiers are as good as ever were; and were the officers half as good as the men, they would beat any army on the globe of equal numbers."[101]

After September 16, 1776, each state was required to contribute regiments in proportion to its population. This measure, passed by the Continental Congress, became known as "the eighty-eight battalion resolve." This decision determined the basic organizational structure of the Continental Army for the rest of the war.[102] Men were promised an immediate payment of twenty dollars and one hundred acres of land if they were willing to sign up for the duration. If patriotism and land should not be enough, George Washington added the phrase "and all the plunder they shall take from the enemy."[103]

Washington pleaded with Congress to extend enlistments to a minimum of three years of service, which he believed was the time needed to build a competent army. Finally, in late 1776, Congress acted by authorizing the states to raise eighty-eight regiments "for three years or the war," starting January 1, 1777. These terms of enlistment remained in effect for the remainder of the war, but the ambiguous language used in the authorization would cause a calamity three years later. The soldiers interpreted it as meaning "either three years or the duration of the war," whichever came first. However, Congress steadfastly maintained that it meant for the duration of the war only.

New England faced other challenges while attempting to fill enlistment quotas. Privateering tempted many men to go to sea, since seductive promises of sharing in the booty captured by government-sanctioned ships attracted many men. These privately-owned armed vessels were commissioned by states to attack enemy ships, usually merchant vessels. Crews were entitled to receive portions of the value of any cargo they seized, so captured hulls and their contents were sold or auctioned, and profits divided with the state. In all, about 55,000 American seamen choose to serve aboard the privateers.

A RELUCTANT DRAFT

George Washington always maintained that voluntary enlistments were the best way to sustain an army, but soon found that monetary payments, land bounties and other inducements were not adequate to entice men to enlist. He reluctantly admitted, ". . . allurements of the most exhorbanent bounties and every other inducement that could be thought of, have been tried in vain and had little other effect than to increase the rapacity and raise the demands of those to whom they were held out. We may fairly infer that the country has already been drained of that class of men whose tempers, attachments and circumstances disposed them to enter permanently or for a length of time, into the army . . . ."[104]

Washington initially requested one-year drafts, since it would have been unrealistic to initiate a draft that committed all men for the duration of the war. Congress then requested the states to fill draft quotas from their own militia regiments. Next, the states required towns or counties to supply a specific quota of men. Often names were drawn from a hat. A typical notice delivered to a draftee might read: "This is to inform you that you are this evening drafted as one of the Continental men to go to George Washington's headquarters, and you must go or find and able bodied man in your room [place], or pay a fine of 20 pounds in law [ful] money in 24 hours."

This notice clearly states that service could be easily avoided by paying a fine or furnishing a substitute. People bought recruits from entrepreneurs, enterprising businessmen who would pay a willing recruit a bounty and then offer him to those seeking a substitute. The high bidder sent the recruit in his place and the entrepreneur pocketed the difference between the amount of the bid for a substitute and the bounty he paid the recruit.

Some masters enticed slaves to serve as their substitutes, offering freedom at the end of the conflict as an incentive, sometimes coupled with a small monetary reward. In general, slave recruits were required to serve for the duration of the war, and they acquitted themselves well. Baron Ludwig von Closen, a French officer on Rochambeau's staff, reviewed the Continental Army at Dobbs Ferry, New York on July 6, 1781. He commented that the 2nd Rhode Island Regiment, which was 75 percent black, was "the most neatly dressed, the best under arms, and the most precise in its maneuver."[105]

About 5,000 free black men and slaves served in the Continental Army, and many more filled supporting billets as waggoners, drovers, and laborers. Early in the war many freemen and slaves came from the New England states, especially Rhode Island and Massachusetts. The Bay State declared slaves and free blacks eligible to enlist in 1777, and the Rhode Island Assembly allowed the enlistment of "every able-bodied negro, mulatto, or Indian man slave" on February 14, 1778. Later in the war, Southern slaves gradually gained the opportunity to enroll, although South Carolina and Georgia generally resisted such enlistments. At the beginning of 1778, nearly 10 percent of Washington's effective force was African-American.

Prisoners of war, as well as British and Hessian deserters, were also eagerly sought for the war effort. Understandably, Washington was wary of these men. In 1778, he warned both military and civil officials, including James Bowdoin, President of the Massachusetts Provincial Congress, and Major General William Heath, that the Redcoat soldiers might desert in battle and escape back to enemy lines.[106] The entire army of British and Hessian prisoners captured by the victorious Americans at the Battle of Saratoga in 1777 was considered fair game. During the war Hessian mercenaries were promised citizenship for enlisting on the American side. Pamphlets, secretly delivered to their camps, offered freedom and land to anyone willing to desert and sign up with the Americans. Before the war ended, Congress offered Hessian deserters farmland, two pigs, and a cow, along with citizenship.[107]

Men in bondage were also stalked by eager recruiters. The mass immigration in the years before the war had created a huge pool of white servants who had been indentured for specified terms. In general, their master's permission was required, but some states allowed servants to enlist without their approval. Vagrants and the homeless were also drafted into the army, and convicted criminals received pardons for terms of military service. As was found in Peterborough, New Hampshire, there were even new soldiers who were listed as being "mentally deranged."

THE PRUSSIAN MARTINET

In December, 1777, a foreign officer arrived on the French ship *Le Flamand* at Portsmouth, New Hampshire, after a rough voyage that had lasted sixty-six days. Harsh conditions had caused the crew to mutiny, and the vessel had caught fire three times. The ship was loaded with contraband weapons for the American cause, so any encounter with a British warship would have meant certain capture and imprisonment of its passengers. Frederick William Augustus Henry Ferdinand, Baron von Steuben, a passenger on this ship, had undertaken the voyage to offer his services to the fledgling army of the newly formed United States of America.[108]

This forty-eight-year-old Prussian gentleman carried letters of introduction addressed to General Washington and the Continental Congress written by Benjamin Franklin during his lengthy diplomatic stay in Paris. The veteran infantry officer claimed to have served in the Prussian Army under Frederick the Great during the Seven Years' War. American history has always proclaimed the British Army to be the mightiest in the world, but at that time many historians have acknowledged that the Prussian Army was even more powerful. This reputation was based on discipline, professionalism and the ability to maneuver in battle. When he stepped off the ship, von Steuben was clad in a dazzling scarlet uniform with blue trim, which he had been led to believe was the proper uniform for an officer in the American Army. Displayed on his chest was a large, ornate, eight-pointed star of the Baden-Durlach Order of Fidelity, a chivalric order similar to British knighthood. His Italian greyhound, Azor, sat by his side.

After debarking, Baron von Steuben informed the Continental Congress, "I am the possessor of some talents in the art of war, they should be much dearer to me if I could employ them in the service of a Republick such as I hope to see soon in America."[109] While flaunting his credentials as a lieutenant general, he approached Congress with humility and a tempting offer. He admitted that he had never been promised a commission in the Continental Army, and had no desire for one. In a nod to George Washington, he also declined pay except for the reimbursement of expenses. His only modest request was the honor to serve Washington in any capacity.

Relying on a bit of flattery, von Steuben insisted that he had been influenced by Washington's skillful leadership in the previous year's Trenton-Princeton

Hessian Soldier, from a set of watercolors by Captain Friedrich Konstantin von Germann, commanding officer of Company 4, Hesse-Hanau Erbprinz Regiment. This unit was captured at the Battle of Saratoga, New York, in October 1777, while serving as one of 8,000 Hessians under General Baron Riedesel.

campaign, since news of that early American victory had spread throughout Europe, and had established Washington's reputation as a brilliant general. After serving under Frederick the Great, the pushy Baron claimed to seek a leader of equal stature and had written to Washington, "Such being the Sentiments I always profest, I dare hope that the respectable Congress of the United States of America, will accept my Services. I could Say moreover that your Excellency is the only Person under whom (after having Served under the King of Prussia) I could wish to pursue an Art to which I have Wholly given up my Self."[110]

However, despite his self-promotion, von Steuben had never been a Prussian lieutenant general. The highest rank he had ever held was captain, under an impoverished German prince who could not afford to continue his services. With gloomy prospects, and a shaky financial future, he regarded America as an attractive prospect. While fervently professing his eagerness to serve only in the American Army, he was doing so because he had previously been unsuccessful in seeking other military appointments in Europe.

THE RIGHT PLACE AT THE RIGHT TIME

Despite his stretch of the truth, the baron had approached Congress at a critical time. The raw forces were ending a depressing campaign. They had retreated forty miles north from the head of Chesapeake Bay after the British invaders under General Howe, with 18,000 men, had landed at Head of Elk, Delaware in August, 1777. During the weeks that followed, the beleaguered Americans were pushed north forty miles, and then crushed in the horrendous defeat at Brandywine. They were then forced to evacuate Philadelphia, the nation's capital at the time. Lack of men and supplies forced Washington to head for winter camp at Valley Forge, eighteen miles northwest of the city. This site was chosen because it was between York, Pennsylvania, where the Continental Congress had fled after the fall of Philadelphia, and American supply depots located in Reading. During that winter of 1777-1778, the British forces would enjoy a comfortable and festive season watching plays and otherwise entertaining themselves in the city.

On December 19, 1777, Washington's army of 12,000 tired, cold, and ill-equipped men marched into the desolate camp. By February, nearly 4,000 of them were sick, or so poorly clothed that they were unfit for duty. Von Steuben arrived in grand style on the dismal scene on February 23, 1778, but the committee that greeted him consisted of freezing, barefoot soldiers clad in rags, or wrapped in thin blankets, chanting "We want meat! We want meat!" Although Martha Washington visited her husband at the camp, and tried to provide comfort, her nurturing was no match for the horrible conditions that prevailed.

When New York's Gouverneur Morris, a member of the Continental Congress, visited the camp, he wrote, "An army of skeletons appeared before our eyes, naked, starved, sick and discouraged," The Marquis de Lafayette commented, "The unfortunate soldiers were in want of everything; they had neither coats nor hats, nor shirts, nor shoes. Their feet and their legs froze until they were black, and it was often necessary to amputate them." A frustrated George Washington would accuse the Congress of ". . . little feeling for the naked and distressed soldiers. I feel superabundantly for them, and from my soul pity those miseries, which it is neither in my power to relieve or prevent." There would be a worse winter and more severe food shortages at Jockey Hollow during the future winter of 1779-1780, but morale would never again be so low.

While the hardships among American soldiers at Valley Forge are iconic images of the Revolutionary War, there was actually a positive aspect to this terrible experience. Washington, after observing the endurance of his men, began to gain confidence that they would survive to fight again, writing, "Contrary to my expectations, we have been able to keep the soldiers from mutiny or dispersion, although in the single article of provisions, they have encountered enough to occasion one or the other." He began to sense an opportunity for retraining and rejuvenation, and the possibility that a confident and professional American army could emerge by spring.

Into this troubled setting stepped Baron von Steuben, the unemployed officer from Prussia who had unconditionally proffered his expertise to the American cause. Although preoccupied with the day-to-day survival of his army, Washington found time to ride out to greet him when he arrived at the bleak campground. Within a few days the German officer had earned his respect, and a close friendship soon developed between the two men although the Baron spoke only German and limited French. In spite of von Steuben's ambiguous credentials, the Commander-in-Chief was impressed by his personal qualities, his professional appearance, and the potential contribution he could make to the Continental Army. He appeared to be the man who could create an expert training plan for the Continental Army in the linear tactics of European-style warfare. These maneuvers were employed on open fields by lines of opposing infantry troops facing each other, as close as fifty yards apart, while firing in unison. The Americans, while unskilled in the use of these formations, were equipped with French-made, bayoneted flintlock muskets, which matched the effectiveness of the renowned British Brown Bess.[111]

At first impression, Baron von Steuben was appalled at the relaxed and disordered nature of the Americans, many of whom were new recruits. Others were wounded or sick. His impatience with their lackadaisical attitude toward discipline often resulted in iconic exasperated tirades. He swore at them in French

Baron von Steuben drilling Washington's army at Valley Forge in the winter by Edwin A. Abbey (Image courtesy of US Library of Congress)

and German, and then would order a soldier to swear for him in English. After just a few weeks his colorful reputation spread throughout the camp, and any lingering suspicion about misrepresentation of his credentials was soon forgotten.

When the war began, most American commanders believed that the best chance for winning was to fight guerrilla-style, a method that used raids and ambushes to rout the enemy, as had traditionally been done by Native Americans. This style was most effective in wooded and mountainous terrain, and could be easily taught to transient militiamen, the citizen-soldiers of the American forces. Employing hit and run tactics, such as "annoying" the rear guard of the British Army, and avoiding large battles was also less expensive than maintaining a large standing army.

There was convincing evidence to prove the effectiveness of guerilla raiders of the militia. Their tactics were successful at Lexington and Concord, and the skirmishes that followed later in 1775, and were victories won by temporary soldiers unaccustomed to discipline. Morgan's Rangers, led by

Daniel Morgan, and the men who served under Francis "Swamp Fox" Marion were all backwoodsmen. Ethan Allen took Fort Ticonderoga from the British with his militia force, the Green Mountain Boys. This band was made up of settlers from southwestern Vermont who had been led by members of his own family. George Washington's celebrated surprise attack on Trenton was another example of guerilla warfare on a larger scale. But Washington soon realized that his only hope to win independence and be accepted by the powers in Europe was to defeat Britain by waging a conventional war with decisive large-scale battles employing linear tactics.

WE CAN'T FIGHT LIKE NATIVE WARRIORS

American guerilla-type warfare was much different than the traditional type of fighting practiced by the British. The linear tactics of the Redcoats meant that they fought face-to-face, in open fields. Opposing armies would face one another at less than a hundred yards, in tight straight-line formations three ranks deep, and commence to firing volley after volley at each other. While keeping up a continuous line of fire, they would slowly move closer together. The engagement usually ended with a bayonet charge, as one force drove the weaker one from the field. Theoretically, this European style of combat could wipe out an entire army, and win a war in one massive battle.

This linear tactic evolved because it complemented the common weapon carried by the British foot soldier—the smoothbore military musket known as the Brown Bess. A highly inaccurate weapon, it could only be effective when used at less than eighty yards from its target. Because of their imprecision, muskets were not aimed at single enemy soldiers, but instead fired on command in the general direction of the opposing formations. Firing rapid volleys in unison was the most effective technique, and a well-trained infantry soldier could load and fire as many as four rounds a minute.

At first glance, training the entire Continental Army in one winter at Valley Forge appeared to be an insurmountable task. Von Steuben solved this problem by creating a model company consisting of 150 handpicked combat-hardened veterans. His idea was to first train them in linear tactics, and then send each of them out as instructors to train other companies. Using this method, he eventually disciplined the entire army.

Soldiers were first taught to march in step. Some of the uneducated farm boys were not able to react quickly to commands of "left" and "right" but responded well when the orders "hay foot" and "straw foot" were substituted. New recruits, many of whom were illiterate, had wisps of hay tied to their left foot and straw on the right. When confused by right and left, they would respond to the order "hay foot-straw foot," and step off in unison on the left foot to march in step. The practice is said to have come from teaching country folks of the day to dance. They were next taught how to rapidly load and reload muskets and fix bayonets, followed by practice in shouldering, ordering, grounding and saluting with their muskets. Each command was broken down into individual motions, so they could be performed in unison by a group. The baron took some shortcuts by reducing the number of individual commands, in order to simplify them. As soon as the soldiers mastered those orders, they could be drilled in larger formations.

While these individual exercises were indispensable, Baron von Steuben never forgot the objective of the training—the ability to maneuver in large groups during battle. He departed from the traditional European approach of concentrating on precision parade-type marching, and advanced the training to maneuver in larger linear battlefield formations. He limited maneuvers to two hours each day to ensure that the accelerated drilling did not exhaust the emaciated soldiers. Progress was astonishing, and it produced an unanticipated result. American officers who were accustomed to relegating the task of drilling to their sergeants and corporals now personally joined the program.

With the warmer spring weather, living conditions at Valley Forge had begun to improve. In May, the fortune of the American cause was revived when Washington learned that the French had signed an agreement to join the Americans. This joyful news was celebrated in the encampment by a "Grand Review," when the entire army of freshly-trained Continentals was paraded in formation. Wearing their tattered uniforms, the gaunt Yankee Doodles marched in flawless cadence to the resonating sounds of fifes and drums. At the end of the parade, their ten thousand muskets were fired in rolling volleys in perfect sequence. The audience of visiting dignitaries was astounded by this precision display, which was rarely witnessed in even the best-disciplined European armies. Colonel John Laurens, a member of General Washington's staff, described the event: "The order with which the whole was conducted, the beautiful effect of the running fire which was executed to perfection, the martial appearance of the troops, gave sensible pleasure to everyone present. The whole was managed by signal, and the plan as formed by Baron von Steuben succeeded in every particular, which in a great measure attributed to his unwearied attention, and to the visible progress which the troops have already made under his discipline."[112]

The ragged Continentals had been transformed into an army that rivaled any in Europe in only three months. This was a jubilant day for Baron von Steuben, who swelled with pride and basked in the complements and congratulatory acknowledgements of his achievement. To add to his delight, that same day Washington surprised him by commissioning him a major general in the Continental Army.

Only seven weeks later, the now rejuvenated Continental Army faced its first major test at the Battle of Monmouth. There, in the longest battle of the war, the energized men who had trained during the dark days at Valley Forge stood toe-to-toe with the elite regiments of the British Army, repulsing their fierce assaults and fighting them to a standstill.

THE LITTLE BLUE BOOK

Encouraged by his remarkable progress at Valley Forge, Baron von Steuben began organizing his ideas into an eighty-one-page manual, *The Regulations for the Order and Discipline of the Troops of the United States*, Because of the war, there was a scarcity of paper when it was ready to be printed in 1779, so the printer decided to bind the book with the blue paper he happened to have on hand.[113] Congress endorsed the "Blue Book" the same year, and ordered it to be distributed throughout the army. Many state militias also adopted the little manual.

The book also explained infantry discipline information, marching procedures, encampments, camp sanitation, health inspections, guarding procedures, and specific responsibilities of each rank and position in the army. This manual of arms, modeled after the 1764 British Regulations, followed European practices, but was greatly modified by the Baron's understanding of warfare in America and his appreciation for the uniqueness of his soldiers. The Revolutionary War was a standup confrontation fought with lines of men facing each other at close range. The way to achieve success was to fire the first volley, withstand the return fire, and then reload faster than the opposition. The series of commands to load and fire a flintlock musket was complicated, but Baron von Steuben's new firing instructions, the twenty motions required to fire the weapon, were each described in sequence in the blue book. They much simpler than those used by foreign armies, and they significantly improved the rate of fire for Americans.

Baron von Steuben's book remained the official manual for infantry command for the next thirty-four years, and was the official US Army guide to military training and maneuvers until it was replaced in 1812. Its contents had a lasting influence on U.S. military doctrine and portions of it are still in use in today's army manuals on drill and ceremonies. The Blue Book provides a fascinating glimpse into the discipline and routine of the Continental Army. Baron von Steuben's influence created a positive change in the attitude of common soldiers. As reflected in the prayerful words of one soldier, "We believe that Baron Steuben has made us soldiers, and that he is capable of forming the whole world into a solid column and displaying it from the center. We believe his Blue Book. We believe in General Knox and his artillery. And we believe in our bayonets. Amen."[114]

Although von Steuben had exaggerated his rank and status, he understood the specifics of European discipline, and the need to shift rapidly from one formation to another while in battle. This ability enabled him to lead the Continental Army away from relying on ambush and skirmishing, which could not win a decisive war. His talent, and his knack at understanding the differences between American and European soldiers, enabled him to mold the troops into a disciplined fighting force that could stand against any army in the world. During the last five years of the war, most Continental soldiers had never been at Valley Forge, but the Baron's influence carried on, and led to the emergence of the long service professional soldier, the War Men who achieved the ultimate American victory.

The intrepid von Steuben would never have had the opportunity to make his crucial contribution to the cause of American Independence had he not presented himself as an high ranking officer with extensive military experience. Inflating his credentials put him in a position to have a lasting effect on the destiny of the United States. He introduced himself to American leaders at a time when their cause seemed doomed. He convinced them he was the right man for what they perceived to be a problematical task—turning the ragged American troops into skilled soldiers. Baron von Steuben is credited with bringing order and proficiency to the Continental Army to a degree that turned the tide of the war. In the words of Alexander Hamilton, Baron von Steuben brought ". . . into the army a regular formation and exact discipline" as well as "a spirit of order and economy."[115]

The Continental Army probably would have been defeated forever in the springtime of 1778, had the Baron von Steuben not arrived to train the troops that winter. George Washington's respect and gratitude towards him is evidenced in this letter in December, 1783, the last letter he wrote as Commander-in-Chief: "Although I have taken frequent opportunities both in public and private of acknowledging your [von Steuben's] great zeal, attention and ability in performing your office; yet, I wish to make use of this last moment of my public life, to signify in the strongest terms, my entire approbation of your conduct, and to express my sense of the obligations the public is under to you for your faithful and meritorious services"[116]

Chapter Eight

Keeping the Campfires Burning

Historians can describe the details of battles and eulogize the thrill of victories, but they often fail to mention the fact that most of the time the soldiers of the Continental Army were actually encamped. Throughout their various campaigns, the men camped out for weeks, while moving to and from each battlefield. The long-held tradition in that era was that hostilities were to break off in the late fall. At that point both sides would go into permanent winter camp for several months, and combat would then resume in the spring. Washington learned the practical value of this seasonal strategy when half of his fledgling army was annihilated while trying to storm the bastion of Quebec City in December, 1775, during a raging snowstorm. The entire Canadian Campaign proved to be a weather-related failure for the American forces, and it was a lesson that they never forgot.

There were a few notable exceptions to the hiatus taken during the winter months. Washington crossed the Delaware River on Christmas night to surprise the Hessians at Trenton, and then followed up with two victories at Princeton. After the fighting broke off, the triumphant Patriots headed immediately to Morristown, New Jersey, to camp until the end of May. The most notable American long-term encampments were at Morristown and Middlebrook, New Jersey, New Windsor, New York and Valley Forge, Pennsylvania. The British forces had a comfortable, and, at times, even jovial winter in the captured rebel capitol of Philadelphia in 1777-1778. Their main army spent the other years of the war safe and sound in New York City.

The locations for American winter camps were selected on the basis of the local terrain. Natural barriers, such as mountains and waterways, were preferred, because they could offer the shelter needed to provide security for an entire army. Two full winters were spent in Morristown, a site that offered obvious logistical, topographical and geographic military advantages. It was protected on the east by three ridges of the Watchung Mountains, and the impassible Great Swamp. Its elevation was hundreds of feet above the New Jersey plains, which stretched fifteen miles to British lines on Staten Island. (To this day the mountains provide an unparalleled view of New York City). In the days when men and horses shuffled all supplies and cannon, its high position made it almost impregnable. Middlebrook, New Windsor, and Valley Forge were similarly selected for their strategic locations, natural protection and proximity to supplies.

In these isolated places the private soldier found camp life difficult, tedious, and often boring. His day consisted of a nonstop round of drilling, guard duty, and "fatigue work." The last type of work included such repulsive chores as burying the remains of butchered livestock, digging latrines and making cartridges. Guard duty was known as *picket duty*. The word *picket*, derived from the early French Army term *picquet*, denoted a sharpened stick or pointed wooden stake. Soldiers assigned to a forward position to warn of enemy approach used these as weapons. This duty required a man to stay awake at night for a specified number of hours on the perimeter of the camp while watching for an enemy attack. They had to remain alert, while watching for and reporting suspicious activities or danger, while the rest of the troops slept. Duties were performed in all kinds of weather, and falling asleep on guard duty was a serious offense, punishable by twenty lashes or more, especially if the enemy was close by.

Orderly books, the daily records of orders, show that strict discipline was observed in camps, despite the harsh conditions. Guard duty was assigned each day no matter what the weather. Parades, musters, inspections, drills and punishments were regularly held on a grand parade ground. Inspections were held on these grounds by General Washington and members of the Continental Congress, and camp parades were conducted there which involved the entire army.

TATTERED TENTS AND RAMSHACKLE HUTS

When the army arrived at an encampment, the first task was to secure shelter. Tents were preferred for temporary shelter. When on the march, soldiers slept in barns or in the open fields, changing campsites as often as every day. Each company within a Continental Army regiment was divided into groups of five to six men, small units known as "messes." Each mess was assigned a common tent to provide for protection from the cold and rain. The size of the mess determined the size, shape and construction of the tent. In order to cover a five-man mess, as well as their equipment, the average size of the enlisted men's tent was six-and-one-half–feet square by five-feet high. In July, 1781, Quartermaster General Pickering stated, "A common, or soldier's tent should be at least 7 feet square, larger a little if it happens to suit the breadth of the cloath."[117] The simple wedge-shaped shelter known as a soldier's tent was the most common type, and was also used by officers. Material needed to create the tents was typically linen duck, a heavy canvas fabric.

Officers had larger tents that were called *marquees*. They were made of canvas or heavy cotton and were usually about ten-feet across by fourteen-feet deep by eight-feet high. The *marquee* was used by generals, colonels, lieutenant colonels and majors, and came in a variety of sizes. Throughout the war, officers, slept, worked, and dined in these large, sturdy, cloth tents, and they received hard use from constant movement during campaigns.

During each year's military campaign season, and when he arrived at Valley Forge, General Washington used a *marquee* for dining. It was likely still in use at the end of the war. A descendent of the Washington family sold pieces of the multi-part marquee to several historic organizations in the early twentieth century. Today, the Smithsonian Institution displays the exterior of this tent. General Washington's original sleeping and office tent was carefully preserved by generations of the Custis and Lee families, following the deaths of George and Martha Washington. This national treasure is now at the Valley Forge Museum of American History.

Washington's home and office for much of the Revolutionary War was another *marquee* tent that some have called the "first Oval Office." It served as both his sleeping quarters and war office. The Museum of the American Revolution has constructed a replica of the historic tent that the general lived in for eight years. This reproduction was fabricated by a team of conservators, fabric experts, and a maker of historic tents.

Due to the lack of transportation, and the necessity to jettison tents as unnecessary baggage during rapid deployment, they often became unavailable. A variety of makeshift shelters were constructed in the field, and in longer encampments, prior to the introduction of log huts. These temporary lodgings were referred to as wigwams, brush huts, booths or bowers. They were fashioned from with frames of light tree limbs, and covered with leafy branches or pine boughs. Open lean-to sheds were similar in construction to brush huts, but covered with lumber, fence rails, cornstalks, or straw, and sometimes sailcloth. Even stone and turf shelters were reported on the outskirts of Boston in 1775.[118]

When the army planned to stay at a campsite for more than a few weeks, cabins or huts were raised. A total of 12,000 soldiers arrived at Jockey Hollow near Morristown at the end of 1779. Within two weeks each brigade had been assigned a sloping, well-drained hillside 320 yards long and forty yards deep, with a forty-yard-wide parade ground in front. Soldiers' huts were built eight in a row behind the parade ground. Men were forced to sleep out in the open and huddle together for warmth until the huts were completed. Given this situation, they wasted no time in cutting down oak, walnut and chestnut trees with which to build them. When the supply of timber ran out, they began pulling down farmers' fences and outbuildings for boards, which soon caused a furor among the local populace. Nevertheless, these dwellings were completed in a month, and served as a place to eat, sleep, and gather for the men who occupied them.

Replica hut at Valley Forge
(US National Park Service)

The huts at Jockey Hollow were held together with notched logs. A mixture of mud and clay was packed between the logs as chinking. The standard floor plan, fourteen-feet-wide, sixteen-feet-long, and six-and-a-half-feet high at the eaves, was carefully calculated to accommodate twelve occupants. Washington required each hut to be built with these exact dimensions, and ordered those that were improperly constructed to be pulled down and rebuilt. Each had a basic fireplace with a chimney at one end, and the sides were lined with wooden bunks. Windows were not cut in until spring, and were shuttered to keep out pests.

Roof shakes were kept in place with heavy tree branches, because nails were a scarce commodity. Boards were used for floors when they were obtainable; otherwise the huts had dirt floors. Larger structures of similar construction were built as hospitals, guard houses and administrative offices. Over time, a surprising 1,000 to 1,200 buildings were erected at the Jockey Hollow campsite.

The substantially lower fatality rate that was recorded at Jockey Hollow can be attributed to the lessons learned at Valley Forge two years earlier. Although the winter was harsh, and clothing and food were in short supply, improved hut construction, sanitary conditions, medical services and a better water and wood supply accounted for the difference. The efficient organization of the campsite made it possible to accommodate the entire Continental Army in an area half the size of Valley Forge. The number of recorded deaths over the winter dropped from 2,000 at Valley Forge to 86 at Jockey Hollow.

During the last years of the war, Washington's army reached a peak of proficiency in establishing permanent camps. In 1782 and 1783, the army was based at the New Windsor Cantonment near Newburgh, New York. There the American soldiers were fed, clothed, and sheltered much better than they had ever been. The seven hundred spacious huts on this site were built with heavy logs to last more than one season, and could be erected in less than a week. A total of 8,000 men, 280 women and 220 children lived on the site for two years. The New Windsor huts received good reviews from senior officers. Major General Gates wrote to Baron von Steuben in November, 1782, "Our men are becoming so adroit and perfect in the art of hutting that I think they will be more comfortable and better lodged, in the quarters they built for themselves than any city in the continent could afford them. This mode of covering an army for the winter is new in the art of war . . . ."[119] General William Heath, commander of the Highlands Department, visited the camp in the spring and commented, "The cantonment for its nature and kind was regular and beautiful."[120]

These huts proved to be so well-built that most were auctioned off to local farmers after the army departed in 1783. Russell Headley, in his *History of Orange County New York*, reported that a few still remained intact over a hundred years later, in 1896. In 1934 one of the original huts was discovered as part of a house in a nearby town. It was disassembled and moved back to its original site, which is now a state park with replica buildings and a museum.[121]

The camp at New Windsor included a hospital and a bakery. Headquarters activities were centered about Temple Hill, where a large all-purpose building had been built of logs at the center of a raised portion of ground. It was 110 feet long and 30 feet wide, and served as administrative offices, an indoor church, and a place for general meetings of the officers. It was even used as a meeting hall for the Masonic Fraternity. It was first named the "The Temple of Virtue," but after uproarious parties had taken place there it was referred to simply as "The Temple." It was the largest structure built by the Continental Army during the Revolutionary War.

A cemetery has never been found at the Cantonment site in Newburgh. Graves may have been purposely concealed so that spies could not count the losses, or the dead may have been buried at either local cemeteries or at the head of the parade ground near the temple. No human remains of any kind have ever been discovered at the camp.

The improved quality of life did little to lessen the hard conditions for the soldiers. While there were no bloody footprints in the snow around the huts at New Windsor, this last winter encampment of the Continental Army was racked with an internal struggle. Having not been paid, and aware that peace was looming, the troops became bored and impatient. Looting, fence-burning and drunkenness by soldiers, combined with a conspiracy by disgruntled officers, posed one of the greatest dangers the Continental Army had ever faced.

After basic shelter had been provided, the men at camps went to work excavating trenches and building other perimeter defenses. Any idle moments were soon filled with cooking and gathering wood.[122] When Benedict Arnold occupied the Fort at Crown Point on Lake Champlain in the winter of 1775, he divided his men into task squads. Some baked bread, others hunted for game or fished, and the rest cut timber or mounted cannon.[123] The army made use of the soldiers who possessed craft skills. Craftsmen were allowed to earn money by making such items as shoes, leather breeches and hats. They worked at their trades during the off-hours between the retreat at sunset and tattoo, the signal that summoned soldiers to their quarters at eight or nine o'clock at night.

Early in the war the quality of life for soldiers was abysmal, especially during the long winter encampments, but conditions gradually improved with practice. Undernourished and poorly clothed, living in crowded, damp quarters, the army was ravaged by sickness and disease. Typhoid, "putrid fever" (typhus), smallpox, dysentery and pneumonia swept through the camps during the winter. These diseases, along with starvation and exposure to the freezing temperatures, contributed to the deaths of nearly 2,000 soldiers at Valley Forge.[124]

Two years later, eighty-six men perished at Jockey Hollow in Morristown. This lower fatality rate can be attributed to the painful lessons learned at Valley Forge. Despite the harsher conditions at Jockey Hollow, hut building, sanitation and administration were greatly improved. Although both camps were near substantial communities in the center of bountiful agricultural areas, they were still unsustainable. Transportation and distribution were hindered by bad weather, and local merchants and farmers were reluctant to accept devalued Continental dollars.

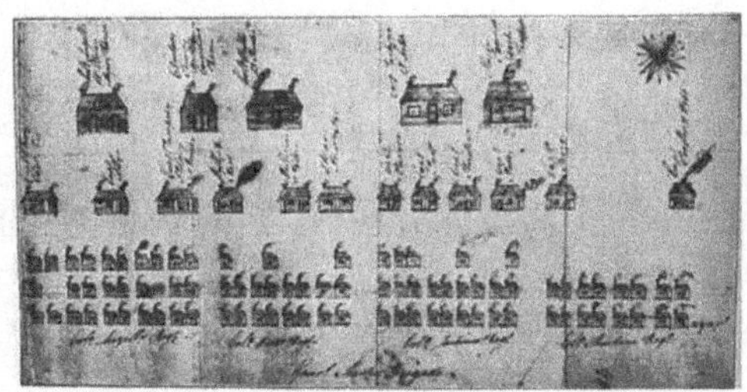

Contemporary sketch of the Stark's Brigade camp in Jockey Hollow during the winter of 1779-1780 (US National Park Service)

Soldiers often provided their own leadership during the winter encampments. Many officers left for home on furlough, senior commanders departed before the holidays, and some of them did not return until spring. The somewhat shaky reason they offered for their absence was that they were returning to their home states to recruit replacements for their decimated units. This left corporals and sergeants responsible for the control of the army during most of the hard winter.

In response to this deplorable state of affairs, a Brigade Order was issued on January 30, 1780, at Jockey Hollow: "His Excellency [General Washington] is displeased that there are so many officers on Furlough on so much as there is not a sufficient number to preserve order and perform the common Rotation of Duty So Several companies are left without a commissioned officer. He directs that a distribution of the remaining officers be made that no company be without a commissioned officer"[125]

Corporal punishment at the winter camps far exceeded that administered at other times of the year. An unusually high number of convictions occurred when the army set up camp for an extended length of time. This occurred because time had not permitted the holding of trials or the inflicting of punishments. When the army was on the march, courts-martial were postponed until the troops settled in camp.

Desertion also accounted for an abnormally high rate of offences. During idle months the soldiers—freezing, hungry and without pay—deserted in droves. At times, the situation became desperate, since the high desertion rate threatened the very existence of the beleaguered Continental Army. Men who had families were willing to even risk the death penalty to return home to care for their starving families and neglected farms.

Other offenses, such as drunkenness and theft from civilians or fellow soldiers, were fueled by boredom and the struggle to survive. Punishments were administered immediately, and over time these became more frequent and severe. At Jockey Hollow in 1779 six privates from the New York Brigade were tried for desertion, only two weeks after they had arrived at camp. All were convicted, and each received one hundred lashes, a severe penalty. This was the first of many harsh sentences that followed during that winter. Flogging was the usual punishment; in the first six months there, the orderly books for the New York regiments at the camp recorded twenty-one floggings. This was a brutal but effective punishment, since men usually survived to fight again.
Sunday was observed as a day of worship in all the camps. Congress promoted devotion by issuing 20,000 Bibles to troops in September, 1777. General Washington was a staunch proponent of piety among his men, and often made this known in his general orders with statements such as, "To the distinguished character of a , it should be our highest glory to add the more distinguished character of a Christian."[126]

The typical day began with public prayers and preparation for the service. The sermon usually started at 11:00 a.m., and stressed the virtues of faithfully performing duties, cleanliness, honesty, temperance and modesty, and was supplemented with biblical references. Some sermons continued for the entire day, and were attended in relay fashion by captive audiences of soldiers. Not all the men attended these orations willingly, so penalties were put in place to encourage participation. Those absent from worship in the New York regiments were forced to spend equivalent time digging out stumps, a measure that caused an immediate rise in attendance.[127]

In mid-winter, when it was too cold for the ragged troops to stand out in the open and listen to long sermons, many chaplains took advantage of this time to return home on furlough. Reverend John Gano, the New York Brigade chaplain, left for the winter from the encampment at Pompton, New Jersey. When he returned to camp in April, 1782, the pious Gano was greeted by a soldier who said, "We have been in want of everything during the winter, clothing, provisions and money, but hardest of all for us was that we did not have the Word of God to comfort us." The conscience-stricken clergyman was distraught after hearing this, until he learned that the incorrigible joker was simply taunting him for having departed for the winter.[128]

CHOAKY FIRE CAKE

The long winter encampments were a test of the army's survival. During 1775, the first year of the war, when the army was besieging Boston, the American forces were well-supplied from nearby New England states. When New York was lost the following year, the ability to provide food to the Continental Army declined. Food shortages remained a serious predicament during the next six years of the war due in part to an inefficient supply chain. Soldiers starved in a land that abounded in agricultural products.

At Jockey Hollow the Continental Army went as long as six days without bread or meat, and up to three days without either. Washington appealed to the nation, "Our soldiers, the greatest part of the last campaign, and the whole of this, have scarcely tasted any kind of vegetables; had but little salt and vinegar, which would have been a tolerable substitute for vegetables; have been in a great measure strangers to, neither have they been provided with proper drink. Beer or cyder seldom comes within the verge of the camp, and rum in much too small quantities. Thus, to devouring large quantities of animal food, untempered by vegetables and vinegar, or by any kind of drink but water . . . are to be ascribed the many putrid diseases incident to the army."[129]

In desperate times extreme measures had to be taken. Soon pet dogs were disappearing from camp. When Colonel William Winds stopped to look at a small campfire and inquired why the men were cooking a stone in their kettle they replied, "There is some strength in stones, if only you can get it out."[130]

The diaries of soldiers clearly indicate that their main preoccupation was foraging for food. In December, 1777, Elijah Fisher, a private in the 4th Massachusetts Regiment, was camped at Whitemarsh, a few miles south of Valley Forge. He wrote in his journal, "We had no tents or anything to cook our provisions in, and that was prity poor, for beef was very lean and no salt, nor any way to cook it but to throw it on the coles and brile it; and the water we had to drink and mix our flower with was out of a brook that ran along by the camps, and so many a dippin and washin in it which maid it very dirty and muddy."

Due to the scarcity of wood, which was stripped from area adjoining the campsite, food was often improperly cooked. Washington himself commented, "I thought that different regiments were upon the point of cutting each others throat for a few standing locusts near the encampment to dress their victuals with."[131]

When food gave out entirely, as it did at Valley Forge, men would beg from nearby farms, or resort to stealing cattle and chickens. At the more permanent camps, sutlers, civilian merchants who traveled along with an army, sold food, liquor and other wares from the back of a wagon or a temporary tent. The sutlers kept their stores within the confines of the camp, and were licensed and regulated by senior officers to prevent overcharging.[132]

The customary food for the army was flour and beef. Once each day men were issued a ration of flour and a pound of raw or preserved meat. They either cooked meals themselves or combined their food with other men's, and then took turns cooking. Usually six soldiers shared either a tent or a hut and created a "mess," or eating unit. Camp followers, who were wives and other women, often served as cooks. Meat was spitted on a convenient bayonet and broiled over an open fire. When no meat was available, the men were only provided with flour or grain. These ingredients were mixed with water to make a paste which was baked in a pan on a flat stone, or skewed on a stick over hot coals. The result was known as "fire cake." During the dreadful days at Valley Forge, Dr. Albigence Waldo lamented, "Fire cake and water for breakfast, fire cake and water for dinner! Fire cake and water for supper!"[133]

A sutler or victualer was a civilian merchant who sold provisions to an army in the field, in camp, or in quarters. They sold their wares from the back of a wagon or a temporary tent, either traveling with an army or to remote military outposts.
(Photograph courtesy of Pricketts Fort Memorial Foundation, Fairmont, West Virginia)

Six months after the Continental Army had been formed, a standard ration for each man was provided. The Continental Congress passed a resolution on November 4, 1775 establishing the ration for each soldier. The menu was high in calories, since men needed the extra energy for physical labor. Transporting the rations without spoilage also required nonperishable items.

> *Resolved, That a ration consist of the following kind and quantity of provisions, viz:*
>
> *1 lb. of beef, or 3/4 lb. pork, or 1 lb. salt fish, per day.*
>
> *1 lb. of bread or flour per day.*
>
> *3 pints of pease, or beans per week, or vegitables equivalent, at one dollar per bushel for pease or beans.*

1 pint of milk per man per day, or at the rate of 1/72 of a dollar.
1 half pint of Rice, or 1 pint of indian meal per man per week.
1 quart of spruce beer or cyder per man per day, or nine gallons of Molasses per company of 100 men per week.
3 lb. candles to 100 Men per week for guards.
24 lb. of soft or 8 lb. of hard soap for 100 men per week.

These ingredients were often in short supply, or unobtainable. Supplements were often added, such as small quantities of milk, rice and butter, a half pint of vinegar and a gill (a quarter pint) of spirits.

Washington was constantly immersed in every detail that affected his men, and particularly showed great interest in the diet of his troops. His concern that the standard diet might induce scurvy caused him to direct that sauerkraut be added, and that regimental quartermasters gather sorrel (a leafy herb) and watercress for salads.[134] This need for fresh vegetables continued, and as late as 1783, at the New Windsor camp, he directed camp commanders to order the men to plant gardens: "It is recommended to the troops to make regimental gardens for the purpose of raising greens and vegetables for their own use, and in order to collect a sufficient quantity of seeds, commanding officers of regiments will give passes to as many trusty soldiers as they may judge necessary to go into the country, and be absent, not exceeding ten days. The General hopes he shall see a suitable attention bestowed on an article which will contribute so much to the comfort and health of the troops. He even flatters himself it will become a matter of amusement and of emulation."[135]

A change in food variety was made possible by purchases from sutlers or farmers at camp markets. General Washington stated in the summer of 1777 that, "Nothing can be more comfortable and wholesome to the army than vegetables, every encouragement is to be given to the Country people, to bring them in . . . ." But the men had to have money or items to barter, so this made it difficult for many of the men to supplement their diet.

Documents such as General Orders list foods sold by local suppliers. A list from August, 1777, included butter, mutton , lamb, veal, milk, potatoes, squashes, beans or peas in the pod, cucumbers, pigs for roasting, turnips, carrots and beets. A later order lists spirits and sugar, turkeys, geese, ducks, "Dunghill fowls," chickens, cheese, eggs, cabbageheads, parsnips, lump, loaf and brown sugar, honey and vinegar.[136]

This example of consecutive entries in the diary of Sergeant John Smith, 1st Rhode Island Regiment, shows the constant preoccupation with food gathering and preparation in the daily life of a soldier:

[December] the 19th [1777] in the morning we marchd to our winter Quarters—we marchd all Day without Victuals having nothing to Eat—we went into the woods & Sleept in huts as usual

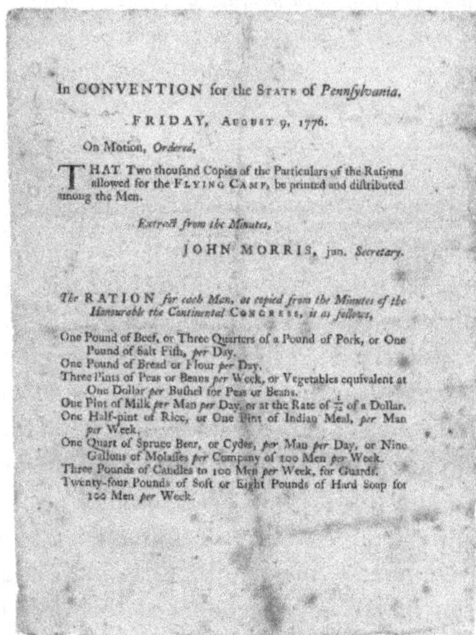

In CONVENTION for the STATE of *Pennſylvania.*

FRIDAY, AUGUST 9, 1776.

On Motion, *Ordered,*

THAT Two thouſand Copies of the Particulars of the Rations allowed for the FLYING CAMP, be printed and diſtributed among the Men.

Extract from the Minutes,

JOHN MORRIS, jun. *Secretary.*

The RATION *for each Man, as copied from the Minutes of the Honourable the Continental* CONGRESS, *is as follows,*

One Pound of Beef, or Three Quarters of a Pound of Pork, or One Pound of Salt Fiſh, *per* Day.
One Pound of Bread or Flour *per* Day.
Three Pints of Peas or Beans *per* Week, or Vegetables equivalent at One Dollar *per* Buſhel for Peas or Beans.
One Pint of Milk *per* Man *per* Day, or at the Rate of $\frac{1}{72}$ of a Dollar.
One Half-pint of Rice, or One Pint of Indian Meal, *per* Man *per* Week.
One Quart of Spruce Beer, or Cyder, *per* Man *per* Day, or Nine Gallons of Molaſſes *per* Company of 100 Men *per* Week.
Three Pounds of Candles to 100 Men *per* Week, for Guards.
Twenty-four Pounds of Soft or Eight Pounds of Hard Soap for 100 Men *per* Week.

Food ration for each man issued by the Continental Congress, August 9, 1776
(US National Archives)

[December 20] we found a Corn field where was Corn which we took & Eat after we Roasted it in the fire some—we Pounded with two stones & made Samp to thicken our Broth—Some we Carried to mill & Got it Ground into meal—towards Night we Drew Some Poor Beef & one Days flower—this Decembr 20th 1777
the 21st Sunday—we had warm Pleasant weather & Nothing to Eat but a Little flower made with Coarse Indian meal& a Little Flower mixd with it—at Night the fortune of war Put into our hands a Poor Sheep which we Roasted & boild which Gave the Company a Good Super which we Eat & turnd in
[December 22]—Sleept Qietly untill morning when we Receivd orders to march in fifteen minits—we Paraded the Regt. & Grounded our arms & Drew flower for one day & Baked it But no meat as yet but a Party of Volenteers turnd out to Goe to get Some Cattle from Toreys—we had nothing to Eat Untill 10 o clock at Night when we had a Ram Cooked roast & boild which 3 of our Company took & killd as they traveld on their way—about 10 o clock A Detachment went from here to Goe Down towards the Enemy etc.
23d—we turnd out a Party of men to Build huts for our winter Quarters—in the afternoon had some mutton Served out to us for one day & Drumd a whore out of Camp & set her over Schullkill River for theaft—this night Capt. Lee took 13 Light horse & 8 Riders of the Enemy & Brought them in.[137]

Sergeant Joseph Plumb Martin related this experience at Jockey Hollow in January 1780: "We are absolutely, literally starved. I do solemnly declare that I did not put a single morsel of victuals into my mouth for four days and as many nights, except for a little black birch bark which I gnawed off a stick of wood. I saw several men roast their old shoes and eat them, and I was afterward informed by one of the officer's waiters, that some of the officers killed a favorite little dog that belonged to one of them."

Dr. Issac Senter accompanied a column led by Benedict Arnold through the Maine wilderness in November, 1775. He reported, "Our greatest luxuries now consist of a little water, stiffented with flour in imitation of shoemakers paste . . . Instead of diarrhea which turned out men most shockingly in the former part of our march, the reverse was now the complaint . . . . In company was a poor dog who had hitherto lived through all tribulations, became a prey for the sustenance of the assassinators. This poor animal was instantly devoured without leaving any vestige of the sacrifice. Nor did the shaving soap, pomatum [perfumed oil hairdressing], and even the lip salve, leather of their shoe, cartridge boxes etc share any better fate."[138]

PAYDAY BLUES

Even before the onset of rampant inflation, the wages of the army were insufficient. In fact, civilian laborers were paid much higher wages than soldiers. Privates earned six and two-thirds dollars per month. A quarter of this was deducted for clothing, so many sold their clothes in order to supplement their meager income. The paper currency that Congress had authorized to be printed in 1775 became unacceptable to many civilian suppliers of provisions, and they soon refused to accept it in payment.

Washington often expressed his apprehension about pay issues, and his fears came true when the Pennsylvania Regiments at Jockey Hollow rebelled. A year later, the New Jersey Regiments revolted at nearby Federal Hill. In August, 1780, Washington reported from his headquarters at Newburgh, New York, that he feared a mutiny was again brewing over the pay issue. A major issue in these mutinies was not only that the suffering men had not been paid at all, but that the few times they had received wages it was in lesser amounts than they were due, and in depreciated dollars. After this time Congress was never able to meet its obligations to the army. By 1780, Continental paper money had become almost worthless, as inflation gripped the American economy. For instance, in 1781 one quart of rum cost $1,200 in paper money.

In the summer of 1781, Washington's army marched south from New York to Yorktown. Regular pay had been discontinued for four years, and Congress, lacking the power to tax, had completely run out of funds. Most men had not received any portion of their pay in over a year. Grumbling began in Philadelphia, and quickly escalated into rumors of mutiny. Some regiments lost 10 percent of their strength due to desertions while on the march. Washington warned Congress that the Yorktown campaign itself might have to be abandoned.

When the war-weary men from New York, New Jersey and Pennsylvania reached Elkton, Maryland, they refused to continue moving further from their home states without receiving pay. They wanted to be paid in coin, the only currency merchants would accept. Washington believed that if he could secure just one month's pay in coin for his army, morale would vastly improve. Twenty thousand dollars was required for this task. Robert Morris, Superintendent of Finance for Congress, tried, but failed to obtain this amount from the states. Finally, Morris audaciously asked General Rochambeau, the top commander of French forces in America, for a loan. The French nobleman graciously ordered the Intendant (controller) of the French Army to give him one. It was even more than he requested; the $26,600 in silver coin that was provided was enough to pay the entire American Army.

On September 8, 1781 the gathered army was paid in hard currency at Elkton. For many of these American soldiers this was the only time they ever received "real" money during all their years of service. This payday was a momentous event that was acclaimed in orderly books and, years later, in soldiers' diaries. Meticulous pay records were kept, and the joyful occasion was remembered in pension applications long after the war. New Yorker Major William Popham wrote, "This day, 8 September 1781, will be famous in the annals of history for being the first in which the troops of the United States received one month's pay in specie."

Sergeant Joseph Plumb Martin, after receiving his coins that day, wrote, "We each of us received a month's pay, in specie, borrowed, as I was informed, from the officers in the French army. This was the first that could be called money, which we had received as wages since the year '76, or that we ever did receive till the close of the war, or indeed, ever after, as wages." Martin recalled only being paid twice in his eight years of service—once when he signed up in 1776, and this time. He may have been paid a few other times between 1776 and 1781, but it was in nearly worthless Continental currency.[139]

Another enlisted man, John Hudson of the 1st New York Regiment, age thirteen, recalled it was at Head of Elk (Elkton) that "I received the only pay that I ever drew for my services during the war, being six French crowns, which were a part of what Robert Morris borrowed on his own credit from the French commander to supply the most urgent necessities of the soldiers. My comrades received the same amount."[140]

Continental troops went months, and even years, without being paid. At the final encampment of the Continental Army at New Windsor, most enlisted men were at least a year in arrears on monthly wages, and many had not been paid since that memorable day on the march to Yorktown, two years before. The restless men at New Windsor knew peace was expected, and with all their idle time bitterness grew in the ranks. Threats from both men and officers culminated with a planned defection of most officers on March 10, 1783.

Washington learned his officers would meet at the Temple of Virtue to approve a passionate petition calling for a mutiny if Congress failed to provide them back pay and pensions. This document declared that if the war continued, they would lead the army into "some unsettled country" and let the American people fend for themselves against the British. On the other hand, if the war ended, they would march on Congress and demand their pay at gunpoint. At the time the British still occupied New York City and other American ports, and could easily restart the war.

Washington narrowly averted this disaster by giving the most emotional speech of his military career. He ordered his men to meet on March 15, and slipped in unnoticed through a side door, so his men were surprised when he suddenly appeared before them. He took out his written address and his spectacles from his coat pockets, saying, "Gentlemen you will permit me to put on my spectacles, for I have not only grown gray, but also blind in the service of my country," and read a passionate nine-page speech, which has become known as the Newburgh Address.[141] In it, he sympathized with their demands, but denounced the methods they were contemplating to achieve them. His actions drew tears from many of the officers, and convinced them not to march on Congress.

Pay continued to remain an issue until the Army was finally disbanded. The mounting unrest among the unpaid soldiers at New Windsor was punctuated by desertions, drunkenness and disobedience. Fearful of a riot among enlisted men, the army began to reluctantly discharge soldiers so that they could return home. About two-thirds of the army, 4,500 men, left the Cantonment in June, 1783. The only pay they received was a few dollars in Continental currency, enough to provide necessities on the way home, and they were also allowed to keep their muskets. Many had hundreds of miles to travel, and most men sold their weapons along the way to avoid starvation.

At that time, Corporal John Allison of the 2nd New York Regiment was released, after serving for eight years. He returned home penniless, but sometime before September, 1785, he finally received a certificate for back pay for his entire time in service, an amount which totaled eighty dollars. There is no evidence that he ever actually received this promised money. Bankrupt New York State usually paid its veterans with land bounties in the western part of the state, which many of them sold to ever-present speculators for a pittance. In the end, Allison received the equivalent of eight dollars for his grant.[142]

The problem of paying the army was compounded by other reasons other than a lack of funds. A prevailing belief held by the American public was that it was greedy and unpatriotic for soldiers to receive any compensation. They felt that American men should be willing to fight for the cause of freedom in the same way as the mythical yeoman farmers did in the first months of the war. Civilians did not recognize that most men had enlisted for economic incentives, and a promise of steady wages. Many depended on their army pay to support starving families at home. Many civilians, and even some officers, viewed the dreadfully low wages of the common soldiers as being sufficient. It was widely believed that the sporadic pillaging of civilian farms proved the soldiers were living off the land, and therefore did not need compensation.[143]

Soldiers themselves considered their lack of pay an insult to their honor, and rightly compared themselves to slave labor. Like slaves, they served for an unspecified period of time, and performed harsh physical labor. Soldiers had to carry identification when leaving the camps, similar to slaves who had to obtain passes to leave their owner's plantation.

The lack of ability to pay the army, and most of the problems confronting American military leaders in their struggle to sustain the army, came from one source. Only the states, not Congress, had the authority to impose taxes and raise revenue. Unfortunately, funds were not often raised by the states, or forwarded to Congress, until long after they were due. Not knowing how much and when states were going to pay their share made establishing a budget for the armed forces nearly impossible, and severely handicapped the war effort. This failing was pervasive from the disastrous year of 1776 until after the British surrender at Yorktown, to when Continental Army officers, camped at Newburgh, considered military action against the Continental Congress and the entire army was near mutiny over the failure of Congress to pay them.

Chapter Nine

Ragged Shirts and Frozen Feet

The year 1776 was one of total disaster for the cause of freedom. An appalled public learned of the suffering and fatalities of the inexperienced army, and the yeomen farmers, now discouraged, stopped volunteering. They would never again comprise the heart of the Continental Army. The thin clothing of the surviving soldiers was in tatters, and many were lame from tramping hundreds of miles in their bare feet. Weakened men became sick from exertion, and from sleeping on the ground without blankets or covering of any kind. Indignant soldiers deserted as they witnessed the bad faith and indifference of state governments and civilians toward support of the war.

Colonel Israel Angell of Rhode Island wrote from Peekskill, New York to his governor in August, 1777. He declared that his regiment was so disheveled that the members of the other corps, and people in the villages along the line of march, poked fun at his men, calling them "the Ragged, Lousey, Naked regiment."[144] Documents of the time often portray the soldiers as "naked," which at that time meant not fully clothed.

At Valley Forge, driving rains turned to snow and sleet, causing great suffering among the shoeless men. Once winter set in, the mud on roads and paths froze, creating sharp ridges along the way. Washington wryly observed that the American Army could have been easily tracked by following the blood stains from their frozen, lacerated feet. During the next winter at Jockey Hollow 2,898 men (about 25 percent of the army), were deemed unfit for duty because they lacked shoes and shirts. At night the freezing soldiers huddled around their campfires, reluctant to sleep far from the source of warmth. The camp hospital and nearby farmhouses were filled to capacity with men whose feet had become too painful to allow walking. Few blankets were available, and those that did reach the camp were a third too short to cover legs.

In the spring of 1779, potential enlistees began demanded exorbitant bounty money when they heard of these shameful conditions. The situation in the South was especially critical. In 1781, nearly half of Nathanael Greene's regiments lacked shoes, and there was only one blanket to be shared among every ten men. As the Siege of Yorktown began, the American soldiers were so ragged that the French troops camped nearby began to made jokes about their appearance. An American soldier predicted that if the war continued, the British troops would become terrified enough to run away from such menacing and disheveled wretches.[145]

Blankets were used for more than just bedding. A soldier of the 2nd New York Regiment at Valley Forge in February, 1778
(Courtesy of *Military Collector & Historian*, Fall 2000)

Unfortunately, there were no logistics experts among the army's leadership who could handle the problems of furnishing the army with supplies. The shortages were caused by the lack of cloth (which used to be imported before the war), and difficulties encountered in manufacturing and distributing finished garments. Army quartermasters aggressively attempted to procure uniforms from any source, and a bounty of twenty dollars was offered to recruits who supplied their own clothing. Procurement of foreign supplies was repeatedly attempted; an order for 40,000 uniforms was placed with France, but it took two years to arrive.

Many uniforms came from captured British stores. In one instance, an American fleet entered Narragansett Harbor in Rhode Island, and captured a British vessel bound for Canada that had thousands of uniforms onboard. In a sea battle with English ships, Spaniards captured 3,000 coats, all of which were shipped to the Continental Army. The ragged but patriotic soldiers refused to wear them, however, because they were the same color red that the British wore. Stores of British uniforms were also captured at St. Johns, Canada in 1775, and at Saratoga in 1777. These garments were also red, but they could be dyed with coffee or worn under other garments to avoid confusion on the battlefield.

The ragged uniforms and poor food discouraged enlistments and hampered the efficiency of American soldiers. They grumbled, threatened mutiny, and grew careless about their appearance and negligent in their habits. In his Orders of the Day for January 1, 1776, Washington wrote, "Our men are brave and good; men who, with pleasure it is observed, are addicted to fewer vices than are commonly found in armies . . . . If a soldier cannot be induced to take pride in his person he will soon become a sloven, and indifferent to everything else. Whilst we have men, therefore, who in every respect are superior to mercenary troops, that are fighting for two pence or three pence a day, why cannot we in appearance also be superior to them, when we fight for Life, Liberty, Property and our Country?"[146]

THE HUNTING SHIRT

During the opening months of the Revolution, the state militia volunteers reporting for duty at the Siege of Boston had no common uniform. Most wore civilian clothing, uniforms they had purchased, or those which their commanders had contributed. When George Washington assumed command, he ordered the use of the hunting shirt as a field garment to provide some uniformity. This shirt was the precursor of the ubiquitous fatigue uniform used in modern wars, a practical inexpensive garment chosen for its durability. It was either made of leather, linen or other homespun cloth, and had rows of fringe hanging down around the edges to help shed rain. It fit loosely, so the wearer could move freely, and almost reached to the knees. Beneath the hunting shirts, men usually wore pants that covered their lower torso and legs. Hunting shirts were shirts, men usually wore pants that covered their lower torso and legs. These garments were used while performing manual work in the field to save regimental uniforms from hard wear and tear. The shirts were all dyed the same color in each regiment, and worn by both officers and men of both Continental and militia troops.

The ever-present hunting shirt worn by American forces was unknown to New Englanders, who made up most of the Continental Army during the Siege of Boston. It was brought to Cambridge in July, 1775, by Daniel Morgan's famed frontier riflemen who came from Pennsylvania, Virginia, and Maryland. The linen hunting shirt was an American frontier article of clothing which had been worn in the backcountry in the years prior to the war. Its original designers were professional hunters, who needed a cheap and light summer garment.

Charles MacKubin Lefferts (1873 1923) was an American artist and army officer who studied and worked almost full-time over thirty years searching the archives of the United States, Great Britain, France and Germany for historical documents. Lieutenant Lefferts studied orderly books, diaries, old newspapers and other accounts, poring over every scrap of information about uniforms and military accoutrements so that he could depict accurate details in his paintings.

Lefferts described the hunting shirt:

> *The rifle dress or hunting frock was preferred by Washington, and was worn by most of the army throughout the war. It was the field dress of almost the entire army. The hunting shirt was made of deer leather, linen, or homespun, dyed in various colors, in the different regiments, such as tan, green, blue, yellow, purple, black or white. They were all of the same pattern, but some had capes and cuffs of different colors. With the hunting shirts were worn long leggings or overalls, also preferred by Washington in place of breeches and stockings. They were made of linen or duck undyed, or of deer leather, and later in the war were furnished in wool for the winter. They were shaped to the leg, and fastened at the ankle with four buttons and a strap under the shoe.*

In 1776, Washington recommended hunting shirts as part of the clothing bounty to be provided to each soldier by the Continental Congress, and as the most practicable garment for troops not supplied with uniform coats. He pointed out the several advantages of the rifle dress in his General Order of July 24, 1776: "No dress can be cheaper, nor more convenient, as the wearer may be cool in warm weather and warm in cool weather by putting on undercloaths which will not change the outward dress, Winter or Summer—Besides which it is a dress justly supposed to carry no small terror to the enemy, who think every such person a complete marksman."

REAL UNIFORMS AND RECOGNITION

In addition to covering the soldier's bodies, uniforms served other vital purposes. During the Revolutionary War armies used black powder weapons, all of which produced smoke when discharged. Thick clouds would form as soon as musket and cannon firing began, so much so that visibility was reduced to a few yards as they drifted across the battlefield. Uniforms had to be brightly colored in order to differentiate between friend and foe, since the smoke was light gray and white. The red-coated British and the blue-coated Continental troops were easily recognizable in the haze of battle, and officers could order tactical maneuvers after defining the size and function of units by uniform color. The Americans preferred dark blues and browns. Other Europeans who later joined in the war effort created their own styles and colors. For example, the French, who arrived in America in 1778, wore white uniforms or different shades of blue.

Distinctive colors also built pride in regiments, which were proud of reputations earned for gallantry on the field. In a sense, this served as a form

A 5th New York Regiment reenactor at Fort Ticonderoga (Courtesy of 5th New York Regiment)

of preemptive psychological warfare, since the unique uniform of a well-known regiment could frighten their opponents, causing them to flee rather than stand and fight.

Brown was the first official color for Continental uniforms, and was adopted by the Continental Congress on November 4, 1775, after approval by Washington and the New England states. Regiments were to be distinguished by facings of different colors.[147] This recommendation, however, was not completely carried out, and the troops uniforms were never all brown, because some of the early organizations had already chosen other combinations. At the same time, there was a shortage of brown cloth, so some regiments dressed in blue and gray. In September, 1778, Congress received a large shipment of blue coats from France trimmed with red collars, cuffs, and lapels. These were from the order for 40,000 uniforms placed with France two years earlier. Regulations published in 1779 retained the blue coats, but added colored facings based on region—white for New England, red for the Mid-Atlantic, and blue for the South.

The design of the Continental Army uniform was based on that of the eighteenth century British Army, and was similar to the soldiers that they were fighting at the time. It featured a tightly-fitted waistcoat (vest) and breeches. Due to lack of supplies, many Continental troops were not clothed according to this standard, so they wore hunting shirts throughout the war, rather than any official uniform.

The uniform of the American soldier was made up of these garments and related accoutrements:

A hat-the vast majority of soldiers wore the traditional tricorn. This was a broad brimmed hat made of black felt that was the turned up on three sides. Others wore woolen caps or no head covering at all.

A shirt made of linen or cotton

A black cloth, normally worn around the neck

A wool coat, usually with collar, cuffs, and lapels of a different color

A waistcoat (vest) made of linen or wool

A pair of wool, linen, or cotton trousers or breeches that were gathered just below the knee

A white belt over the left shoulder held the cartouche-box. This box, typically made of leather, contained a drilled wood cartridge holder. It was designed to be worn pushed to a soldier's back while on the march, and then slid to the front in combat. Most American soldiers carried twenty bullets in the cartouche box and another forty in a haversack, or small single-strap backpack.

Stockings and leather shoes, when available. At the time, shoes did not come in left/right pairs, so the same shoe would fit either foot. Most soldiers wore moccasins, or whatever was at hand, including pieces of hide from recently-slaughtered cattle. The iconic images depicting shoe shortages at Valley Forge show the soldiers wearing strips of blankets on their feet or going barefoot in the snow.

In desperation, blankets were often used for clothing, when no other garments were obtainable.

Twenty men of one regiment had "... no Breeches at all, so that they are obliged to take their blankets to cover their nakedness ... the poor fellows are obliged to fetch wood and water on their backs, half a mile with bare legs in snow or mud."[148]

With little alteration, blankets could serve as overcoats. In December, 1777, the Marquis de Lafayette recommended that, "The [mens'] blanckets must have one or two buttons to surround the breast and be a kind of great coat ...."[149] In the winter of 1779-1780 at Jockey Hollow, Washington's troops would have welcomed the option of wearing blankets.

HASH MARKS AND THE FIRST METAL OF HONOR

In August, 1782, Washington issued orders establishing the first combat decorations. A "Badge of Distinction" was the first honor awarded to the common soldier on a regular basis. It consisted of a strip of white cloth sewn above the left cuff of the soldier's regimental coat. The general especially valued the services of those soldiers, who had long and honorable service, and who had participated in active combat.

The second award, the Military Badge of Merit, was created to reward both soldiers and officers for "Singularly meritorious service, instances of unusual gallantry and extraordinary fidelity and faithful service." Washington designed the award personally, and specified that it be the figure of a heart in purple cloth, or silk, edged with narrow lace or binding and worn on the left breast. Soldiers awarded this decoration had their names entered in the army's special "Book of Merit." These men, regardless of their rank, were permitted to pass all sentinels and receive salutes as if they were officers. In today's military, such honors are reserved for recipients of the Medal of Honor, our country's highest military award for personal acts of valor above and beyond the call of duty.

The "Badge of Military Merit" was created to reward soldiers for meritorious service. (Courtesy of New Windsor Cantonment Historic Site, New York Office of Parks, Recreation and Historic Preservation)

At the New Windsor Encampment two soldiers from Connecticut were selected to be the first recipients of the Military Badge of Merit. The first, Elijah Churchill, was cited for gallantry in action at Fort St. George, on the southern coast of Long Island, in November, 1780, at Tarrytown, New York, in July, 1781, and at Fort Salonga, also on Long Island, on October 2, 1781.

The second soldier selected was Sergeant William Brown of the 5th Connecticut Regiment of Foot. No record of his citation has been uncovered, but it is believed that he participated in the assault on Redoubt No. 10 during the siege of Yorktown. The award ceremony took place on May 3, 1783 at Washington's Headquarters at Newburgh with the 1st New York Regiment, the Commander-in-Chief's Guard, and other units in attendance.

It is remarkable that the first awards for valor in America were presented to common soldiers. The practice of recognizing ordinary soldiers for courage or extraordinary service never occurred in European countries, where the tradition was to award such honors honor only to high-ranking officers who won battles. But it was not all work and no play for private

Men may have endured physical suffering and privations while in camp, but even in the worst of times they managed to find creative ways to provide fun and recreation. The next chapter will explore these in greater detail, and provide a glimpse into the private life of Yankee Doodle.

Chapter Ten

Rum, Sex, and Jollification

Continental soldiers had few occasions for fun or recreation, but based on the evidence in diaries and orderly books, they did find ways to entertain themselves and pass the time. They tossed balls to one another, and played whist and other card games. An amusement called pitch penny was also popular in camp, although most men had no betting money, so buttons was substituted for coins. There were marksmanship contests and ice skating in the winter, and swimming was popular during the summer months.[150] Permission to fish, hunt and gather nuts was usually granted only to officers. Wives visited the camp if soldiers' homes were nearby, despite the danger of enemy attack.

Common games played in the Revolutionary War era were Leap Frog, Blind Man's Bluff and Hop Scotch (Courtesy of 18th Century Material Resource Center collection)

Mahitable Pride, the wife of Sergeant James Pride of the 5th New York Regiment, was at Fort Montgomery sharing a picnic lunch with another soldier's wife when they heard the sound of gunfire. This barrage was the start of the British assault on the fort. This statement appears in her surviving spouse pension application filed in 1837: "Mahitable Pride says that her late husband James Pride was stationed at Fort Montgomery at which place this deponent and Lieutenant Furman's wife [John Furman, an officer in Hutchings 2nd Company, was captured on the day of the battle] went to see their husbands.

While we were at the Fort there was an alarm that the British were coming and we left the Fort ,and this deponent says that in all probability her husband would have been taken prisoner had he not just before the British came been ordered out with a detachment of men to guard a weak place about the fort."[151]

Even the act of taking a bath in a body of water was such a noteworthy occasion that it was recorded in orderly books. It also led to a few problems: "Complaints having been made by the inhabitants situated near the mill pond that some soldiers come there to go into swimming in the open view of the women and that they come out of the water and run to the house naked with a desire to insult and wound the modesty of female decency, 'tis with concern that the general finds himself with the disagreeable necessity of expressing his disappropriation for such beastly conduct."[152]

The social highlights of life in camp were the celebrations that took place around the holidays, since these were the only officially-sanctioned diversions for the common soldiers. Fourth of July was considered the top event of the year. On that day the entire army was placed on parade, and massed artillery fired thirteen salvos, one for each of the colonies. This was followed by running volleys of musketry, and a rousing speech was given by a senior officer. The ceremony ended with three huzzas from the hundreds, or even thousands, of gathered troops. Routines were relaxed for the rest of the day and a gill (a quarter pint) of rum was issued to each man. So great was the sound of gunfire at the celebration in 1778 in New Brunswick, New Jersey, that it was noticed twenty-five miles away on Sandy Hook. When the British heard it, they thought they were being attacked.

Elijah Fisher, a member of Washington's Life Guard, describes this event in his journal, "July 4th. We celebrated the Independence of America the howl army paraded and at the right of every brigade there was a field peace [cannon] placed, then was the signal given for the howl army to fire and they fired one round a piece and the artillery discharged thirteen cannon and we gave three cheers. At night his excelency [Washington] and the gentlemen and ladys had a bawl at head Quarters with greate pompe."[153]

Thanksgiving and Christmas were observed with religious services, light duty and an extra allowance of liquor. Washington issued this proclamation near Valley Forge in 1777: "Tomorrow being the day set apart by the Honorable Congress for public Thanksgiving and Praise; and duty calling us devoutly to express our grateful acknowledgements to God for the manifold blessings he has granted us. The General directs that the army remain in its present quarters, and that the Chaplains perform divine service with their several Corps and brigades. And earnestly exhorts, all officers and soldiers, whose absence is not indispensibly necessary, to attend with reverence the solemnities of the day."[154]

Among the more unusual celebrations was St. Patrick's Day, which Washington proclaimed to be a holiday in 1780. Because of the large number of Irish immigrants and deserters of Irish descent from the British Army who had joined the Americans, it was specifically set aside for their benefit.

Special occasions were also observed. The wonderful news that France had joined the American cause and the anniversary of the great victory at Saratoga were commemorated each year. Congress and local governing bodies often contributed a gift of rum to the celebrations. Thirty hogsheads (a large barrel containing about sixty gallons) were sent by Congress to the army to honor the survivors of Brandywine on September 12, 1777, the day after the battle.[155]

Bands of captives passing through camp, such as prisoners of war and local Tories, also provided amusement for the soldiers, who taunted the unfortunates. This occurred around Fishkill on the seven-hundred-mile march from Massachusetts to Virginia of the thousands of prisoners of the "Convention Army." These were the troops of Burgoyne captured after his defeat at Saratoga in 1777. In addition, soldiers were fascinated by important or curious visitors, such as members of the Continental Congress sent to inspect the army, foreign diplomats, and even Indian chiefs. Private David Howe was excited when one such chief visited his camp. He wrote in his diary, "The King of the Ingans, with five of his Nobles to attend him, come to Head Quarters to Congratulate with his exelency."

Displays of corporal punishment provided a grim diversion in the otherwise uneventful life in camp. Officers believed that witnessing hangings and floggings would set an example and teach a lesson, so attendance at these punishments was mandatory. Audience participation was often required for such penalties as firing squads and "running the gauntlet," a form of punishment in which men were forced to run between two rows of soldiers while being pummeled and hit by sticks and other objects. Frequent last minute reprieves of prisoners added a measure of theatrics to the drama.[156]

One can imagine the energized young men, many of whom were teenagers, making their own fun while in camp. The following entry appears in a regimental orderly book of the New York Brigade when it was preparing for the campaign against the Iroquois Nations in western New York State during 1779:

> *The Comdg. Officer is under the disagreeable necessity of informing his Soldiers of that which in his Opinion their own good sence and time of Service ought long before this to have Convinc'd them of the unpropriety of . . . their noisy unsoldierlike conduct when in their Tents . . . seems to encrease daily to such a degree as to render the situation of their Officers verry disagreeable & expose themselves to the illnatured observations of the Soldiers of Other Regiments in their passage thro' the Camp. He therefore expects that they will behave with more propriety for the future, and moderate their Mirth so as to render the situation of those whose duty Obliges them to be near not so disagreeable as it has hitherto been, he has not the least Inclination to lay them under any restrictions that will check their Mirth provided it is kept within due bounds but on the contrary would rather incourage it as far as it is consistent with good order & Military discipline.*

VIRTUOUS YANKEE DOODLE

The Continental Army, along with its corps of dedicated chaplains, enforced church attendance and insisted that its soldiers remain virtuous. This policy may help explain why little evidence of carnal matters can be found in soldier's diaries, and why there is even less indication of immoral conduct in other army documents. Although temptations must have been in attendance, detailed written accounts indicate that licentious attractions were viewed with indifference. The fact that few common soldiers could afford sexual entertainment might also account for this fact. The accounts of immoral behavior that do exist often consist of adamant denial of participation.

Colonel Loammi Baldwin of the Massachusetts Line wrote to his wife from New York soon after the army arrived from Boston in June 1776: "The whores continue their employ, which is become very lucrative. Their unparalleled conduct is a sufficient anecdote against any desires that a person can have that has one spark of modesty left in him . . . Perhaps you will call me censorious and exclaim too much upon bare reports when I say that I was never within the doors of nor exchanged a word with any of them except in execution of my duty as an officer of the day in going the grand round with my guard of escort have broke up the knots of men and women fighting, pulling caps, swearing and crying, 'Murder!' etc., hurried them off to the provost dungeon by half dozens, there let them lay mixed till the next day. Then some are punished and some get off clear. Hell's work."[157]

Sergeant Joseph Plumb Martin passionately admired the New Jersey belles as he passed through New Jersey on his way to the Battle of Monmouth in 1778: "The Young ladies of the town Princeton and perhaps of the vicinity had collected and were sitting on the stoops and in the windows . . . I chanced to be on the wing of a platoon next to the houses, as they were chiefly on one side of the street, and had a good chance to notice the ladies, I declare that I have never before nor since seen more beauty considering the numbers I saw at the time. They were all beautiful. New Jersey and Pennsylvania ladies are in my opinion, collectively handsome, the most so in the United States"[158]

Georg Daniel Flohr, a French soldier serving with Rochambeau's forces, described this scene as the French Army marched through Suffern, New York on the way to Yorktown in 1781: "Suffrantz [Suffern] is a little town in a very pleasant area where everyone would have liked to stay. In that area males are very welcome since one did not meet many of them, when entered a house there the first thing they did was to ask whether one did not want to stay with them they would hide you until the French were gone."[159]

The role of camp followers has been misunderstood by historians and others, who often assume that they were all prostitutes. Thousands of women accompanied the Continental Army, and although some were indeed illicit sexual partners, the majority of them were wives of the soldiers. They traveled with the baggage train, and provided vital services to the army, such as sewing, washing and mending. They also went in search of the food, clothing, and other supplies that the soldiers needed from local towns. Washington knew that forcing these women from the camps would in all likelihood reduce the ranks of his volunteer army, so he did not make a big issue of it. A few desperate women may have turned to prostitution, but most likely avoided it since it would have resulted in their being permanently barred from traveling with the army.

Piety in Pattens, or, Timbertoe on Tiptoe, a 1773 etching published in London

Prostitution was a constant worry for army leadership because of the fear of the spread of venereal diseases. New York City presented a serious problem when it was occupied by the Continental Army in 1776. Venereal disease had become so widespread that the army began deducting pay from afflicted soldiers as punishment. Soldiers slipped away to visit the "Holy Ground," an extensive and squalid district of bars, brothels, and gambling halls, where more than five hundred prostitutes plied their trade to soldiers and sailors. If there was violence and thievery in New York after dark, it more than likely occurred at the Holy Ground. A week after the Continental Army occupied the city, in April, 1776, the mutilated bodies of two soldiers were found hidden in a brothel there; both had been hideously murdered. In response, soldiers protested by rampaging through the area tearing down houses and rioting in the streets.

Lieutenant Isaac Bangs, of Massachusetts, toured the Holy Ground out of curiosity and concern for the health of the soldiers in his regiment. He described the place in his journal: "When I visited them [prostitutes], at first I thought nothing could exceed them for impudence and immodesty, but I found the more I was acquainted with them, the more they excelled in their brutality."

He went on to question how any man could have "intimate connections with such creatures," and was amazed by how soldiers and officers were attracted to the women "till the fatal disorder [syphilis] seized them."[160]

Despite Washington's orders of curfews and threats of punishment for soldiers found drunk in "red light" districts, prostitution continued to flourish in New York. William Tudor, Washington's judge advocate, wrote to his fiancée, " . . . every brutal gratification can be so easily indulged in this place that the army will be debauched here in a month, more than in twelve at Cambridge [Boston]."[161]

A GILL FOR COURAGE AND COMFORT

Rum, or its equivalent in whiskey, hard cider or brandy, was a beverage of daily consumption in the Continental Army. References to liquor appear frequently on official requests for supplies, and in general orders. Alcoholic drinks were used to celebrate all special occasions and to encourage enlistment. They were often issued after a day of extra work, a job well-done, following a long march, during bad weather, or in battle. The standard allowance per day was a gill (one-quarter pint). This was often mixed with three parts of water, and carried in canteens. A gill was just enough to induce mild euphoria but was not enough to get a man drunk.

The army's liberal distribution of alcohol reflected the accepted belief at the time that drinking in moderation promoted health and reduced fatigue. Major General Henry Knox insisted that quartermasters at Valley Forge provide daily allotments: "We have found by experience that this [alcohol] would support the men through every difficulty."

In addition to imbibing on a regular basis in camp, the Continental Army, like most other armies in the world at that time, fought while under the influence of alcohol. A few days before the Battle of Brandywine, General Peter Muhlenberg wrote in his orderly book, "Many soldiers are making a practice of getting drunk regularly, once a day and therefore rendering themselves unfit for duty."[162] Minutes before the Battle of Eutaw Springs in South Carolina in 1781, General Nathanael Greene was preparing his inexperienced troops for the upcoming fight. Colonel Otho Williams reported, "We . . . moved in order of battle about three miles, when we halted and took a little of that liquid which is not unnecessary to exhilarate the animal spirits on such occasions."[163]

Robert Steele was a young drummer boy at the Battle of Bunker Hill. In the thick of the fighting he remembered being ordered by his sergeant to procure rum:

You are young and spry, run in a moment to some of the stores and bring some rum. Major Moore is badly wounded. Go as quick as possible . . . we however immediately passed on and went into a store, but see no one there. I seized a brown, two-quart, earthen pitcher and drawed it partly full from a cask and found I had got wine. I threw that out and filled my pitcher with rum from another cask. Ben took a pail and filled with water, and we hastened back to the entrenchment on the hill, when we found our people in confusion and talking about retreating. The British were about advancing upon us a third time. Our rum and water went very quick. It was very hot, but I saved my pitcher and kept it for sometime afterwards.[164]

This astonishing invoice was sent to the New York Provincial Congress in 1776 from the 2nd Orange County Militia Regiment, a unit consisting of from seventy to two hundred men, some of whom were part-time soldiers. A similar bill had been submitted the previous month.

2 Hogsheads of rum, (220 gallons) at 9s 4d
7 1/2 Gin of John Waldron
case of gin at 9s 4d
67 1/2 gals spirits at 12s
5 1/2 gals of gin at 13s

British Soldiers drinking at a sutler's booth (Courtesy of Brown Military Collection, Brown University Library)

Drunkenness was the chief offence in camp. Additional liquor, not distributed by the army as rations, was readily available from sutlers. These civilian merchants with portable shops near camps always had liquor available to those who could afford it, and some sold it to those without money as an advance against their pay. As a consequence, men could drink up their entire pay before they even received it. At other times, soldiers traded blankets and items of their own clothing for alcohol. As a result, regulations put in place for sutlers in 1782 stipulated, "For liquors or other articles sold to non commissioned officers & soldiers, artificers and waggoners, nothing shall be taken in payment but money."

Washington realized that it was impossible to outlaw these shops, so he licensed them, and then carefully monitored and regulated their prices: "The gin shops and other house where liquors have been heretofore retailed with in or near lines are strictly forbidden to sell any in the future to any soldier in the army . . . . If any soldier of the army shall be found disguised with liquor, as has been too much the practice heretofore, the General is to have him punished with the utmost severity, as no soldier in such situation can be either fit for defense or attack. The General orders that no suttler in the army shall sell to any soldier more than one half pint of spirit per day. At the beating of the tattoo, each suttler is to shut up his stores, and sell nothing more until after Reveille the next morning."[165]

Sergeant Joseph Plumb Martin recounted wading through chest-high water when crossing the Schuykill River on the way to Valley Forge after the Battle of Germantown, Pennsylvania in October, 1777:

> *When we had crossed and it became dark, we met the Quartermasters, who had come out to meet us with wagons and hogsheads of whiskey, thinking perhaps that we might take cold for being so much exposed in the cold water . . . . The casks were unheaded, and the Quartermaster sergeants stood in and dealt out the liquor to the platoons. Each platoon halting until it came up to be served. The intention was to give each man a gill of liquor, but as measuring it out by gills was tedious, it was dealt out to us in pint measures with direction to divide a pint between four men. But it was dark and the actions of the men could not be seen by those who served out the liquor, each one drank as much as he pleased: some, perhaps half a gill, some a gill and as many as choose it drained the pint.*

A resentful British lieutenant, upset by the unexpected and courageous resistance of the raw American troops at the Battle of Harlem Heights in September, 1776, offered this disparaging comment while praising the abstention of his own men: ". . . an opportunity of showing the difference of British and American spirit. Every one of the enemy's killed and wounded stunk infamously of rum. Their canteens still contained the remains of sheer spirits and even their officers were in this manner urged on; while ours . . . had not, I dare say drank their allowance of grog, which is four waters to a good deal less than a half pint of rum."

Years after the war, the miniscule American Navy had a propensity for tippling that seems to have even exceeded the thirst of the Continental Army. The USS *Constitution* (Old Ironsides), a warship, carried enough fresh water for her crew of 475 officers and men to last six months of sustained operations at sea, as well as plenty of rum. According to her ship's log, "On July 27, 1798, the ship sailed from Boston with a full complement of men, 48,600 gallons of fresh water, 7,400 cannon shot, 11,600 pounds of black powder and 79,400 gallons of rum." By November, she had defeated five British men-of-war, captured and scuttled twelve English merchant ships, and had salvaged all the rum stores aboard each of these vessels. In January, with her ammunition supply now exhausted, the unarmed ship made a night raid up the Firth of Clyde in Scotland. There her landing party captured a whisky distillery, and liberated 40,000 gallons of single malt Scotch. The Constitution then headed home for Boston in February, 1799. The ship arrived without food and liquor of any kind. The sole cargo remaining was 38,600 gallons of water.

Historic USS *Constitution* freesails in celebration of her 200th birthday.
(File photo from *Herald Sun*, 1997, photograph by Charles Krupa)

Abuse of liquor was a problem during the entire war. As late as May, 1782, at the New Windsor Cantonment, General Washington ordered each regiment to maintain a liquor log, ". . . from which the name of every soldier shall be struck off who addicts himself to drunkenness," and condemned, "the practice of swallowing the whole ration of liquor at a single draught."[166] But perhaps some "false courage" was helpful in warfare, an activity which required soldiers to stand close to the enemy and absorb direct gunfire, or engage the foe with the bayonet, all of which took an enormous amount of nerve and daring.

Chapter Eleven

The Sting of Battle

Yankee Doodle in Combat

Muskets and cannon were the primary weapons of the Revolutionary War, and these armaments determined the tactics on the battlefield. Because they were smoothbore, muskets were inaccurate at distances beyond fifty yards, and their trajectory was very unpredictable. This required soldiers to stand dangerously close to the enemy while withstanding a barrage from their opponent. After firing, they had to reload their weapon; an experienced soldier could only shoot three volleys in one minute. For the common soldier of the time, this conventional approach to fighting required an enormous amount of fortitude and concentration.

In March, 1781, Sergeant Roger Lamb of the Royal Welsh Fusiliers described a terrifying moment he experienced when confronted by American soldiers at the Battle of Guilford Courthouse, North Carolina: "When we arrived within forty yards of the enemy's lines it was perceived that their whole force had their arms presented and resting on a rail fence . . . they were taking aim with nicest precision . . . . At that awful period a general pause took place. Both parties surveyed each other for the moment with most anxious suspense. Colonel Webster rode in the front of the regiment and said 'come on my brave fusiliers.' . . .they rushed forward amidst the enemy's fire. Dreadful was the havoc on both sides."[167]

In the early days of the war, the untried citizen-soldiers were awed and intimidated by the professionalism of the well-equipped British regulars. While the Americans prided themselves on their superior marksmanship, they were terrified by their enemy's deadly and effective use of the bayonet. This apprehension was soon confirmed by the dismal performance of the fledgling Continental Army at Kips Bay in New York City during 1776, when Washington's men panicked and fled without firing a shot at the first sight of Sir William Howe's Redcoats. A discouraged General William Smallwood described this event, "I have often read and heard of cowardice but hitherto have had but a feint idea if it . . . I could wish the transactions of this day blotted out in the annals of America. Nothing appeared but flight, disgrace and confusion."[168] Even though there were often officers placed in the rear, with orders to shoot anyone who retreated, this too failed to create stability among the poorly-trained men led by inexperienced officers.

Yankee Doodle's greatest challenge on the battlefield was overcoming fear, and its cousin panic. In European-style armies, it was acceptable, and even encouraged, for men to fear their own officers as much as the enemy. All eighteenth century armies had a series of penalties extending from fines and demotions all the way to executions. The most common punishment was flogging, which could range up to 1,000 lashes. The commanders of the free-spirited American soldier could never hope to achieve such a high level of intimidation. If they had, the Yankee Doodles would likely have deserted in even greater numbers.

Washington always issued a General Order to his troops before battles. It typically invoked patriotism and God, and ended with a stern warning that those who ran would be shot. There is little evidence of Continental soldiers ever admitting to fear. They were taught that fear was a sin, and that the best way to control it was by displaying reverence and patriotic ardor. Reverend Robert Cooper, in a sermon delivered to the Pennsylvania Regiments in 1775, offered this guidance to soldiers: "To draw back, if you were even before the cannon's mouth, would fix both awful guilt and indelible disgrace upon you . . . . If you would escape deep guilt before God, and lasting contempt among men, forward you must go wheresoever the drum shall beat and the trumpet sound for battle."[169]

American soldiers overcame their trepidation when they became convinced of their skill to fight as trained professionals. The ultimate test, however, was the ability to stand fast and not run away in fear in the heat of battle. Fear in battle was never proof of their lack of bravery, and the independent and freethinking nature of American soldiers served them well when courage was enhanced with discipline and professionalism.

Evidence of self-reliance is often found in narratives of smaller engagements. In 1776, a small patrol of twenty Americans, without officers, stumbled onto a Hessian position at King's Bridge, a vital crossing located in what is now the northwest part of the Bronx. Two privates charged up the hill, followed by a handful of their fellow soldiers, and were successful in taking the position. But the retreating Hessians were soon reinforced by about fifty men, and they were able to recapture the hill. The Americans discussed the situation, and decided to split up and attack the rocky position again from the rear. This time they were successful; the Hessian force retreated for good, and the Americans overran and held the rocky stronghold.[170]

HIT AND RUN OR STAND FAST - BATTLEFIELD TACTICS

The traditional opponents of the American soldier and his pioneer ancestors were the Native Americans, whose hostility was continuously provoked by relentless encroachment on their tribal lands. The primary tactic that the Indians used in warfare was sniping, especially when concealed behind trees and rocks, or ambushing the opponent by surprise. Soldiers learned these Native-style guerilla tactics throughout the one hundred years of hostilities prior to the Revolution.

Americans used guerilla tactics effectively on a number of occasions. At Lexington and Concord this approach was very successful. Shortly thereafter, at Bunker Hill, the Patriots hunkered down in tall grass, Native-style, until the British were within forty yards, and then effectively slaughtered elite companies of grenadiers. Later, in the South, where much of the fighting was done by militia forces, concealment and surprise was used to great advantage.

American riflemen were deadly at Cowpens and Saratoga, since they were led by qualified officers, such as Daniel Morgan and Nathanael Greene, who knew how to exploit their marksmanship. Partisan leaders, such as Francis Marion, often surprised the British and then quickly vanished into the swamps before they could organize a defense. These fighting bands led by the "Swamp Fox" managed to destabilize the forces of Cornwallis with hit-and-run tactics before they confronted the main Continental Army at Yorktown.

While guerilla warfare provided obvious advantages, its tactics did have some dangerous drawbacks. Forces could become completely disorganized and suffer heavy casualties from friendly fire. Wounded men might find themselves disoriented, or without a nearby comrade to assist them. Unfortunately, these woodsmen's tactics did not win decisive battles.

More traditional eighteenth century battles were primarily fought in two ways. The first was a "war of posts," attacking or besieging fortifications or attempting to defend them. The other method was with troops exposed on the open field, a "war of maneuver." In general, the latter was more prevalent, and the backwoods skills and superior marksmanship that Yankee Doodle brought to the war were inadequate for that brand of European style.

Starting with George Washington, all of the American military leadership recognized that battles were going to have to be won European-style in order to be decisive. This meant that troops had to fight using "linear warfare," standing in ranks and exchanging volleys of musket fire at close range, the aim of which was to blast opponents off the battlefield with concentrated firepower. The true test of a regiment was to deliver a hail of musket fire, and then manage to survive after receiving a barrage in return. Those soldiers still standing could then swarm over the enemy with fixed bayonets and dispatch them. The Continental Army could only start winning battles when it mastered these types of skills. This did not occur until the American forces were drilled by Baron Frederick von Steuben. Based on his experience in the Prussian wars, he was able to demonstrate techniques that American soldiers could use to counter British tactics on the open ground.

The concept of linear warfare had been developed in Europe, where the terrain mostly consisted of large flat fields. This tactic made it effortless to command and control troops. Massed firepower at short range, concentrated on a specific area, could inflict great devastation on the opposing enemy's front lines. Many American officers were familiar with this type of warfare, since they had served under British commanders during the French and Indian War. Among the senior commanders who had filled the ranks of the British Army were George Washington and many members of his staff, including Generals Montgomery, Gates, Alexander, Mercer, Putnam, Van Schaick and Charles Lee. Until the arrival of von Steuben, none had had the foresight to train American soldiers in this tactic.

Upon analysis, linear tactics were a ridiculous method of conducting warfare. Entire armies were formed into two lines of men, two or three ranks deep, standing shoulder to shoulder. The opposing sides would then march toward each other in tight formation. Both sides, in effect, were offering each other as a huge "sitting duck" target. Once within range, typically less than one hundred yards, the soldiers in the first row would drop on one knee, present arms, and fire in unison on command. Limited by their inaccurate muskets, soldiers aimed at general areas rather than at individual targets.

The battlefield became obscured by thick smoke after the first volley. Adversaries continued to fire volley after volley, moving closer together after each barrage. When one side gave way, the force with the most survivors could then cohesively surge forward in a charge with bayonets at the ready. The broken line could usually not withstand such an organized charge, and the fray typically ended with the bayonet attack deciding the winner.

Speed in maneuvering around the battlefield was critical, and discipline was needed to move together in one line, coordinate barrages, and confront oncoming bayonet assaults. A fast pace was required to fire as many rounds as possible in order to decimate the enemy before it could attack. Surprisingly, linear tactics remained the rule throughout the nineteenth century, and even into the first part of the twentieth century. The continued use of these identical approaches caused the horrific carnage of the Civil War, even after repeating rifles and other weapons with much greater fire power were introduced. It was not until the mass slaughter caused by the invention of the machine gun in World War I that time-honored linear tactics were finally abandoned.

The training initiated by von Steuben leveled the fighting field during the Revolution, and soon the British regulars found themselves opposed by audacious Americans armed with comparable fighting skills. The victories at Bennington and Saratoga, the face-off at Monmouth, and the amazing surprise attack at Stony Point, New York were followed by the successes in the

South at King's Mountain, Cowpens and Eutaw Springs. The engagements proved to the British that American troops could repel an assault in the open field against their most elite regiments.

RUSTY MUSKETS AND BLOODY BAYONETS

The two principal weapons of the American Revolution were the muzzle-loading flintlock musket with attached bayonet, and the cannon. Less important were the rifle and pistol, and swords and other cutting weapons. By far, the flintlock musket, an icon of the struggle for American independence, was the most common firearm employed. The "shot heard round the world" fired at Lexington Green in 1775, came out of the barrel of a smoothbore musket. The French Charleville musket was widely used by Continental soldiers, the English version of which was called the Brown Bess. These two types of muskets were similar in accuracy, length and caliber.

Linear battlefield tactics were actually developed in order to use the flintlock military musket to the best advantage. Instead of the large square formations of pikemen moving as a block, men with muskets lined up in three ranks to bring the maximum number of weapons to bear on the enemy. Firing rank-by-rank, the massed musketmen could fire a devastating nine volleys per minute. Linear tactics were designed to blast opponents off the battlefield with this concentrated musket fire.

When war first broke out, muskets from the French and Indian War were relied upon, but these worn-out arms soon deteriorated. The Continental Army then turned to weapons either smuggled in or captured on the battlefield, which explains why the English Brown Bess served as the primary musket of the American forces. Officers in the Continental Army were also authorized to buy guns from militia regiments. Desperate for muskets, Congress sent Silas Deane to France in January, 1776, to plead for assistance, and large consignments of firearms began to arrive in 1777 as a result of his efforts. More than 100,000 Charleville muskets were purchased from France during the Revolutionary War, and within a short period of time this gun replaced the Brown Bess as the main musket for the Continental Army.

Due to the technology used in weapons of the period, accuracy was not critical on the battlefield. Soldiers did not specifically aim at another person, but instead pointed muskets in the general direction of the enemy. A more critical aspect was rate of fire. A well-drilled company could load and fire four volleys a minute. All members fired on command, in unison. Firing was synchronized by the drum command, "company (or battalion) prime and load," typically followed by the shouted command "fire!"[171] The drum served as a means of signaling and conveying orders above the din of battle more effectively than the human voice. During battles, drums signaled troops to take up weapons, move their position, form lines and retreat.

By today's standards, the military musket was very inaccurate, since it proved difficult to hit a target as big as a man beyond seventy-five yards. The typical gun weighed over ten pounds, and had roughly the caliber of a twelve-gage shotgun. Its barrel was at least three feet long, which made it difficult to aim. Flints lasted for only about twenty firings, and often had to be replaced in the thick of battle. Musket balls were made of lead, and could be made to be more lethal by splitting them along the molded seam. This caused them to scatter into pieces when fired, similar to today's hollow point bullet. Men also used bits of iron, nails and glass shards to load muskets, and this fragmentation had the devastating effect of buck shot.

To technique of loading a musket consisted of opening a cartridge box, grabbing a cartridge, and biting off the end to expose the powder. The soldier then poured a small amount of the powder into the pan of the lock, closed the pan and dropped powder and a cartridge into the barrel. The last step was to use a ramrod to seat the powder and cartridge in the barrel. He "made ready" to shoot by cocking his lock and "presenting" (pointing) his piece at the enemy. There were no sights except for the bayonet lug near the muzzle, so the soldier just looked down the barrel and hoped for the best result. With each shot fired, there was more and more fouling in the barrel from the black powder, which made shots harder to load. After firing about five rounds, soldiers slowed down because of the fouling, and because the barrel was now quite hot. The delay to clear the barrel with a ramrod and patch, or hot water, resulted in many casualties in the heat of battle. A lubricant was sometimes used to soften the fouling in the bore so that it was dislodged during loading.

There were problems with the flintlock musket. It took so long to reload after firing that the enemy could easily overrun a position with a swift bayonet assault. Gunpowder was often difficult to obtain (only about 10 percent was produced domestically), and lack of an adequate supply haunted the army throughout the entire war. There were only three powder mills in operation in all of the colonies, so gunpowder was imported from French colonies in the West Indies.[172] The shortage was so serious in 1776 that Benjamin Franklin suggested that pikes (a long thrusting spear used in the Middle Ages) replace muskets. He also argued that bows and arrows should also be issued, since a man could shoot four arrows for every one bullet; opponents, with their vision obscured by smoke, he reasoned, would be distracted by flying arrows.[173]

The phrase "lock, stock, and barrel," meaning the "whole thing", refers to the three main parts of a musket. The stock is the wooden base, the barrel is the tube where the musket ball accelerates and exits the weapon, and the lock is the mechanism that causes the weapon to fire. The expressions "going off half-cocked" and "flash in the pan" are also derived from the use of the musket. The weapon had a long life in America; the last flintlock firearm was supplied to the army in 1840, although obsolete flintlocks were used in action in the early days of the American Civil War.[174]

THE RIFLE

Why was the musket the predominant weapon of the Revolutionary War, when the rifle had vastly superior accuracy and range? Rifles were formidable firearms that had been used on a daily basis for about one hundred years prior to the war to put food on the tables of American colonists. They were accurate at two to three hundred yards, about three times the range of the musket. The process called "rifling" created groves in the rifle barrel which caused the ejected bullet to spin, thus vastly improving its accuracy. Riflemen could then aim at specific targets on the battlefield with increased precision. Since they could be so far from the field of battle, riflemen firing from positions in the woods or on rough ground had ample time to fall back and hide if they wanted to avoid hand-to-hand combat. Rifle companies attached to regiments were used as skirmishers to engage the enemy in advance of the main army, after which they would withdraw.

American riflemen were so feared that British officers were advised to remove the gold trim from their coats since it could be used as a target. The Bradford brothers, Loyalist Philadelphia printers, ominously reported to the *London Chronicle* on August 17, 1775 that "This province has raised 1,000 riflemen, the worst of whom will put a ball into a man's head at a distance of 150 or 200 yards, therefore advise your officers who shall hereafter come out to America to settle their affairs in England before their departure."

However, the flintlock rifle had considerable disadvantages when compared with the musket. It had a significantly longer reloading time, since a minute or more was needed to carefully ram the ball down the barrel to tightly engage the rifled grooves that spun it and gave it trajectory. And like muskets, rifles became very difficult to load, since after a few shots the gunpowder quickly fouled the barrel.

In June, 1775, the Continental Congress authorized ten companies of riflemen to be recruited. Daniel Morgan's famous corps of riflemen consisted of handpicked marksmen selected from the ranks of the entire Continental Army. Their great speed and mobility made them effective for scouting and rapid deployment over great distances, and Morgan used these advantages to engage in guerrilla tactics. His snipers first killed the enemy's Indian guides, and then picked off the British officers. While targeting officers was considered dishonorable by both sides, it proved to be extremely successful in breaking up Redcoat formations. Morgan's men were indispensable to the American victories at Saratoga and Cowpens, South Carolina.[175]

The fighting began at Saratoga when an advance party of four regiments of British regulars heard a chorus of turkey gobbles that seemed to be coming from shadowy figures in fur caps in the surrounding woods. Suddenly the sharp crack of rifles broke the stillness. Within minutes every British officer was killed or wounded, and then privates began to fall. The riflemen disappeared into the woods when the Redcoat reserves rushed to the rescue of their comrades. Later in the battle, General Simon Fraser, a top British Commander, was killed by a bullet from Timothy Murphy, one of Morgan's riflemen. The death of Fraser contributed to the surrender of more than 5,000 British and German soldiers, and was one of the war's greatest victories.[176]

Riflemen are also credited with the overwhelming victory at King's Mountain in October, 1780. A force of more than 1,100 Loyalists, trained and equipped by the British, and commanded by Scottish Major Patrick Ferguson, were opposed by an American force of 1,400 backwoodsmen. Each carried a rifle and a bag of parched corn. At first, the Americans were beaten back by bayonet charges, but they managed to surround the Loyalist force after dispatching most of their officers. Major Ferguson himself died after being hit by eight bullets. The Tories surrendered after an hour of intense fire, and as many as eight hundred were killed and wounded. In comparison, one hundred riflemen fell in the action.

Major Ferguson's death was a setback to British small arms technology. He was the designer of a unique repeating rifle, the first in the western world used by an organized military force. The weapon, known as the "Ferguson Rifle," fired six to ten rounds per minute, an exceptionally high rate of fire for its day. Only two hundred of the weapons were made by British firms, and issued to a rifle corps commanded by Ferguson in 1776. The rifle was first used in New Jersey at the Battle of the Short Hills in June, 1777, and later that year at Saratoga and Brandywine. After limited use at the Siege of Charleston in 1780, it was discontinued. While far ahead of its time, the gun was not appreciated by the British War Office. In the field the linear tactics of the period were better suited to the standard muzzleloader. The rifles were difficult and expensive to produce and easily broke down in combat. In battle, rifle units were singled out as priority targets, and took high casualties, especially among officers.

Prior to becoming a renowned Indian fighter, Daniel Boone had been a militia officer. In 1778, he shot at a British officer in Kentucky who had stuck his head out from behind a tree, and the bullet hit the Redcoat commander in the forehead, killing him instantly. The shot, confirmed by witnesses on both sides, was from a distance of 250 yards. Boone attributed his accuracy to having carefully measured the exact load of black powder in his rifle.[177]

American riflemen, considered an elite special force, had a reputation for being arrogant, unruly and boisterous, and their disruptive behavior was resented by the regular troops. They were physically tough, and many were over six feet tall. They wore white hunting shirts and distinctive round hats.

One company from Maryland is described in *The Pennsylvania Gazette* of August 16, 1775: "I have had the happiness of seeing Captain Michael Cresap marching at the head of a formidable company of perhaps one hundred and thirty men, from the mountains and backwoods, painted like Indians, armed with tomahawks and rifles, dressed in hunting shirts and moccasins, and though some of them had traveled near 800 miles from the banks of the Ohio, they seemed to walk light and easy, and not with less spirit than at the first hour of their march. Health and vigor, after what they had undergone, declared them to be intimate with hardship, and familiar with danger . . . ."

Many riflemen were volunteers. When five hundred marksmen signed up in the mountains of Virginia in 1775, the commander wished to select the most skillful from among them. A board one foot square, with a chalk drawing of a nose was nailed to a tree at a distance of 150 yards. Those who came nearest the mark with a single bullet were to be chosen, but this was not such an easy decision after the first forty or fifty men who shot cut the nose entirely out of the board.[178]

These marksmen were armed with the "Kentucky long rifle," a weapon actually made in Pennsylvania by German gunsmiths for settlers trekking through their state en route to the frontier. They were artfully crafted with a carved stock that was often made of curly maple. Usually they were engraved and decorated personally for the owner. These types of rifles also had ornate engraved brass inlay with a brass patch box fitted into the stock.[179]

Light in weight and economical in consumption of powder and lead, the Kentucky rifle was fatally accurate and uniquely American, and it was used with little modification for a hundred years after the war. Riflemen also carried tomahawks and large knives, both of which substituted for the lack of a bayonet.[180]

The smoothbore musket continued to be the principal weapon for Continental infantry because of fundamental difficulties, as already mentioned. Bayonets, an essential infantry weapon, could not be fastened to rifles, and the longer range and better accuracy of the rifle was of little value on battlefields that were quickly obscured by powder smoke. Riflemen were also required to carry powder horns, needed to measure the precise amount of powder required. Soldiers often wryly commented that rifles were indeed excellent for shooting at things that wouldn't shoot back—like deer.

WITH PASSION AND BAYONETS

In modern warfare, bayonets have been considered weapons to be used only as a last resort, in rare instances where firearms become useless. But in the Revolutionary War they played a major role on the battlefield. These spikes or blades fastened to the end of a musket were some of the most useful and ubiquitous weapons of the war. Since most of the lead that was fired never hit its intended target, bayonets often accounted for a third of all casualties. This weapon could be used during hand-to-hand fighting, and allowed infantrymen to defend themselves from cavalry charges in much the same manner as spears and pikes did in earlier times.

American soldiers had no bayonet training in the early months of the war, and a limited number of bayonets were issued to the army. The few that were distributed ironically found better use as tent stakes or spits for roasting meat over the campfire. The American preference for fighting behind foliage or some type of defensive protection forced the British to change from reliance on gunfire to the speed and shock of the bayonet charge. British generals soon learned the Patriots were terrified by the weapon, and especially intimidated by the lack of mercy shown to those surrendering or helplessly wounded. Bayonet charges caused American troops to panic even without a preliminary softening up with gunfire.

During two valiant but ineffective advances against the hastily formed American defenses, the Redcoats took heavy losses at Bunker Hill, and had to rely on the bayonet for their third successful assault. At that battle most British troops were equipped with bayonets on their muskets, while few Americans had the weapon. Colonel Prescott, one of the last officers to withdraw, defended himself from bayonet thrusts with his ceremonial sword.

The British used the bayonet with deadly effect on Long Island in 1776. They first absorbed a volley from American muskets, and then charged before the Americans had a chance to reload. Christopher Ward described the engagement: "The British really relied on cold steel, this ineffective volley firing being usually only a prelude to a charge with the bayonet. Such an attack, carried out by a body of trained men, terrible in their brilliant uniforms, their compactness, their grim courage, was time and time again in this war, enough to put the untrained American militia, most of whom had no bayonets, to flight even before the charge fell on them."[181]

The British Brown Bess and the French Charleville were fitted with triangular bayonets. They were lightweight and strong, since their triangular shape resisted bending. The three-sided wounds they made were bloody, and they left a gaping hole that was impossible to stitch completely closed, and thus open to infection. Body movements would constantly open up the wound, and even if the bayonet did not puncture a vital organ, the loss of blood alone could cause enough shock to kill.

It is popularly believed that triangular bayonets were outlawed by the second Hague Convention in 1899, which prohibited weapons that were inhumane or caused unnecessary suffering. However, bayonet configuration was never specifically mentioned in the Geneva Accords. Triangular, cross-sectional and spike bayonets were still in use by several countries, including the United States, during the world wars of the twentieth century.

American soldiers had to master the use of the bayonet and learn how to stand firm against the British onslaughts before they could win battles. In the assault on the British fort on the Hudson River at Stony Point, New York, in 1779, the troops were ordered not to load their muskets and to only use their bayonets. Since this was a surprise attack, General Anthony Wayne did not want to risk the accidental firing of a musket. One-hundred-fifty men of the Pennsylvania light infantry stormed the fortifications at bayonet point and captured the bastion without firing one shot. The soldiers at Stony Point were more compassionate than their British opponents, and they spared the enemy wounded. British Commodore George Collier reported in his journal, "The rebels had made the attack with a bravery they never before exhibited, and they showed at this moment a generosity and clemency which during the course of the rebellion had no parallel."[182]

With the introduction of repeating rifles, the bayonet became obsolete in the 1800s, but its use continued until recent times. On February 18, 1967, three hundred soldiers from the Royal Australian Regiment mounted a two-day bayonet attack on a fortified Viet Cong stronghold in Phuochold Tuy Province, South Vietnam. As recently as October, 2011, a British Army lance corporal named Sean Jones led a squad of soldiers from the Prince of Wales Royal Regiment in a successful bayonet charge against Taliban fighters in Helmand Province, Afghanistan.

CANNON - KINGS OF THE BATTLEFIELD

Cannon were the kings of the battlefield throughout the Revolutionary War, and the "weapon of mass destruction" of the day. Any infantry that was not supported by artillery usually lost battles. By besieging fortifications or laying down fire on a battlefield, artillery companies and their cannon could control the outcome of battles. Cannon were used extensively by the Continental Army and were crucial to several major victories. They could fire a ball for hundreds of yards and hit dozens of enemy soldiers with a single shot. These large guns used gunpowder to shoot a round projectile on the battlefield, in forts, and on ships. Mounted on a sturdy wooden carriage, they were designated by the weight of the ball they fired. A three-pounder, for instance, was capable of shooting a three-pound cannon ball.

Cannon fired either solid ball or small shot. Solid balls were cast of iron or bronze at a foundry. Artillerymen would insert a bag made of paper or cloth containing gunpowder into the gun barrel, followed by the cannon ball itself. It was fired by igniting a goose-quill tube filled with gunpowder that had been inserted into a vent-hole that led to the gunpowder in the barrel. When the goose quill fuse was lit, "Fire in the hole!" was shouted by the gunner to warn the crew to stay clear of the recoiling gun when it fired. Cannon had to be wrestled back into the firing position by the gun crew after recoiling. As many as fourteen soldiers were required to operate one cannon. When fired, they erupted with a sharp ear-shattering concussion, and long daggers of flame shot out of their barrels. Their booms surpassed the volume of the worst thunderstorm, and could be heard for miles.

American Artillery Crew in Action during the Revolutionary War, a drawing by Alan Archambault (Courtesy of Center of Military History, United States Army)

Cannon not only provided firepower against personnel and fortifications; they had a psychological advantage as well, since few men were willing to stand up to them. The effects of small shot were devastating, since cannon were turned into giant shotguns by stuffing them with a canvas bag loaded with small musket balls or grapeshot. Scattershot composed of chain links, nails, shards of glass, rocks or other similar objects was loaded into a canister, a tin or brass container, and had the same effect. The projectile burst as soon as it left the gun barrel. A close range blast could destroy an entire enemy company of thirty men in seconds.

The cannon used by the American Army were smooth-bore, muzzle-loading guns, the design of which had changed little over the previous two hundred years. They included field cannon and siege cannon. The former were mounted on wooden carriages with wheels. They were lightweight mobile pieces capable of firing solid shot or small shot, and when fired in a flat trajectory they could devastate infantry or cavalry. Although cannon shooting ordinance up to twelve pounds were occasionally used, the Continental and British Armies rarely fielded anything larger than a six-pounder because of the difficult roads in America.

Siege cannon, on the other hand, were heavy and had limited mobility. They fired the solid shot needed to destroy fortifications, and were typically mounted permanently in forts or on ships. The largest ordinance used in the war fired balls weighing forty-two pounds. "Hot shot" was used by siege cannon crews on ships, since a red hot cannon ball could set an enemy ship on fire. "Bar shot" and "chain shot," (two halves of a cannon ball attached by either a bar or chain) could splinter a ship's mast and tear up rigging, thus disabling the vessel.

A number of critical battles of the war were little more than artillery duels. At Yorktown, the British fielded an impressive 244 artillery pieces, but they were mainly lightweight field cannon, and proved ineffective against the large mounds of earth that comprised the American and French earthworks. The victorious allied forces had a lesser number of guns, approximately 131, but most were heavier gauge cannon that could penetrate the enemy fortifications. The three-pounder was the most widely used field gun by both sides during the Revolutionary War. It had a range of up to eight hundred yards with solid shot and two hundred yards with grape shot. Its combined weight, when mounted on a carriage, was five hundred pounds. The three-pounder could be pulled by one horse, or carried by eight men to positions too rugged for towing. This type of cannon was often called a "grasshopper," since it reminded soldiers of that insect when outfitted with handspikes and moved up and down a battlefield to match the flow of action. When fired, the gun would recoil, or jump backward, again similar to the action of a grasshopper.

Mortars and howitzers, two other types of artillery, were also used in the war. Mortars were mounted weapons with a chambered firing system. This meant that a powder chamber was bored into the breech (rear) end of the inside of the barrel, a chamber smaller in diameter than the bore of the barrel. The powder charge went into the chamber, and the weight of the shell rested on the ledge above it. In this way the great weight of the shell would not compress the powder, and prevent ignition, or worse, cause accidental ignition when loading. This design allowed exact amounts of powder to be loaded. By varying the amount of the powder charge a trained soldier could adjust the range of the shot. This provided more predictable results than with the muzzle-loaded cannon.

With mortars, gunners in the field used a fixed elevation of forty-five degrees and varied the charge to reach the target. This high angle trajectory gave mortars another great advantage over standard artillery. These weapons had a maximum range of 1,300 yards. With plunging fire, they could hit targets behind obstacles, in fortifications, or concealed in cover. The high trajectory, with near vertical descent of projectiles, could wipe out infantry protected behind hills, walls or in trenches. Sighting was simple. A line would be painted down the center axis of the barrel. This would be aligned with the target by use of a plumb line. Mortars also had the advantage of being able to fire from the protection of a trench or other type of cover.

Tactical movement of heavy artillery over the battlefield was difficult. The speed at which the guns could be redeployed was limited to the pace of the gunners dragging them. Cannon were usually set in position to fire on a critical sector of the battlefield, with little opportunity to shift them to take advantage of a sudden enemy move.

Few foundries existed in the colonies in 1775, and none were forging cannon when the war began. Forging and other metalworking was not

Eighteenth century mortars (Courtesy of Military Collector and Historian)

specifically prohibited, but the American colonies had always exported raw materials to England's factories, and then served as a market for the finished goods. Thus, only a few manufacturing facilities needed to produce arms existed on this side of the Atlantic. Those that did exist were small, and produced steel inferior in quality to the British forges. The Continental Congress quickly realized that a war could not be waged without these weapons, so they encouraged mill owners to forge steel to manufacture cannon. American-manufactured guns were largely copies of British standard models, since these were the easiest to obtain for copying patterns.

The acquisition of a large number of captured British cannon led to America's first decisive victory of the war. Washington arrived in Boston in July, 1775, to direct the siege of the city and to drive out the British occupation forces. He was impressed with siege lines engineered by a young officer, Henry Knox, a former Boston bookseller. Knox presented him with a plan to recover and transport the big guns from Fort Ticonderoga, the British bastion that had recently been captured by forces led by Ethan Allen and Benedict Arnold. The audacious proposal proposed by Knox to attempt to move the heavy weapons over rough terrain in the deadly Northern winter was approved by Washington.

Knox reached Fort Ticonderoga on December 5, 1775, after encountering heavy snows and ice on the shores of Lake Champlain along the way. He commenced building ox-drawn sleds to haul sixty tons of cannon and other armaments from the fort. The route crossed some three hundred miles of ice-covered rivers and the snow-covered Berkshire Mountains. He reached the Boston siege camps six weeks later, with seventy-eight cannon, two howitzers, eight mortars, thousands of cannonballs, and 18,000 pounds of musket balls. This was one of the most awesome feats of logistics of the entire war.

Over the course of one night the weapons were positioned on Dorchester Heights, overlooking the city of Boston. The next morning, General Howe, the British senior commander, was stunned by the sudden appearance of these fearsome weapons, and ordered his forces to begin abandoning Boston. The victorious American Siege of Boston ended on March 17, 1776, a day still celebrated as Evacuation Day in that city. Some of these same guns were used throughout the New York campaign, and were hauled across New Jersey to be put to use in the American victories at Princeton and Trenton. Fifty-six historical markers have been placed to indicate Knox's route across New York and Massachusetts.[183]

An artilleryman was called a *matross*. The word is derived from a German term meaning *sailor*, since his tasks of loading, firing, sponging and manning dragropes were considered to be similar to that of a sailor. The skills of the matross were highly valued, and these men were considered to be choice troops. Few soldiers had the skills to compute the simple geometric calculations necessary to place a cannonball on target, and this ability was considered an art. Older men were often assigned to the artillery, since these duties were less physically demanding than those of foot soldiers. The intricate procedures for firing and commanding a gun crew made artillery officers essential men to a successful campaign, and they were often the best-read and trained in the art of war.

The "fog of war" is a cliché, but in the eighteenth century, it had a specific meaning. The amount of smoke generated by dozens of cannon on a battlefield, together with the gun smoke created by hundreds, or even thousands, of muskets firing in volleys, caused enormous confusion, since it was almost impossible for officers to follow troop formations. Cannon technology would continue to advance and increase the destructive power of artillery to unimaginable heights in the Civil War, and World War I and II.

THE SMALL BOYS - HANDGUNS AND OTHER SIDE ARMS

Small arms were weapons that could be carried in a soldier's hand, and employed in face-to-face interaction with the enemy. These included pistols, sabers, and spear-like weapons called pole arms. Spear-like pole arms, called spontoons or pikes, were often carried by officers and sergeants as a sign of rank, and were often used to point out the direction of advance for the troops to follow.

Flintlock smoothbore pistols had barrels about six inches long. They were extremely inaccurate except at close range, and difficult to load. Cavalrymen were equipped with preloaded pistols and usually used them defensively. American officers carried the handguns as side arms but rarely used them except when in hand-to-hand fighting. Pistols were expensive to make, and were manufactured without army specifications, so parts were not interchangeable and this made repairs difficult.

Swords were in wide use during the Revolutionary War. Large, decisive battles, such as Guilford Courthouse, were fought with swords, axes and bayonets, in bloody hand-to-hand combat. Riflemen had no bayonets, so they relied on knives and tomahawks. For the common soldier or sailor, swords were weapons of last resort, when firearms were not available, or as an alternative to the bayonet. Some of these weapons had been borne in battle by other family members and had sentimental connections. General Washington sometimes presented swords as rewards for valor. In September of 1782 he awarded dress swords and a brace of pistols to John Pauling, David Williams and Isaac Van Wart, the soldiers who had captured British Major John Andre. Edged weapons included cutlasses, sabers, and infantry swords, or "hangers." Foot soldiers carried cutlasses. These short, broad, slashing swords had a slightly curved blade and were sharpened on the cutting edge. Cutlasses were also commonly used at sea during close engagements, such as when boarding another vessel. Sabers were carried by cavalrymen, and had a thinner curved blade with a single cutting edge. They were longer than swords to provide extended reach for slashing from horseback. Many swords were fashioned by local blacksmiths from steel saws.

Tomahawks were hatchets that were introduced by Native Americans. These weapons were used in hand-to-hand fighting, or were thrown at the enemy. Pole arms were blades placed on the end of a long wooden shaft to extend the soldier's reach. These cutting or thrusting weapons were favored for close combat, since cavalry horses would abruptly stop charging when confronted by a row of pole arms. These weapons were in a category which included pikes, spears, spontoons and halberds. Pikes were typically fourteen or fifteen feet long. The spontoon was only six or seven feet overall, and had a more elaborate head which gave it the look of a trident. Halbreds consisted of an ax blade and a sharp spike mounted at the end of a pole. These enabled a foot soldier to confront a man on horseback; the spiked head kept the rider at a distance, and the ax blade could inflict a cleaving blow. Pole arms served both as combat weapons and symbols of rank.

ALL IN SHORT SUPPLY

Supplying the American troops with weapons was extremely difficult during the Revolution. Before the war, most guns had been manufactured in England, since the mother country discouraged Americans from competing with English manufacturers. There was only a small startup gun industry in America during the Revolution, and often European parts were used. By July, 1776, a little over two months into the war, during the *rage militaire*, when huge numbers of men were joining up, nearly one-fourth of the army had no arms. The situation was so critical that the New York Congress required enlisting men who did not bring their own guns to report for duty with shovels, spades, pick-axes and scythes. Soldiers returning home at the end of their enlistments felt entitled to keep their muskets, which further depleted supplies. Washington specifically issued an order to stop this practice late in 1775. There is no evidence that discharged men were allowed to keep their weapons after that time, until the war ended. In June, 1783, Congress could not raise three months back pay that was promised to troops departing from the New Windsor Cantonment, and in an effort to appease the disgruntled veterans Congress voted to allow them to keep their muskets. This gesture did not cost anything, but bought some much-needed short term goodwill.[184]

Supplying the American troops with weapons was an extremely difficult task. There were very few factories in the colonies that could produce the weapons needed by an army. The money necessary to pay for supplies was issued by the new state governments and a new central government. This Continental currency was often not acceptable to suppliers. Another challenge was the transport of arms to the soldiers. When the Continental Army was able to obtain supplies, they had to be shipped great distances, usually by wagon across rugged trails and roads. Without the contributions of foreign allies and the capture of enemy arms, the war would have come to a hasty end.

Chapter Twelve

African-American Patriots

The Last Integrated Army for 175 Years

The mob that attacked British soldiers on King Street in Boston in March, 1770, was described as "A motley rabble of saucy boys, negroes and mulattos, Irish teagues and outlandish Jack tars." Five years passed between the Boston Massacre and the start of the American Revolution, but this incident has always been perceived by Americans as one of the most important events that led to war. Crispus Attucks, an African-American, was one of the five Boston residents killed in that incident. Later, at Lexington and Concord, both slaves and free black men served bravely. The promotion of liberty produced high expectations in the minds of thousands of slaves, and many were ready to fight for a cause that might offer them freedom. In 1775 between ten and fifteen black soldiers, some of whom were slaves, fought against the British at the battle of Bunker Hill.

The men who served in the Continental Army over the eight years of the war were completely different soldiers from those that the Founding Fathers had envisioned. African-Americans and other ethnic minorities joined a pool of impoverished, transient, free white men to form a cadre of professional soldiers who served long-term and far from their home states. These farm hands, drifters, and men in bondage were without property or any other substantial stake in American society, and yet they formed a racially integrated fighting force, the last the United States would see until the Korean War 175 years later.

A group of men, less privileged than most, initially volunteered for service when the call went out to join the cause for independence. Among them were free black men and slaves who came from the New England states, especially Rhode Island and Massachusetts. Prior to the war, both free and enslaved

A 19th century lithograph shows Crispus Attucks (c.1723-March 5, 1770), the first casualty of the Boston Massacre and widely considered to be the first American casualty of the Revolutionary War . He may have been an African-American slave or freeman, merchant seaman and dockworker of Wampanoag and African descent.

African-Americans had served in colonial militias, defending their villages against attacks by Indians. At the war's onset, approximately 500,000 African-Americans lived in the colonies, of which some 445,000 were enslaved, one fifth of the entire population of the thirteen colonies.[185]

These Americans viewed military enlistment as a pathway to freedom and equality, so they were eager to volunteer. This state of affairs prompted an immediate response that reflected the mores of that time. The Massachusetts Provincial Congress quickly resolved that only *free* Negroes could serve with the American forces. The next month over one hundred African-American and Native American soldiers enlisted and served heroically in the Battle of Bunker Hill, the first major battle of the war.

Salem Poor, a former slave who had purchased his freedom, performed so courageously at Bunker Hill that fourteen army officers wrote to the Massachusetts Congress commending him as a "brave and gallant soldier" who deserved a reward for his actions. Poor is credited with fatally wounding British Lieutenant-Colonel James Abercrombie as he led a grenadier battalion in a charge on the Americans' left wing. Poor may also have served at Saratoga and Monmouth, and perhaps spent the winter at Valley Forge.

PETER SALEM SHOOTS MAJOR PITCAIRN AT BUNKER HILL.

An African-American soldier at Bunker Hill. At dawn on June 17, 1775, British Gen. William Howe ordered fire on American forces three times, and drove them northward across Bunker Hill. In this battle, the Americans had 400 dead and wounded men, and the British lost more than1,000. Freed slave Peter Salem was credited with the shot that killed British Maj. John Pitcairn. (Image courtesy of Manuscripts, Archives and Rare Books Division, Schomburg Center for Research on Black Culture, The New York Public Library)

The valor of black Patriots such as Private Poor was overtly overlooked, and discriminatory practices were put in place. Slaves were first excluded in some states. In 1781, French-American writer J. Hector St. John de Crevecoeur remarked that the idea of training and arming slaves and risking a slave rebellion was far more terrifying for Americans than for the British.[186]

Soon after his appointment as Commander-in-Chief, George Washington extended the position of the Massachusetts Provincial Congress and barred *all* African-Americans, both slaves and free, from serving. This policy of exclusion soon yielded to the desperate need for manpower in the distressed Continental Army, and the ban on black enlistment was lifted a few months later, in January, 1776.

Washington, along with most Southern and many Northern slave owners, had been a vocal opponent of recruiting black men, especially slaves. He soon reversed his position, in view of the active recruitment of enslaved blacks by the British and the ever-weakening state of the Continental Army, especially at Valley Forge in the winter of 1777-1778. By the beginning of 1778, nearly 10 percent of Washington's effective forces were African-American. As the war dragged on, in order to meet manpower quotas for the Continental Army, all New England regiments began recruiting slaves, promising freedom to all those who served.

During the course of the war, about one-fifth of the Northern Army was black. Free blacks enlisted voluntarily, or were drafted, and slaves also entered the forces after being offered up by their masters as their substitutes. Most were promised freedom, although this was not always the case. The opportunity for freedom was always a forceful motivation for slaves to join both the American and British Army. Sadly, many had been promised their freedom for political convenience, and they were sent back to their masters after the war was over. George Washington, a Southerner, received pleas from these re enslaved veterans, but decided to ignore them.

Unfortunately, enslaved blacks were accepted only during desperate manpower shortages or when "volunteered" as substitutes. Despite this reluctance, roughly 5,000 African-American soldiers and sailors, both free and slave, served the cause for independence. Many more African-Americans also acted as guides, messengers, and spies, and filled vital support roles as wagoners, drovers (cattle herders), and laborers. This number might have been many times greater if American leaders had not vacillated on accepting blacks, and if the British had not immediately recognized the value of recruiting both free and enslaved African-Americans.

It is difficult to trace the identity of the thousands of Negroes who served in the forces, and the additional thousands in the ranks of the state militias.[187] In practice, most soldiers of all races were listed by name and home state. Race can only be identified in muster rolls, and even then only by occasional designations such as "a Negro Man," or "Negro." Often only a single name, such as "Caesar" or "Pompey," would be provided when a black soldier was recorded in military documents.

The terms "African-American" or "black" were not in use in that day and age, so a variety of pejorative names appear on muster rolls. Since the majority of military documents do not give any indication of a man's race, this suggests that the number of African-Americans serving in the Continental Army is vastly understated.

Benjamin Lattimore enlisted in the Continental Army at age fourteen and fought at White Plains and in other actions in the New York Campaign of 1776. The following year he was taken prisoner at the fall of Fort Montgomery. After being employed by his British captors as a servant, he was recaptured by Americans. He was initially assumed to be a traitor, but soon reenlisted in the 5th New York Regiment and served on the Sullivan-Clinton Campaign against the Iroquois Nations in 1779. There is no reference to his race in any military documents, but his hometown was a predominantly African-American community. Lattimore waited until he was age seventy-two to apply for a pension. His adventures, and the battles and campaigns he witnessed, are vividly described in his pension application.

Emanuel Leutze's famous painting, *Washington Crossing the Delaware*, depicts the Commander-in-Chief with a black soldier at his side. This man is believed to be Prince Whipple, one of his bodyguards. When William Whipple of New Hampshire joined the Continental Army as a captain, his slave Prince accompanied him. He was with General Washington on Christmas Night, 1776, when the legendary crossing took place. The ensuring surprise attack on Trenton, New Jersey was a badly-needed victory for America, and served as a boost to Washington's sagging military reputation. Another black soldier, Primus Hall, also made the crossing, and a week later he was captured by several British soldiers at the Battle of Princeton.[188]

In 1777, William Whipple was promoted to brigadier general, and ordered to drive British General John Burgoyne out of Vermont. At the time, Prince said to his master "You are going to fight for your liberty, but I have none to fight for." As a result, General Whipple agreed to free Prince after the

According to legend, Prince Whipple accompanied General Whipple and George Washington in the famous crossing of the Delaware River, and is the black man portrayed fending off ice with an oar at Washington's knee. *Washington Crossing the Delaware* was painted seventy-five years after the event by German American artist Emanuel Leutze.

campaign was over, but historians differ on whether William Whipple made good on his promise. New England author Valerie Cunningham asserts that Prince was kept in service to the Whipple family for another seven years before his eventual release.[189]

A WARM WELCOME - BUT FROM THE WRONG SIDE

On November 7, 1775, Lord Dunmore, the Royal Governor of Virginia, offered freedom to any owned slave who ran away to join the British forces. This occurred only seven months after the outbreak of the war. Dunmore's Proclamation declared that he would free all black and white indentured men if they would fight with the British. "Indentured" in this case was meant to include slaves and free white or black men working for an employer under contract for a fixed term of years. Dunmore believed that encouraging slaves to defect would be a tremendous military advantage. Escaped slaves could swell the ranks of the British Army, and with their intimate knowledge of the terrain and infrastructure of the country, they could provide invaluable intelligence. While the British side welcomed African-Americans into their armed forces, they also had a grander motive.

The American rebellion was supported and financed to a great extent by the plantation economy, which the British believed would become paralyzed by the loss of slave labor. They thought that destruction of this infrastructure would effectively end the war. Three hundred slaves did enlist in the British Army in the month following Dunmore's Proclamation. They were designated as "Lord Dunmore's Ethiopian Regiment," and their uniforms included a sash with the inscription "Liberty to Slaves." The regiment soon grew in size to eight hundred men. It had tremendous propaganda value for the British, and was regarded as a major threat by the terrorized military leadership.

Lord Dunmore's Ethiopian Regiment. Detail from *The Death of Major Peirson, 6 January 1781*, an oil painting by John Singleton Copley.

At this point, Washington began to completely reverse his previous position. He wrote a letter to Colonel Henry Lee in December, 1775, stating that success in the war would come to whatever side could arm black men the fastest. He then issued orders to recruiters to begin encouraging free blacks who had already served in the army to reenlist, before they decided to join the British side.[190]

Dunmore's Proclamation was expanded four years later by Sir Henry Clinton, the top British general in America, and it inspired thousands of runaways to unite with the British throughout the duration of the war. Clinton's Philipsburg Proclamation declared that all slaves in the United States belonging to Americans were to be freed, regardless of their willingness to fight for England. The law also promised protection, freedom and land to any slaves who left their masters, stating that "Every Negro who shall desert the Rebel Standard, [is granted] full security to follow within these Lines, any Occupation which he shall think proper."[191]

There was an overwhelming response to Clinton's plan, and tens of thousands of slaves fled behind British lines. So many slaves escaped that the British General had to reluctantly order many to return to their masters. In reply, in 1778 the Patriots instituted a similar plan granting freedom to escaped slaves of Loyalists. Sadly, slaves who did not die from disease or warfare and escaped to one side or the other generally ended up being sold back into bondage when the war ended.[192]

A PATRIOT DILEMMA

The race issue became a dilemma for American leaders. They feared that slaves who were armed would rise up, and that military service would entitle black soldiers to broader rights, or even freedom. This was a paradox recognized by many prominent Patriots. Abigail Adams, the future First Lady, wrote to husband John in 1774: "It always appeared a most iniquitous scheme to me to fight ourselves for what we are daily robbing and plundering from those who have as good a right to freedom as we have."

Plantation owners in the South anticipated an immediate rebellion should slaves become armed. Before the war, most Southern militias, which later became an integral part of the forces, had been created for the sole purpose of resisting slave uprisings. Ultimately, despite some opposition from Georgia and South Carolina, Southern slaves gradually gained the opportunity to enlist so blacks could be substituted for their masters.

At the Valley Forge encampment, dozens of African-Americans served in every state regiment, freezing, starving and dying beside their white comrades. By February, 1778, they were also drilling with Baron von Steuben. When the von Steuben-trained army proved itself later at Monmouth, about seven hundred black freedmen and slaves were serving in place of their masters, fighting side-by-side with whites.[193] Ironically, they were fighting for a freedom that they would never gain, and often their enlistment bounties or their meager pay went directly to their masters.

SEGREGATION BUT A CHANCE FOR FREEDOM - THE 1st RHODE ISLAND REGIMENT

Rhode Island's leaders were having difficulty enlisting white men to meet their troop quotas, so they reluctantly decided to enlist slaves. General Washington, with an army starving for manpower, agreed, and convinced Congress to approve plans for that state to raise a regiment of slaves and free blacks. In February, 1778, that state's Assembly voted to allow the enlistment of "every able bodied negro, mulatto, or Indian man slave" that chose to do so, and that "every slave so enlisting shall, upon his passing muster, be immediately discharged from the service of his master or mistress, and be absolutely free."[194] The owners of slaves who enlisted were to be compensated in an amount equal to the market value of the slave.

A total of eighty-eight slaves enlisted in the 1st Rhode Island regiment over the next four months, as well as a small number of free blacks. Over time, 140 African-Americans joined the regiment, along with a lesser number of white soldiers. It was the only segregated unit during the war, as it had white officers and separate companies for black and white men. In all other units of the Continental Army, black soldiers were fully integrated, and they fought, trained, marched, lived and shared these hardships alongside their white comrades.

The 1st Rhode Island remained a part of the Continental Army for five years. The unit fought at the battles of Fort Oswego, Red Bank, Saratoga, and Yorktown, and several other clashes. At the Battle of Newport in 1778, when expected reinforcements failed to arrive, the American forces retreated under a fierce enemy attack. The regiment repelled three enemy assaults by positioning itself between retreating units and advancing Hessian mercenary forces. This mostly-black unit inflicted five casualties upon Hessian forces for every one casualty of its own. The Hessians suffered so many losses that one of their officers refused to lead his men to slaughter, and resigned his commission on the spot.

Colonel Christopher Greene, Nathanael Greene's third cousin, was the commanding officer of the Rhode Islanders. He was responsible for guarding Pines Bridge in Westchester County, New York, with about two hundred men, many of whom were black recruits. On the morning of May 14, 1781, Loyalist forces slipped across the Croton River and advanced toward Col. Greene's position at the Davenport House headquarters. The surprised Patriots were only able to get off a few shots before being overrun, and in the end, although the regiment put up fierce resistance, it was ultimately defeated. Col. Greene and many others were killed in the battle, several were wounded, and over twenty soldiers were taken as prisoners of war. Greene's body was later found in the woods, about a mile from his tent, cut and mangled, apparently as punishment for having led black soldiers against the British Crown.[195]

A mass grave, somewhere near the Davenport House, contains the remains of an unknown number of black soldiers from Greene's 1st Rhode Island Regiment. A monument has been erected on the site which includes three statues—a Native American soldier, an African-American soldier, and a white soldier.

Baron Ludwig von Closen, a French officer, wrote in his journal that the Rhode Island Regiment was "the most neatly dressed, the best under arms, and the most precise in its maneuver." While at the American camp at White Plains in 1781 he recorded: "I had a chance to see the American Army, man for man. It is really painful to see those brave men, almost naked with only some trousers and little linen jackets, most of them without stockings, but, would you believe it, very cheerful and healthy in appearance. A quarter of them are Negroes, merry, confident and sturdy. It is incredible that soldiers composed of men of every age, even children of fifteen, of whites and blacks, unpaid and rather poorly fed, can march so fast and withstand fire so steadfastly."[196]

Foreign officers were unanimous in commenting favorably on the presence of black American troops. In December, 1777, a German officer wrote "The negro can take the field in his master's place; hence you never see a regiment in which there are not a lot of negroes, that are well-built, strong, husky fellows."[197] Ironically, at Yorktown, black soldiers fought alongside Southern militiamen whose previous job had been to round up runaway slaves. After their valiant service at Yorktown, and as the war drew to a close, the black soldiers from the 1st Rhode Island began to return home. A handful enjoyed new lives as freemen, but many were doomed to resume their former lives as slaves.

LOYAL SERVICE UNREWARDED

After the war, the American public did little to reward African-Americans. Unhappily, the close of the war did not bring the changes that these soldiers had hoped for or had been promised. While some were granted their freedom, many slave owners reneged on their promises. Racist attitudes resumed after the war, and the states again began banning blacks from service. Connecticut and Massachusetts banned all blacks, free or slave, from the military in 1784 and 1785. Southern states excluded all slaves, but allowed free black men to serve in their militias. In 1792, the United States Congress formally prohibited all African-Americans from military service, specifically allowing only "free able-bodied white male citizens" to serve. The 1792 law became the United States Army's official policy until 1862.

Some African-Americans who had defected to the British side in exchange for promised freedom were forced to work as farm hands and domestics for white Loyalists, many of whom were former slave owners. After seven years of living under deplorable conditions in a socially hostile environment, many even opted to relocate to West Africa. About 15,000 Loyalist black men, women, and children sailed from New York, Charleston, Savannah and Nova Scotia to the country of Sierra Leone. The British government encouraged the Loyalists to settle in this new colony by establishing the Sierra Leone Company, which provided ships to transport the migrants, and to help manage the development of the community of Freetown. When the British evacuated Loyalist refugees, many American slave owners attempted to recapture their former slaves, but British military leaders kept their promise of freedom made to Black soldiers despite this American resistance. Free blacks who had joined the British Army were transported to Nova Scotia and England, but former slaves were sent to Florida, Jamaica, and Nassau, where they were soon re-enslaved under new masters.

It is estimated that about 20,000 slaves defected to the British Army. About 8,000 died from disease or wounds, or were recaptured by the Patriots. Roughly 12,000 left the country for freedom in Canada, or were kept in slavery in the West Indies at the end of the war.[198] Some blacks who fought in the Continental Army and state militias were granted freedom after the war. This was done by honorable masters who remembered promising to free them if they served. The black soldiers of the 1st Rhode Island started new lives as freemen. In 1782, the Virginia Assembly had passed a law permitting manumission. Between 1782 and 1792 only about 1,000 Virginia slaves were freed, including some who had fought as Patriots. In 1783, the Assembly passed a bill condemning owners who "contrary to principles of justice and to their own solemn promise" had retained their soldier substitutes as slaves. These men were freed by legislative decree. How many slaves received their freedom as a result of this bill is not known, since a slave could not himself initiate his own legal proceedings.

When the war ended, African-Americans were bitterly disappointed, but not surprised. For them it had been a war for freedom, for their country and for themselves, and they had been forgotten. The agenda of both the American and British Armies had been to win, not to encourage equality. However, serving in an integrated army gave African-American veterans the confidence to unite in their desire for freedom. The fact that they had chosen to fight for American independence, despite the fact that the same America denied them their freedom, became the issue for those who fought emancipation in the decades leading up to the next great American struggle, the Civil War.

Chapter Thirteen

Integrated Patriots

Native Americans Join the Fray

Both sides initially urged Native Americans to stay out of the war. On the same day that the first shots of the war were fired at Lexington and Concord, the Second Continental Congress announced its position about the Indians to representatives of the Six Iroquois Nations: "We desire you will hear and receive what we have now told you, and that you will open a good ear and listen to what we are now going to say. This is a family quarrel between us and Old England. You Indians are not concerned in it. We don't wish you to take up the hatchet against the king's troops. We desire you to remain at home, and not join on either side, but keep the hatchet buried deep."

Tribal leadership correctly deduced that if Americans gained their independence, settlement on their lands would expand and accelerate. With its Proclamation of 1763, the British government had attempted to restrict colonial expansion to the east side of the Appalachian Mountains, and to protect existing Native lands. The Proclamation honored Native rights and did not encourage American westward expansion. While this action was well-received by the various tribes, it angered American settlers who were rapidly encroaching into frontier land in western Virginia, Pennsylvania and New York. The British also had available funds to purchase tribal loyalty through generous donations of food, guns and other gifts, and they had influential agents and traders embedded with the tribes. Their long friendship was due in good measure to the efforts of William Johnson, who began trading with the Six Iroquois Nations back in 1738. He was the only European they would trust, and in 1755 he was eventually appointed by the Crown as Superintendent of Indian Affairs.

In 1775, Chief Joseph Brant, or Thayendanegea, was invited to England to meet King George III. In London, Brant was treated as a celebrity, and the king honored him by presenting him with a medal, a standard practice at the time. While in public, he dressed as a Mohawk chief. He was also accepted into a prestigious Masonic lodge, and the king personally presented him with a

Joseph Brant / Thayendanegea at age thirty-four. From a mezzotint of 1779, now in Lenox Library in New York City, after a portrait by Romney painted in London in 1776.

ritual apron. The British government also promised him land in Quebec if the Iroquois Nations would fight on the British side. There is no evidence that he received the land in Quebec, but in 1798 Brant was granted 3,450 acres at Burlington Bay, Ontario, for his services during the American Revolution by King George III. Here he built a mansion and ran a prosperous farm for the rest of his life. Brant died in this house at the head of Lake Ontario on November 24, 1807 at age sixty-four.

Native American leaders, influenced by the British, believed that the Revolutionary War was as much about the acquisition of their land as it was independence, so with few exceptions they joined the opposite side during the entire war. As a result, the Indians were soon vilified by American leaders. The Declaration of Independence specifically mentioned King George III's incitement of "merciless Indian Savages" against men, women, and children settlers. Thomas Jefferson, although known as a champion of equality, belittled them in 1776, when he wrote, "Nothing will reduce those wretches so soon as pushing the war into the heart of their country. But I would not stop there. I would never cease pursuing them while one of them remained on this side of the Mississippi."[199] When Washington dispatched a third of his army on the Sullivan-Clinton Campaign against the Iroquois Nations in 1779, he called for "a total destruction of their settlements and the capture of as many prisoners of every age and sex as possible." The country, he stated, was "not to be merely overrun but destroyed."[200]

Cruel warriors committing atrocities became the stereotype of Indians during the Revolution, and this concept was fueled by a single incident. In 1777, in the town of Fort Edward, a supposedly beautiful young New Yorker named Jane McCrea was planning to meet her fiancée, a British soldier. Two friendly Native scouts were assigned to escort her safely to the British lines. Along the way the warriors quarreled over the expected reward for escorting her in, and Jane was shot, brutally tomahawked and scalped.

When the escorts showed up in the English camp with her bloody scalp and demanded the promised payment, the British were aghast. However, no one was ever punished for the crime, since the warriors were associated with General John Burgoyne's army. When the Americans learned of this atrocity they were horrified. Newspapers throughout the colonies responded with inflammatory rhetoric and shocking illustrations of the deed. Artists portrayed Jane as being sensuously beautiful, with long golden hair. After the war this image continued to be exploited by the new nation to justify the cruel treatment of Native Americans and the subsequent occupation of their tribal lands. As a consequence, some of the bounty lands awarded to veterans were lands formerly stolen from Native tribes.

Two of the Indian nations—the Oneidas and Tuscaroras—attempted to stay out of the conflict, and at times even supported the American cause. The British, on the other hand, succeeded in persuading the Mohawks, Cayugas, Onondagas, and Senecas to join them. The Oneidas supplied food to General George Washington's starving army at Valley Forge, and fought in battles at Fort Stanwix, Oriskany, and Saratoga against other Iroquois nations.

Indian warriors fought with the American light infantry in the Battle of Van Cortlandt Woods (also called the Battle of Kingsbridge) on August 31, 1778. Chief Ninham led sixty Mohican warriors on a patrol to track the movements of the British Army. They crossed over enemy lines into a no-man's land located between the Bronx and Yonkers. They were discovered, and soon surrounded by five hundred British and Hessian troops. The Natives somehow

The Death of Jane McCrea, an 1804 painting by American artist John Vanderlyn (1775-1852)

fled through open fields, but were hunted down by cavalry, and once again surrounded by infantry. The braves, although completely overwhelmed, still refused to surrender. They fought valiantly by climbing onto the enemy's horses and pulling off the riders, and attacking with tomahawks and knives because there was no time to reload their muskets. The battle ended with the deaths of seventeen Stockbridge Mohicans, among them Chief Ninham.

Indian children were trained to fight at an early age. They played aggressive games that had been passed down over hundreds of years. This mock warfare toughened them, and they matured into fearless fighting men. Taking captives, often women and children, was a common practice in Indian warfare. Victorious braves then selected their personal captives from among survivors and then slaughtered those that remained. This practice provided a source of replacements for those warriors of the tribe who had been killed in battle, and ensured a steady source of victims for ritual sacrifices. Vanquished opponents were often scalped in the process.

The Natives believed their mission was to kill anyone who had white skin and was not wearing a British uniform. The warriors also believed that as victors they were entitled to all the possessions of a conquered enemy, so they ruthlessly plundered entire villages. At first, Americans were appalled by their barbarity, but soldiers soon adopted their practices on the frontier, including the taking of scalps. On the Sullivan-Clinton Campaign into western New York in 1779, two New Jersey officers embellished their boots with the skins of enemy warriors.

African-Americans had been assimilated directly into the ranks of the Continental Army, but Indians, with few exceptions, served in other ways. Their warriors were used for scouting, raiding, and defending against enemy patrols. Most of these actions took place on the frontier where they could use their unique style of combat to best advantage. They developed tactics that compensated for their lack of manpower, while also minimizing losses, by engaging in raiding parties instead of large battles. If the party became overwhelmed, braves simply disappeared into the nearby woods. Hand-to-hand fighting was commonly employed by warriors, since the killing of an opponent bestowed prestige on any victor, especially if they could display a scalp as proof of his bravery.

Indian warriors disregarded the orders of white officers, but did obey the commands of their own leaders. Braves were difficult for American officers to keep in the field for long periods. They had very little tolerance for military routine and discipline, and during inactive times they became easily bored, and soon disappeared into the forest and headed home.[201]

Both the Natives who joined the Patriots, and the majority who fought with the British, lost everything in the peace that followed. In the end, they probably would have fared better if America had lost the war. The first Articles of Peace of 1782, which ended hostilities, made no mention at all of the Native Americans. Their leaders believed that they had fought in the war to save their homelands, and became irate when the British failed to set aside the areas that had been promised in treaties. Under the terms of the Treaty of Paris of 1783, Britain handed over all of its territory east of the Mississippi, south of the Great Lakes, and north of Florida to the United States, a huge tract that included Native lands.

The Native Americans who had joined the cause were looked down upon after the war, since American society did not differentiate between those who served and those who had not. All were lumped together as supporters of England, so the newly-formed nation dispossessed and expelled those who had supported the cause of independence, along with those who had opposed it. Americans eventually continued their massive move westward, disregarding treaties along the way. They acquired Native lands by force, or simply squatted on them. Despite their important role and visible presence, they had receded into the shadows of European diplomacy. Recognition of their existence and status was easier to ignore or deny in Europe than in America.

In their succeeding negotiations with the Indians, the Americans attempted to convince them that by choosing the losing side in the struggle they had lost all their rights. The resistance and strength of the Indians had refuted the notion that conquest could be asserted rather than won. The American negotiators rejected the Natives' claims to their territories, and asserted the full authority of the colonies to possess the lands west to the Mississippi. By 1783 it did not really matter whose side Native Americans had fought on, since they had lost the majority of their traditional grounds.

BREAKING THE BRITISH ON BOTH SIDES OF THE SEA - THE SCOTS-IRISH

People of Scots-Irish descent were the largest immigrant group to arrive in the colonies during the 1700s. Estimates are that one quarter or more of the Continental Army was Irish by birth or ancestry, and nearly half of the regiments from Pennsylvania and Maryland were Irish. The early immigrants were from the Northern county of Ulster, although their descendants in America usually referred to themselves simply as Irish. The Ulster immigrants were predominantly Protestant Presbyterians who settled in the Appalachian uplands. A century later, following the great wave of Irish immigration during the Irish Potato Famine of the 1840s and 1850s, the descendants of the Protestant Irish began to refer to themselves as "Scots-Irish" in order to differentiate themselves from the predominantly Catholic surge of impoverished immigrant families in that time period.

According historians' estimates, more than 200,000 Scots-Irish migrated to the Americas between 1717 and 1775. When they realized that land in the coastal areas was either already claimed or too expensive, they quickly left for western hill country, which was the limit of the American frontier at that time. Life in the mountains was one of poverty and hardship, accompanied by the constant fear of attack by hostile Indian tribes. The descendants of these people have sometimes been called "hillbillies," a derogatory term that has connotations of poverty, backwardness and violent behavior. But their qualities of "make-do" for themselves, their original music, and tendency towards independence have been admired by many.

Long after they settled in America, the Scots-Irish harbored a great resentment against the Crown. Joshua Pell, a British captain, called them "born rebels, chiefly composed of Irish Redemptioners and Convicts, the most audacious rascals existing."[202] Their position in the backcountry of the southeast wedged them between belligerent tribes on their west, and antagonistic English officials to their east. The colonial government in Charleston, South Carolina ignored these mountain people, and considered them backward and crude. With little support from their government, and as the target of frequent Native raids, these early settlers soon developed a strong militia. Although this militia system provided valuable training to the men of the backcountry, it never developed enough strength or cohesiveness to wage an all-out war on its own. However, the militia system in the South, when combined with the Continental Army, enabled the Patriots to turn the tide of war against the British.

Ireland, like America, was striving for independence from the British Empire, so these people were entirely sympathetic to the cause during the American Revolution, especially since they had originally been driven from their homeland by British oppression. In 1770, Pennsylvania, Virginia, and most of the Carolinas unanimously supported the Revolution. That year marked the height of the "America Craze," when great numbers of Scots-Irish arrived in America fleeing from poverty created by the collapse of the weaving industry, the high rents demanded by landlords, and a potato and grain failure.[203]A Hessian officer commented, "Call this war by whatever name you may, only call it not an American rebellion; it is nothing more or less than a Scotch Irish Presbyterian rebellion." A British major general testified to the House of Commons that ". . . half the rebels in the Continental Army were from Ireland."[204]

Records of the war are replete with the exploits of the valor of Scots-Irish immigrants. Five days before the Battle of Bunker Hill, Jeremiah O'Brien, while leading a raiding party that included his four brothers, seized the British warship *Margaretta* in Machias, Maine. This event is considered the first naval battle of the American Revolution. Afterwards, O'Brien and his brother John were commissioned as privateers, ship captains authorized to seize enemy ships.

Hercules Mulligan was a master spy. He was born in County Derry, Ireland. When the British occupied New York City, he posed as a Loyalist and lived among them. He gathered vital intelligence while listening to British soldiers during their frequent meetings in his clothing store. He warned General Washington of plans to kidnap him, and uncovered another British plan to invade Pennsylvania. Washington publicly praised Mulligan as a true friend of liberty.

Sharpshooter Timothy Murphy, of Pike County, Pennsylvania, was a sergeant in the Continental Army's 12th Pennsylvania Regiment and a member of Colonel Daniel Morgan's Rifle Corps, the fierce group of sharpshooters and snipers. Murphy had fought at the battles of Trenton and Princeton, and later at the Battle of Saratoga. He was an expert marksman, able to hit a seven-inch target at 250 yards. At Saratoga, Murphy is reputed to have shot and killed British officers Sir Francis Clerke and General Simon Fraser. Murphy took these shots from a tree at the extreme distance of three hundred yards.[205] In the Southern theater, the Scots-Irish mountain men of Virginia and North Carolina formed a militia force known as the *Overmountain Men*, because they came from the wilderness west of the Appalachian Mountains ridge. This unit was responsible for the victory at the Battle of Kings Mountain in North Carolina in 1780. This win forced the British to abandon their Southern Campaign, so some historians believe that Kings Mountain was the turning point of the American Revolution.

When the British Army evacuated Boston on March 17, 1776, George Washington, in recognition of his many Irish soldiers, named John Sullivan the officer of the day, and made "Saint Patrick" the password for those on guard duty. The dual holiday on March 17—Evacuation Day and St. Patrick's Day—is a state holiday in Massachusetts to this day. Later, generals born in Ireland, or were sons of Irish parents, commanded seven of the eleven brigades of the Continental Army wintering in Morristown, New Jersey in 1779-1780.

Mecklenburg County, North Carolina, with its large Scots-Irish population, may have been the first place in the thirteen colonies to declare independence from Britain. The Mecklenburg Declaration of Independence was supposedly signed on May 20, 1775, at Charlotte, North Carolina, by a committee of citizens after they learned of the outbreak of hostilities at Lexington and Concord. While most historians have debunked this story, if it is true, the Mecklenburg Declaration predated the better-known Declaration of Independence by more than a year.

A thousand mountain men under Richard Caswell successfully defended Moore's Creek Bridge in North Carolina against 1,600 British Loyalists on April 12, 1776. This was the first major battle in the South, and was a crucial factor in determining the early course of the American Revolution. The Loyalists quickly surrendered and gave up 850 prisoners. This engagement gave the Patriots an important morale boost and ended British authority in that colony.

GERMAN-AMERICAN SOLDIERS IN THE REVOLUTION

In May, 1776, General Washington wrote to the Continental Congress recommending that companies of German-Americans be recruited to oppose the German-Hessian mercenaries who were expected to arrive to join the British forces. He believed that many of the Hessian soldiers would desert when they encountered their own countrymen in his ranks. Although he appreciated the fact that a vast number of American colonists were German immigrants, he did not realize that the greater part of them spoke southern German dialects, which would have been extremely difficult for Germans from other regions to understand. In addition, the incoming mercenaries were from the central German territory of Hesse, and may have been disliked by the country folk from Pennsylvania.

In the late seventeenth century, one third of the population of Pennsylvania, many of whom were descendants of German immigrants, spoke a dialect known as Pennsylvania Dutch.[206] William Penn, the Quaker founder of the Province, had welcomed persecuted Europeans who wanted to settle there. In general, at least 100,000 Germans had entered the colonies by the time the Revolutionary War began. Large numbers of them also lived in western Virginia, the Carolinas, the Shenandoah Valley, the Mohawk Valley of New York, the Raritan Valley of New Jersey, and on the outskirts of Savannah, Georgia. Most of them came from the Rhineland Palatinate, Swabia and Salzburg in western Germany.[207]

In 1776, some German Americans were pacifists of the Mennonite faith, while others were revolutionaries of the Lutheran and Reformed faiths. The latter immediately responded when the Continental Army first called for volunteers. On June 14, 1775, Congress requested the colony of Pennsylvania to provide six companies of sharpshooters to join the fighting around Boston. Pennsylvanians had a reputation for being hardy men from the frontier, who often used their rifles to bring in food and provide defense against Natives. The colony responded enthusiastically, and soon nine companies had been raised. The first to arrive to join Washington's army were sharpshooters from Berks County. All of these units were composed of German-American soldiers, and were commanded by German-American officers.

In his 1919 book, writer and illustrator Rudolf Cronau described these soldiers: "These splendid fellows, everyone would have been welcomed by King Frederick the Great into his famous body-guard of giants. These sunburnt backwoodsmen, dressed in deer skin or homespun hunting suits, and wearing fur caps, armed with rifles, tomahawks and hunting knives, created a great sensation everywhere. On the breast of each, written in large letters, appeared their watchword: Liberty or Death!"[208]

These sharpshooters rushed six hundred miles to Massachusetts, completing the trip in an astonishing twenty-one days. When Washington spotted them in the distance, he galloped up and jumped from his horse to greet them, with tears of joy streaming down his face. During the Siege of Boston, these men inflicted heavy casualties on the British lines. Most carried unique rifles made by the German gunsmiths of Pennsylvania, not the inaccurate smooth-bored musket. Snipers with these weapons wreaked havoc among the British regiments by targeting their officers. The early effectiveness of the German marksmen induced Congress to create an entirely German regiment consisting of eight companies, a unit that played a vital role in major engagements at Trenton, Princeton, Brandywine and Germantown.

PALATINES OF THE MOHAWK VALLEY

The "Palatines" were natives of the Electorate of the Palatinate region of Germany. At the end of the seventeenth century, this prosperous region had been invaded by the French, which resulted in continuous strife, devastation and famine. As a result of this intrusion, about 13,000 German refugees fled to England in 1709. However, the British Government had difficulty integrating the Palatines, so they shipped 3,000 of these people to their colony of New York in 1710. Many of them were forcibly assigned to labor camps in the Hudson River Valley to work off the cost of their passage. In 1723, families from the camps migrated west to acquire land along the Mohawk River in present-day Herkimer County.

Emigrants leaving the Palatinate for America, Nuremberg: Buggel, 1735. (Courtesy of PD Dr. Helmut Schmahl, Mainz University)

The spring of 1777 was a critical time for the American cause. The British were ready to launch a strategy to split the country in half by separating New England from the other colonies. They hoped to achieve this by occupying the waterway that extended from the St. Lawrence River down a chain of lakes south to the Hudson River, and ultimately New York City. The Crown forces planned a simultaneous attack from three directions—General Burgoyne, along with 8,000 men, would move down from the north, Sir Henry Clinton was to move up the Hudson River from the south, and from the west, Lieutenant Colonel St. Leger would capture the Mohawk Valley. The three armies would then theoretically converge at Albany. If this strategy was successful, the forces would become paralyzed, and the War for Independence would soon be over.

St. Leger's expedition force of 1,800 men was a mixture of British regulars, Hessian Jäegers, Loyalists, and Indians from several tribes. In August, 1777, they traveled up the Saint Lawrence River and along the shore of Lake Ontario to the Oswego River. When they arrived at present-day Rome, New York, they besieged Fort Stanwix, a Continental outpost at the headwaters of the Mohawk River, the homeland of the Palatines.

The German settlers knew that the fort had to be relieved, and the enemy prevented from joining Burgoyne. Leaving only the aged and women to protect their homes, eight hundred citizen-soldiers from the local militia, along with a small number of Onieda warriors, converged on the fort to end the siege. The Tyron County militia was under the command of General Nicholas Herkimer.

The Loyalist troops and Iroquois Nations' forces, led by Mohawk Chief Joseph Brant, set up an ambush in the swamp west of Oriskany Creek.

As the American soldiers crossed the swamp, the enemy attacked. The Palatines soon noticed that the Indians always noted the location of the tree from where a shot had been fired at them. Knowing full well that as soon as their opponent had fired, he would need time to reload, they charged and tomahawked the man. The Palatines promptly countered this tactic by posting two men behind each tree. One shot the attacker while the other reloaded. As a result, the Indians suffered heavy losses, and soon fled into the woods, and the British forces, fearing an attack from the fort, also retreated.

The German Patriots had fought in brutal hand-to-hand combat, and in spite of heavy casualties, had forced the enemy to retreat. The losses they suffered were so severe that they were unable to pursue the fleeing enemy and follow up on their victory. The Palatines lost 240 men in the engagement. All the males of several families had been killed, and almost all of the survivors were wounded in some way.[209] General Herkimer himself was wounded in his leg, and died ten days later.

The Battle of Oriskany was one of the bloodiest battles of the war. It was one of the few battles in which almost all of the participants were North American. Loyalists and allied Natives fought against German-Americans and the Oneida Tribe in the complete absence of British soldiers. In the end, western forces failed to join Burgoyne. This caused the failure of the ambitious British master plan, and resulted in the first great American triumph at Saratoga, New York. This significant victory can be largely attributed to the stiff resistance of the New York troops in the Hudson River Valley, and to the German Palatines of the Mohawk Valley who stopped St. Leger's forces at the Battle of Oriskany.

Afterwards, the survivors of the German militia forces headed east to Saratoga to support the main American forces against Burgoyne, and helped to achieve the new nation's first great victory on October 8, 1777. Washington himself acknowledged the great services of the Palatines by stating that General Herkimer and his men had turned the darkest hour into one of his brightest prospects, "Herkimer first reversed the gloomy scene of the northern campaign."[210]

German troops were conspicuous in many actions of the American Revolution. The French Army under Rochambeau included a unit of Germans—the Royal Deux-Ponts Regiment. Military leaders on the American side hoped they could attract Hessian deserters. These attempts, and other efforts, caused the British desertion rate to sharply increase in 1782.[211] The Germans in Georgia, as well as those in the Carolinas, Virginia, Maryland, Delaware, New York and New England colonies, were plentiful in regiments that they furnished to the Continental Army. Washington's personal bodyguards, who accompanied him during the seven years of the war, consisted of 150 Germans from Berkshire and Lancaster Counties, Pennsylvania. Commanded by Major Bartholomaeus von Heer, a former Prussian officer, they were considered to be exceptionally trustworthy, reliable, and tough.

Long service in the Continental Army blurred racial and ethnic identity and created unity in the ranks. American soldiers—red, white and black—believed their service in the Continental Army and their valorous contributions would entitle them to freedom, or a better quality of life, when the war ended. While they fought with the same intensity and suffered the same hardships as the larger group of transient, landless men that they joined, there is little evidence of patriotic fervor or nationalism in their conduct. These men, regardless of their ethnic and racial differences, considered themselves free volunteers. They defied the authority of their officers and other powers when they perceive they were being treated unjustly. When the war ended they expected to be rewarded with a better place in society. Tragically, for many this did not occur, but these expectations may have planted the seeds for their struggles for equality over the next two centuries.

Chapter Fourteen

In Their Own Words

Diaries

To better understand their lives, a historian can find nothing more valuable than documents written in a soldier's own words. Although hundreds of accounts were kept by common soldiers during the Revolutionary War, very few have survived. These accounts were written for personal or family interest, with no thought of public distribution, and were simply lost over the years. Most of a soldier's time was spent in inhospitable surroundings, where even the act of composing a simple document with quill and ink would have been a daunting chore. Many private soldiers were illiterate.

In his iconic 1902 book, Charles K. Bolton described the difficulty of writing diaries during the War for Independence: "Some of those who could write kept diaries. These journals have many references to the weird and the unusual, and they show a rough humor. Keeping a diary in all kinds of weather, with no table to write upon, poor quills and thick ink, and hands numb with cold, or stiff from guard duty, was an achievement which must command respect. As the scratchy pen was driven slowly across the fibrous paper in the flickering glare of the camp-fire, the writer, with brows puckered to concentrate his thoughts and keep a cacophony of voices from his mind, put down much that was instructive and amusing. To one the Sunday text was worthy of note, to another the current price of shoes or the details of an execution for crime."[212]

For the most part, those writings that did survive are the products of humble country boys. From them we can learn from their reactions to daily experiences, empathize with their frustrations, and take delight in their occasional happy and amusing experiences. Unfortunately, most extant diaries are filled with an endless litany of entries, such as "it rained today" or "we marched 12 miles" or "nothing remarkable." But a choice number of them reveal the everyday life of Yankee Doodle, and the dynamics that motivated him to carry on through desperate times. Several even depict, in graphic detail, significant events of the war that have received little attention because no prominent military leaders were in attendance.

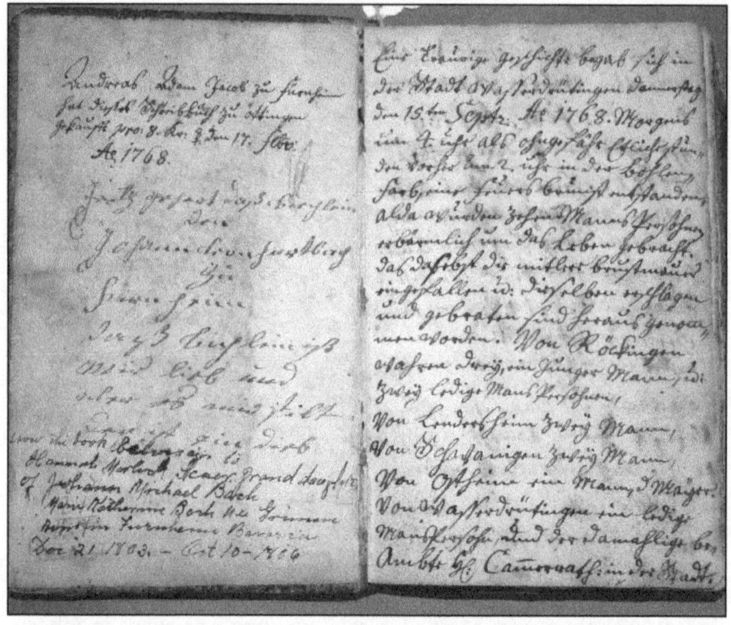

Inside cover of a German language Revolutionary War period diary beginning in 1768 (Photograph courtesy of The Commons Getty Collection Galleries)

These documents confirm that the minds of soldiers were constantly preoccupied with their struggle for survival. They portray hunger, thirst, and suffering, ordeals in severe weather, exhausting marches and punishments. Experiences such as a rare payday, a decent meal, or being issued a ration of rum were considered extraordinary occasions. The men wrote these diaries only for their personal use, and never expected them to be read by anyone other than perhaps their immediate family. They never imagined that their writings would appear in print, and be recognized as outstanding literary accounts of the war. This probably explains why they spoke with complete openness, and at times even provided erroneous or embellished information.[213]

GRAMMAR AND WRITING STYLE

A small number of unique diaries written by enlisted soldiers of the Continental Army have been discovered. Reviewing several of these works reveals a number of common patterns in both content and grammar.

The soldiers spelled many words phonetically, i.e., by the way they sounded. Their errors are generally consistent within each diary, and if read orally dialects can sometimes be detected. For example, *ware* for where, *pecking up* for picking up, *ridgment* for regiment, *battree* for battery, *whept or whipt* for whipped. We see *Fryday* for Friday, *milds* for miles, *scin* for skin, *wether* for weather and *howers* for hours. An *a* is used for *e*, as in *sarten* for certain, *prants* is used for prints, *lave* for leave, *sands* for sends, and *wall* for well.

On February, 1780, Elijah Fisher, a private in the Massachusetts Line, wrote this entry in his diary: "I stayes [with Mr. Wallis] and follows my Riting and sifering the same as I had Dun the Evnings before, for Every Evning from six of the Clock till Nine I used to follow my study." Under the date of October 17 this quaint note appears: "I agreed with Sarjt Sm. Whippels to stay one month with him after my time was out and so do his Duty and he was to larn me to Rite and sifer and what other larning would be easy."[214]

Diaries were often written as a continuous narrative, without sentence structure or punctuation. Some can be perplexing, especially when obvious chronological entries are not separated by date or place. Capitalization was haphazard within sentences. This practice also appears in orderly books and pension applications, and in many other forms of eighteenth century writing, regardless of the literacy level of the writer. The only pattern of capitalization that does emerge in many writings is that most nouns and many verbs are capitalized, regardless of where they appear in a sentence.

The following slang was often found in diaries of the period. It is taken from *The 1811 Dictionary of the Vulgar Tongue:*

beetle-headed: Dull, stupid.
brown bess: A soldier's firelock. "To hug Brown Bess" is to carry a firelock, or serve as a private soldier.
chicken-hearted: Fearful, cowardly.
cur: A cut or curtailed dog, disabled from chasing game. Figuratively used to signify a surly fellow.
English burgundy: Porter.
flip: Small beer, brandy, and sugar.
grog: Rum and water. "Groggy" or "Groggified" is to be drunk.
huzza: Said to have been originally the cry of the huzzars or Hungarian light horse; but now the national shout of the English, both civil and military; to give three cheers being to huzza thrice.
jack tar: A sailor.
lobster(back): A soldier, from the color of his clothes.
loggerhead: A blockhead or stupid fellow, also a double-headed, or bar-shot of iron.
neck weed: Hemp.
scaly: Mean, sordid.
tattoo: A beat of the drum, or signal for soldiers to go to their quarters, and a direction to the sutlers to close the tap.

RECURRING THEMES

A common theme found throughout all diaries is that men displayed unusual courage and resilience in their day-to-day lives, and retained their sense of humor while enduring harsh conditions. Patriotism, or any other reason for their motivation, is rarely mentioned, but much is said about their daily challenges to stay warm and to get enough food to eat.

They regularly disparaged the enemy, whom they referred to as "Lobsterbacks," "Philistines," "the wicked enemy," or "the butchers of the tyrant of Great Britain." During the Siege of Boston, soldiers called British General Gage "that Crocodile." At the burning of Charlestown during the Battle of Bunker Hill he was referred to as "that infernal Villain Thomas Gage." Light Infantry Colonel Banastre Tarleton was called "Bloody Ban," and became the subject of a propaganda campaign after his men slaughtered surrendering Continental Army troops at the Battle of Waxhaws in South Carolina in 1780.

Theft of personal possessions or food was a common practice, and was regarded as a grave offense. The loss of an article of clothing could mean the difference between freezing to death or survival. At Jockey Hollow, Lieutenant Burton lost his "cotten" shirt by a "bold Theefe" and a soldier "was whipped thirty lashes for stealing a cheese."[215] Samuel Haws recorded in October, 1775, that in a camp near Boston a rifleman "was whipt 39 stripes for Stealing and afterwards he was Drummed out of the camps."

Cursing was a habit that annoyed and shocked George Washington. A clergyman, when referring to the language of the New York troops who accompanied General Benedict Arnold in 1776, remarked that "It would be a dreadful hell to live with such creatures forever." Washington issued a General Order against profanity on August 3, 1776: "The General is sorry to be informed that the foolish and wicked practice of profane cursing and swearing, a vice hitherto little known in our American Army is growing into fashion. He hopes that the officers will, by example as well as influence, endeavor to check it and that both they and the men will reflect that we can little hope of the blessing of Heaven on our army if we insult it by our impiety and folly. Added to this it is a vice so mean and low without any temptation that every man of sense and character detests and despises it."

Frequent references to crime and consequent punishment appear in enlisted men's journals. For the month of September, 1777, the diary of Sergeant John Smith, 1st Rhode Island Regiment, Continental Line, shows an astonishing record of twenty-three sentences over a three week period:

> *Septemr. the 2d—Seven Searjts. 5 Corporals one Drums. & one Privat was tried By a General Court Martial Whereof Colo. Angel[l] was Presedent for Behaving Disorderly—the Searjts. were Ordred to Be suspended During the Pleasure of the Commanding Officer—the Corporals& Drum & Privats was Reprimanded & Dismisd*

& one henery forsigtte was tried & sentenced to Receive 100 Lashes & sent on Board one of the Ships to Serve During the war—John fly for Disserting was tried& sentenced to Receive 100 Lashes on his Naked Back & william Taylor provost Martial tried for Disobeying General Orders & was aquitted from further Punishment—sd. Taylor was Released

Septemr. 4th—James Gduggen was tried By a Genll. Court Martial for Attempting to fire his Gun at a Party of fategue men as they was Coming in from work thinking their was one Barns who had threatned to Kill his wife was their—he was Sentenced to sit on the Gallows half an hour & to Be whipt 50 Lashes on his Naked Back at the Gallows

Septemr. the 6th [5th]—the above sd. Prisoners Gdaggen & forsight & fly & one Stadwant was whipt & Sat on the Gallows & Received his other Punishment at sd. Place & was Ordred Back to the Provost Guard—in the after noon the Searjts. & Corporals was Brought out & Reprimanded—the Searjt. was suspended the others Aquited& went to their tents

Tusday the 9th—the Several Brigades to Parade on the hill at the Gallows to see the Execution of amos Rose who was Condem'd to Be Shot for Cocking his Gun at a Leiut. who struck him with his Cane & abuse'd him when in Liquor & Lemmuel Arkly who is an Enemy to his Country& took a Commission under General howe to inlist in the Service of the King of Great Brittian is under the sentence of Death to Be Executed at sd. time& Place—the Regmts. Paraded & the sd. Prisoners were Brought up& their sentences were Read—the Minesters Pray'd with them & they for themselves & Kneeld Down by their Graves to Be Shot—then the General sent them a Pardon & they were to be Carried on board of the Ships in the River their to Serve During the Present war—then they was Conducted By the Guards to the Provest Guard again—then we all went to our tents again

Saturday the 13th—three men Belonging to Col. Greens Reget. was whipt for Being Absent on muster Day & Frances Baptist for staying out of Quarters all night Received 30 stripes [i.e., lashes] [the] other[s] 25 Each & william Telley was tied to a tree Naked & to stand ten minits—John Congden & Daniel Ellice & Amos Gardner [were tried] for Letting the Cattle out of the Pen at Peeks Kills when on Guard & was acquitted

Sunday 14th this afternoon one Joseph Owens & one [blank] was teaken up about 6 miles from this incampment & Confind under the Provost Guard—sd. Owens Belonged to Col. Groons Rogot. & Dosortod on tho march to this Placo & wont to tho Enomy and Came as a spy with the sd. [blank]—Likewise Edward Murfey who Diserted from this Place & was teaken up over Kings ferey & Brought here & put in irons --the Prisoners was sent on board the ships in the River them who was Repreiv'd from the Gallows on the 9th of this instant [i.e., this month]—Several Others was sent to Sopas Goal [i.e., jail]

Sept 20th—at 8 o Clock A M. Edward Murfy& Epraham Simmons Receiv'd 100 Lashes Each on his Naked Back & sent on board the ships of war in the River to serve During the war & william Mathews & Frances Foster both whipt 100 Lashes Each & foster sent on board the Galley from whence he Disserted & Joseph Codose sentenced to Receive 50 Lashes for getting Drunk & Leaving his Post when on sentry was acquitted & Joseph Owens tryed at the same Court martial is Condemd to Die the 3 Day of October next

Novbr 1st, 1777, John muclevain an Irishman & Dick Ellise was hanged at Red Banck for Traytors to their Country & for Piloting the Hesians to this Garrison the 22d of Octor. Last—they were hanged Between the hours of 10 & 11 O clock A.M—they hanged untill [al]most Night then they were Cut Down & buried under the Gallows

NOTEWORTHY DIARIES OF SOME COMMON SOLDIERS

Several diaries stand out as being especially interesting and valuable because they realistically portray of the lives of common soldiers. All cover significant events, and have the length and chronological continuity to make them important contributions toward understanding the war. Those that have been partially transcribed below preserve the original substance and writing style.

Private Elijah Fisher

This diary spans almost the entire war, from May, 1775, until April, 1781. The content of the concise entries is fascinating, and covers several major events of the conflict, including the winter at Valley Forge and the major battles of Saratoga and Monmouth.

Fisher was born on June 18, 1758, in Norton, Massachusetts and served three times during the war for a total of nearly six years. He joined the militia a few days after the battles of Lexington and Concord in April, 1775. On his seventeenth birthday his regiment, the 12th Massachusetts Infantry, saw action at Bunker Hill. This unit helped build the defensive works there, a feat which was accomplished in one night; British officers were astonished when they saw the defenses the next morning. Fisher's regiment lost five men and had twenty-one wounded in this action.

The following year, Fisher fought in the Battle of White Plains in November, 1776, and afterward was discharged for illness. He recovered, and then reenlisted for three more years in January, 1777, in the newly formed 4th Massachusetts Regiment, commanded by Colonel William Shepard. This unit saw action at the American victory at Saratoga.

When Commander-in-Chief Washington increased his Life Guard from fifty to one-hundred-fifty men on March 19, 1778 at Valley Forge, Fisher was selected to serve in this elite unit. The purpose of the guard was to protect General Washington, as well as the money and official papers of the Continental Army. Washington specified that the group be a "corps of sober, intelligent, and reliable men."[216] Because it was an honor to be a member of the unit, care was taken to ensure that soldiers from each of the thirteen colonies were represented.[217]

Fisher recorded his acceptance into the Guard in 1778:

March 19th: There was orders that there should be three men sent from each Reg't to jine His Excelences Gen. Washington's Life Gard and Seth Lovil was sent out of our Company but after being there a fue days and did not like to be there he said, but I sepose that he was afeared that the Reg't would go to Rhode Island which they did afterward and he could not go with them and he come back to the Company....

March 30th: I jined the Life Gard and liked being there much better than being in the Ridgement let them go where they would.

Fisher was discharged from the Guard at Morristown, New Jersey in January, 1780. He returned home, but reenlisted one more time in October, 1780, in the 1st Massachusetts Regiment of the Continental Line, commanded by Colonel Benjamin Tupper. On December 15, 1780 he was promoted to first sergeant. He was discharged in April, 1781, at West Point. After the war he settled in Livermore, Maine where he resumed farming, married, raised a family, and received a pension for his war service. An extensive file covering his war years is housed at the United States National Archives.[218]

Jeremiah Greenman

Greenman's diary spans September, 1775, to December, 1783. He was born in Newport, Rhode Island in 1758, and served in the military for the entire span of the war. Some parts of his journal appear to have been revised at a later date. His manuscript remained unpublished until 1978, when it was identified in the possession of a direct descendent. Greeman was unskilled, and barely literate, when he joined the 2nd Rhode Island Regiment of the Continental Army in May, 1775. Over the course of the war he traveled from Quebec to Philadelphia. His diary shows the maturing of a naive young man into a seasoned veteran who provided a detailed record of the hardships he suffered.

Jeremiah was with a small force of American soldiers commanded by Benedict Arnold when they crossed Maine's freezing wilderness to invade Canada in late 1775. In December, this group was crushed while attempting to take Quebec. Greenman, and four hundred others, were held prisoner in that city until August, 1776. He continued to write regularly in his journal, even while a prisoner.

He later participated in the Battle of Red Bank, in Delaware, 1777, and spent the bitter winter at Valley Forge in 1777-1778. He received three combat wounds during his enlistment, and was promoted four times in the field. By 1781 he held the rank of lieutenant.

After the war, he held several jobs, but eventually went to sea for twenty years and eventually became a ship captain. He left Rhode Island when nearly fifty years of age and moved his family to Waterford, Ohio, where he took up farming, and lived there for another twenty-two years. He was a Mason for nearly fifty years in the Mount Moriah Lodge in Waterford. He applied for a pension in 1819, and an extensive file of documents appear in his service record in National Archives.

He died November 15, 1828, and is buried on the highest hill on his farm. The grave is marked with a sandstone monument and the inscription: "Revolutionary Soldier-In memory of Jeremiah Greenman Esq. an active officer in that army which bid defiance to Britons power and established the independence of the United States."[219]

John Smith

Sergeant John Smith, from Bristol, Rhode Island, wrote his account in two segments. The first one spans from August, 1776, to January, 1777, and covers his service in Colonel Christopher Lippitt's Rhode Island Regiment. The second covers July, 1777, to January, 1778, and records his service with Colonel Christopher Greene's First Rhode Island Regiment.

The first diary describes the conclusion of the disastrous New York Campaign and the tragic retreat across New Jersey which followed, and closes with the critical American victory at Trenton. The latter diary describes the service of the 1st Rhode Island Regiment near Peekskill, New York, the Hudson Highlands, and in the Philadelphia Campaign, when it joined with the main army. Smith's recording of the Hessian attack on Fort Mercer at Red Bank, New Jersey on October 22, 1777, is especially vivid and highly-valued, since it is the narration of a common soldier. Following that action, he documented the reduction of Fort Mifflin, the Whitemarsh encampment, and his experiences during several weeks of the winter at Valley Forge.

Company muster and pay rolls verify that Sergeant Smith was on detached command in Rhode Island from January, 1778, through September, 1779. He continued in service with the 1st Rhode Island Regiment until the expiration of his three-year enlistment, and was discharged in May, 1780. His diary seems to have ended with his departure from Valley Forge, but subsequent volumes may have been lost since the account ends abruptly on the last day of 1779 and Smith continued in service for two-and-a-half years beyond this time. Little is known about his personal life, except that he lived in East Greenwich, Rhode Island in 1785, and is documented as still living there in the 1790 Federal Census. He died before 1803, based on the marriage record of his son Samuel.[220]

Ebenezer Fletcher

Fletcher was born in New Ipswich, New Hampshire in 1761. He attended school there, and became an apprentice to a mill owner when he was age fourteen. In 1777, he enlisted for three years as a fifer in a New Hampshire regiment. His diary begins in the spring of 1777, when the unit was assigned to a garrison at Fort Ticonderoga, in a battalion commanded by the famous Nathan Hale. The fort was evacuated at the approach of the British Northern Army when it advanced south toward Saratoga. British forces under General Simon Fraser overtook the retreating American rear guard at Hubberton, in the disputed territory of New Hampshire (now Vermont). During the fierce fighting Fletcher was severely wounded and taken prisoner.

Fletcher describes his captivity: "Some of the enemy were very kind; while others were very spiteful and malicious. One of them came and took my silver shoe-buckles and left me an old pair of brass ones, and said exchange was no robbery but I thought it robbery at a high rate. Another came and took off my neck handkerchief. An old negro came and took my fife, which I considered as the greatest insult I had received while with the enemy. The Indians often came and abused me with their language calling us yankees and rebels; but they were not allowed to injure us. I was stripped of everything valuable about me."

He was confined by the British for a few weeks, and after partially recovering from his wounds he was able to escape. After a perilous trek of over one hundred miles alone through a wild mountainous area, without food, the now-exhausted boy somehow reached his home in New Ipswich. There he fully recovered, and was later able to rejoin his company and serve the remaining part of his enlistment. Fletcher went on the Sullivan-Clinton Campaign against the Iroquois Nations in the fall of 1779, and was discharged in March, 1780. He then returned to New Ipswich, where he started a trunk-making business. He prospered, and was eventually able to purchase a mill. He died in New Ipswich, in May, 1831. His diary "written by himself and published at the request of his friends" was first made available in 1813 by S. Wilder, Printer, New Ipswich. A fourth edited edition was released in 1827 by Wilder. In 1866 Charles L. Bushnell of New York reissued the diary, "Taken from the original 1827 imprint-the authors best revised and improved edition." Fletcher is not listed at the National Archives as having applied for a veteran's pension.[221]

Solomon Nash

Private Solomon Nash kept his diary from January, 1776, through January, 1777. No personal details are known about his life, except that he was a resident of Abington, Massachusetts, where he had relatives. During wartime he served in the Massachusetts and New York campaigns with Captain Jotham Drury's artillery company, part of Henry Knox's artillery regiment. He was a man of limited education, and probably kept his record for his own amusement. His diary was published in 1865.

Research by this author in pension archives documents tragically revealed that Nash was killed in the Battle of Rhode Island in 1778. The encounter took place in Newport on August 29, 1778. Continental Army forces under the command of General John Sullivan were attacked by British forces supported by Royal Navy ships, while withdrawing after abandoning their siege of Newport. After being hit in the leg by grapeshot, Nash was carried by two soldiers in his platoon to a nearby hospital set up at the College of Providence. His comrades were privates Joseph P. Guerney and Whitcom Pratt, both from his home town of Abington. Nash died a few days later.[222]

Nash wrote of his daily routine in the army, and his experiences at the Siege of Boston and the action at Bunker Hill. He described his voyage from Boston to New York after the British evacuation, and records the personal events in his life during New York Campaign and the evacuation of Long Island. He relates the plot to poison General Washington and the destruction of the statue of King George in New York City, the activities of the American artillery on Governors Island, and the actions of British ships in the harbor.

Nash faithfully describes the weather each day. Many of his entries simply read, "nothing remarkable happened." His forty-six-page account covers a remarkably eventful period of the war, and provides fascinating glimpses of the daily lives of ordinary soldiers. He laments the desertions and fatalities, and the suffering of sick comrades whose only aid came from their fellow soldiers. His entry of October 30, 1776 reads: "Today it being rainy, Luke was taking not well, I still being not well . . . we both set out for North Castle hospital . . . and we got within 4 miles of the hospital and put up for this night." The men slept in the woods and then completed their arduous journey, unaided, in the morning.[223]

David Howe

David Howe was born in Methuen, Massachusetts in 1758. All six sons in the family of ten children served in the war, and three of them fought at Bunker Hill. He was a currier (a dresser and finisher of leather after it has been tanned). A Minute Man at age sixteen, he responded to the British attack at Lexington and Concord. In June, 1775, he joined other militia troops at the Battle of Bunker Hill. During that fray, after firing his musket, he continued fighting by using the weapon of the man who had died beside him.

Howe wrote his fifty-one-page diary in two parts. The first begins in December, 1775, when he enlisted in the Continental army, and provides the details of his voyage along the New Jersey coast to New York and the campaign that followed, including the Battle of Harlem Heights. He describes the army's desperate retreat across New Jersey, and the astonishing American victory at Trenton. After that action he marched from New Jersey back to Massachusetts. He concluded his narrative when he reached his home at Methuen in January, 1776. The second part begins nine months later, in September, 1777, and covers his experiences at the Battle of Saratoga, and also ended when he returned home to Methuen.

The diary was not published until 1865, when it was discovered by a local historian. Henry B. Dawson, in his introductory remarks to the first addition of Howe's diary, describes the work: "It is the work of a plain unassuming country boy who responded to the call of his country in the days of her great trouble, and the picture which it presents of the routine of camp life in the earlier period of the War of the Revolution. [Howe's] dickering in trade, his social visits, the fatigue, escort duties, sermons and penalties, rumors and realities—will afford to the careful and intelligent reader both amusement and instruction." Dawson's description can be augmented by these typical entries:

[October] the 6 [1775]. The enemy fired between 80 to 90 Canon at our men but killed nine onely cut of one mans arm and killed too cows So much for this day.

November 1775 the 1. Last night the fire ran over Samuel Hawes's hair and that provoket him to wrath Nothing very remarkable hapnd this day that I know of.

At the conclusion of the war Howe returned to the town of Haverhill, about five miles from Methuen, and opened a small currier shop. The business prospered and became a large establishment, and it manufactured shoes for the army during the War of 1812. Over the years Howe invested in land, and eventually became one of the largest landowners in Essex County, Massachusetts. There is no evidence of Howe or his survivors filling for a pension, no doubt due to his affluence.[224] He died in Haverhill in 1842.

Joseph Plumb Martin

The most famous and comprehensive account of the war by a common soldier is that of Sergeant Joseph Plumb Martin. It has become the most widely-read, informative and best-loved classic writing by a Continental soldier. It is also the most-referenced first person account of the war and is endlessly quoted. The diary has been published in several print editions and was even portrayed in a PBS documentary. The reason for its popularity is that the work is written in a lively, colorful style that is entertaining to all, not just hard-core military history buffs. It is full of anecdotes and amusing vignettes from the life of a teenage soldier, as well as descriptions of historic battles and stories of legends, such as Molly Pitcher.

This account was written many years after the war, and as such is not considered a contemporary diary composed while in the field. However, with its chronological daily entries, the writing appears to be based on an actual diary. It has an immediacy that has led many historians to assume that it was composed soon after the events described, and not a half-century later. *A Narrative of Some of the Adventures, Dangers and Sufferings of a Revolutionary Soldier* is

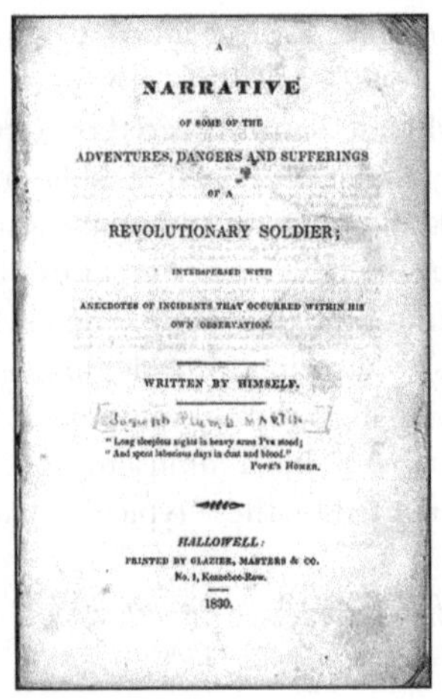

A

NARRATIVE

OF SOME OF THE

ADVENTURES, DANGERS AND SUFFERINGS

OF A

REVOLUTIONARY SOLDIER;

INTERSPERSED WITH

ANECDOTES OF INCIDENTS THAT OCCURRED WITHIN HIS OWN OBSERVATION.

WRITTEN BY HIMSELF.

[Joseph Plumb Martin]

"Long sleepless nights in heavy arms I've stood;
"And spent laborious days in dust and blood."
Pope's Homer.

HALLOWELL:
PRINTED BY GLAZIER, MASTERS & CO.
No. 1, Kennebec-Row.
1830.

Title page from *Narrative of Some of the Adventures, Dangers and Sufferings of a Revolutionary Soldier...* by Joseph Plumb Martin, Hallowell, Maine, 1830.

an absolute "must read" for anyone having the slightest interest in the life of the Continental soldier, and deserves a place in the short list of notable Revolutionary war diaries.

Martin was born in Becket, Massachusetts, in 1760, and lived with his maternal grandparents near New Haven, Connecticut. He ran away at age fifteen to join the Connecticut Militia and a year later enlisted in the Continental Army. He fought in dozens of battles, and wintered at major encampments. His narrative provides eyewitness accounts of numerous battles, including Long Island, White Plains, Fort Mifflin, Monmouth, and Yorktown. He encamped with the army at Valley Forge, Jockey Hollow and New Windsor. He also depicted several critical actions that are obscure, since no major commanders were present. Martin served until the war ended in 1783.

The narrative was first published anonymously in 1830. At that time only a small number of people in his town knew who had written it, and at first it drew little notice due to its homespun grammar. After the book became more widely distributed, the public found that the accounts of battles, travels, and hardship proved surprisingly accurate when compared to other records. Although Martin wrote his book nearly fifty years after the war, he displayed total recall with regard to timing and small details. By the beginning in the twentieth century the book began to be embraced by historians as a primary source document of the war.

The immediate emotional appeal of Martin's observations had an impact on our understanding of the entire war. His reminiscences of cold and starving soldiers have served to enshrine common soldiers as symbols of patriotic sacrifice. His colorful description of Molly Pitcher at the Battle of Monmouth has spawned much of the literature about this fighting female Patriot, and substantiated that she was more than just a legend. He described how he had observed a woman firing cannon in the midst of the battle: "A woman whose husband belonged to the artillery and who was then attached to a piece in the engagement, attended with her husband at the piece for the whole time. While in the act of reaching a cartridge and having one of her feet as far before the other as she could step, a cannon shot from the enemy passed directly between her legs without doing any other damage than carrying away all the lower part of her petticoat. Looking at it with apparent unconcern, she observed that it was lucky it did not pass a little higher, for in that case it might have carried away something else, and continued her occupation."

Martin's presence as a sapper (digger of trenches and tunnels) and miner at the Siege of Yorktown provides an astonishing ground-level view of one of the most celebrated victories in American history. His eyewitness portrayal of George Washington provided evidence of the general's appeal as a man of the people who interacted with ordinary soldiers without condescension.

After the war, Martin relocated to Maine to claim his bounty land, and in 1784 settled on one hundred acres in Stockton Springs. He cleared the land and began farming, but soon learned that General Henry Knox, who served with Washington, had secured legal control of the entire area. Martin and other war veterans who had occupied the land were then treated as squatters. After the land was appraised by the state, he had to pay the difference between the unimproved and improved values. For Martin, this penalty amounted to $100, which for him was a significant amount of money.

In 1811, records show Martin living on fifty-six acres in Maine. In 1818, he applied for a veteran's pension, but reported owning no real estate. He served as town clerk in nearby Prospect for twenty-eight years, as a selectman in that town, a representative to the Massachusetts General Court, and a captain in the Maine militia. Martin was obviously a smart, intellectually inquisitive man. He established a church in Stockton Springs, composed a hymn that is still sung to this by the congregation, read extensively, and, as an amateur naturalist, painted birds and flowers. He was also an antiquarian, preserving some artifacts that are still in Maine historical collections. He died in Stockton at age ninety.[225]

Most images from the Revolutionary war depict events from a distance, with senior officers and historians providing overviews and assessments. Soldiers' diaries provide a rare eyewitness view of Revolutionary War-era combat and camp life. The experiences of each individual evoke the reality of battles, marches, surrenders and comradeship. For the soldier, reality was hunger, freezing, the sting of battle and the boredom of camp life. With the killing range of the musket, and reliance on the bayonet, the eighteenth century battlefield was a very personal experience. These writings reveal much about the authors and the circumstances in which they found themselves in war and peace.

Chapter Fifteen

Who Won the War?

Many people do not understand the major difference between the citizen-soldiers of the militia and regular soldiers of the Continental Army. Both of these forces fought during the entire war and both suffered heavy casualties, and there are supporters for each who claim that one or the other was responsible for winning the war.

One major distinction between the two groups was in their administration—the militia forces were sponsored by each individual state, while Washington's Continental Army was directed by Congress. About 100,000 men served in the Continental Army during the Revolutionary War, and in all probability twice that number soldiered as militiamen. In Abraham Lincoln's famous Lyceum Address, delivered in 1838, he stated, "At the close of that struggle, nearly every adult male had been a participator in some of its scenes." This claim appears to be true.[226]

The local militia existed long before the American Revolution took place. As early as 1691, state legislatures began organizing regiments in each county. The colonists relied on these part-time citizen-soldiers to defend them from the Native Americans and hostile French troops. The militia also served as a type of police force, often called upon to maintain law and order outside of major cities. On July 18, 1775 the Continental Congress recommended to all colonies "that all able-bodied, effective men, between 16 and 50 years of age be formed into companies of militia." Typically, the age for militia service in most states during the war was between 16 and 60. However, each individual state passed its own legislation regarding age. For example Pennsylvania passed The "Act to Regulate the Militia of the Commonwealth of Pennsylvania" on March 17, 1777. It required all white men between the ages of 18 and 53 capable of bearing arms to serve. The 1775 federal guideline remained in effect until May 9, 1792 when the Uniform Militia Act required all free, able-bodied white men, age 18 to 45, to sign up. The militiamen were assembled from all segments of free white male society. Only clergy, slaves, and often free blacks, were forbidden to join. The militia consisted of farmers with small land holdings, farm laborers, and tradesmen. This last category commonly included tailors, boot makers, blacksmiths, carpenters and shopkeepers, joined by clerks, lawyers and tutors. Large land owners and affluent citizens served as officers in the various militia regiments.

The state militias were, in effect, standing home armies, prepared to defend the areas near their homes. They met at regularly scheduled times to train with weapons and perform military maneuvers, often on the town green or in some other open space. These gatherings were regarded by the men as jovial social events. During the Revolution, they monitored enemy troop movements, and opposed and harassed neighboring Tory activities. These men joined the Continental Army at the front lines, but usually remained mobilized for no more than ninety days, and frequently supplied their own provisions.

Each militia regiment was structured to conform to its mission. A regiment's task could consist primarily of suppressing Loyalists, or, in Southern states, preventing slave uprisings. On the frontier they were called out to fight Native Americans, and were used to relieve Continental forces at nearby garrisons. Some militia duties involved nothing more than gathering provisions or rounding up herds of cattle to feed the Continentals. Others served mainly as a handy pool of potential recruits for the Continental Army.

The terms *militia* and *Minutemen* are often used interchangeably, and sometimes incorrectly. Many people, including members of the Continental Congress, confused the special forces of Minutemen with ordinary militiamen. The Minutemen were elite special units within the militia system. Their members received additional training, and were required to report quickly for urgent events; hence their name. Minutemen were usually less than thirty years old, and were handpicked for their enthusiasm, patriotic zeal, and physical prowess. They trained vigorously during the sixteen months between the Boston Tea Party of December, 1773, and the first combat at Lexington and Concord in April, 1775. The state of battle-readiness of most militia forces never approached that of the selected Minutemen.

Americans preferred this type of military force over a permanent army. Animosity for standing armies began with the resentment hurled at the British Army when they tried to enforce the 1765 Stamp Act. Hatred accelerated afterwards, and Americans regarded any regular army as a symbol of monarchy and tyranny, and as a menace to civilian rule.

Significant differences can be found when comparing the typical militiaman with his counterpart in the Continental Army. Most Continentals were poor, landless transients with an average age of about twenty. The citizen-soldiers were landholding farmers of the lower to middle class, and tradesmen. Militiamen were older, typically in their late twenties. This age difference likely resulted from the practice of primogeniture, where estates were typically passed from father to eldest son.

Few militiamen had any combat experience before their first action.[227] Unskilled soldiers, called from home on short notice, often lacked confidence on the battlefield. But Washington admitted that if they had a regular army to support them, these amateurs could fight effectively and inflict significant damage on the enemy. Some generals, notably Daniel Morgan and

Nathanael Greene, learned to use the militia as auxiliary troops around a core of regulars with triumphant effect at battles such as Cowpens and Saratoga.

Militia officers were often elected from the ranks by popular vote. In New England non-commissioned officers and those up to the rank of captain were elected in this manner. The practice varied in other states. In Pennsylvania, for example, men in each battalion elected their own field officers, with ranks of major, lieutenant colonel and colonel. These officers were then commissioned by the state, and each served for three years. Within each county, the field officers drew lots to determine their date of rank or seniority. Elected officers tended to avoid discipline, and fraternized with enlisted soldiers. They did not want to alienate fellow citizens, who could simply opt to elect another person, and they always had to keep in mind that they would once again be neighbors after the emergency had passed. In most cases, the Continental soldier, subjected to more authoritarian leadership, respected the status of his officers to a greater degree.

RESTING ON A BROKEN STAFF

At the end of the summer of 1775, only six months after the war had begun, skirmishes moved away from local areas, and the New England citizen-soldiers began to lose their fighting spirit. Washington deplored the lax discipline that resulted from the popular election of officers, and the fact that the once-patriotic farmers did not remain in service long enough to be adequately trained. Washington commented on the New England militia, writing that "Their officers generally speaking are the most indifferent kind of people I ever saw." Discouraged by the way militiamen tended to run away at the first sight of a British soldier, Washington informed the Congress in late 1776: "If I were called upon to declare . . . whether the militia had been most serviceable or hurtful upon the whole, I should subscribe to the latter."[228]

Washington insisted that a decision to ". . . place any dependence on Militia is assuredly resting on a broken staff. Men just dragged from the tender scenes of domestick life; unaccustomed to the din of arms, totally unacquainted with any kind of military skill, which followed by want of confidence in themselves, when opposed to troops regularly trained, disciplines and appointed superior in knowledge, and superior in arms, make them timid and ready to fly from their own shadow."

Other generals concurred with him. General Nathanael Greene stated that militiamen had ". . . all the tender feelings of domestic life . . . not sufficiently fortified with natural courage to stand the shocking scenes of war. To march over dead men, to hear without concern the groans of the wounded, I say few men can stand such scenes unless steeled by habit and fortifies by military pride"[229]

After the Revolution, American political leaders began to eulogize about the heroism of the citizen-soldiers while at the same time denigrating the Continental Army. This went along with the pervasive belief that the Revolution had been a "people's uprising," in which everyone was a soldier in some way, and that the Continental Army only played a peripheral role. Even the "Spirit of '76" was redefined to include civilians. Opinions of the effectiveness of militia were often disputed by the former Continental Army officers and soldiers who had ascended to positions of prominence.

Many Continental Army veterans also defamed the militia, and took every chance to remind the public of the reputation of citizen-soldiers for running away when attacked. These veterans even disparaged the legendary militia successes at Lexington and Concord, Bunker Hill, King's Mountain, and Cowpens. They maintained that these occurred by chance, when the militia troops were under cover, or up against poorly-trained Tories, as opposed to British regulars.

Most Americans chose to remember the citizen-soldiers at Concord and Lexington, who gallantly fired the first shots of the war and fell at Bunker Hill in 1775. Thomas Paine, the renowned American political activist and revolutionary, called them "summer soldiers," since so many of them went home to harvest their crops later in the year: "These are the times that try men's souls. The summer soldier and the sunshine patriot will, in this crisis, shrink from the service of their country; but he that stands by it now, deserves the love and thanks of man and woman."[230]

Private Joseph Plumb Martin wrote, ". . . the militia did good and great service . . . on particular occasions, I well know, for I have fought by their side, but still I insist that they would not have answered the end so well as regular troops. They would not have endured the sufferings the army did; They would have considered themselves (as in reality they were and are) free citizens, not bound by and cords that were not of their own manufacturing, and when the hardships of fatigue, starvation, cold and nakedness, which I have just mentioned, begun to seize upon them in such awful array as they did on us, they would have instantly quitted the service in disgust, and who could blame them?"[231]

General Washington never championed the militia. He complained that they had failed to exhibit "a brave & manly opposition" while engaging British or Hessian regulars in the early campaigns of 1776 in Manhattan and on Long Island. At the Battle of Brooklyn Heights in August, 1776, for instance, thousands of militiamen retreated. Washington believed that their sniping at the enemy from behind stone walls was not the way to defeat an organized army trained in European-style tactics. He was especially disturbed by militia privates ignoring orders issued by officers of the regular army.

Following the devastating defeats of the New York Campaign, the now-frustrated Washington refused to rely on militia forces and their fighting methods, and implored the Continental Congress to create a standing army.

He remained steadfast in his belief that only a standing professional force whose private soldiers enlisted for the long-term could hope to prevail against an enemy army that was the finest, most disciplined, and effective in the world.

At the Second Battle of Saratoga in October, 1777, many militiamen vanished on the morning of the battle, since it was the same day that their enlistments expired. At Camden, South Carolina, in August, 1780, militiamen were blamed for one of the worst defeats of the war. At the onset of the battle, they panicked, threw down their weapons, and fled when confronted by advancing Redcoats.

But while the ill-trained, part-time soldiers often lacked confidence on the battlefield, Washington eventually discovered a way to use these forces effectively. He learned that if militia maneuvers on the battlefield were synchronized with the tactics of the regular army, the citizen- soldiers could develop into valiant fighters.

A GOOD AND GREAT SERVICE

While the militia did have their shortcomings, America could not have won the War for Independence without these part-time soldiers. British General Cornwallis wrote from Yorktown in 1781, "I will not say much in praise of the militia, but the list of British officers and soldiers killed and wounded by them . . . proves but too fatally they are not wholly contemptible."

Documented evidence of militia service is scarce, and usually fragmentary, compared to Continental Army records. The best method to learn what militiamen actually did during the Revolution is to study their applications for pensions. The men of the militia were not allowed access to this benefit until long after it was provided to Continental soldiers in 1818. Militia requests were not permitted until 1832, almost four decades after the war. Reviewing the descriptions of their service, in their own words, reveals that the role of the citizen-soldier in the Revolutionary War has not been fully appreciated, and that their deeds often matched the valorous exploits of the regular army.

Many of these records contain interesting details about the myriad duties a typical militiaman might perform, in addition to joining regular troops in combat. Some were called up for as many as four or five tours, each lasting about three months. They were intimately familiar with local terrain and its challenges, and were responsible for guarding hundreds of miles of coastline and riverbank. Inland, they garrisoned forts and conducted scouting patrols. The hit and run tactics of the militia men in forested areas on the frontier were effective against similar fighting methods used by hostile Indians.

Once the regular troops departed from a combat zone, only the locally-organized militia units, acting independently, had the ability to keep control

Heroes of "76" marching to the fight (Currier & Ives, c. 1876. Library of Congress Prints and Photographs Division, Washington D.C.)

over it. With its limited manpower, the main Continental Army could not afford to leave behind large occupation forces, especially in geographically-dispersed areas. When the war shifted to the South, the Southern Continental Army was devastated by defeats at Savannah, Charleston and Camden. At that time, the militia stepped up to meet the challenge, under the leadership of experienced soldiers such as Thomas Sumter of South Carolina. In the end, these men became the mainstay of American resistance in the South. Unfortunately, their lack of discipline, and fondness for plunder, alienated as many people as their battlefield valor encouraged.

The service of militia forces frequently degenerated into brutal internecine warfare to settle local disputes and old resentments. In areas such as Bay Shore in New Jersey, and along the highlands of the Piedmont, members of the same family, now divided into Whigs and Tories, sometimes clashed. The Battle of Kings Mountain in South Carolina in October of 1780 was a battle between Americans, but it would be more appropriate to call the savage encounter a massacre. Loyalists had 290 men killed, while the Patriots lost fifty-nine. After the fighting, he victorious militiamen demanded retribution against the Loyalists they had captured, and condemned thirty of their prisoners to death for atrocities committed against them, their friends, and kin. Nine Tories were hung before officers stopped the slaughter. Ultimately, it took the Southern Continental Army, under General Nathanael Greene, to make a decisive impact on the war in the South.

When Washington marched to Yorktown in 1781, he depended on the militia to protect New Jersey, despite the looming threat of half of the British Army in nearby New York City. In a sense, the militiamen served as a military government, opposing and punishing Loyalists, forcing reluctant citizens to sign oaths of allegiance, and intimidating merchants who were supplying the enemy or refusing to accept continental currency. Many served as guards for British prisoners of war, and also gathered provisions or drove herds of cattle to supply the regular army.

The major advantage of maintaining a large reserve of citizen-soldiers was that they could be called on to reinforce, support and swell the numbers of the Continental Army during critical times. The number of regular American troops was inadequate during the war, but before decisive battles American commanders could add thousands to their ranks. They accomplished this by rapidly mobilizing this plentiful pool of militiamen who were ready and willing to fight on short notice. This lethal potential always kept the enemy guessing as to the strength of American forces. In the end, even if the militias tried the patience of American generals, their numbers were needed.

No one can dispute the fact that in 1775 militiamen fought with courage along the Concord Road and at Bunker Hill. Nearly 40 percent of soldiers serving under Washington in his legendary Christmas night victory at Trenton in 1776 were militiamen. The decisive victories at Bennington in 1777, and King's Mountain in 1780, were fought solely by militia. In both instances the militia, led by experienced officers, scored victories without any help from the Continental Army. Half of the American forces in the wildly successful Saratoga Campaign of 1777 were militiamen. At that great American victory, the militia poured in after the Continentals had fought the British Army to a standstill. Their huge numbers tipped the balance and convinced General John Burgoyne that his position was hopeless and that surrender was his only option.

A print showing a man on horseback pointing to the distance as two other men prepare to leave with their rifles. A woman on the porch passes a rifle to one man as a younger woman with a child looks distraught. (Currier & Ives, c. 1876. Library of Congress Prints and Photographs Division Washington, D.C.)

Washington and his generals, Daniel Morgan and Nathanael Greene, had great success after they learned to effectively use militia riflemen in conjunction with Continental infantry. At the Battle of Cowpens, South Carolina in 1781 General Daniel Morgan crushed the despised Banastre Tarleton and his dreaded cavalry, who had consistently slaughtered Americans after they had surrendered. Morgan's unusual technique was to position his troops with their backs toward a river so they could not fall back, and then threaten to shoot any of his men who broke ranks. He then positioned the weakest six hundred of his eight hundred troops in the front line. Knowing that they would probably crumple, he ordered them to fire only two volleys before retreating, and then take position behind the seasoned Delaware and Maryland Continental divisions who were hidden from view. When Tarleton's dragoons saw the militia withdrawing, they believed that the Americans were on the run, so they charged into a barrage of musket fire, shot with deadly effect, from about thirty yards. The British assault collapsed, with some troops surrendering while others fled. The Cowpens victory was won after engaging some of the most elite troops of the British Army. This was the turning point of the war in the South, and it ultimately led to the chain of events leading to the final victory at Yorktown.

The tactics used at Cowpens were successfully repeated in the South in the battles that followed. In March, 1781, at the Battle of Guilford Courthouse near present-day Greensboro, North Carolina, General Nathanael Greene skillfully deployed his militiamen using the Cowpens techniques, and this caused the British to suffer such devastating losses that they evacuated the entire state.

Washington continued to lament the weaknesses of the militia, but high-ranking officers such as Morgan and Greene held a more realistic appraisal of the citizen-soldiers. They understood that while the militia could not always stand up against trained enemy forces, they could perform other critical roles that decided the outcome of battles. The militiamen were essential to the war, and its most numerous participants. However, except for the first six months of the war, Washington's Continental forces formed the core of the American army.

Alexander Hamilton summed up this view of the militia five years after the end of the war:

> *The steady operations of war against a regular and disciplined army can only be successfully conducted by a force of the same kind. Considerations of economy, not less than of stability and vigor, confirm this position. The American militia, in the course of the late war, have, by their valor on numerous occasions, erected eternal monuments to their fame; but the bravest of them feel and know that the liberty of their country could not have been established by their efforts alone, however great and valuable they were. War, like most other things, is a science to be acquired and perfected by diligence, by perseverance, by time, and by practice.*[232]

The decision to commit to a regular standing army, rather than a fragmented militia force, gradually gained broad support among the American public. They soon accepted the fact that the Continental Army protected the civilian population from sending family members away for long-term service, and participating in some of the worst combat. The reality was that only a reliable and organized standing army could endure long campaigns and confront the well-trained British regulars and their professional Hessian mercenaries on a regular basis. The only possible conclusion is that the militia could not have won the war alone, but the war probably could not have been won without them.

Chapter Sixteen

Ms. Yankee Doodle

The Women Who Followed the Army

The "camp followers" who accompanied Washington's army ranged from influential people, such as Martha Washington, across the gamut to less-than-desirable women, such as prostitutes. The term *camp follower* has been used to identify civilians and their children who trailed behind the armies during the Revolutionary War, although the expression itself was not used in the eighteenth century. Generally, camp followers were wives and children of soldiers who followed their husband's or father's army, and provided some type of service to encamped soldiers such as laundering, cooking, mending and nursing. The females who came behind Washington's army were seeking safety, shelter, food, and work. Most were deprived and accustomed to doing house or farm work, so they were well suited for these duties. Another type of camp follower, the *sutler*, was a service provider who sold goods or services that the military did not supply. These included coffee, sugar, liquor and sometimes sexual services. But there appears to have been little military prostitution in the American camps because of the poverty of American soldiers, the religious idealism that pervaded the Army, and penalties in the form of pay deductions for soldiers afflicted with venereal disease.

Females were never recruited, or even encouraged, to follow the army, so little was recorded in American records concerning the rules and regulations that governed them. While the Commander-in-Chief welcomed his own wife's long visits during the war, he was initially reluctant to allow other women to join the troops. In August, 1777, he suggested, "The multitude of women in particular, especially those who are pregnant, or have children, are a clog upon every movement. The Commander in Chief therefore earnestly recommends it to the officers commanding brigades and corps, to use every reasonable method in their power to get rid of all such as are not absolutely necessary . . . ."[233]

Washington soon learned that by driving these women away he would reduce the ranks of his volunteer army, and at the same time lose some of his best men: "[I]was obliged to give Provisions to the extra Women in these Regiments, or lose by Desertion, perhaps to the Enemy, some of the oldest and best Soldiers In the Service."[234] John U. Rees, a Revolutionary War historian, examined several regimental records, particularly those which enumerated the women that were present. He found that, on average, adult female camp followers amounted to about 3 percent of the strength of each unit, i.e., one woman for every thirty-three men.[235] At that rate, women in the Continental Army numbered between 2,000 and 3,000 at various time periods.

Army wives who followed their soldier husbands on campaign earned their living by washing clothes. (Image courtesy of www.allthingsliberty.com)

Although few eyewitness descriptions of camp followers exist, those that can be found show that their backgrounds were vastly different, although nearly all of them were the wives of soldiers and officers. Orderly books, kept by both Continental Line and militia regiments, show that commanding officers requested all of the names of women and children, and recorded to which soldier they "belonged." Unattached women did not receive rations, and relied on the soldiers to give up a portion of their food, or else fended for themselves. Their best chance to subsist, therefore, was to become emotional involved with a soldier, and to do so some of these women may have resorted to providing sexual favors.

When husbands fell in battle, their wives suddenly found themselves far from home, and all alone. In this event, some women quickly remarried to one of their husband's comrades, in order to ensure that their subsistence would continue. Many American women and their children found themselves rejected and harassed in their local Tory communities, so they were forced to join their husbands for protection. Many went home in the late fall, however, to avoid the hardship of upcoming winter encampments.

Camp followers were not members of any one social class. Educated women, who were typically officers' wives, provided services such as copying

New York Regiment reenactors at Monmouth Battlefield, June 2014, Patriot Lass "Julie Christine" with author on right. (Photograph by the author)

correspondence and managing field hospitals. Martha Washington, Catherine Greene, Lucy Knox and other wives of high-ranking officers traveled to the winter encampments to spend time with their husbands. In fact, Martha Washington joined her husband for every winter of the war. The value of these women to the army was mostly symbolic, since their presence inspired the public as evidence that everyone should make sacrifices for the cause for independence. They were usually billeted in private homes that had been appropriated for the use of their husbands.

Maria Cronkite was one classic example of the women who followed the army. She joined her husband, a fifer in the 1st New York Regiment, in 1777, when she was thirty-two years old: "Mrs Cronkite served as washerwoman for the officers until the close of the war when her husband was duly discharged . . . [and] had while in said service several children . . . ."[236]

Slaves were among the groups of camp followers. An advertisement posted by the colonel of the 3rd Maryland Regiment, in October, 1778, described a courageous woman who had run away from his unit:

Mulatto slave, named Sarah, but since calls herself Rachael; she took her son with her, a Mulatto boy named Bob, about six years old, has a remarkable fair complexion, with flaxen hair: She is a lusty wench, about 34 years old, big with child; had on a striped linsey petticoat, linen jacket, flat shoes, a large white cloth cloak, and a blanket, but may change her dress, as she has other cloaths with her. She was lately apprehended in the first Maryland regiment, where she pretends to have a husband, with whom she has been the principal part of this campaign, and passed herself off as a free woman.[237]

The presence of women in the ranks of the troops was only acceptable if they were willing to work. An entry in the orderly book of the 2nd Pennsylvania Regiment in 1778 states: "Should any woman refuse to wash for a soldier at the rate [specified by the army] he must make a complaint to the officers commanding the company . . . who [if they] find it proceeds from laziness or any other improper excuse he is immediately to dismiss her from the regiment. No women shall draw ration unless they make use of the endeavors to keep the men clean."[238]

At times women loaded muskets, or assisted cannon crews, in the heat of battle, but most spent their time providing mundane, but vital, services. They cooked, sewed, washed and mended clothes, and cared for the sick and wounded. They often scavenged for food, clothing and other supplies in local towns to help the soldiers survive in times of shortages. Their presence alone, as well as their ability to ease the tedious day-to-day burdens of the troops in the dreary camps and during exhausting marches, must been an enormous boon to morale.

General Washington tried not to publicly encourage women to follow the army, but over time he officially recognized their efforts by allotting them food. Each woman was authorized to receive half-rations each day "without whiskey." Children were allowed a quarter of a ration daily. Except for this allotment, the women were not compensated directly by the army in any other way for performing their essential services. They could, however, charge for performing special chores. Most often this entailed laundry services, and the frugal army precisely regulated the prices for this work. Overcharging soldiers for washing was always a serious offense, and numerous Regimental Orders make it clear that offenders would be ordered out of camp and not allowed to return. Although some officers feared that laundresses extorted the soldiers, they still recognized the need for the services washing women provided, and tried to regulate them to assure the quality of their work.

Laundry rates were fixed by officers at West Point in 1780 when they believed women were overcharging: "The following Prices be paid for

Washing; to the Women, who draw provisions, with their respective Companies; For a Shirt two Shillings; Woolen Breeches, Vest and Overalls, two Shillings, each; Linen Vest, and Breeches, one Shilling, each; Linen Overalls, one Shilling and Six Pence each; Stock, Stockings and Handkerchief, Six Pence each; the Women who wash for the Companies, will observes these regulations."[239] The equivalent of shilling in today's money is about fourteen cents, and five pence were equal to one shilling.

Life with the army was arduous and, at times, very unpleasant. Camp followers were frequently sent out onto battlefields to strip the dead for supplies. Following the Battle of Saratoga, American women were seen stripping the clothing from the dead and the dying.[240] After Burgoyne's defeat there, in November, 1777, his captive troops and their attendant camp followers were marched to Boston. Hannah Winthrop described the female British prisoners as they entered the city:

> *To be sure, the sight was truly astonishing, I never had the least Idea that the Creation produced such a sordid set of creatures in human Figure—poor, dirty, emaciated men, great numbers of women, who seemed to be the beasts of burthen, having a bushel basket on their back, by which they were bent double, the contents seemed to be Pots & kettles, various sorts of Furniture, children peeping thro the gridirons & other utensils, Some very young Infants who were born on the road; the women with bare feet, cloathed in dirty raggs such Effluvia filled the air while they were passing, had they not been smoaking all the time, I should have been apprehensive of being contaminated by them.*[241]

While carrying pots and pans, personal belongings, and small children, these women were expected to keep up with the pace of the marching soldiers, so they struggled so that they would not be left behind. The female followers and children had to walk alongside or behind the troops, as they were forbidden to ride in the supply wagons that followed the columns of soldiers. Continental Army General Orders of September 13, 1777 directed, "No woman under any pretence whatsoever is to go with the army, but to follow the baggage." There are accounts of women who stopped along the way to give birth, then hurriedly rejoined the columns in order to catch up to their husbands.

Traditionally, nursing was a female responsibility, so women could earn money and rations with the Continental Army by tending to the sick and wounded. Washington commented to General John Stark on August 5, 1778: "I cannot see why the soldier's women in Albany should be supported at public expense. They may get most extravagant wages for any kind of work in the country and to feed them, when that is the case, would be robbing the public and encouraging idleness. If they would come down and attend as nurses to the hospitals they would find immediate employment."

The army preferred female nurses to male ones, since every woman nurse freed one more man up for fighting. Washington's request for one nurse for each ten patients was authorized by the Continental Congress in 1775. At large winter encampments, such as Valley Forge, the sick and wounded could number between 5,000 and 7,000 men. Nursing was also service with pay, and it too generally meant caring for the troops by cleaning. The nurses usually came from nearby communities, and were paid two dollars each month and provided with full rations. These women were not trained professionals, so few of them could prescribe medicine or treat wounds. Their value was their ability to bathe patients and keep the facilities clean. Their efforts made an enormous contribution to sanitation during all years of the war. Nursing was hard, dangerous work and the women were subjected to constant exposure to diseases, such as smallpox and pneumonia. Germs, rather than enemy fire, were a constant danger, and women, like men, wound up in the military hospitals suffering from various sicknesses. They washed patients, swept floors, and emptied chamber pots. Without the help of these women both the American and British Armies would have had to hire or assign men to these chores-and that meant diminishing the ranks of soldiers.

Camp followers typically dressed in the simple clothes of the poorer classes—garments of wool, linen, and hemp, colored with natural dyes—since most were regarded as being at the bottom of the social scale. Although the common soldiers appreciated their services, officers generally belittled them. They were described by one officer as, "the ugliest in the world to be collected . . . some with two, others with three and four children, and few with none . . . the furies who inhabit the infernal region scan never be painted half so hideous as these women."[242]

In contrast to the American forces, camp followers were officially accepted by the British Army, and disembarked off the same transport ships that brought the troops to America. The British found that allowing wives with families to accompany their husbands or partners provided a significant incentive to enlistment. Many children were born during the American campaigns, and these transient families flourished in American.

The women of the British Army seemed to have been more rebellious and unruly than their American counterparts. They often dropped out of the line of march to plunder abandoned houses in nearby towns, and were accused of spreading smallpox into the camp when the homes they pillaged had been quarantined. Specific orders were issued to control this practice, specifying that the women suffer the same punishments as the soldiers. For instance, women were often flogged for selling liquor to the troops.

An entry in the orderly book of a Maryland Loyalist regiment, dated July 3, 1778, described how camp followers Mary Colfritt and Elizabeth Clark were tried for plundering. Mary Colfritt was found not guilty, but no compassion was shown toward Elizabeth Clark. She was sentenced to "Receive 100 Lashes on her Bear Back and to be drummed out of the army in the Most Publick manner." Women were often flogged for selling liquor to the troops.

General Washington was always uneasy about the image of his troops, especially at times when they were exposed to review at large public events. When the army marched through the capitol city of Philadelphia in 1777, he was embarrassed by the ragged camp followers who walked behind them, surrounded by pitiful children. He ordered, "Not a woman belonging to the army is to be seen with the troops on their march thro' the city."[243] But after the soldiers had passed, the defiant ladies appeared out of the alleys where they had been hiding, and brashly paraded down the main streets.

Molly Pitcher, as published by H. Mann, 1797.

SOME NOTABLE WOMEN OF THE REVOLUTION

Deborah Sampson

One of the most remarkable individuals of the Revolution was Deborah Sampson, a woman who impersonated a man and joined the Continental Army. The disguised young lady had little difficulty in doing this, since she was five-feet-seven inches tall, which was unusual for a female at the time. She was wounded twice in the fighting in the Hudson River Valley, but somehow managed to conceal her identity. She was finally discovered during the summer of 1783 by a physician who treated her when she became seriously ill. Nonetheless, after she recovered she was given an honorable discharge from the army. She returned to Massachusetts after the war, where she married a farmer and had three children.[244]

Molly Corbin (Photograph courtesy of West Point Museum Collection, United States Military Academy)

Two other women have been positively identified as having masqueraded as men to fight for their country. Sally St. Clare was a Creole girl who died with her husband during the British capture of Savannah in 1778. Ann Bailey of Massachusetts, known as "Samuel Gay," attained the rank of sergeant before being discovered and discharged for being a woman. There may have been other women who impersonated men to be of the service to their country, and in some clever way remain undetected. The real challenge for them, of course, was when they became injured and had to be examined by doctors. The easy part about concealing their gender was that soldiers slept in uniform and rarely bathed.

The following are some of the women who fought valiantly in the war, undisguised:

Margaret Cochran Corbin

Molly Corbin was the wife of John Corbin, an artilleryman in Captain Thomas Proctor's 1st Company of Pennsylvania Artillery. She became a camp follower at age twenty-one, and along with her husband, learned how to load and fire cannon. In November, 1776, she fought in the Battle at Fort Washington, New York, where she stood with the gun crew in the front line. During an assault by the Hessians, when her husband was mortally wounded, she took his place sponging and loading the cannon. Margaret herself was wounded by grape shot in the arm, chest and jaw. Captured by the British when the fort fell, she was transported by her captors to Philadelphia. After she was later released on parole, she returned to the army and was transferred to West Point.

Completely disabled from her wounds, she found life difficult. In 1779, the state of Pennsylvania granted her a lump sum of $30, and passed her case on to Congress. The Board of War was impressed with her service and bravery, and granted her half the monthly pay of a soldier in the Continental Army, along with a new set of clothes. This act made "Captain Molly" the first woman in the United States to receive a military pension from Congress. She remained at West Point until her death in 1800, and was buried there.

Mary Ludwig Hays

Hays accompanied her husband John, a member of the 1st Pennsylvania Artillery, into the Battle of Monmouth in 1778. During the fighting, she supplied water to the troops who were manning the cannon, so they called her "Molly Pitcher." Like Margaret Corbin, when her husband was wounded, she assumed his duties and assisted the other artillerymen. Shortly after the war ended, John died, and Mary remarried. Unfortunately, her second marriage did not last long. She received a small annual state pension and, prior to her death in 1832, supported herself as a servant, cleaning and painting houses, washing windows, and caring for children and sick people. She lived in the town of Carlisle, Pennsylvania and was well-liked by the people, even though she "often cursed like a soldier."[245] Some scholars believe "Molly Pitcher" was a generic term for all women of the army who may have assisted soldiers in this way.

Anna Maria Lane

Anna Maria accompanied her husband John when he enlisted in the Connecticut Line, though it is unclear if she did so as a camp follower or disguised as a soldier, since she was dressed like a man during the Battle of Germantown in 1777. After the war, Lane and her husband relocated to Virginia, where both eventually drew pensions for their service. According to the Virginia General Assembly records, Lane, ". . . in the garb, and with the courage of a soldier, performed extraordinary military services, and received a severe wound at the battle of Germantown."[246]

Sarah Osborn

After her first husband was killed in an early battle of the war, Sarah Mary Matthews married Aaron Osborn, a sergeant in the 1st New York Regiment, in 1780. She followed him while he was in the army and worked as a seamstress, washerwoman, and baker. She was with the American Army on the Yorktown Campaign in 1781. At the Siege of Yorktown, she cooked for her husband and four other soldiers, carried water, and tended wounded soldiers. Forty years later, in 1837, she applied for a pension under the first pension act for widows. As part of her claim, she submitted an astonishingly detailed autobiography of her Revolutionary War experiences. She described a chance encounter with

General Washington on the front lines, and provided a fascinating account of the siege and subsequent British surrender at Yorktown. Her pension application was approved, and she lived to enjoy it for another twenty years. Sarah Matthews died on April 26, 1858, at about the age of eighty-one.[247]

Camp followers shared the dangers with the troops on the battlefield, and were as likely to be killed or wounded as the soldiers. They were also exposed to the epidemics of smallpox and other diseases that swept through the camps. They went hungry when food was scarce, and suffered when shelter was not obtainable. The women who followed the army left the security of their homes to enter a difficult life filled with stress, danger and physically harsh conditions. They worked hard so their families could survive, and supported their men and the cause of independence. Some concealed their gender to fight in battle. Despite Abigail Adams's plea to ". . . remember the ladies . . .,"[248] the role of camp followers has not been recognized and celebrated as well as that of the men of the Revolution.

Chapter Seventeen

War and Punishment

The Politics of Punishment

General George Washington's image is typically that of a benevolent military leader who was obsessed with the welfare of his admiring troops. It seems out of character, therefore, that he took a hard line approach when it came to corporal punishment. He defined a suitable punishment for each type of offense, and often expressed frustration when he believed that a court's sentence was too light. Washington also insisted that the existing one hundred lash limit be raised to five hundred lashes after the Pennsylvania Line mutinied at Jockey Hollow in 1781, but this proposal met with strong opposition from Congress. Punishment limits were ultimately set by Congressional regulations, and even the Commander-in-Chief was not allowed the power to authorize an increase in sentences.

Crimes and punishments in the American military were defined by the Articles of War, regulations which govern the conduct of the country's military and naval forces. With the outbreak of the Revolutionary War, the Second Continental Congress adopted the "American Articles of War" on June 30, 1775. The document was written by John Adams, an attorney, and representative from Massachusetts. It was drawn largely from the codes governing the Royal Navy and the British Army. There were sixty-nine Articles of War, the purpose of which was to govern the conduct of the Continental Army. The first twelve articles described the behavior that was expected of members of the armed forces. Most of the others cover specific offences and define what kinds of punishments were to be meted out to offenders, or left to be decided by a courts-martial trial. The original articles went through several revisions, but formed the basis of what was followed until 1951, when the Uniform Code of Military Justice was instituted.

Any soldier who was arrested or confined had to be brought to trial within eight days, or as soon as a court could meet. When the army was on the move, it was impossible to obtain prompt hearings, but Washington insisted on trials being held without delay as soon as his forces settled into camp. This explains why such an excessive number of courts-martial and sentences appear in orderly books during winter encampments.

The dilemma facing American military leaders was that the existing military legal code did not specifically provide details for any punishment between one hundred lashes and death. When court-martials believed the level of punishment warranted more than a one hundred lash penalty, their hand was forced, and they had to recommend the death sentence. This oversight resulted in an inordinate amount of death penalties. Many officers agreed with Washington, when he said that this lash limit was inadequate for more serious crimes, so they tried to circumvent it. One way was by convicting for multiple offences committed during a single crime. For example, desertion, insubordination, and striking an officer resulted in three separate floggings. Another way to increase the severity of the sentence was for the hundred-stroke allowance to be spread out over four successive days. This would inflict the maximum pain by preventing healing of the inflicting wounds.

Washington did not have the power to unilaterally change the Articles of War. In 1781, Congress declined to raise the maximum penalty to five hundred strokes, so they directed him to allow a Board of General Officers to consider the dilemma. The board unanimously recommended to Congress that hard labor be the intermediate punishment. This commutation of the death sentence, when applied, usually meant serving aboard a Continental frigate for the duration of the war.

Although he supported corporal punishment throughout the war, Washington always insisted on restraint, ". . . lest the frequency of punishment should take off the good effects intended by it." He warned his generals "not [to] introduce capital executions too frequently," and reminded them that if executions were too common they would "lose their intended force and rather bear the Appearance of cruelty than Justice."[249]

Soldiers could be punished for the slightest offenses, but Washington mercifully discouraged any extra-legal punishments, or those not authorized by court-martial tribunals. With few exceptions, most sentences prescribed flogging. The average number of lashes in the Continental Army in 1775 had been thirty-nine, but in 1776 the maximum number allowed by Congress was increased to one hundred. This was a result of Washington's intense lobbying, and his opinion that thirty-nine might as well be zero for all the effect they had on insubordinate troops. It was considered unusually light by soldiers who joked that they would take another's thirty-nine for a pint of rum. The hundred lash maximum was officially followed throughout the war. Desertion to the enemy was considered a major offense, and offenders could be sentenced to death, or relegated to remain on a warship for the duration of the war.[250]

Washington and his officers were constantly attempting to balance harshness and leniency. They tried to define levels of punishment that could be effective in enforcing discipline and subordination, without provoking mass desertions or mutinies. Corporal punishment was the way to enforce absolute obedience and respect for rank, but it was of no value, and might inspire rebellion, if soldiers regarded it as too severe. When soldiers believed that sentences were too harsh they became mutinous, made threats, and openly voiced their discontent. The 1780-81 mutinies of Connecticut, Pennsylvania and New Jersey troops were, in part, caused by resentment of severe sentences on their comrades.

Although the death penalty was often imposed, in practice it was frequently counteracted by reprieves, so it was rarely carried out. Historian Caroline Cox analyzed executions, and estimated that only 17 to 30 percent of capital sentences actually resulted in executions.[251] A practical reason for this softening of death penalties was that each one meant the loss of one soldier, whereas offenders eventually recovered from floggings and lived to fight again. Washington would order ten men shot, then give nine a reprieve, moments before the execution. At Jockey Hollow, in January 1780, eleven soldiers were condemned to death for various crimes, and ten were pardoned.[252]

At times, General Washington pardoned large groups of offenders. On Independence Day, 1779, he released all prisoners who were under sentence of death. Mass pardons to deserters were also occasionally granted—Washington offered general pardons to this group four times. During the final days of the war, in 1782, he took the extraordinary step of offering a pardon to deserters who had joined the enemy.

The army clearly understood that men would be hesitant to enlist, and hence would more readily desert, if the word spread that harsh punishments were inflicted for relatively minor violations. Stories brought home by returning soldiers and deserters had a chilling effect on recruiting efforts. Reports that cruel and arrogant officers were handing out sentences of fifty lashes for cutting up a blanket, or urinating near huts, tended to discourage military service. Clemency was usually granted when leaders feared repercussions from other soldiers after seeing their comrades punished. Mercy was frequent, but not altruistic.

Generally, officers conformed to the official rules of punishment, combined with military traditions. Striking a soldier during drill was accepted, but sentencing men to flogging without following legal procedure was not tolerated. Washington enforced the one hundred lash limit imposed by Congress, even though he did not agree with it. Courts-martial sometimes tried to circumvent the limit by sentencing a prisoner to receive lashes for several crimes at a single trial. The Commander-in-Chief usually stopped this practice. A court martial in 1776 sentenced a soldier to receive three hundred lashes, one hundred for each of his offenses—desertion, fraudulent reenlisting to obtain bounty money, and perjury. Washington did not approve of the court's decision, and reduced the sentence to a one hundred lash total.

This all begs the question: How many lashes can a human being endure? It is unpredictable, and depends on such variables as the type of whips used, the number of knots on the whips, and the temperature of the day. The experience of the flogger also came into play. They were often trained by substituting a tree trunk for a body. They also learned how to avoid breaking the skin, and thus prolong consciousness. Several dozen lashes could cut a man to the bone, so Washington's proposal for five hundred lashes was, for all intents and purposes, a death sentence.

Sergeant Joseph Plumb Martin recounted that in 1776 a Connecticut sergeant was convicted of mutiny and sentenced to death. Although the prisoner received a pardon at the last moment, Martin describes the rebellious behavior of the troops: "But the sergeant was reprieved, and I believe it was well that he was, for his blood would not have been the only blood that would have been spilt: the troops were greatly exasperated, and they showed what their feelings were by their lively and repeated cheering after the reprieve, but more so by their secret and open threats before it." Martin also mentioned another incident where soldiers hurled stones at an executioner who was not properly respecting the body of his dispatched victim.[253]

While the punishments inflicted by the Continental Army seem barbarous by today's standards, British Army penalties were even more severe. Punishments of five hundred to one thousand lashes were allotted, surely enough to kill a man. In 1803, the maximum number of lashes that could be imposed was limited to 1,200, an amount that always permanently disabled or killed the offender. This maximum sentence was only inflicted nine or ten times by general courts-martial, but sentences of one thousand lashes were administered about fifty times; penalties of nine hundred, seven hundred, five hundred or three hundred lashes were more frequent. In the British Army and Navy, these brutal punishments were often inflicted for trivial offenses. One soldier was sentenced to seven hundred lashes for stealing a beehive. These draconian measures were abandoned in the early eighteenth century in England, but both military and civilian offenders were then shipped to the penal colony in Australia, where more whippings often awaited them.[254] During the era of the American Revolution, the British Army set the maximum number of lashes which could be ordered at 1,200.

A vast number of courts-martial proceedings appear in all orderly books of the Continental Army. For many regiments, the records are a continuous litany of crimes and penalties. Entries regarding desertion, insubordination, theft, the destruction of local civilian property, all followed by a variety of barbarous corporal punishments, are especially frequent.

Offending American officers received significantly lighter sentences than those meted out to enlisted men. This blatant discrimination and favoritism was modeled on the British Articles of War and was unquestioned, and in fact formally codified, under American military law. For the most part, soldiers were meted out physical punishment, while officers, when engaging in "ungentlemanlike behavior," were punished by reprimands or humiliation. For an "officer gentleman" of that time, public humiliation in front of civilians, as well as the army, was considered a truly severe punishment.

At times, General Washington broke all the rules, and insisted on prompt punishment without a hearing. At Valley Forge, a no-doubt exasperated Washington ordered: "Any soldier who shall be found discharging his musket without leave, and in an irregular manner, is to receive 20 lashes immediately on the spot." For straggling or falling out, wandering away or failing to keep up with the march, officers were authorized to order an immediate fifty lashes. For looting or plundering, Washington directed that each "delinquent [be] punished immediately on the spot with any number of lashes not exceeding one hundred."

The Commander-in-Chief also bypassed trials at Harlem Heights in September, 1776, when he declared: "Any Officer, or Soldier . . . who (upon the Approach, or Attack of the Enemy's Forces, by land or water) presumes to turn his back and flee, shall be instantly shot down, and all good officers are hereby authorized and required to see this done, that the brave and gallant part of the Army shall not fall a sacrifice to the base and cowardly part, or share their disgrace in a cowardly and unmanly Retreat." Ten days later, he ordered his generals to place officers at the rear of the battalions, with orders "to shoot any Officer, or Soldier, who shall presume to quit his Ranks, or retreat, unless the Retreat is ordered by proper Authority."[255]

Soldiers charged with minor offenses were tried by a regimental or garrison court, which consisted of five officers appointed by the commander of the units. More serious offenses were tried by a general court-martial, which was made up of thirteen officers. These could be convened by brigade and division commanders, generals, Congress, or the Board of War. If offenders believed that a member of the court was prejudiced against him, they were permitted a challenge, and if successful, another officer was compelled to take the place of the one rejected.

Judge advocates, officers with some legal training, often served as prosecutors during court-marital hearings. They called witnesses and presented evidence. Witnesses testified under oath and could be cross-examined by the accused. The accused could call his own witnesses to testify on his behalf, and was permitted to bring a lawyer or some other person into court to give him advice. Responsibility for the defense had to be done personally by the accused; the defense lawyer was not permitted to address the court. Given this scenario, cases were often lost due to incompetent pleading by terrified defendants.[256]

'TIL DEATH DO US PART

There is a vast difference in the frequency of capital punishment in the Revolutionary War, when compared to all wars that followed. At times, it seems as though this was a standard form of punishment. Desertion, spying, and mutiny were considered the worst crimes under the Continental Articles of June 30, 1775. These offenses carried a mandatory death penalty by either hanging or firing squad. The British Articles of War went much further than this, and invoked the death penalty for many other offences—mutiny, striking a superior, disobeying an order, deserting, sleeping while on guard, or raising a false alarm, In addition, corresponding with the enemy, plundering, misbehaving in battle, revealing the watchword, and forcing a commander to abandon his post to the enemy were all punishable by death. Executions were usually performed in front of the largest possible audience. The public display and simultaneous humiliation associated with this most extreme form of military punishment was meant to terrify anyone who might be contemplating these crimes.

Washington approved hundreds of death sentences during the war to demonstrate the strength and power of military authority. The first instance in which he did this came a year after he assumed command. The offender was Thomas Hickey, a member of his personal guard. Hickey attempted to enlist soldiers of the Continental Army into British service, and to start an uprising when the British Army arrived to occupy New York. There were rumors that his plot had also included the assassination of Washington. A court-martial sentenced Hickey to death, and Washington approved the sentence. Hickey was hanged on 28 June 1776, the day following his trial.[257]

In his diary, Surgeon James Thacher recorded the tragic punishment of men of the New Jersey Brigade who mutinied in January, 1781, at Federal Hill near Pompton, New Jersey. The men had not been paid in over a year, and lacked warm clothing. Many of them suffered from frostbite and scurvy. Most had enlisted for "three years or the duration of the war," and had assumed that these terms meant "whichever comes first." They soon learned that they would not be going home, and were instead compelled to continue serving until the war was over. Neglected by both military leaders and the Continental Congress, these men felt that they could not endure another winter. After their rebellion at Federal Hill was exposed and suppressed, three men were judged to be the ringleaders and were promptly sentenced to be shot:

Twelve of the most guilty mutineers, were next selected to be their executioners. This was a most painful task, being themselves guilty, they were greatly distressed with the duty imposed on them, and when ordered to load, some of them shed tears. The wretched victims, overwhelmed by the terrors of death, had neither time nor power to implore the mercy and forgiveness of their God, and such was their agonizing condition, that no heart could refrain from emotions of sympathy and compassion.

The first that suffered, was a sergeant, and an old offender, he was led a few yards distance and placed on his knees; six of the executioners, at the signal given by an officer, fired, three aiming at the head and three at the breast, the other six reserving their fire in order to dispatch the victim, should the first fire fail; it so happened in this instance; the remaining six then fired and life was instantly extinguished.

The second criminal was, by the first fire, sent into eternity in an instant. The third being less criminal, by the recommendation of his officers, to his unspeakable joy, received a pardon. This tragical scene produced a dreadful shock, and a salutary effect on the minds of the guilty soldiers. Never were men more completely humbled and penitent; tears of sorrow, and of joy, rushed from their eyes, and each one appeared to congratulate himself, that his forfeited life had been spared.[258]

Surgeon Thacher also vividly described a scheduled mass execution that occurred at Jockey Hollow in May, 1780. Eleven men were to be put to death, all but one for desertion. Their graves were dug, and eight of them were positioned on ladders with ropes around their necks. Thatcher's diary explains the outcome:

This was a most solemn and affecting scene, capable of torturing the feelings even of the most callous breast. The wretched criminals were brought in carts to the place of execution. Mr. Rogers, the chaplain, attended them to the gallows, addressed them in a very pathetic manner, impressing on their minds the heinousness of their crimes, the justice of their sentence, and the high importance of a preparation for death. The criminals were placed side by side, on the scaffold, with halters round their necks, their coffins before their eyes, their graves open to their view, and thousands of spectators bemoaning their awful doom. The moment approaches when every eye is fixed in expectation of beholding the agonies of death, the eyes of the victims are already closed from the light of this world. At this awful moment, while their fervent prayers are ascending to Heaven, an officer comes forward and reads a reprieve for seven of them, by the Commander-in-Chief.[259]

Washington ultimately issued reprieves to ten of the men. One man, James Coleman, was executed. He was considered the worst of the offenders because he had forged discharges enabling more than one hundred soldiers to leave the army, including himself.

AT THE LAST MINUTE

Although reprieves were common, they were held back until the last possible moment to maintain a high level of apprehension among the spectators. Executions were carried out with enough frequency that anxiety and doubt always existed in the ranks. One study found that of 225 death sentences, only forty to seventy-five were actually carried out.[260] On October 26, 1777, Washington ordered the execution of a man sentenced to death for desertion. Later the same day, he granted a postponement for three more days. Four days later he granted another stay. On November 1 he pardoned the man, saying that he expected him to ". . . show himself worthy of this act of clemency." Washington said that he hoped that "Gratitude to his Clemency will induce them in the future to behave like good soldiers."[261]

Ebenezer Wild, a corporal in the 1st Massachusetts Regiment, described a typical execution in his diary. The event ended favorably, but must have been suspenseful and agonizing for the witnesses: "The culprits marched to the place of execution to the strains of the 'Dead March,' with their coffins carried before them. The guilty men stood in front of their entire brigade. Their death sentences were read in a loud voice. Their graves were dug, the coffins were laid beside them, and each man was commanded to kneel beside his grave while the executioners received their orders to load, take aim and ___. At this critical moment a messenger rushed in with a reprieve which was read aloud."[262]

THE STING OF THE CAT

The ghastly task of inflicting lashes was assigned to the drummers and fifers under the direction of the regimental drum-major. This would have been a daunting task for boy musicians. However, a study of 292 drummers and fifers by Revolutionary War historian John U. Rees shows that most of the army's musicians were, in fact, more mature. He found that the men's average age was eighteen-and-a-half years. Boy musicians, while they did exist, were the exception rather than the rule, and it seems that the legend of early teenage or pre-teenage musicians in the Continental Army is a false one.[263]

The cat o' nine tails, commonly named "the cat," was a type of multi-tailed whip that originated as an implement for severe physical punishment for 18th century soldiers. (Image courtesy of Suzanne Adair)

The offender was tied to a tree or post, and encouraged to bite down on a piece of lead. The whip, formed of several small knotted cords, would cut through the skin of the naked back at every stroke. The stinging blows were usually absorbed in silence. To increase the severity of the penalty, the prescribed number of stripes was often administered in installments, so the flesh of the victim had time to become inflamed or to heal partially between each flogging. Although the number of stripes should have been related to the severity of the offense, in reality most offenders received the maximum of one hundred lashes for all types of transgressions.

In 1780, Surgeon Fisher described this method of flogging, together with the bravery and defiance of the soldiers subjected to this cruelty:

> *However strange it may appear, a soldier will often receive the severest stripes without uttering a groan, or once shrinking from the lash, even while the blood flows freely from his lacerated wounds. This must be ascribed to stubbornness or pride. They have however, adopted a method which they say mitigates the anguish in some measure, it is by putting between the teeth a leaden bullet, on which they chew while under the lash, till it is made quite flat and jagged. In some instances of incorrigible villains, it is adjudged by the court that the culprit receive his punishment at several different times, a certain number of stripes repeated at intervals of two or three days, in which case the wounds are in a state of inflammation, and the skin rendered more sensibly tender; and the terror of the punishment is greatly aggravated.*[264]

CRUEL AND UNUSUAL

Since the regulations did not provide any stipulation of the penalties between one hundred lashes and death, the void was filled by the creation of brutal new punishments. These extremely cruel practices were usually applied when nervous and frustrated officers found that conditions were out of control, and were terrified by the threat of rampant desertions or even mutiny.

Running the gauntlet. This punishment was carried out by assembling a large number of men in two parallel lines to form a type of narrow lane. This "gauntlet" was at times a half-a-mile long. The offender was stripped to the waist and forced to run down this path, while being struck with fists or lashed on his back by switches or sticks. Soldiers often tried to spare their comrades by applying light blows, and well-liked men had a better chance to make it through the line. If the prisoner could run quickly, the punishment would be less severe, so to slow a guilty man down a junior officer would hold a bayonet on his chest and back him through the line. The offender might also be pulled by a rope tied around his hands, or prodded along by a pursuer. Curiously, running the gauntlet was considered to be a more honorable form of punishment, far less of a dishonor than a flogging, since the person was not bound and could show his courage and stamina to others.

James Smith runs the gauntlet outside Fort Duquesne. In May. 1755, Smith was taken captive by Delaware Indians, and brought to Fort Duquesne at the Forks of the Ohio River. There he was forced to run a gauntlet before being given over to the French.
(Image courtesy of www.brooklineconnection.com)

The piquet. This brutal punishment required soldiers to be hung by one wrist from a tree and allowed to support their weight by standing on a wooden peg in the ground. The wrist was tied to the tree, while the sole or heel of the opposite bare foot was balanced on the peg. The top of the peg was narrow but not sharp enough to draw blood. To relieve pressure upon the foot, the prisoner had to hang by his wrist and could only be relieved by shifting weight back onto the foot. The piquet soon fell out of favor because it resulted in too many permanently disabling injuries.

Riding the Wooden Horse. This cruel punishment was usually inflicted for rioting or being drunk. A horizontal board was mounted on legs high enough so that the soldier was forced to sit astride it. With his hands tied behind his back, he could not touch the ground with his feet. Sometimes the upper edge of the board or pole was sharpened to intensify the cruelty and often heavy weights were tied to each foot. Punishments could last as long as three days with a fifty-pound weight tied to each foot for such small crimes as stealing chickens. The practice injured men so severely that it was discontinued early in the war.

Less Brutal and More Often Used. Offenders were often fined. A month's pay was the maximum permitted by the Articles of War. Orderly books are replete with sentences of fines for minor infractions. An ensign lost a month's pay for being absent without leave. A soldier found guilty of stealing, and of using abusive language to the quartermaster, was fined. A deserter was given fifteen lashes and fined one month's pay to defray the expense of apprehending him.[265]

The picquet did not require any sophisticated tools. All that was needed was to place a stake in the ground, and then tying the victim's thumb far above his head. The stake was never sharp enough to draw blood, but it was meant to be very painful. This torture method usually only lasted a few hours, but could be carried on indefinitely. (Image courtesy of www.medievality.com)

Confinement and restriction to a bread and water diet was also a common sentence for enlisted men. One man received this sustenance for six days for raising a disturbance in the streets. Another man received eight days of this punishment for threatening the life of a lieutenant. Another, a deserter, was given only bread and water for a full month.[266]

Noncommissioned officers frequently were "reduced to ranks" for their crimes. A deserter was demoted from corporal to private and fined one month's pay. A combination of these penalties was often imposed. A sergeant who abused and struck a captain was broken to private and flogged. For mutiny, a sergeant was reduced to private and fined, while a corporal involved in the same affair was whipped and demoted.[267]

Men were "drummed out" of the army to humiliate them. They were followed through camp by drummers and fifers and ejected at the front entrance. In one instance, a man convicted of theft was mounted on a horse without a saddle, his coat turned inside out, and his hands tied behind him as he was and drummed out of camp. A sergeant underwent the same process with a sign on his back that read "Mutiny."[268] This practice was continued in the Marine Corps until it was finally banned in 1962.[269]

Punishments were apparently personally painful to Washington. When considering the crime of mutiny he begged his men not to commit crimes that would force him to inflict punishments:

The General addresses himself to the feelings of every man in the army; exhorting one and all, to consult their own honor and welfare—to refrain from a conduct that can only serve to bring disgrace and destruction upon themselves, and ruin to their country—He intreats them not to sully the Arms of America, by their Infidelity, Cowardice or Baseness, and save him the anguish of giving Guilt the chastisement it demands—They

> *are engaged in the justest cause men can defend—they have every prospect of success, if they do their part—Why will they abandon, or betray so great a trust? Why will they madly turn their backs upon glory, freedom and happiness?"*[270]

He was always mystified as to why soldiers misbehaved. In a moment of frustration he complained, "Why will Soldiers force down punishment upon their own heads? Why will they not be satisfied to do their duty, and reap the benefits of it?"[271] Although he favored administering punishment for infractions, his objective was to have ". . . the business of the Army conducted without punishment."[272]

Chapter Eighteen

Caring for the Sick and Wounded

During the Civil War one man in five died, and in World War II one in forty American servicemen perished. In the Continental Army, while bearing arms in the War for Independence, one in four soldiers, about 30,000 Americans, died. Many more men succumbed to illness, rather than wounds. In the first year of the war, one in five died, not in battle, but from illness. For every ten men who joined the Continental Army, one perished miserably in a wretched hospital or in an abominable prison.

Many young Patriots took their last breath after exposure to unsanitary conditions, such as lying on filthy straw pallets. Their wounds were not mortal until becoming infected, especially after being sliced with the grimy instruments of surgeons. The few doctors who traveled with the army were equipped only with the surgical tools they could carry in their knapsacks, and if a wound was severe they performed the only useful procedure they knew—amputation. As a result, Continental soldiers prayed to be shot in the head, where death would be quick.

Medical issues had a major impact on the entire war. At that time, much was unknown about the causes and treatments of even common ailments. Therefore, anyone with even a rudimentary level of medical knowledge was accepted into the Continental Army to tend the vast numbers of sick and wounded. Army doctors had only a basic idea of how to treat wounds and diseases, and most had had no formal training, since there was no requirement for this to become a doctor. Smallpox and other diseases were another major issue, since these afflictions determined strategies and influenced battles. Over the course of the war, these diseases killed thousands of people. Smallpox was even used as a biological weapon when infected people were sent to infiltrate enemy camps.

Each regiment appointed its own physician; such men were usually local doctors who skills were of varying degrees. Fewer than three doctors in the entire country had a medical degree. A few had graduated from the ten-year-old Philadelphia Medical College, while others were graduates of European medical schools in France and Germany. These schools were expensive, and had daunting admission requirements, including knowledge of classical literature and other scholarly subjects. Most students had never been exposed to a live patient, and were routinely instructed in the inaccurate practices of the time. Despite this deficient training, Revolutionary War surgeons did a commendable job of attempting to save lives. Most were brave, honest, and well-intentioned, but the unhygienic conditions and shortages in medical supplies overwhelmed them.

Doctors on both sides cared for both friend and foe. After the Battle of Monmouth Court House the British forces evacuated, but left behind forty-four severely wounded officers and men, with only one surgeon to tend them. They were taken to nearby Tennant Church, which was being used as a makeshift hospital, and were cared for by American medical personnel alongside their wounded opponents. Soldiers killed on the battlefield on both sides were collected by the Americans and buried together in the Tennant Churchyard.

Illustration of surgeon treating wounded soldier (Courtesy of US National Park Service Museum Collections)

AN ARMY CRIPPLED BY DISEASE

Disease first began affecting the outcome of campaigns during America's major opening offensive. In 1775-1776, American forces had to abandon their planned invasion of Canada, and retreat south from Quebec, a distance of over three hundred miles. While they were not militarily defeated, they were decimated by disease. On this particular expedition, a third of the men in some regiments died of smallpox.[273] John Adams described the condition of the retreating American soldiers when they gathered at Crown Point at the south end of Lake Champlain: "Our Army at Crown Point is an object of wretchedness to fill a humane mind with horror; disgraced, defeated, discontented, diseased, naked, undisciplined, eaten up with vermin; no clothes, beds, blankets, no medicines; no victuals, but salt pork and flour."[274]

The army was crippled and hindered by disease in nearly every campaign during the remaining seven years of the war. One of several reasons that Washington hesitated to approve the plan for the Yorktown Campaign, the final decisive operation of the war, was that epidemics were sweeping through the Southern states. After the victory there, he feared the army would fall prey to disease, so he rushed his troops north to the more healthful regions of the Hudson River Valley.

There were only nine army hospitals in the northeast in March, 1780. Death rates were high in these primitive facilities, with their close quarters, poor sanitation and contaminated food and water supplies. Only small amounts of medical supplies were available, most likely smuggled in from the West Indies, supplied by the French, or captured from the British. Food and clothing shortages added to the problem. Medical care deteriorated even further in the last years of the war, when completely untrained people were assigned to care for injured and sick soldiers. Medical supplies continued to be scarce, and pain killers of any kind were rare. The dead were carried out of the primitive hospitals and replaced by others, without changing straw or sheets or applying any types of sanitizing precautions.

Military leaders were desperate and confused over the uncontrollable losses; they rationalized by attributing illnesses to causes they could understand. Illness from hunger, cold and homesickness was referred to as "Army Sickness." Major General Philip Schuyler stated early in the war, "Of all the specifics ever invented there is none so efficacious as a discharge, for as soon as their faces turn homeward nine out of ten are cured."[275] Dr. Benjamin Rush, Surgeon General of the Middle Department of the Continental Army, maintained that the mass desertions and withdrawals of entire New England regiments were caused by homesickness. As a prevention against illness in harsh weather, a half-gill of rum was issued to the men each day, and they were cautioned against drinking "new cider" (non-alcoholic unfiltered apple juice).[276] During the dark days at Valley Forge this remedy was suggested by an army doctor: "Mutton and grog, proved to be as useful as anything to aid in resisting the germs of disease that everywhere threatened the camp with pestilence."[277]

The complete lack of understanding of the causation of illness led to exposure to smallpox, typhoid, dysentery, typhus, pneumonia and tuberculosis. Whooping cough and measles were often fatal. Boils and other skin infections resulted in gangrene and "bodyitch" caused by lice spread over the entire body, which soon developed into impetigo.

Floors of huts where soldiers lived during the winters were often below ground level, cold and damp. Rats, mice, cockroaches and other pests quickly invaded these crude dwellings. Latrines were rarely available, and human waste was frequently deposited nearby. This occurred even where strict orders prohibiting the practice were written in orderly books. At the winter encampment at Jockey Hollow a private was given one hundred lashes for urinating in the living area. After animals were slaughtered for food, their remains were left unburied, or even thrown into water sources.

Sanitation was a complete mystery to the army. Purification of huts was attempted by filling dwellings with wood smoke, burning tar fumes or sulfur from burnt cartridges. Vinegar was sprinkled over the floor and furnishings. Washington personally ordered huts sanitized by burning the powder of blank musket cartridges each day or by burning pitch or tar.[278]

BETTER A BLAST TO THE HEAD - THE DOOMED WOUNDED

At times wounded men lingered on battlefields for days before being assisted. It was standard practice to amputate arms and legs if bones were shattered. Those with stomach wounds usually died in hours, while others lingered in agony for a few days. The use of unsterilized instruments and dirty dressings caused the mortality rate to escalate.

In his pension application, Corporal John Adlum described the experience of a comrade after the devastating American defeat at Fort Washington in Manhattan in 1776: "Ens. Jacob Barnitz of Stake's company was shot through both legs and lay on the field of battle all night naked, having been stripped by the Hessians or their trulls [prostitutes]. He was taken up the next day after the battle by those appointed to bury the dead and taken to the hospital in New York, where one leg was cured, and he would not suffer the British surgeons to amputate the other. He carried the ball a little below his knee for thirty-two years when it became so painful he was obliged to have his leg amputated above his knee."

Musket balls, or the bayonet, caused most wounds. In cases where a limb could not be saved, an amputation was performed. This procedure was done without any attempt at sterilization or anesthesia, except possibly rum, brandy or a tobacco juice concoction, if any of these was available. All too often, however, the patient simply "bit the bullet." A lead musket ball or a wood stick was given to the person to bite down on, and to stifle his screams. Two surgeon's assistants held the soldier as the process was undertaken. The surgeon used a small bone saw to remove arms, and a larger one to remove a leg above the knee. A leather tourniquet was placed above the point of amputation, and the surgeon cut down to the bone of the damaged limb, and moved arteries aside with curved needles. A leather retractor was placed on the bone, and then pulled back to allow the surgeon a clear area to continue. Arteries were buried in the skin flap, which was then sutured. The end result was bandaged with white linen cloth, and a wool cap was placed on the stump.

During this barbarous operation the majority of soldiers went into shock. Regimental surgeons were not well-trained at the beginning of the war, but they soon learned to work fast. Some were able to perform an amputation in less than forty-five seconds. After losing a quantity of blood from the injury, the patient was further weakened by being bled. Surgeons mistakenly believed that this procedure would prevent further disease. In the end, only about 35 percent of amputees survived. Most died of gangrene or from infection that rapidly spread throughout their bodies.

The scene after a battle was appalling. When the battle of Guilford Courthouse ended, the dead and dying were scattered over a thousand acres. Shortly after the fighting was over, a torrential rain fell, and finding and treating the wounded became increasingly difficult. There were few doctors present, and little medicine of any kind. Quakers other civilians in the area, along with British surgeons, cared for the wounded of both sides. Houses within an eight-mile radius of Guilford Courthouse were commandeered as hospitals. Arms and legs were amputated, lead balls extracted, and broken bones set. Many wounded died within the week from infections and blood poisoning. A smallpox epidemic then swept through both armies and claimed yet more lives.

THE POLITICS OF MILITARY MEDICINE

The Continental Congress was so overwhelmed by other issues that little attention was given to establishing a military medical organization. This neglect was compounded by rivalry among the top medical officers, congressional politics, and corruption by lower level medical officials. They continuously argued about the correct chain of command, and most other issues. The result was that the army medical staff was a mix of militia, civilians, and regular army personnel.

Dr. John Morgan, a famous surgeon, was the first Director General. He was a bitter rival of Dr. William Shippen, Director of Hospitals for the Continental Army, a precursor to the Surgeon General of the US Army. Shippen served from April 11, 1777, to January, 1781. He was eventually court-martialed for misappropriating supplies intended for recovering soldiers, and for underreporting deaths. Other medical personnel did a brisk business selling medical discharges.

General Washington was appalled at the lack of training and the poor level of competency of the army's medical personnel, and attempted to require surgeons and surgeon's mates to take examinations to qualify. Various states fought this screening of their political appointees, so no action was taken until 1782, a year before the war ended, when Congress established a board to scrutinize the qualifications for military surgeons. Washington also persuaded Congress to have surgeons report the number of casualties, so that commanders could separate the dead and wounded from those who had deserted.

Because of the inconsistent procedures of regimental surgeons, Director General Morgan was forced to issue these incredibly rudimentary regulations on how to handle combat casualties:

- Dress the wound by a hill 3,000 to 5,000 yards to the rear of the battlefield. (To keep patients and caregivers beyond the range of artillery and musket fire.)

- Regimental surgeons are to be stationed with their men when in a fort or on a defense line. (To prevent them from being too far away from the action).

- Give emergency care only. In the heat of battle, amputation or any capital operation is best avoided.

Emergency duties to be carried out directly on the battlefield include:

- Stop bleeding with lint and compresses, ligatures, or tourniquets. Remove foreign bodies from the wound. Reduce, or set, fractured bones to realign them. Apply dressings to wounds. If the dressings are too tight, blood flow is decreased and will increase inflammation and excite a fever. If the dressings are too loose, fresh bleeding may recur or set bones may displace. If you move someone and the bones are not set tightly enough, the bones will slip out of alignment.

- Before each battle, check with the regimental officers for men to carry off the wounded. A supply of wheelbarrows, other convenient biers, or whatever transport is available, is to be secured in order to carry off the wounded.

DISEASE AND VACCINATION

The prevalence of smallpox during the Revolution posed a very real danger to the success of the war. The risk of this deadly disease was a critical factor in military decision-making, and impaired American efforts in the campaigns of 1775 and 1776. Smallpox was a major factor at the Siege of Boston and during the American invasion of Canada. Rumors over the British use of biological warfare, controversy over inoculation, and attempts to control the spread of smallpox all had a major impact on the progress of the war. Recruitment was diminished, desertions increased, and commanding officers were forced to continue operations with decimated forces. This invisible killer affected civilian populations as well.

Similar to the Native Americans, the men of the Continental Army came mostly from rural areas, and had little immunity to the disease. Because the population was less dense, Americans often reached adulthood without coming into contact with the smallpox virus. Men sometimes deserted for fear of contracting the deadly disease when it erupted in a camp. In 1775, both Washington's army outside Boston and the British Army inside the city had their options limited by so many of their men becoming sick.

In Europe, smallpox was less of a menace; most people had been exposed to the disease at an early age, so the majority of the adult population was immune. This gave the British Army a major advantage. Most of its troops had already had the disease previously, or had been inoculated. However, the Crown forces were not completely immune. Smallpox has been cited as the reason that the British did not continue to advance inland after they won the major opening battle of the war at Bunker Hill.[279]

FIGHTING INFECTION - INOCULATION

One of the most important advances in medicine during the American Revolution was the initiation of inoculation in the American Army. George Washington ordered everyone who had not previously been inoculated, or had survived smallpox, to report for inoculation. The procedure in that era was known as *variolation*, a method of intentionally exposing someone to a mild form of the smallpox virus (Edward Jenner would not develop the smallpox vaccine until 1796). Variolation was an inoculation in which pus from an infected person was injected under the skin of an uninfected one. The process had some risks. Those who had received inoculation would be contagious for a few weeks, so they were isolated. Others could actually die of the disease that they were trying to avoid. Apprehensive soldiers resisted his controversial order, but despite the uproar, it reduced the rate of smallpox deaths in the Continental Army from 17 to 1 percent.[280]

John Adams, a delegate to the Continental Congress, had been inoculated against smallpox in 1764, but it had made him extremely ill. In the summer of 1776 Adams' wife Abigail informed him that she and their four children were going to be inoculated. John Adams wrote back saying that he was terrified, but because of the urgent activities at Congress he could not be with them in Boston during that critical time. He requested daily updates. Fortunately, the inoculations for the Adams family were successful. One of the four children inoculated was John Quincy Adams, who later became the sixth president of the United States.

As commander, Washington had seen first-hand the tragic effect of the disease on both the civilian and military population. This prompted him to convince his wife, Martha, to be inoculated in 1776. She underwent the procedure in Philadelphia, where she was treated by Dr. William Shippen. Washington wrote to his brother John from Philadelphia, "Mrs. Washington is now under inoculation in the city; and will, I expect, have the smallpox favourably, this is my 13th day and she has had very few Pustules; she would have wrote to my sister but thought it prudent not to do so, notwithstanding there could be little danger in conveying the Infection in this manner." Martha underwent a three week quarantine following the procedure, and Washington remained with her for about a week in the rooms they had rented in a local inn.[281]

Washington was initially hesitant to inoculate the troops, as such a large scale effort presented problems. He feared that his army would be vulnerable during the short period they were incapacitated following the procedure, noting that, "Should we inoculate generally, the enemy, knowing it, will certainly take advantage of our situation." He also feared that those who were temporarily disabled might spread the disease.

Faced with spreading epidemics, delays in troop movements, and the fear of contracting smallpox from potential enlistees, it finally became clear that the spread of smallpox through the ranks would kill more men than the enemy. After more than 100,000 people in North America died as a result of smallpox epidemics, Washington made the controversial decision in 1777 to have all of his soldiers inoculated. In January, he wrote to Dr. William Shippen, the Director of Hospitals for the Continental Army, "We should have more to dread from [smallpox] than from the Sword of the Enemy." John Adams concurred, and in April, wrote to his wife, Abigail, that "Disease has destroyed Ten Men for Us where the Sword of the Enemy has killed one." Adams also expressed his hope that the situation would improve, "We have at last, determined a plan for the Sick, and have called into Service the best abilities in Physick and Chirurgery [surgery], that the Continent affords."

By February, Washington had designed a plan to deal with the disease. He wrote to John Hancock on February 5, 1777, "The small pox has made such Head in every Quarter that I find it impossible to keep it from spreading thro' the whole Army in the natural way. I have therefore determined, not only to inoculate all the Troops now here, that have not had it, but shall order Docr Shippen to inoculate the Recruits as fast as they come in to Philadelphia. They will lose no time, because they will go thro' the disorder while their cloathing Arms and accoutrements are getting ready." He did not wait for a reply from Congress; he issued orders to begin mass inoculation the very next day.

Although the procedure produced only a mild infection, soldiers could be sick for days, so all recruits who had not already contracted the disease were inoculated and quarantined in special camps, before they were combined with the main army. Hospitals were set up to perform mass inoculations, and the program was conducted with great secrecy. Thousands of soldiers were inoculated at Valley Forge in the winter of 1777-1778, but as the year began in the dreary camp 3,000 to 4,000 troops still had still not been vaccinated, so in

January, 1778, the program was expanded. Washington's personal involvement in this massive health issue is one of his most impressive accomplishments of the war.[282] Washington had his own immunity to smallpox, acquired in the "natural way." He survived a case of smallpox when still a teenager and the pock marks on his face were a testament to this.

The program was highly successful; smallpox was no longer a major problem for the remainder of the war. It is interesting to hypothesize that if smallpox inoculations had been performed earlier, the outbreak among Continental soldiers in Quebec could have been avoided. This could have ended the Revolutionary War and allowed Canada to be annexed by the United States.

THE HORROR OF HOSPITALS

A soldier's chances of dying on the battlefield during the American Revolution have been calculated at about 2 percent; but this rose to 25 percent if he was admitted to a crowded army hospital.[283] Private William Hutchinson of the 2nd Delaware Regiment described this scene at a hospital after the Battle of Germantown, Pennsylvania in 1777: "[I] had the occasion to enter the apartment called the hospital and where necessary surgical operations were performing and there beheld a most horrid sight. The floor was covered with human blood; amputated arms and legs lay in different places, in appalling array, the mournful memorial of a most unfortunate and fatal battle, which indeed it truly was."[284]

Military hospitals were houses of disease and infection during the Revolutionary War, and confinement therefore aggravated the problems of the sick and wounded. Men admitted to hospitals for battle wounds usually died from illnesses that they were exposed to there. Typhus spread quickly in the crowded, unsanitary conditions. Dr. Benjamin Rush stated: "Hospitals are the sinks of human life in the army. They rob the United States of more citizens than the sword."

On the long retreat of American troops south from Canada in 1776, Anthony Wayne, a colonel at the time, wrote to General Horatio Gates from Fort Ticonderoga: "Our hospital, or rather house of carnage, beggars all description, and shocks humanity to visit. The cause is obvious; no medicine or regimen on the ground suitable for the sick; no beds or straw to lay on; no covering to keep them warm, other than their own thin wretched clothing."[285]

Medical treatment facilities had to travel with the fighting forces on campaigns, advancing or retreating with the army. Mobile field facilities became known as "Flying Hospitals." The wounded were carried or hobbled into these huts, tents, or at times barns, homes, colleges, and churches. Attempts were made to place them in relatively secure areas away from any action. They were equipped with a few emergency beds, and a surgeon's table. These were the crude precursors to the M.A.S.H. units in recent wars.

General Hospitals were more permanent, and were located in public and private buildings. Major facilities were located in Providence and Newport in Rhode Island, Peekskill, Fishkill, and Albany in New York, Hackensack, Fort Lee, Elizabeth, Morristown, Perth Amboy, New Brunswick, and Trenton in New Jersey, Bethlehem, Bristol, Reading, Lancaster, Manheim, and Philadelphia, Pennsylvania, and Alexandria and Williamsburg (the Governor's Palace) in Virginia. The dead were buried in unmarked graves in grounds adjoining the hospitals. The Continental Army managed these sites, and often assigned soldiers who were not suited for military life to work in the hospitals.

Many of the wounded died in transit. After the battle of Brandywine, in October, 1777, the retreating army was the shield which protected the six hundred wounded while they were being evacuated. It was a torturous forty-mile-long trip to Valley Forge in hard-riding open wagons, sleds, carts and wheelbarrows. The trip was especially hard on those carried on stretchers made of muskets connected with coat and blankets. After the Battle of the Short Hills in June, 1777, in present day Scotch Plains and Metuchen, New Jersey, the British counted thirty-seven rebel wagons filled with wounded. At the time, these wagons were laboring up a hill through a pass to reach the secure route behind the first ridge of the Watchung Mountains that led to the Middlebrook Encampment. Even today local historians refer to the pass as "Bloody Gap."

General von Steuben, the ubiquitous Inspector General, published the first Army Regulations dealing with health care in 1778 and 1779. He stressed compassion, the importance of cleanliness, and the duty of regimental commanders to preserve the health of troops. To prevent overzealous officers from prematurely sending wounded men back to fight, he authorized regimental surgeons to determine when a soldier had sufficiently recovered from his illness to resume his duties: "There is nothing which gains an officer the love of his soldiers more than his care of them under the distress of sickness: it is then that he has the power of exerting his humanity in providing them every comfortable [necessity] and making their situation as agreeable as possible. When a soldier has been sick he must not be put on duty until he has recovered sufficient strength, of which the surgeon shall be the judge. The surgeons are to remain with their regiments, as well on a march as in camp, that in case of sudden accidents they may be at hand to apply the proper remedies."[286]

In remote regions conditions were worse. There was no hospital at Peekskill, New York during a period when 5,000 men were stationed there. The hospital at Albany, New York, in 1781, was completely without supplies except for bad vinegar, and patients went without food for days at a time. Those who could walk were encouraged to beg for food in the town. In 1780, no military hospital at all existed in the entire state of Virginia.

During the Southern Campaign in 1781, General Nathanael Greene reported that the few army hospitals that did exist were "shocking to humanity." He appealed to Congress for assistance: "Without medicine and destitute of stores and every article of necessity to render the sick comfortable, for want of a surgeon and supplies soldiers were being eaten up by maggots." He stated that sickness among troops in the South was over five times that in the North. He never received a response.[287]

DISEASE AS A WEAPON

Many American leaders, including Franklin and Washington, believed that the British had a plan to deliberately spread smallpox in the Continental Army. When a commission appointed by Congress sent reports on the war to Benjamin Franklin in France, they commented favorably on the mass inoculation initiated by Washington. They also reported that the program would, ". . . frustrate a Cannibal Scheme of our Enemies who have constantly fought us with that disease by introducing it among our troops."[288] Suspicion of a covert British effort to spread disease among the American troops remained persistent throughout the war.

As mentioned, smallpox was a major cause for the failure of American forces to capture Quebec. It was rumored that General Guy Carleton, a British commander, sent people infected by smallpox to the American camp. Thomas Jefferson was convinced of this and wrote: "I have been informed by officers who were on the spot, and whom I believe myself, that this disorder was sent into our army designedly by the commanding officer in Quebec."[289]

The evidence against the British is convincing. Just before Virginia's last royal governor, Lord Dunmore, departed from his base at Norfolk to exile in England in 1776, the *Virginia Gazette* reported that he had infected two slaves and sent them ashore in order to spread smallpox, ". . . but it was happily prevented."[290]

When the American Siege of Boston began in April, 1775, smallpox was raging among civilians there. Washington suspected that some of them were leaving the city on purpose, in hopes of spreading the disease among the Continentals. He believed that the British had deliberately infected people with smallpox, and then they sent them out to mix with the American forces. At first Washington and his staff thought these reports were ridiculous, but he soon wrote to John Hancock, "The information I received that the enemy intended Spreading the Small pox amongst us, I could not Suppose them Capable of—I now must give Some Credit to it, as it has made its appearance on Several of those who last came out of Boston." In December deserters arriving at the American lines reported that "Several persons are to be sent out of Boston that

WILLIAMSBURG, *June* 15.

WE learn from Gloucefter, that Lord Dunmore has erected hofpitals upon Gwyn's ifland; that his old friend Andrew Sprowle is dead, and that they are inoculating the blacks for the fmallpox. His Lordfhip, before the departure of the fleet from Norfolk harbour, had two of thofe wretches inoculated and fent afhore, in order to fpread the infection, but it was happily prevented.

The Virginia Gazette reported the failed smallpox plot of Lord Dunmore.

have been inoculated with the small-pox" with the intention of spreading the infection. A Boston physician admitted "that he had effectually given the distemper among those people" who were leaving the city.[291]

It is evident that the British had few qualms about infecting the American army, or the population in general, with smallpox. In 1777 a British officer, Major Robert Donkin, published a small book in New York entitled *Military Collections and Remarks*. In a footnote he offered this suggestion: "Dip arrows in matter of smallpox, and twang them at the American rebels, in order to inoculate them; This would sooner disband these stubborn, ignorant, enthusiastic savages, than any other compulsive measures. Such is their dread and fear of that disorder!"[292]

When the British expedition arrived in Virginia in 1781, General Alexander Leslie plotted with Cornwallis to spread disease among the Americans. He planned to send "about 700 Negroes down the River with the Small Pox, the Rebell Plantations." It is not known if he carried out his plan.[293]

In the last years of the war, the British began reneging on their promise of freedom. African Americans, who had staked their lives on British promises of liberty, were forced to return to their masters. American leaders, however, suspected the enemy had an ulterior motive, and insisted that the British had sent a large number of Negroes with small pox from Yorktown for the purpose of communicating the infection. If the British were trying to spread smallpox to the American Army at Yorktown they were too late—the Patriots there were immune, since they had been inoculated in 1777 and 1778.

Although the army was successful in eradicating smallpox, many other health issues had a major impact during the Revolutionary War. Doctors' knowledge of medical issues was very basic and generally faulty, and many lacked any formal training. There were few hospitals, surgical instruments were rudimentary, and much was yet to be discovered about the causes and treatments of common ailments. Living in close quarters with poor sanitation and hygiene, eating contaminated food and drinking from foul water supplies, all contributed to the rampant spread of disease in army camps.

Although medical practices were appalling during the Revolutionary War, they did result in some long range positive effects. Basic principles of sanitation and hygiene were initiated, and the importance of smallpox inoculation was accepted. A policy for battlefield treatment and evacuation of the wounded was established, and a military medical department created. However, significant and adequate advancements in the practice of surgery and anesthesia for the army did not occur until many years in the future.

A General Return of the Sick and Wounded in the Military Hospitals belonging to the Army commanded by his Excellency

Places where military hospitals are open	Admitted during the Month	Discharged during the Month	Deserted during the Month	Dead during the Month	Remaining in hospital March 1					
					Convalescant	Wounded	Sick of Acute Diseases	Sick of Chronic diseases	Venereal	Total
Yellow Springs	21	10	-	1	5	4	-	45	1	55
Philadelphia	12	69	-	-	8	-	-	1	-	9
Danbury	-	-	-	-	17	6	3	4	-	30
Trenton	1	2	-	-	3	1	6	1	1	12
Pluckemin	32	32	3	2	12	1	8	40	29	90
Baskingridge	15	10	-	3	5	2	14	10	2	33
Fishkill	-	-	-	-	30	2	6	47	10	95
Albany	4	3	3	1	6	8	13	44	15	86
Camp (Morristown)	-	-	-	-	128	9	123	246	57	563
	85	127	6	7	214	33	172	439	115	973

General George Washington, from Feb. 2 to March 1. 1780.[294]

Chapter Nineteen

Demobilization and Abandonment

Of the two-and-a-half million Americans who fought in Iraq and Afghanistan, an estimated 900,000 of them are being treated for post-traumatic stress disorder, as well as other service-connected disabilities. Revolutionary War soldiers shared the same emotional strains and physical dangers as the soldiers of today, and in surprisingly similar conditions. Overextended armies fought in brutal places over vast regions, with the pervading insecurity of being unable to tell the enemy from the people they were defending. Morale waned in the largely volunteer force, with multiple deployments, vacillating public support, and brave deeds overlooked.

Unlike most other American wars, there was no support system for the returning veterans of the War for Independence. Worst yet, an ungrateful public did not credit the soldiers of the Continental Army with achieving the astonishing victory that created the new nation. Impoverished and disabled, the Yankee Doodles were sent home, and did not receive support of any kind until many years after the war had ended.

Few facts remain about the postwar problems of the surviving Patriots and their readjustment to civilian life, compared to all other wars waged by America. These men deserve to be remembered with those who took up arms during the Civil War, the shell-shocked doughboys of World War I, the "Greatest Generation" of World War II, the silent men of the Korean Conflict, and the tragically maligned veterans of the Vietnam War.

In October, 1782, General Washington moved his Northern Army to the New Windsor Cantonment near Newburgh, New York for the winter. Rumors of peace were circulating as the fighting subsided, but an attack by the British, who held New York City, only sixty miles south, was still a possibility. Thus, a wartime state of readiness prevailed in the camp, and the drilling and training of the troops for a potential spring offensive continued through the winter months.

In November, 1782, Preliminary Articles of Peace were approved in Paris.[295] The agreement provided for the release of all prisoners on both sides after a final treaty was ratified. Both parties promised to do so within six months, or sooner. This caused Washington to become apprehensive. The British still had time to reopen hostilities. Following the ceasefire, 26,000 Crown troops still occupied New York City, Charleston and Savannah, with naval support plying the waters off the coast. The French army and navy had already sailed for home, so the outnumbered Patriots at New Windsor were on their own. The impending release of 6,000 British prisoners who would rejoin their units added to Washington's apprehension.

On March 18, 1783, news that the Continental Congress had agreed to a cessation of hostilities and a possible peace treaty reached the Cantonment. Since Washington feared the enemy still might strike, he waited a month before making any official announcement to the troops. It was a momentous occasion when the news was finally released, and a time for great celebration. All regiments were formed up on the parade ground and given a generous ration of liquor. A toast was made to "perpetual peace and happiness for the United States of America."[296] Although the Commander-in-Chief issued ceasefire orders a week later, this did not end the war.

SHOULD WE LET THEM GO HOME?

The men anticipated that the disbanding of the Continental Army would follow the ceasefire, but with the possibility of British prisoner releases it would have been imprudent to break up the army. Congress decided that the War Men, the soldiers who had enlisted for the duration of the war, would be required to remain until a binding treaty of peace had been ratified. The prospect of holding the restless men at the Cantonment was also risky. The unpaid soldiers grew edgy to the point of mutiny, and with its treasury empty, Congress was unable to placate them in any way. Regular payouts to the troops stopped in 1777, and few paydays followed after that time. Discussions to provide each departing soldier with three months' pay soon stalled, and the now-disgruntled armed forces had every right to rebel against civil authority.

General Washington now faced a tough choice. By holding the army at New Windsor, he risked a mutiny. But how could he allow it to disband when British occupation forces still posed a threat? At this critical point, he conceived a brilliant strategy. He recommended to Congress that the army be granted "furloughs," not final discharges, and be permitted to leave on a gradual basis. Furloughing meant that the soldiers could return home but could be recalled at any time. This approach had two huge advantages: the troops from nearby states could hastily be recalled if the British decided to resume the war, and a diminishing, but sufficient, core of American troops would remain at New Windsor. This site would be a safe haven until all the British forces sailed away because it was on the vital Hudson River, and within striking distance of New York. Finally, in May, 1783, fearing a riot in the ranks at the Cantonment, Congress agreed to allow furloughing of the "War Men." The furloughed soldiers would not be paid, but they were promised a discharge when a final treaty of peace was concluded. This did not occur until January 14, 1784.

During those tense interim months, the irritated soldiers at New Windsor were yearning to leave for home. Many had assumed that the war would be over after the victory at Yorktown a year-and-a-half earlier. After news of the impending peace treaty spread through the ranks, the men suspected that they were being held unnecessarily. They disregarded orders, became defiant, and taunted their officers. The low morale and lack of discipline led to widespread drunkenness and massive desertion. To maintain control, daily courts-martial were promptly held to punish offenders. Extra guards were posted to keep the agitated men from roaming out of the camp at night in order to leave or plunder local farms, and the sale of liquor by sutlers was restricted. The men were treated as virtual prisoners, and memories of their glorious accomplishments began to fade. With the cessation of hostilities, a relaxed American public began to regard their army with suspicion, and as a drain to the economic system.

Getting back pay and going home were endless topics of discussion for the discouraged men who gathered around the huts. A tense General Washington wrote to Alexander Hamilton about his unruly troops: "We are obliged at this moment to increase out guards to prevent rioting and the insults the officers meet with when attempting to hold them to their duty."[297] General Orders' entries followed: "Until further order there is to be a camp guard mounted by each Brigade in this Cantonment for the preservation of good order." Although American fighting men had matured into disciplined, professional soldiers, they never had practiced the blind obedience of European soldie[illegible] Most were realistic, and expected little from Congress, but not all were wi[illegible] to return home empty-handed.

Defiant Continental troops were also billeted in Philadelphia [illegible] nearby Lancaster, Pennsylvania. On June 21, 1783, they mutinied. [illegible] four hundred armed men, led by their sergeants, surrounded the [illegible] in Philadelphia, where Congress was in session. The angry me[illegible] settlement of their long overdue pay. This entry in the Jou[illegible] describes the state of affairs of that day: "The mutinous [illegible] themselves, drawn up in the street before the State House [illegible] assembled. The executive Council of the State sitting [illegible] called on to interpose and to bring in the state militia." John Dickinson, President of the Supreme Executive Council of Pennsylvania, refused to do this, based on his belief that the militia could not be relied on, and in fact might support the mutineers. The terrified Congress fled to Princeton, New Jersey and the mutineers eventually disbanded. This suggests that peace had actually weakened Congress; it continued to struggle on without financial resources or the authority to raise taxes.

The final peace terms would not be agreed on until September 3, 1783, at the Treaty of Paris, five months later. The final evacuation, when all British forces boarded ships to sail back to England, did not occur until November of that year.

On November 25, 1783 Sir Guy Carleton, Commander of British forces in North America, executed the provision in the Articles of Peace that provided for evacuation of British forces in America, "And His Britannic Majesty shall, with all convenient Speed, and without causing any Destruction or carrying away any Negroes or other property, of the American Inhabitants, withdraw all his Armies, Garrisons and Fleets, from the said United States . . . ."[298]

A much-relieved Congress approved the furlough plan suggested by General Washington, and British soldiers actually began to embark on ships and sail for England. After these events, no time was wasted in implementing the measured demobilization of the Continental Army.

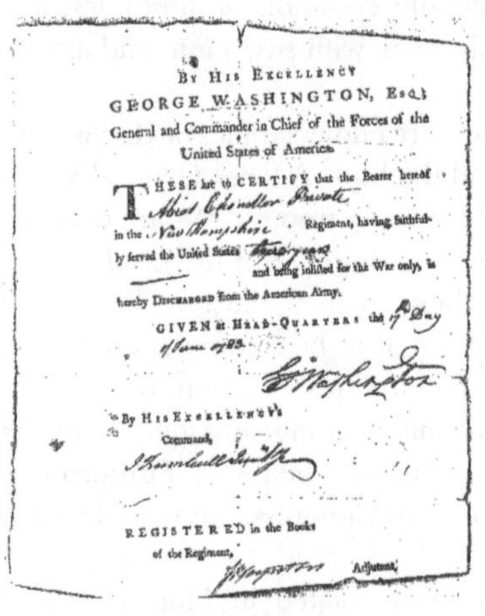

By His Excellency
GEORGE WASHINGTON, Esq;
General and Commander in Chief of the Forces of the United States of America.

THESE are to CERTIFY that the Bearer hereof [illegible] in the New Hampshire Regiment, having faithfully served the United States [illegible] and being inlisted for the War only, is hereby Discharged from the American Army.

GIVEN at Head-Quarters the [illegible] Day of [illegible]

G Washington

By His Excellency's Command,
[illegible]

REGISTERED in the Books of the Regiment,
[illegible] Adjutant.

Revolutionary War Discharge Certificate signed by General George Washington (US National Archives)

The furlough certificate given to each man clearly stated that his release as conditional. But this scrap of paper really amounted to a discharge, since v would ever return to the army. For many, this certificate became their only dence of service after the war, and served as an honorable discharge. More rtantly, it provided evidence for veterans to claim warrants for promised ty land. The simply wording of each certificate stated:

> Headquarters, (date of release) The within certificate shall not avail the bearer, as a discharge, until the ratification of the definitive treaty of peace: previous to which time, and until the proclamation of thereof shall be made, he is considered to be on furlough.[299]

Congress eventually approved three months pay for the departing troops, but by that time some of them had already left. The final settlement of the army's obligations to its common soldiers was made over the course of many years. In May, 1778, a certificate for $80 had been promised to enlisted men who continued to serve for the duration of the conflict. Corporal John Allison, 2nd New York Regiment, received his promissory note about two years after he was released from New Windsor, in June, 1783. However, without funds, Congress had no provision for paying principal or interest on the certificates, and they depreciated like the almost-worthless Continental currency. The promissory note did not entail a land bounty grant of any kind. Congress did not actually redeem the paper until the 1790s, but by then most impoverished veterans had sold these notes to speculators for about 10 percent of their face value. There is no evidence that Allison received any other outstanding back pay for his eight years of service.

Disbanding of the Continental Army at New Windsor Cantonment, June 1783. (By H.A. Ogden, published in *Harper's Weekly* in 1883 to commemorate the centennial of the end of the Revolutionary War)

Warrants for one hundred acres of bounty land were promised to all Continental Army soldiers in 1776. Continental and militia captains were granted three hundred acres, while non-commissioned officers and privates were granted one hundred acres. Congress did not have the funds to survey these lands, so the first titles for the bounty lands were not issued until fifteen years after the war.

Muskets and tattered uniforms were the only items of any value that the separation terms provided to the furloughed soldiers. Congress reasoned that this meager gift would not cost anything and it might even create some short-term goodwill. A few men were doled out a small amount of dollars as they left, and others were provided with a food ration that would last only a few days. Luckily, this gradual release of the troops over several weeks, before the definitive treaty was concluded in September, was successful. A large portion of the army was disbanded while continuing to maintain security.

After hostilities had ceased, few soldiers expressed any desire to remain in the army as a career. Most enlisted men left the Cantonment peacefully. Accounts of their parting show that the men were remorseful when the time came to bid farewell to their comrades. Despite the deplorable conditions they had suffered, the men remembered acquiring skills as soldiers, and surviving together through difficult times. Sergeant Joseph Martin reminisced about leaving New Windsor: "The soldiers . . . were as strict as band of brotherhood as a Masons and, I believe as faithful to each other. We were young men and had warm hearts, I question if there was a corps in the army that parted with more regret that ours did, The New Englanders in particular."

General Washington continued to pressure members of Congress and the state legislatures to provide pay for the veterans as they prepared to depart. He reminded them that they had pledged that their country would finally do the army justice. In the end, veterans received very little for their enormous sacrifices. Amazingly, while aggressively demanding compensation for his veterans, Washington continued to remain loyal to Congress. With very little effort, he could have could have easily incited his angry army to rebel, and our current form of democratic government would probably never have been achieved.

Major Christopher Richmond wrote to Major General Horatio Gates on June 15, 1783: "Men of the war have been sent off agreeable to the directions of Congress . . . . Without thanks they have been sent-without a farthing of money in the pockets of either Officer or soldier-and without provision to help them on the way home-'tis shocking I can say no more about it."[300]

General Robert Howe attempted to rationalize this pitiful situation in his last general order at New Windsor: "If they meet with no other reward, will retire with a heartfelt consciousness of having amply filled the measure of their duty, and having deserved, though they should not obtain the rewards, applause and gratitude of their country."

The optimistic Washington took a more positive view. He was convinced that a major accomplishment of the war was the blending of men from all of the states into one patriotic family:

For who has before seen a disciplined Army form'd at once from such raw materials? Who, that was not a witness, could imagine that the most violent local prejudices would cease so soon, and that Men who came from the different parts of the Continent, strongly disposed, by the habits of education, to despise and quarrel with each other, would instantly become but one patriotic band of Brothers, or who, that was not on the spot, can trace the steps by which such a wonderful revolution has been effected, and such a glorious period put to all our warlike toils?[301]

YANKEE DOODLE MARCHES HOME

The mass exodus of men from New Windsor began in early June, and by the end of the month 4,500 men, about two-thirds of the Continental Army, had departed, marching off to the familiar sounds of fifes and drums. Women and children, many of whom had been with the army for several years, followed the columns. On their way home, the stamina of the men of the Continental Army would be tested one final time.

Some of the soldiers lived hundreds of miles from the camp, so they had to endure a long trip. Food was soon depleted, and their muskets were soon sold. Many of the soldiers were able to reach home only by begging along the way; prisoners of war who had been released in New York City in April, 1783, walked the streets looking for handouts. One reported that ". . . some of them would pity us and give us something, some half a dollar, some a quarter, some less, some nothing but frowns."[302]

The "War Men," the long-service soldiers, were allowed to leave first. In the first two weeks of June, 1783, the Massachusetts, Maryland, New Hampshire, and New Jersey troops were freed from service, and by December the entire army had been disbanded. Since their releases were staggered, the departing soldiers remained under the command of their officers as they marched for home. This precaution was taken for fear that thousands of armed, penniless men, suddenly turned loose on the countryside, would resort to a frenzy of pillaging.

The intrepid Baron von Steuben urged General Washington to hold a final massive review before the men marched out of the New Windsor Cantonment. But the regiments left without any ceremony or fanfare. As the troops left camp, the Baron roamed through the site and attempted to lift their spirits. He was appalled at seeing the demise of the fighting force that he had played a large part in molding, from unorganized farm boys to a first rate professional fighting force. He lamented, "This disbandment of their army . . . was so thoroughly comic that you would have laughed yourself sick if you had seen it."

By the end of the summer in 1783, the entire Continental Army had been reduced to about the 2,500 men whose enlistments had not expired, all of whom were garrisoned at West Point. Although Congress declined to make any decision about the army in peacetime, it did address the need for some troops to remain on duty until the British had evacuated New York City and their frontier posts. On November 15, a detachment of men from West Point reoccupied New York.

Since the enlistments of most of the remaining soldiers were due to expire by June, 1784, Washington ordered the discharge of all but five hundred infantry, and one hundred artillerymen, before winter set in. On June 2, Congress ordered the release of all remaining men, except twenty-five caretakers at Fort Pitt and fifty-five caretakers at West Point. The next day, it created a miniscule peacetime force composed of seven hundred men from four states, all serving for one year. That was all that remained of the once-glorious Continental Army.[303]

Washington bid farewell to his remaining officers on December 4, 1783, at Fraunces Tavern in New York City. As each officer came forward to personally say goodbye, many wept, including Washington himself. On December 23 he appeared before Congress, and returned his commission as Commander-in-Chief: "Having now finished the work assigned me, I retire from the great theatre of Action; and bidding an Affectionate farewell to this August body under whose orders I have so long acted, I here offer my Commission, and take my leave of all the employments of public life."

Congress officially ended the War of American Independence on January 14, 1784, by ratifying the definitive peace treaty that the English had signed in Paris on September 3, 1783. In his final address, Washington appealed directly to each veteran, "to console himself for any unpleasant circumstances by recollecting uncommon scene in which he has been called to act no inglorious part, and the astonishing event to which he has been a witness"[304]

Chapter Twenty

Returning to an Ungrateful America

As the men drew nearer to their homes, they dropped out of their lines of march, and stood alone listening as the familiar sounds of the fifes and drums faded into the distance. At that moment they must have realized that their war life was over, and a feeling of uneasiness about their future must have set in. After the long, traumatic years filled with danger and adventure, resumption to their former lives, although of a much more tranquil nature, would take some adjustment. In the process, their emotional scars would not be recognized by anyone except fellow soldiers.

Only veterans returning from a lengthy and arduous tour of combat duty in the military, or perhaps travelers back from a prolonged and perilous journey, can appreciate the emotions associated with being suddenly thrust back into society. The soldiers must have experienced an initial feeling of exuberance and freedom. Their days, at first filled with the joy of being with loved ones, and the resumption of old patterns of living, were soon touched with a sense of emptiness.

The sudden absence of unrelenting stress and fear strangely created a mood of depression. They struggled to discern and understand the many changes that had occurred in their absence, and awkwardly tried to relearn the little amenities of civilian ways. While trying to stay occupied with constant activity, they may have done needless tasks in order to block out haunting memories. They became sensitive and were easily offended, and their anger could explode if they perceived an affront from someone who had not suffered as they had.

Habits acquired as a soldier, such as food cravings and a heightened awareness of anything threatening, tended to linger. They crouched at any sound that was similar to gunfire, and cowered at the crash of thunder in their attempts to escape from something unknown. They wept when they heard the cadence of drums or the beat of a marching band.

Everyone wanted to hear about their experiences, but these accounts were often met with skepticism or horror, or a mixture of both. People were repelled by the dreadful events which the soldiers had witnessed. The men soon stopped describing their harrowing experiences, and when asked about wartime adventures, they would describe the few humorous incidents that had happened to them along the way.

Confronted with ordeals most others had never faced, soldiers knew each other as few other people did. They noticed that many of their friends and neighbors had not returned, or had disappeared entirely in their absence. Although former brothers-in-arms often lived close to one another, they made little effort to spend time with one other. Chance meetings, if they did occur, were often uncomfortable and painful. Eventually, with time, the memory of the grim days began to fade, but an aching loneliness for lost comrades always remained.

In 1838, fifty-five years after the Revolution, seventy-year-old Sergeant Joseph Plumb Martin, of the Connecticut Line, reminisced about his days in the Continental Army. He remembered his personal sufferings even more than the combat he endured:

> *How many times have I had to lie down like a dumb animal in the field, and bear the pelting of the pitiless storm . . . could I have the benefit of a little fire, it would have been deemed a luxury. It is fatiguing almost beyond belief, to those who never experienced it, to be obliged to march twenty-four or forty-eight hours, and often more, day and night without rest or sleep, wishing and hoping that some wood or village, I could see ahead might be a short resting place. How often have I envied the very swine their happiness, when I have heard them quarrelling in their warm dry sties, when I was wet to the skin and wished in vain for that indulgence. Believe me that I have felt more anxiety, undergone more fatigue and hard ships, suffered more in every way in performing one of those tedious marches than I ever did fighting the hottest battle that I was ever engaged in.*[305]

Shunned by society in the years following the close of the war, Continental Army veterans received little credit for winning the Revolution. When Washington's victorious Yankees Doodles reached home, they were openly regarded as pariahs, or conveniently ignored. The impoverished veterans returning from years of sacrifice often had to depend on friends or their own children for support. Many of them, wounded or traumatized, roamed from town to town, telling their war stories at the village inns, or by firesides, to anyone who would listen. A thankless society did not support any type of financial assistance for needy veterans or surviving dependants.

A large segment of the population had vacillated between being Loyalist sympathizers and Patriots. This often had a pragmatic aspect to it, since it depended on which side offered the most economic incentives or security at any given time. Some people even went so far as to portray the public as the saviors of the army at Valley Forge, but in reality their failure to supply the starving soldiers was the main cause of suffering during that endless winter. American farmers in the vicinity of the camp had openly exchanged grain and livestock for British hard coins, rather than sell them to the Continental Army in return for ever-depreciating paper currency. Merchants always traded with the British when they had the opportunity, and since taxes were very low, they enjoyed wartime prosperity in the midst of suffering. Furthermore, relatively few Americans had made any willing sacrifices; after the first six months of the war, many found ways to avoid military service.

Financial difficulties, unemployment, and old age adversely affected these veterans' lives as time went on, and tended to keep them at an economic disadvantage. Physical disabilities from wounds or illnesses experienced while in service prevented many veterans from earning a living after the war. Public ungratefulness kept them in depressing poverty, and many were unaware that governmental help was even available. Veterans, or their widows and orphans, who attempted to apply for assistance, were discouraged by the daunting application procedures. These proved to be so arduous that most failed to follow up on the claims they managed to submit. Often benefits went uncollected due to administrative red tape, which insisted on proof of service that might no longer exist.

Electa Campfield, of Hanover, New Jersey, the widow of a Continental soldier, first wrote to her county court in 1785. She claimed that she was left destitute with a child, and had no means of sustenance or support. After forwarding her claim to the state legislature, widow Campfield then waited seven months for final approval of her application. Then, for further consideration for a benefit, she had to obtain a deposition from her husband's officers and provide his service record. The minister of her church also had to testify as to the legality of her marriage and the local overseer of the poor had to swear to her poverty. This information was then submitted to a court for review. She was finally awarded half-pay ten years later.

Historian Howard Peckham has assembled Revolutionary War casualties figures based on the records of 1,331 military and 218 naval engagements. He concludes that 7, 174 men were killed, and 8,241 were wounded, during the eight year war.[306] Many of those who were wounded in battles lived on. They were crippled, had lost limbs, suffered loss of vision and hearing, or had other handicaps that kept them unemployed or underemployed. Veterans vividly described disease, wounds and other injuries in their appeals for assistance to the government.

One modest form of relief did provide for a few veterans. The passage of a national pension law on August 26, 1776, promised half-pay for life, or during their current disability, to any soldier who had lost a limb or was totally disabled. This payment, about four dollars per month for privates, has about the same buying power as seventy-one current dollars, and thus was hardly enough for one person to live on.

James Starr petitioned the state of Pennsylvania for a pension in 1820, stating that he was "... still suffering with wounds received in the service." He was "not one third of his time capable of pursuing his trade and at best not capable of doing half work" due to war injuries and other "pains."[307]

Levi Starling received two flesh wounds and was "severely wounded" while on the Sullivan-Clinton expedition against the Iroquois Nations in 1779. Starling did not describe the nature and extent of his wounds in any detail, but maintained he was "not able to pursue" labor because of his service-related injuries.[308]

Isaac Lewis was wounded in his thigh by a musket ball on August 22, 1776, while setting fire to wheat stacks that had fallen into possession of the British in an action on Long Island: "It was with great difficulty that his comrades even rescued him. As a result of the wound inflicted, "he has been a cripple ever since, entirely unable to walk but with a crutch."[309]

Military service did not eradicate the poverty of the underprivileged men of the American Army. Most soldiers returned to civilian life as impoverished as when they enlisted, so few were able to achieve any financial stake in their new nation. A study that traced the lives of 658 Virginia soldiers concluded that the majority of veterans in that state led paupers' lives after the war.[310]

Of the 302 Maryland soldiers who enlisted in 1782, the Federal Census of 1790 showed that 80 percent had not established a household, and likely had become landless laborers.[311] There were no opportunities generated by the war that were sufficient to satisfy the aspirations of Revolutionary War soldiers.

FINALLY! SUPPORT FOR THE AGING VETERANS

For the three decades following the war, Americans continued to cling to the traditional belief that the citizen-soldiers of the militia were the key military force that had won the war. Over time, though, they finally began to accept that the war had been won by the Continental Army. What had caused this shift in public opinion?

The War of 1812 proved that the new nation was in need of some type of a standing army. By the early 1800s, Revolutionary War veterans had grown old and frail, and most were poor. An outpouring of sympathy for them from a new generation after the War of 1812 created a wave of patriotism that swept the nation, and in the process completely altered the public's collective memory of the Revolution. With these events, the Continental Army veterans became regarded as heroic warriors who embodied the ideals of fervent patriotism and civic virtue, and who were owed a debt of gratitude. Finally, the aging, infirm, and disadvantaged veterans were gaining acknowledgment. And even more importantly and fortuitously, there happened to be a US Treasury surplus at the time.[312]

By 1818, thirty-five years after the war, many of the Yankees Doodles were in their sixties. Most no longer owned land, or were unable to work at full capacity. Debt-burdened and disabled veterans and their families had not enjoyed material success in the decades after the war. Most Americans believed that pensions, not just hand-outs, were a proper way for the nation to repay those who had fought to create it.

THE PENSION ACTS

In 1818, the Federal Pension Act finally provided support for a large number of veterans. The act provided $96 per year to any male veteran who had served more than nine months in the regular army. To the delight of historians everywhere, this law tremendously increased the amount of testimonial evidence about the lives of veterans. Pension applications provide a plethora of information about the soldiers who were still alive at the time. In 1836, the act provided that widows could also claim the veteran's benefits if married during the term of the soldier's active service in the Revolution and as long as they had remained unmarried. These widow's applications also provide a remarkable picture of the lives of the soldiers' families.

In 1820, due to an overwhelming response, an amendment was added to the law to reduce cost and prevent fraud. A supplementary act of 1820 disqualified any pensioner not in dire poverty by requiring applicants to submit a certified schedule of personal property and income. This condition provides a fascinating view of the aging, reduced survivors of the Revolutionary War and their households. It tallies the amount of land held, the extent of improvement, and an accounting of livestock, tools, and implements. Each list contains the court-assessed value of all property, real and personal, excluding only "necessary clothing and bedding." Veterans submitted letters, copies of deeds, bills of sale, and court decisions relating to indebtedness to prove that any transfer of property had not been intended to defraud the government.

By 1820, Corporal John Allison was sixty-six years old. In that year, he was involved in four lawsuits for nonpayment of small debts. He defaulted on his mortgage, and his land was sold in a sheriff's sale. He dictated this list of all his possessions to a scribe who composed the document: "Nor do I have any income other than what is contained in the following inventory viz-that he has one cow that he has bought with his pension money-one bed-three knives and forks- four old chairs which he has bottomed with bark-one corn hoe-that he has a wife of about 70 years of age-no other family, no support but what he obtains by labor."[313]

Allison and his wife Sarah somehow subsisted on his eight dollar monthly pension for the rest of their lives. When he died in 1828 at age seventy-four, his total assets amounted to $36, all of which represented uncollected pension money due to him. The old soldier probably lived alone, and was too ill to claim his pension money in the last months of his life.

The paperwork for the 1820 act also revealed that some veterans who applied were not destitute, and so were disqualified, which reduced the number of pensioners from 18,800 to 12,331. Congress believed few veterans would apply for the benefits under the pension laws, but the number of applicants over the next two years completely overwhelmed the War Department.

The pension acts of 1818 and 1820 excluded many deserving individuals. Because they required proof of nine months of service, thousands of militia veterans and irregular troops were automatically eliminated. Most African-American veterans did not qualify because it was commonly alleged that they had served to win freedom from slavery, and therefore did not deserve additional rewards. Women camp followers were not mentioned at all. No effort was made to promote eligibility, and thousands more who might have qualified did not even submit applications.

In the study of 302 soldiers from Maryland who enlisted in 1782, it was found that less than ten applied for pensions. This paltry amount suggests that a vast number of veterans, many of whom were illiterate, were either not aware of the laws, or were discouraged by the complexity of the process. In the intervening years since the war, many men had lost documents that would have proven their enlistment. Many had also sold their land warrants and other bounty entitlements papers to unscrupulous investors.

Pension legislation really came too late to improve the quality of veteran's lives, and served to sustain them for only a few years. However, this steady source of benefits was welcome, and in many cases was the sole source of income. Aside from being honored by this outburst of patriotism and nationalistic spirit, another encouraging, but unanticipated, result occurred. Elderly widowed or unmarried pensioners, aided by the security of this guaranteed income, easily attracted young wives.

Sergeant Joseph Plumb Martin summed up his treatment by the United States government: "The country was rigorous in exacting my compliance to my engagements to a punctilio, but equally careless in performing her contracts with me, and why so? One reason was because she had all the power in her own hands and I had none"[314]

Pensions for Revolutionary War service were the first federal program to grant direct relief to a large group of poor people, until Roosevelt announced his "New Deal" on July 2, 1932. This series of projects and programs provided economic relief during the bleak years of the Great Depression, when at least one-quarter of the American workforce was unemployed. On June 7, 1832, Congress finally granted all remaining veterans, including militiamen and state troops, unrestricted pensions. In his annual report to Congress in 1834, the Commissioner of Pensions reported that there were then 27,978 Revolutionary

War pensioners on the rolls claiming pensions. The entire federal pension roll in 1834 for veterans of all wars contained about 43,000 claimants.

The poverty of Revolutionary War veterans initiated the depressing and thorny history between the United States and its veteran soldiers. During the Great Depression, an army of World War I veterans camped in Washington while demanding a bonus. Vietnam Era veterans faced public contempt for a war that many of them did not choose to fight. Veterans of the United States Army in Iraq and Afghanistan continue to face threats of cuts to their medical and other benefits. History repeats itself in many ways.

Chapter Twenty-One

The Anatomy of an Infantry Company

The everyday life and ordeals of a Continental Army soldier can best be followed by tracking the activities of an actual Revolutionary War infantry company. The company was the smallest unit in the American Army, and the 2nd Company of Foot is a perfect case in point. The majority of its men were young New York farm laborers from Orange and Ulster counties, and they participated in many of the momentous events of the eight-year war. A complete account of their activities may be found in the modern biography of Corporal John Allison by this author, *The War Man*.[315]

On paper, in the table of organization, a fully-staffed infantry company had about sixty men, but because of disabilities and chronic difficulties in recruiting during the war, it normally had less than forty, and losses in battle could cause this to shrink even further. For example, twenty of the 2nd Company's forty-two men, as well as three of its four officers, were killed or taken prisoner at the tragic defeat at Fort Montgomery in the Hudson Highlands in October, 1777.

For many of the men of the 2nd Company, the war had started long before they joined the unit. They had enlisted in the spring of 1775, about two months after the war began, and had marched north in the 3rd New York Regiment on General Richard Montgomery's disastrous invasion of Canada. During most of 1776, they suffered through the series of humiliating defeats at Manhattan and Long Island.

The 2nd Company was one of ten groups that made up the 5th New York Regiment of Foot. This large unit was formed on November 30, 1776, and it joined the other four regiments of the state to form the New York Line of the Continental Army. The 2nd Company continued to serve as an identifiable unit until the 5th New York Regiment was merged into the 2nd New York Regiment

5th New York Regiment reenactors at the Battle of Bound Brook April, 2007.
(Photograph by the author)

a t

the end of 1780. During those four years its activities and turbulent history can be traced through a review of its muster rolls and payrolls.

Muster rolls were the method that the American Army used to keep track of its available fighting strength; they were prepared as often as twice each month. These documents provide the main source of comprehensive information to track the adventures of the 2nd Company. Twenty-four muster rolls can be found in the collection of the US National Archives for the period that the 2nd Company was in existence. Each roll contains the name, rank and dates of enlistment for all officers and men. What are most informative and interesting are the soldier's status and their duties.

Comments associated with each man might note that he was "on command" (on duty at a different location) or "on guard" (assigned to protect a high-ranking officer). Alternately, a man might be listed as being "sick in camp" (or at a particular army hospital), "in the enemy's captivity," "on furlough," "absent with leave," or "deserted." Any changes in status since the prior roll was taken are also recorded. Thus, these entries could also include notations such as "died from illness," "wounded" or "killed in combat."

ORIGINS

In June, 1776, the Continental Congress promoted Major Lewis Dubois to the rank of colonel, and directed him to recruit a new regiment that would be added to the four that already existed in New York. DuBois, a veteran officer, was a carpenter from Ulster County. He enlisted in the militia at the age of eighteen years, and when war broke out he was promoted to captain. At that time he formed a company in Nicholson's Regiment that became a part of Colonel James Clinton's 3rd New York Regiment during the Canadian Campaign.

The 5th New York Regiment had been authorized in June, 1776, but a dispute arose over who had the authority to appoint New York officers—the New York Provincial Congress or the Continental Congress. The Continental Congress finally prevailed, but this delayed the appointment of Dubois, so the regiment was not assembled until November, 1776. Almost all of its members signed up for the duration of the war, believing that this option would be a shorter term than a three-year enlistment, the alternative that was offered. In late 1776, Dubois appointed Amos Hutchings as captain to command the forty-six men of the 2nd Company of the 5th Regiment.

AT THE TWIN FORTS

Early in 1777, the new regiment was garrisoned on the Hudson River in two forts; both were located about forty miles north of New York City in the rugged terrain of the Hudson Highlands. These defenses, Fort Montgomery and Fort Clinton, stood on adjacent hilltops. They were known as the "Twin Forts," and they were still under construction when the 5th New York Regiment arrived. The fortresses were perched on rugged cliffs one hundred feet above a narrow spot in the river (today's site of the Bear Mountain Bridge). Their battery of heavy thirty-six pound cannon had the fire power to destroy any British ship that attempted to sail up the river to attack West Point or Kingston, which was the New York provincial capital at the time. This formidable bastion appeared to be impregnable.

In order to fill the ranks, an energetic recruiting drive was conducted during the first half of 1777, but afterwards the regiment still remained under strength. The 2nd Company's four officers were Captain Amos Hutchings, First Lieutenant Patton Jackson, Second Lieutenant James Furman, and Ensign Henry Weaver. They all had been appointed officers on November 21, 1776, the same day that the 5th Regiment had been authorized. Non-commissioned officers included four sergeants and three corporals.

Captain Hutchings was a native of Haverstraw, New York, eight miles south of the Twin Forts. He had previously served on the Canadian Campaign with the 3rd New York Regiment, and had fought in the Battle of White Plains in October, 1776. Lieutenant Patton Jackson was a farmer from Clarkstown, near Haverstraw. He served in the Orange County Militia before enlisting in the 5th Regiment in February, 1776, and had fought in Hutching's company at White Plains. Lieutenant John Furman also served with Hutchings at the Battle of White Plains. Ensign Edward Weaver, the junior officer, from Waterloo, Albany County, was new to the army and was sent on recruiting duty during the summer of 1777.

The survivors joined Brigadier General George Clinton in pursuit of the British up the Hudson, but were too late to prevent the October 16 burning of Kingston by the British. After Burgoyne's surrender, the 5th wintered in the Fishkill supply depot and healed its wounds. The regiment camped at White Plains in the summer of 1778, and took part in the Sullivan-Clinton Campaign of 1779 against Tories and Natives in western New York. After that successful campaign, they were reviewed in Pompton New Jersey with the rest of the New York Brigade by General Baron von Steuben and General George Washington. The winter of 1779-1780 was spent at Jockey Hollow in Morristown, New Jersey. The 5th was again assigned to garrison duty when they arrived at West Point in 1780. The New York Line was consolidated in January, 1781, and the 5th New York was merged into the 2nd New York. Members of the original 5th New York were present at Yorktown. They avenged the loss of the Highland Forts when they comprised part of the second wave at the storming of the redoubts there.

Most of the enlisted men in the 2nd Company came from Haverstraw Precinct, an area that encompassed the greater part of what is now Rockland County, New York. Others were from the New Paltz area in Ulster County. Some of them had served together previously, while others were neighbors or friends in civilian life, and a few were even relatives. Captain Hutchings was the brother-in-law of Corporal John Allison, and both Private and Corporal John Allison (same name) were cousins. William and Lawrence Bonker and Jacob and Hermanus Crum also are shown on the company muster rolls, however, their familial relationship, if any, is unknown.

The men of the 2nd Company were kept busy constructing the defenses at the Twin Forts and subduing Tories during the spring and summer of 1777. Others were "on command"—patrolling the river bank for signs of an invasion up the Hudson from the British stronghold of New York City. The British Army under Sir Henry Clinton was expected to sail north to launch an amphibious attack and join forces with "Gentleman Johnny" Burgoyne, who was making his way south with an accompanying army from Canada. If successful, this drive would split the colonies in two, and effectively end the American rebellion.

Life was good at the Twin Forts during the warm season of 1777. Evidence discovered in archeological digs shows that the enlisted men had been housed in barracks and had eaten from earthenware plates. Clothing and supplies were issued regularly, and soldiers were able to purchase personal items from traveling sutlers. Since many of the men were close to home, they may have been allowed furloughs for short visits, and family members probably visited the soldiers in return. The pension application of the widow of 2nd Company member Sergeant James Pride states that she was at Fort Montgomery with the wife of Lieutenant Furman on the morning of October 6, 1777. While there, the ladies had heard gunfire, signaling that an attack was taking place on the Twin Forts.

THE SKIRMISH AT DOODLETOWN

The 2nd Company would make history on that fateful day, as it had been selected for a perilous reconnaissance mission to gather intelligence about the invading enemy's strength and movements. The company was probably selected for this critical mission because of its abundance of seasoned combat veterans from the area, men who were familiar with the narrow mountain passes and local terrain. Captain Hutchings remained at Fort Montgomery, while Lieutenant Patton Jackson led the patrol. The thirty chosen men moved cautiously through the woods, heading south for about two miles, until they reached the small crossroads hamlet of Doodletown. There they came face-to-face with the entire enemy assault force—more than 2,000 battle-ready Redcoats—who were advancing to attack the Twin Forts.

Given these overwhelming numbers, the men of the 2nd Company disregarded their orders to simply gather intelligence. Instead, while concealed in the underbrush only twenty-five yards away, they fired a barrage of musket fire directly into the British lines. The company was the first to engage the combined British, Hessian and Loyalist forces, and the first to fire the shots in the day-long battle that ensued. After the enemy realized that they were being attacked by so few men, they returned the gunfire, and three men of the 2nd Company fell.

The sounds of gunfire at Doodletown alerted the defenders back at the forts, and warned them that a British assault was in progress. Jackson and his men also noticed that the enemy was dividing its force in preparation for striking at the forts from two sides, and this critical intelligence was quickly relayed back. This alarm caused the British to lose the advantage of surprise, and allowed the inhabitants of the forts a short time to prepare for the two-pronged attack.

After the skirmish at Doodletown, the survivors of the company fell back toward the forts, with 1,200 Redcoats of the right wing of the assault in close pursuit. To slow the onslaught, the courageous company made a second bold stand once they reached a stone wall that crossed an open field, only a half-mile from the safety of Fort Clinton's single redoubt that faced west. The now-exhausted men rested their musket barrels on the wall to steady their aim, and stood alone for the second time on that tragic day. Somehow they managed to slow the aggressive British advance for about an hour.

Lieutenant Henry Pawling of the 5th New York Regiment provided this eyewitness account in his journal: "Lieut. Jackson was sent out with a small part, being about 11 o'clock in the forenoon, in order to watch the motions of the enemy. About 12 o'clock a small firing was heard supposed to be Lieut Jacksons's who it was thought had met the enemy, the drums were immediately ordered to beat to arms, the men paraded."[316]

Today the site of the stone wall is on the picnic grounds of the Bear Mountain Inn. A bronze plaque mounted on a large boulder nearby reads: "When the British attacked Forts Clinton and Montgomery Oct. 6, 1777, the first fighting occurred over the outworks at this point."

The survivors of the 2nd Company were driven back into Fort Clinton, where they joined other defenders from their regiment, as well as local militia forces. The outnumbered Patriots were either stretched along the defenses in a thin line, or clustered in the redoubts. As afternoon gave way to evening, waves of attackers smashed through the barricades and engaged the Americans in hand-to-hand fighting, and British warships on the Hudson River bombarded the forts with their heavy guns at the same time. The forts were entirely surrounded, but fortunately for the struggling Americans, oncoming darkness caused confusion and disorder.

The 2nd Company fought fiercely while defending the north redoubt, and it was the last position to be taken. The men desperately tried to stave off the onslaught by using the butts of the slow-loading muskets as clubs, but this failed to stop the hundreds of brutal Redcoats swarming over the ramparts with fixed bayonets. As the position was overrun, many men with bayonet wounds were pinned to the ground, and as darkness fell the remnants of the company were encircled by British bayonets and captured or killed. While half of the defenders did manage to escape through the British lines into the woods, the forts finally fell after a combined assault by British forces. Previous offers to surrender had been rejected, and no American order was given to surrender; no doubt many lives would have been spared if the Americans had capitulated. This mismatched action later became known in history books as the Battle of Fort Montgomery.

TRAGIC AFTERMATH

The losses to the 2nd Company at the Twin Forts were appalling. The muster roll taken after the battle shows that half the privates, twenty men, were killed or taken prisoner. Of the four sergeants, two were missing. Only two of the corporals survived, and three of the company's four officers were listed as missing. The valiant Lieutenant Patton Jackson was taken prisoner in the north redoubt, along with the unit's other lieutenant, John Furman. Ensign Edward Weaver was arrested five days after the battle, and charged with desertion and conduct unbecoming an officer. He had fled from Fort Montgomery before the main assault, after he had heard the gunfire from the clash at Doodletown. Captain Amos Hutchings was the only officer left.[317] (Refer to Appendix C-2nd Company muster roll after Twin Forts battle).

Governor Clinton reported on the performance of the 2nd Company to the New York legislature the day after the battle, but exaggerated the size of the enemy force: "I am only briefly to inform you that only yesterday at 10 am an advanced party was attacked by the enemy at Doodletown about two and a half mile from Fort Montgomery. They consisted of 30 men. The enemy by appearance and accounts after received [appeared to number] five thousand. They receive the enemies fire and returned it and retreated to Fort Clinton." The heroic stand of the 2nd Company at Doodletown was described in several other reports by eyewitnesses at a court of inquiry which was held after the tragic American defeat.[318]

The British killed or captured 98 out of 312 men of the 5th New York Regiment when the Redcoats stormed the forts. The surviving regiment, joined by about three hundred Ulster and Orange County militia, held off multiple British attacks and inflicted numerous casualties on the British, Hessian, and Loyalist forces. The victorious Crown forces paid dearly for the triumph. Three days after the battle Governor Clinton reported that the enemy had lost seven officers and as many as three hundred men.

The day after the battle the bodies of the American dead were stripped and dumped in a pond a few yards from the north redoubt. Lieutenant Henry Pawling had been captured in the redoubt with the officers and men of the 2nd Company. After being beaten, he was placed in a makeshift jail in the barracks. He gave this account of what he saw from a window ". . . also we saw the enemy carrying our dead across snaggy poles naked as they were born and heels hanging down, also saw the enemy walking about the fort with our clothes, selling them to each other.."[319]

The American prisoners were well-acquainted with some of their captors. They were neighbors who fought in a Loyalist regiment that had joined the British Army to join the attack on the forts. Pawling writes, "The officer who had guard over us the first night was Richard Vanderburgh a Lieut. in the new corps, who gave Lieut. Mott a blow aside the head and knocked him down for calling him by his former familiar name, being well acquainted with him heretofore."

The captured Patriots were herded to the river to be transported forty miles to New York City. As the dejected men marched to the dock, their coats, hats and shoes and anything else of value, was taken from them. They were then were forced to pass through an unruly mob of about 2,000 Loyalist civilians. The Tories made threats, erected a gallows, shouted insults, and spat on them. After they reached the city, they were herded into the notorious Sugar House Prison, where many later died of starvation and sickness. From there they were transferred to the prison ships out in the East River, where many more perished over the next four years from cruelty and neglect.[320]

Captain Amos Hutchings was the only officer of the 2nd Company who remained after the carnage at the Twin Forts. A month later his company was reduced to ten men. Adding to those lost in the battle were the sick men unfit for duty. Others, stunned by the barbarity of the British, had fled when the forts fell and had not returned. They were mercifully listed on the roll as "absent" not "deserted."

Hutchings must have been devastated by the carnage at the Twin Forts, and may have become depressed and discouraged. He is listed as "absent" during the months that followed the battle, and may have simply headed for home. He returned for a brief time in January, 1778, and was assigned to Fort Constitution, an island fortress near West Point. He promptly got into trouble there, and was charged with disobeying an order from Captain Mott, an artillery officer. Hutchings was arrested, but later exonerated. He resigned on May 9, 1778 and returned to Haverstraw, where he continued to serve as an enlisted man in Hay's 2nd Regiment Orange County Militia. After the war, he became a carpenter and was a founder of the Presbyterian Church in the town.[321]

Lieutenant Patton Jackson was held on prison ships for three years and three months. The journal kept by Lieutenant Henry Pawling mentions Jackson, and describes their incarceration. Patton Jackson was exchanged on January 10, 1781. He did not return to service, and applied for a pension in 1818.

Lieutenant Furman was also taken prisoner at Fort Montgomery, and held on prison ships. He was exchanged on November 9, 1780, after almost three years in captivity. A pay receipt dated November 21 shows him on the prison ship *Cornelia*, opposite Kings Bridge. After his release Furman rejoined the army, on January 1, 1781, in the 1st New York Regiment. He was with this regiment at Yorktown in 1781, and was discharged from at New Windsor on June 3, 1783. He received a land grant for 200 acres in 1791, but apparently neither he nor and his family survived to apply for a pension in 1818.

The 2nd Company, 5th New York Regiment played a vital role at the Twin Forts. The battle, while a devastating American defeat, was actually a strategic success. History credits the event on having a significant effect on the outcome of the entire war. If the British forces had not been delayed at the Twin Forts they could have swept north in time to join the Battle of Saratoga. As reinforcements they could have tipped the scale and cost the Americans this great victory. Saratoga is regarded as the turning point of the Revolution, and the reason France entered the war on the side.

A HARSH YEAR 1777-1778

During the week after the battle, the shattered 2nd company straggled north twenty miles to New Windsor, a few miles from Newburgh, New York, to join Colonel Dubois and the remnants of the 5th New York Regiment. There were only 162 men available for duty in the entire regiment after the heavy losses at the Twin Forts. The survivors joined Brigadier General George Clinton in pursuit of the British as they sailed up the Hudson, but were too late to prevent them from burning Kingston on October 16, 1777.[322]

As the winter of 1777-1778 approached, the New York troops attempted to survive by building makeshift shelters and procuring food, warm clothing, and blankets from supportive civilians in the local area. The Continental soldiers were alone. The local militia forces who had fought with them at the Twin Forts had returned home to assist their families during the winter months. All their supplies had been lost at Fort Montgomery, and conditions were desperate. In January, General Putnam reported, "Dubois regiment is unfit to be ordered on duty, there being not one blanket in the regiment. Very few have either a shoe or a shirt and most of them have neither stockings."[323]

The 5th New York was without senior officers for that entire winter. Most of the discouraged commanders went home on furlough rather than endure the cold with their soldiers. This practice was not unusual, and was justified by the fact that hostilities were usually discontinued by both sides in the winter months. There were also better opportunities at home for recruiting new men. Colonel Dubois, recovering from a bayonet wound in the neck sustained at Fort Montgomery, was among the few who remained. The 2nd Company was among the small number of Continental troops that remained in the Orange, Ulster County area. This ghost force, traumatized by the horror of Fort Montgomery, attempted to patrol forty miles of riverbank between Newburgh and Kingston, New York, since the threat of another British invasion up the river still existed.

In the spring, some of the men that had been "absent' had rejoined the company. Then another calamity hit the regiment. The roll for March, 1778, lists nine men who had come down with smallpox. From New Windsor, the 5th New York crossed the Hudson River to join the main Continental Army camped at Peekskill and White Plains. There, the Americans could keep the British forces penned up in New York City and prevent them from advancing north up the waterway. By January 1779, there were only twelve men left in the 2nd Company, and no officers, since Captain Hutchings had resigned seven months earlier. Leadership of the group was provided by two sergeants and a corporal.

THE CONQUEST OF THE IROQUOIS NATIONS

In the summer of 1779, the 2nd Company moved with its regiment to the frontier, which in those days was western New York State. The local public was outraged by the atrocities and brutal attacks on settlers by the Indian tribes of the Iroquois Nations, supported by the Loyalists of the region. The company moved down the Susquehanna River, as part of the New York Brigade under General James Clinton, to join a larger force under General John Sullivan. The combined force of 3,800 men then marched north into the heart of Native American county in northwest New York State.

The Sullivan-Clinton Campaign was a major offensive. The army destroyed Indian villages and crops, and defeated their forces at the Battle of Newtown, near present day Elmira. The army went on to destroy the capitol of the Iroquois Nations at Genesee, New York. The 2nd Company started out on the expedition with twenty-seven men. After six harrowing months on the frontier, and a two hundred mile trek back to New Jersey, only fourteen, remained fit for duty. Seven men were left behind in field hospitals in Scranton and Albany. Private James Titus, for instance, was listed as "shot at Canajoharie." This frontier town was an assembly point for Clinton's forces at the beginning of the campaign, but there is extant record of fighting having taken place there.

JOCKEY HOLLOW AND BACK TO THE FRONTIER

The 5th Regiment arrived at the winter camp at Jockey Hollow, Morristown, New Jersey in December, 1779. Lieutenant Henry Vanderburgh was assigned to the 2nd company in late 1779. Vanderburgh has served with the 5th New York since 1776. He was the first officer that the unit had had since Hutchings had resigned. At Morristown they would suffer hunger and bitter cold in the worst winter of the century. By January, 1780 the 2nd Company had dwindled down to a handful of men.

Two men were sick in hospitals in Newburgh and Haverstraw, and seven were on duty on the front lines, guarding the mountain passes east of Morristown. Five men who had enlisted for three years, but not for the duration of the war, were discharged. Corporal John Allison personally wrote to General Washington about the confusion of his enlistment terms. His former captain, Amos Hutchings, signed an affidavit stating that Allison had only enlisted for three years, and not for the duration of the war. This appeal was not acknowledged, and Corporal Allison continued to serve with other War Men in his company, until the end of the war.

In the spring of 1780, the 5th New York marched north again to the New York frontier, this time to confront a new wave of Indian atrocities. At the time the 2nd Company had sixteen privates. Jasper Allen and George Marks had deserted during the winter at Jockey Hollow, and Sergeant James Robinson's three year enlistment had expired. Only six men remained from the original forty-three that had been engaged at the Battle of Fort Montgomery. Colonel Lewis Dubois resigned in May, and was replaced by Lieutenant Colonel Marinus Willet.

In June, 1780, after the Native attacks along the Mohawk towns had subsided, the New York troops trekked east 170 miles east to West Point, which they arrived at in time to greet the fort's new commanding officer, General Benedict Arnold. They spent the summer at West Point, and from there patrolled forty miles of Hudson River bank south to Hackensack, New Jersey. In September the men of the 2nd Company learned of the defection of Benedict Arnold. Most common soldiers were staggered and heartbroken by the treason of this popular officer.

In October of 1780, Indian raids once again erupted on the frontier, and the 5th New York marched north for the second time that year. On the way they passed through Doodletown, and by the stone fence where they had made their stand three years before. The regiment camped one night at the ruins of the Twin Forts, and must have been haunted by the memory of that tragic day in October, 1777, when the forts fell and so many of their comrades were lost.

On December 31, 1780, the 5th New York Regiment was "deranged" (merged) into the 2nd New York Regiment under Colonel Philip Van Cortlandt. Eight men from the 2nd Company, along with sixteen others, formed the 7th Company of the 2nd New York under Captain Henry Dubois. The regiment was assigned to Fort Schuyler on the Mohawk frontier. This military outpost, garrisoned by New York regiments throughout the war, was originally known as Fort Stanwix.

YORKTOWN AND VICTORY AT LAST

In the summer of 1781, the 2nd New York Regiment marched off to the Battle of Yorktown with men from the 2nd Company, 5th New York Regiment in its ranks. Five men who fought in the battle of Fort Montgomery remained together, four years later, to avenge the loss of the Twin Forts at this great victory. They were in the second wave at the storming of Redoubt Number 10, an historic event that is considered the high point of this final decisive battle of the war. Thomas Jones, formerly of the 2nd Company, was with Alexander Hamilton's light infantry brigade, the unit that captured the redoubt.

Four men of the original 2nd Company were discharged in 1783 from New Windsor, after peace had been declared and most of the Continental Army was being demobilized. They had served together for six years after the battle of Fort Montgomery. Sixteen men and two of the officers who were at the Twin Forts survived, or had family members, who applied for pensions starting in 1818.

THE 5TH NEW YORK REGIMENT TODAY

Today's 5th New York Regiment, a dedicated group of living historians based in the Hudson Valley of New York State, recreate the events of the American Revolutionary War, as well as honor the sacrifices of those who served in the original 5th New York. The regiment was organized in 2001 by Colonel James M. Johnson, Ph.D., Ret., Joe Ryan and Ed Burr, who transformed an inactive unit of the Orange County, New York Shore Guard unit into the new regiment. The 5th New York has joined the Brigade of the American Revolution and the Continental Line, the two largest Revolutionary War organizations in the country, and partners with the Living History Foundation and the Fort Montgomery Battle Site Association. Jon Svibruck, President/Commander, typically schedules about twenty-five battlefield reenactments and "living history" displays throughout the northeast each year, designed to both educate the public and honor those who served in the War for Independence. Richard McGuinness, Unit Historian, has carefully researched the fragmentary supply records of the original regiment to ensure that the clothing, weapons, ammunition and accoutrements are accurate representations.

Chapter Twenty-Two

Lest We Forget

Searching for Your Yankee Doodle
Did My Ancestor Serve in the War of the Revoltuion?

The Revolutionary War lasted for eight years, from 1775 until 1783. If your family lived in America during this time period, you are very likely to be the descendant of a soldier. Any male ancestor who was between the ages of sixteen and sixty years old during the war years is a potential candidate.

The pension acts are the richest source of information about the lives of Revolutionary War soldiers. The first congressional legislation authorizing the payment of pensions for Revolutionary War service was passed August 26, 1776. It provided half-pay for officers and enlisted men who were disabled in the service of the United States and incapable of earning a living. Disability typically meant the loss of a limb. The pensions were paid for and processed by each state until 1789.

Application procedures and information requested was varied from state to state. The process usually required the applicant to appear before a court of record and describe his service and the nature of his disability. These early applications are mostly scattered lists, and when they can be found, they are of marginal value to the historian or genealogist. Many that had been filed at federal facilities were destroyed by fires in 1800 and 1814. Some of these original applications, as well as those generated subsequent to pension legislation, are now located at the National Archives. These can be requested in the same manner as all other pension records. The treasure trove of information about veterans really begins in 1818, when the US Congress granted pensions to Continental Army veterans without service-related disabilities.

In the years that followed 1818, benefits were extended to members of the militia and their widows. A high proportion, between 80 and 90 percent, of the eligible surviving Continentals and militia men submitted applications. However, in 1820, when property lists were added as a requirement to substantiate the claims of poverty, a large number of applicants were found to have substantial wealth, so roughly one third of the 18,000 names on the list were removed. Since few common soldiers left diaries, wills or other documents, pension data, when it can be found, is considered to be the most important source of documentary evidence about the veterans.

The Revolutionary War Pension and Bounty-Land Warrant Application Files collection is available in National Archives and Records Administration (NARA) microfilm publication M804. The collection contains an estimated 80,000 pension and bounty-land warrant application files for American military, naval, and marine officers, and enlisted men, from the Revolutionary War. For an individual veteran, a file can range in size from a single bounty land warrant card to hundreds of documents. These records may reveal details about each veteran's history and service, as well as information about his family, state of health, and life after the war.

A typical compiled military service record includes the person's name, rank, military unit, date of entry into service, and, occasionally, the date of separation. It may also include personal details, such as age, physical description, date and place of birth, and residence at time of enlistment. These records are of great value to genealogists, historians and sociologists, since they vividly portray the lives of ordinary Americans in the nineteenth century.

Information about the details of the lives of Revolutionary War veterans can also be found in state archives, as well as county and town sources. Records of lineage societies and research libraries dedicated to preserving the history of the period should always be investigated.

FINDING YOUR VETERAN-THE PROCESS

The best place to start your search is by accessing the NARA records. This can be one by requesting the record by mail or by accessing the collection online.

If you want to apply for the record by mail, you will need to complete your request on Form NATF-86. To obtain this form write to General Reference Branch (NNRG), National Archives and Records Administration, 8th and Pennsylvania Avenue N.W., Washington, DC 20408. You can also find and submit the form online at www.archives.gov/contact.

Since NARA has consolidated all documents relating to service of veterans during the Revolutionary War, the NATF-86 form will generate a request for all of the information in the collection for a specific veteran. Allow up to ninety days for processing your order. You will receive a postcard acknowledging receipt of your order, which will provide a tracking number. If the NARA staff locates the service record for a specific veteran's name, they will copy the document(s). The cost for copies of all records pertaining to a single soldier is currently $30 (there is no charge for an unsuccessful search). If successful, NARA will mail you an invoice with your copies. You can also opt to receive the record on a CD or DVD.

While NARA is the largest federal repository of military service records, pension records and bounty land records, similar documents related to the American Revolution are also available at the state, county and town levels. State archives or the individual state's Office of the Adjutant General may contain records for individuals who served with the state militia, rather than the Continental Army, as well as records for bounty land issued by the state. The Revolutionary War pension application files have been microfilmed by the National Archives. Copies are also on file at select libraries throughout the country, as well as the LDS Family History Library in Salt Lake City, Utah.[324]

USING ONLINE RESOURCES AND WEBSITES

FOLD3.COM

This site derives its name from the third fold in the flag-folding ceremony that traditionally honors veterans for their sacrifice in defending their country. If you know the state where a veteran served, you can locate the person through the alphabetical hierarchy in the browse menu. Select the state, the first letter of the person's last name, and then locate the person's surname, followed by the person's given name in the next section of browse titles. The Fold3 collection contains the following records for online viewing:

- "Compiled Service Records of American Army Soldiers during the Revolutionary War 1775-1783" contains scanned documents of the service records (from National Archives Microfilm Publication M881).
- "Revolutionary War Pension and Bounty-Land Warrant Application Files" contains scanned documents of these records (from National Archives Microfilm Publication M804 mentioned above)
- "Numbered Record Books Concerning Military Operations and Service, Pay and Settlement of Accounts, and Supplies in the War Department Collection of Revolutionary War Records" (from National Archives Microfilm Publication M853)
- "Revolutionary War [muster] Rolls, 1775-1783" (M246), and other historical records

ANCESTRY.COM

This collection contains all of the NARA records mentioned above, plus other major sources:

- U.S. Compiled Revolutionary War Military Service Records 1775-1783 (from National Archives Microfilm Publications M880 and M881)

- Revolutionary War [muster] Rolls 1775-1783. Nearly 426,000 names (M246)
- Daughters of the American Revolution Lineage Books-152 Volumes
- Sons of the American Revolution Membership Applications 1889-1970
- Revolutionary War Pension and Bounty-Land Warrant Application Files 1800-1900. M804)
- Rosters or other Revolutionary War related records for Alabama, Connecticut, Georgia, Illinois, Maine, Maryland, Massachusetts, New York, North Carolina, Tennessee, Vermont, and Virginia

LINEAGE SOCIETIES

Members of the following national groups have traced their family tree back to an ancestor who supported the cause of American Independence during the years 1774-1783 and are required to document their lineage.

DAUGHTERS OF THE AMERICAN REVOLUTION (DAR)
The National Society, Daughters of the American Revolution is one of the oldest organizations in the United States dedicated to the preservation of American Revolutionary War genealogies.

The DAR Index contains the names of male and female Patriots whose Revolutionary War service (1774-1783) and lineage have been proven by the National Society, Daughters of the American Revolution. Not everyone who served in the Revolution will be listed in this index. Only Patriots whose service has been proven by documentation, and submitted by descendants applying for membership, are included. The index generally provides birth and death data for each individual, as well as information about their spouse, rank, area of service, and the state where the Patriot lived or served. The DAR also has an index that lists all spouses of the Patriots, so it is an excellent source for information about eighteenth and nineteenth century women.

Members of the National Society Daughters of the American Revolution (NSDAR) have been looking for the graves of soldiers and Patriots of the American Revolution since the 1890s. Their names and locations were first published in 1900 in the DAR's Annual Report to the Smithsonian Institution. Every year since then, additional names and locations have been added, and 58,500 have now been reported. Genealogist Patricia Law Hatcher has compiled an alphabetical list of these Revolutionary War soldiers, along with the name and location of the cemetery where they are buried or memorialized.[325] This list can also be accessed online at Ancestry.com.

You can request information from the DAR by completing a simple online form. If your ancestor is located in the index, you can request a copy of the DAR application form, which includes the information about your ancestor, for a modest fee. The website even allows you to learn the identity of people who have previously requested or submitted information about the soldier. You may obtain a photocopy of an application of related descendants by writing to: Office of the Organizing Secretary General, NSDAR, 1776 D Street, N.W., Washington, DC 20006. There is a small fee per record; your order must include: date of request, name and address, name of ancestor and page number in the DAR Index. It is always best to check DAR.org to verify current prices for these services.

The DAR also houses a non-circulating library at their headquarters in Washington, D.C. that can provide photocopies of microfilm, book pages, files, and membership applications. However, you must find out in advance which materials you would like copied, and then send in a specific request. The Index, and some other indexes to materials, are available in large genealogy libraries. Check with your local genealogy library, or a local Church of Jesus Christ of Latter Day Saints (LDS) Family History Center. If you are interested in doing in-depth research in the Daughters of the American Revolution Library, or wish to have a more detailed overview of the library, review their 180-page book titled *American Genealogical Research at the Daughters of the American Revolution, Washington, D.C.* In it you can find details about how you can make the most of your time there doing genealogical research.

The DAR Library also handles requests via fax and postal mail. All of the services require a completed request form with payment by check, money order or debit/credit card. If you have a question, contact them by email first, before mailing your written request and payment.

While the DAR indexes can be very valuable resources, they are not complete. Your ancestor may indeed have served, but may not be mentioned in any of these references. If you do find that your ancestor is listed, it means someone has been approved for DAR membership based on the service of this person.

NATIONAL SOCIETY SONS OF THE AMERICAN REVOLUTION (NSSAR)

Over the past century prospective members of NSSAR have submitted applications documenting the Revolutionary War service for thousands of men and women. Its national headquarters is at 1000 South Fourth Street, Louisville, Kentucky, 40202. The current edition of the SAR Index lists more than 100,000 Patriots and several hundred thousand of their descendants. Over the past several decades, information on the locations of more than 100,000 graves has also been reported to and collected by the SAR Revolutionary War Graves Committee, and several editions of the searchable database have been published—first in print and later on CD—as the SAR Revolutionary War Graves Registry. Both of these indices can be accessed online.

The SAR also maintains a Genealogical Research Library located at 809 West Main Street Louisville, KY 40202. To date the library collection has grown to 58,000 items, and includes family histories, state genealogy materials, federal censuses, Revolutionary War pension applications, and CD collections. An online catalog allows you to see what is available. The library provides an hourly-based research service, which searches the various resources available within the library. In addition to those mentioned above, there are NSSAR applications, documentation records, and family Bibles.

DEDICATED COLLECTIONS

The David Library of the American Revolution (www.dlar.org) in Pennsylvania is a specialized research library dedicated to the study of American history from roughly 1750 to 1800. Here you will find virtually all the primary sources about the American Revolution. This collection includes documents not found anywhere else, such as records microfilmed at the British Archives. This material is in one building, serviced by a small, but highly-knowledgeable and dedicated staff. The library is located on 1201 River Road, Washington Crossing, Pennsylvania, 18977.

The William L. Clements Library, University of Michigan [www.clements.umich.edu] houses a vast collection of original resources for the study of the American Revolution. It is located on the central campus of the University of Michigan, 909 S. University Ave, Ann Arbor, MI 48109

The Digital Collections of the Library of Congress [www/loc.gov/library/libarch-digital.html] is a guide that contains a wide variety of material associated with the war, including manuscripts, broadsides, government documents, books, and maps. This online resource compiles links to digital materials related to the American Revolution that are available throughout the Library of Congress website. In addition, it provides links to external websites focusing on the American Revolution, and a bibliography containing selections for both general and younger readers.

STATE ARCHIVES AND LOCAL SOURCES

Archives of the state where your soldier lived may also keep relevant records, since militias were not included in federal records (although militiamen did qualify for federal pensions in 1832). State archives may house bounty land records, because many veterans received bounty land at the state level. In addition, states also awarded individual pensions to some veterans.[326]

Libraries with a genealogical or historical section will often shelf numerous published works on the American Revolution. These may include military records, such as unit histories, roster lists, and other service records, county histories and genealogical studies. A centralized source for Revolutionary War records is James Neagles' *U.S. Military Records.* This book contains source information for the National Archives, the Department of Veterans Affairs, state archives, libraries, historical organizations and the Daughters of the American Revolution. Also included are extensive bibliographic listings of published sources for the United States military in general and published sources for each state.[327]

To learn more about your Revolutionary War soldier, visit local historic and genealogical societies, most of which have local archival documents. Another excellent source are local reenactment societies, since they often have published histories or websites dedicated to the military units that they represent. If you are fortunate to find that your soldier was a member of a reenacted group, this source will provide valued information about his experiences during the war.

TYPES OF REVOLUTIONARY WAR RECORDS

PENSION FILES

During and after the Revolutionary War, the US Government provided three principal types of pensions to servicemen and their dependents:

1. Disability or Invalid Pensions - awarded to servicemen for physical disabilities incurred in the line of duty.
2. Service Pensions - awarded to veterans who served for specified periods of time.
3. Widows' Pensions - awarded to women whose husbands had been killed in the war, or were veterans who had served for specified periods of time.

Each pension file is identified by a number. The letter "S" before a file number indicates "survivor," and usually means that the file contains one or more post-1800 approved applications of a veteran for an invalid or service pension. "B. L. Wt." signifies a bounty-land warrant, and an "R" in the file number indicates that it was rejected.

Pension applications provide information about the claimant's income, debts, occupation, age, and disabilities. In addition, soldiers often provided the names, ages, and disabilities of all persons in their household, and disclosed any sources of charity. The amount and variety of data in the pension application files varies from case to case. Service data includes rank, organizations, terms of service, the names of officers with whom the applicant had served, and battles in which he had fought. Wounds and instances of capture were also frequently noted. Personal data also references social status, as indicated by military rank and stated occupation.

Economic data, for those who were required to submit a property list in 1820, can be quite detailed. It includes the acreage of land held, the extent of improvement, and a listing of livestock, tools, and implements. Many such lists meticulously recorded the number and condition of household items. Each compilation contains the court-assessed value of all property, real and personal, excluding only "necessary clothing and bedding." Such data about the common soldiers provides an intriguing view into the lives of the aging survivors of the Revolutionary War and their households.[328]

PENSION LEGISLATION

Pension amounts were paid monthly, with the amount of the payment based on rank. Before 1818 the acts provided for half-pay for pensioners. The March 18, 1818 act provided all officers with twenty dollars a month, and former enlisted men eight dollars per month. In 1828, monthly payments were raised to full pay received while in active service, not to exceed the pay of an army captain. To determine your soldier's eligibility for a pension, it will be helpful to review the following summary of pension legislation pertaining to the Revolution.

August 26, 1776

The first pension legislation enacted in the first year of the war was a resolution by the Second Continental Congress that provided half-pay for officers and enlisted men who were disabled in the service of the United States, and who were therefore incapable of earning a living. The half-pay was to continue for the duration of the disability.

May 15, 1778

As a direct response to an appeal by General George Washington, who was desperate to retain officers and men in the Continental Army, Congress unanimously voted on May 15, 1778 to provide for half pay for seven years after the war to all officers who remained in the service until its conclusion. Enlisted men who remained until the end of the war were to receive a one-time payment of $80 at that time.

April 10, 1806

The scope of earlier invalid pension laws pertaining to Revolutionary War servicemen was extended to allow veterans of state troops and militia service to be eligible for Federal pensions.

March 18, 1818

President James Monroe introduced legislation granting lifetime pensions to all Revolutionary War veterans who had served until the close of the war, or at least nine months in the Continental Army, and who were in "need of assistance from their country." Pensions granted under this act were to continue for the lifetime of the veteran. Privates could receive $8 a month, and officers $20 each month.

The act was passed when the country was in the midst of a postwar economic boom that created an unexpected surplus in the treasury. It passed both houses of Congress by overwhelming majorities, in response to a public outpouring of emotion for Revolutionary War veterans, and a swelling of nationalistic pride following the War of 1812. For the first time major pension legislation rewarded veterans, and had not been enacted in order to encourage enlistment.

To receive this payment, each veteran had to swear before a nearby court that he had served "against the common enemy" and that he was in need of aid. He had to identify the unit in which he served, and when he had entered and left the military. Many documents in the pension file consist of fellow soldiers' depositions to support these facts, as well as testimony from friends and family attesting to the service. Occasionally, an official paper was submitted as proof of honorable discharge at the conclusion of the war, or a letter was included from officers. The majority of the testimony was oral, and was recorded in the script of court stenographers. In many cases, it was signed only by the applicant's mark, either due to illiteracy or debility.

Supporters in Congress of the 1818 act believed that the program would have a very limited response, and had assured the public that only a few needy veterans of the Revolution still survived thirty-five years after the war ended. Although they estimated that only a few thousand veterans would apply, they were completely overwhelmed by a flood of applicants; soon 18,800 claimants were granted pensions.

May 1, 1820

The unexpected demand in 1818 led to an amendment in the law to reduce cost and deter fraud. The supplementary act passed in 1820 stiffened the poor law provision, with the addition of a means test that required applicants to submit a certified schedule of personal property and income.

At this time the War Department began vetting eligibility more carefully, and in addition to the newly-required list of property, many other documents were mandated. These included depositions confirming the length and type of military service, letters, copies of deeds, bills of sale, and court decisions relating to indebtedness. The last requirements were to prove that any transfer of property had not been intended to defraud the government by making the veteran eligible for a pension. Medical records were even attached to some files, as former invalid pensioners, no longer eligible for service pensions because of their wealth, were returned to the invalid rolls and were required to submit to biannual medical examination by two surgeons or physicians.

The Secretary of War received a copy of all depositions and made the determination of whether each veteran was "in his opinion, in such indigent circumstances as to be unable to support himself without the assistance of his country." Men who did not qualify were stricken from the rolls. This had the effect of reducing the total of Revolutionary War service pensioners by several thousand. Over the course of the next decade, proof of poverty remained the basis of eligibility for a service pension.

May 15, 1828

Congress passed another service-pension act which granted full pay for life to surviving officers and enlisted men of the Revolutionary War who were eligible for benefits under the terms of the Continental Congress resolution of May 15, 1778, as amended. This gave privates in the Continental Line who had served to the close of the war the amount of their full pay, whether in need of help or not.

On June 7, 1832 Congress granted pensions to all remaining veterans of any Revolutionary military service, including militiamen. The 1832 act provided a yearly grant to every man who had served for six months or more. This act gave full pay for life to all citizens who had served for at least two years in any military unit. Those who had served less than two years, but more than six months, were entitled to receive proportionately smaller pensions. To be eligible under this more liberal 1832 act, soldiers no longer had to be disabled or poor, and service in any military organization was satisfactory, as long as service could be proved beyond a reasonable doubt. While there were no requirements in pension legislation for "cost of living" adjustments, payment amounts were increased by changing provisions in the various acts. This 1832 act raised many pensioners to full pay from lesser amounts. Shortening eligibility periods, extending duration of benefits, and lifting need and disability tests all had the effect of adjusting for inflation. Actually requiring adjustments should not have been a problem during the time this legislation was being approved, since the United States' inflation rate declined 59 percent between 1800 and 1840.

These acts were followed by what were known as "the widows' acts." An 1836 act stated that widows could claim the veteran's benefits if she had married the soldier during the term of his active service in the Revolution, and if she had remained unmarried after his death. This legislation added 22,600 widows' pensions to the rolls, all women who had survived veterans who did not live to file claims. Later widow's acts lengthened the term of eligible marriages to the year 1800.

PENSION PAYMENTS

In order to trace pension payments, the complete service record of the veteran from the National Archives Microfilm Publication M804 is needed. Pension payments provide many clues about the life of a veteran, including home locations, names and relationships of family members, and health condition.

Collecting pension money was a daunting chore for many aging veterans. It could entail traveling long distances to appear in person before the US Government agent who distributed pensions. If the pensioner could not travel due to poor health or inconvenience, his attorney or agent could collect the payment on his behalf. The agent could be a family member or a paid representative.

Researching the records relating to pension payments is somewhat difficult, requiring an understanding of obscure and un-indexed records. For Revolutionary Army veterans, the research process primarily involves two record groups, Record Group (RG 15), Records of the Veterans Administration, and (RG 217), Records of the Accounting Officers of the Treasury. It is not surprising that these records have never been published, due to their complexity. A recent guide to the research process uses a veteran of the 15th Massachusetts Regiment, William McCullar, and his widow, Chloe, as a case study.[329] Pension payment certificates are often included in each veteran's service record, (NARA Publications M880 and M881).

By the autumn of 1834, fifty-one years after the Treaty of Paris, approximately 40,000 pensioners were on the rolls. This was nearly 22 percent of those who had enlisted for Continental, state, and militia service.[330] The Revolutionary War pension acts were the first federally-legislated welfare program in the country, and the first federal pensions for all soldiers. They paved the way for the government to grant compensation for military service in all subsequent wars.[331]

BOUNTY LAND WARRANTS

The Federal Government offered free bounty land to those who had served in the military during the Revolutionary War, and nine states did the same.[332] Veterans or their heirs were entitled to claim this land. The Federal Government reserved tracts of land in the public domain for this purpose, and several states set aside tracts of bounty land for their veterans. As a result, there may be bounty land files for soldiers in the Continental Line and militia at both the federal and state levels. Bounty records can provide evidence of military service in cases where a veteran or his widow did not apply for a pension, since not all Revolutionary War veterans and widows met the qualifications for these during their lifetimes.[333] Since there was no requirement to demonstrate poverty for bounty land, many of these veterans and widows were successful in their claims.

A bounty land warrant application for a veteran of the Revolutionary War will include the person's rank, military unit and period of service. It will also generally provide his age and place of residence at the time of application. If the application was made by the surviving widow, it will usually include her age, place of residence, the date and place of marriage, and her maiden name.

Bounty land warrants were not automatically offered to every veteran. The veteran first had to apply for a warrant. Once received, the land warrants could also be transferred or sold to other individuals. A veteran requested bounty land by filing out an application for a warrant, usually at the local courthouse. If it was granted, he could use it to apply for a land patent. The land patent is the document that granted him ownership of the land.

The application papers and supporting documents were placed in bounty land files, which were then maintained by the federal or state agency. These files contain information similar to pension files, including the veteran's age and place of residence at time of application. Later laws allowed for the sale or exchange of warrants. Because of this, very few soldiers actually received title to bounty land or settled on it, and many sold or exchanged their warrants for a pittance.

Searching bounty land patents can also determine if your soldier moved west to the frontier in the early to mid-1800s. The frontier in those days was considered to be the western portions of New York, Pennsylvania, Ohio and Virginia. It is useful to review histories of those areas to see if they were designated as a military district, and then attempt to identify if a grant was from the state or Federal Government. Deeds later recorded at the county level usually do not record military land patents.

Federal bounty land applications and warrants for the Revolutionary War can be requested in the same way as pension records. They are available at the National Archives, its regional branches, "Revolutionary War Pension and Bounty Land Warrant Application Files," (Record Group 15) and various online sources.

The warrants for Revolutionary War service were issued under acts of July 9, 1788, March 3, 1803, and April 15, 1806. The 1788 act gave free land in the public domain to officers and soldiers who continued to serve during the Revolutionary War or, if they were killed, to their representatives or heirs. The resolution provided that a private or noncommissioned officer would be entitled to one hundred acres of bounty land. Officers received additional land based on their rank. Ensigns were allotted 150 acres, lieutenants 200 acres, captains 300 acres, majors 400 acres, lieutenant colonels 450 acres, colonels 500 acres, brigadier generals 850 acres, and a major generals 1,100 acres. A 4,000 square-mile tract (2,539,110 acres) was surveyed in the Northwest Territory, and was set aside for these land warrants. This area came to be known as the US Military District of Ohio. Originally the lands in this district were to be distributed by January 1, 1800. By the end of 1802 about 14,000 warrants had been issued.

FOLLOWING YOUR SOLDIER'S ADVENTURES IN THE WAR ORDERLY BOOKS

Regiment orderly books can provide a way to track your soldier's army life by following the activities of his unit on a day-by-day basis. These books are handwritten copies of official orders that flowed down from higher-ranking officers and locations to the lower units; they served as mass communication to transmit essential information to troops at all levels. They provide a digest of the operations of the Continental Army, and an insight into the lives of its common soldiers. These records have been described as "the diary of the army." They provide firsthand accounts of places and geography where military units camped, marched, and fought, how the men behaved, and how they were disciplined. Detailed soldier's diaries and contemporary regimental histories are scarce, so orderly books are the major source for understanding the "real" Continental Army.

The Continental Army initiated the keeping of orderly books when the war broke out in 1775. The system was based on the record keeping practices of the British Army that American officers had learned during the French and Indian War. Senior officers of the Continental Army began the practice in April, 1775. The initial regulations were issued by New England army commander Artemas Ward, and by General Washington when he arrived at Cambridge in early July of that year. The orderly book soon became the controlling document of day-to-day life in each regiment. "General Orders" originated at the headquarters of General Washington and other higher-ranking officers, and were passed down through the ranks by commanders, lieutenants, and captains. Other orders would be initiated at the regimental level by colonels. When the Continental Congress or state legislatures issued directives relevant to the army, these proceedings were also entered in the orderly books. What makes these documents additionally significant is that all orders show the place and date of issue.

In these writings the reader can detect the effects of exhaustion during long marches, boredom, and bravery in battle. They contain constant reminders of the persistent shortages of clothing, blankets, tents and ammunition, as well as the hardships and the privations which eventually led to mutinies. Minute details of camp life are frequently documented, including fun, amusements, pranks, petty thievery from civilians, and the theft of food and personal property from fellow soldiers. Even the astonishingly large quantities of rum consumed by the troops can be found in these records. Orderly books, however, are not the best sources for genealogical research. Except for court martial proceedings and sentences, it is relatively rare for common soldiers to be mentioned.

General Washington was in some ways a micromanager, and was in the habit of being personally involved with many insignificant issues. Orderly book entries can be found with his comments about prices to be charged by camp followers for laundry, the amount of fines against enlisted men for the loss of a single musket cartridge, and the charges by settlers and civilians selling produce to the army. When a practice is explicitly prohibited by an order, it is usually evidence that's subject was a widespread problem.

Thoroughly detailed accounts of all general court martial cases, including charges, case dispositions, and sentences are plentiful on the pages of orderly books. Many books, in fact, are primarily catalogs of criminal activity and Continental Army justice: they contain many examples of the barbarous corporal punishment meted out to common soldiers, and the comparatively painless sentences of officers.

The orderly book of the 2nd and 4th New York Regiments kept between 1778 and 1783 typifies what can be found in these rich resources. The book actually covers the activities of the three other New York regiments, and the brigades of several other states that were on the same campaigns, or were encamped with them. Day-to-day accounts of many significant historic events of the war are discussed, and provide insight on their impact on the lives of the troops. Included are orders given during the periods of the Sullivan-Clinton Campaign against the Iroquois Nations in 1779, the treason of Benedict Arnold, the winter at Jockey Hollow, New Jersey, the siege and victory at Yorktown, and the peace treaty in 1783.

This entry typifies the content of orderly books. It relates to the sentencing of three soldiers, two of whom were apparently related, for desertion and theft from a civilian. Their court martial took place during the grueling winter at Jockey Hollow. All original spelling, punctuation and sentence construction have been retained.

Head Quarters Morristown Feb,y 25th 80 [Ford Mansion, Morristown]
Genl orders
Parole Holland [password] C.S. [counter sign] Honnour, Honesty
Brigade Maj. From 1st Pennsylvania Brigade [duty officer]
The Pennsylvania Division furnished the Morris Town Picquet [guard duty] and Fatigue for the new orderly room to Morrow and the Next Day.
Division Orders Feby 25 80
By a Division Gen'l Court Martial whereof Majr Thayer is President, Henry Hines of the 3rd N York Regiment Was tried for Desertion and found Guilty of a breach if the 1st Article 6 section of the Articles of war and sentence to Receive 100 lashes on his

bare back and to be put under a stoppage of one half of his monthy pay till the Expance incurd in Conquiance of his Desertion be paid. By the same Court James Lighthall was tryed and charged with stealing a piece of brown Lining from an inhabitant of Paramus. Found guilty and sentenced to receive 100 lashes on his bare back and return a shift of the same linnin to the owner.

By the same Court, Malangdon Lighthall soldier of the 3rd NYork regiment was tried and charged with being concerned in the robbery of Mr Cornelious Bogert family at paramious [Paramus, New Jersey] found not guilty and ordered to be released form his confinmennt.

By the Same Court Henry Pilgart of the same Regiment was tried and Charged with Desertion and found guilty it being a breach of 1st article 6 section of the Article of war and sentenced to receive a100 lashes on his Bare Back.

The Commanding Officer approves the Sentence and orders the Corpl Punishment inflicted to morrow Morning at Roll Call on the Regimental parade to which they belong.

Brigade Orders Adjt to Morrow Hardenburgh Officer of Camp Guard Ensign V Deburgh

MUSTER ROLLS

Muster rolls are perhaps the best source for tracking the military career of an individual Revolutionary War soldier. Bi-monthly muster rolls were prepared at the company level to track the army's strength in detail. They also provided basic information about the identities, numbers, condition, equipage, and pay status of the men and units that comprised the army in order to determine its strength. Each roll contains the names of all officers and men, the dates of their enlistment, and a description of their assignments. They constitute the largest collection of Continental Army records that exist and provide a vast amount of information about individual soldiers.

The vast majorities of muster rolls consist of lists of names in descending order of rank of all officers and men of the company present or absent on the day the unit was assembled for muster. This collection can be accessed online at Fold3.com and Ancestry.com, and are listed as "Revolutionary War Rolls, 1775-1783" (NARA M246). The full collection is composed of 138 microfilmed reels of American Army units that existed between the years 1775-83. The documents are the original wartime manuscripts, and contain bi-monthly muster rolls and payrolls, weekly strength returns, descriptive rosters, periodic inspection reports, and clothing returns, as well as other unit-related archival records.

The columns of each roll had standard notes—"sick," "on guard," "on furlough," or "on command" (absent from camp on official business). A man might also be assigned to a general's guard. Special conditions included being listed as "sick in camp," or at a specified army hospital, "in the enemy's captivity," "absent with leave," or the more shocking alternative of "deserted." Changes since the prior roll might include a note of transfer to a light infantry company, "on wagon duty," "promoted," "reduced" or "broken," "died" if due to disease, "wounded" or "killed." Frequently, these entries were supplemented by dates of absence, death or transfer and the locations of those absent, sick, or on command.

Names of soldiers who were dropped from the rolls because of transfer, discharge, desertion, or death appear at the end of the roll. On the reverse of each muster roll is a tabulated statement titled "Proof of Effectives." This provides the number of officers and men of each rank present and absent, excluding those who were to be purged from the rolls. The date and place where the roll was taken are frequently listed at the bottom.

One of the most enlightening muster rolls is the rare "descriptive roster." For each soldier, it lists the date and term of enlistment, age, height, race ("complexion"), civilian occupation, home town and/or country of birth and, at times, special "comments." For example, "A Muster Roll of the men Raised and Pass'd Muster in the County of Orange [New York] for Capt Johnston's Company 4th August 1775. Peter Ellison, date of enlistment- July 23, age 23, born Orange, Farmer, height-5 Foot 10 inches, complexion-fair, eyes-blue, hair-black, A scar on ye right cheek."

The army had a hidden agenda in preparing "descriptive rosters," since these records were also compiled to assist in identifying and apprehending deserters. They are the most uncommon type of muster roll. Although forty-five entries were found on muster rolls for Corporal John Allison, who served for the entire eight years of the war, only one was on a descriptive roster.

PAYROLLS

Pension files of Revolutionary War veterans and their widows are well-known as excellent genealogical and historical research sources. Few researchers, however, venture beyond the pension file to follow the "money trail" of records documenting the actual pension payments. Unit payrolls can be found The "Revolutionary War Rolls, 1775-1783," (NARA M246). Unit payroll data can be accessed online on the Fold3.com database.

Payroll lists document the amount of wages paid to each soldier. The heading shows the same data as muster rolls, i.e., the company, regiment, commanding officers and often the place of the payment. The name and rank of each man appear with his pay rate and the amount paid on that payday. Comments are often included regarding absence during the pay period, and withdrawals reflecting penalties for lost or damaged clothing, arms, and equipment. Charges for as little as twenty-five cents for a wasted musket cartridge are tabulated. While regulations called for the troops to be paid bi-monthly, paydays were very intermittent, and months, or even years, might elapse between paydays.

Payroll data appears in a wide variety of formats, and some rolls contain many more details than others. Information on some vouchers may include the name of a spouse, county of residence, and previous residences. The record lists length of service, final pension payment amount, and the date. Some vouchers may also include children's names and the dates of death for the veteran or his spouse.

Payrolls that require a signature to acknowledge receipt of funds can reveal if the soldier was literate. Those who could read and write signed their names, whereas other entries appear with an "X." Generally, muster rolls provide more information about individual soldiers than payrolls, and beyond each man's date and terms of enlistment, very little data of genealogical research value are to be found within payrolls.

Record keeping efforts at the federal and state level generated a huge amount of military documents which contain relevant personal information about Revolutionary War soldiers. The importance of military records was first recognized by genealogists, since they often served as the only evidence of the life of common soldiers and their families. Births were never recorded for many American men who lived during the Revolutionary War era, and public identification was found only in tax records or other record relating to the possession of property. As a result, identification in these records is the only place we find evidence for the soldiers' existence. Some are only mentioned once, whereas for many others there is a trail of documentation that followed their entire lives. After the demobilization of the fighting forces, pension legislation, claims for bounty land, and back pay extended the creation of these records through most of the nineteenth century.

Acknowledgments

Research is the heart of this work. The soul of Yankee Doodle can only be found in papers written at the time of the American Revolution. The true image of the common soldier emerges not only from military and public documents, but from the most valued sources—eyewitness accounts found in diaries and pension records in the soldier's own words.

My search to find the real Yankee Doodle led to many locations where he lived and died during our country's most important war. At many of these revered places I met living witnesses, local historians who truly keep the spirit of the brave men of the American Revolution alive. They shared their insights about the lives of the common soldier, and provided little-known details about their own experiences. They included the staff at national and state parks, re-enactors, archeologists, members of historical societies, and people who still live on the land near to where their soldier ancestors rest in local cemeteries.

Fortunately, for historians visiting this turbulent time, vital information is available in a few major repositories. Most of my research was focused on the collections of the National Archives and Records Administration, the William I. Clements Library at the University of Michigan, the David Library of the American Revolution at Washington Crossing, Pennsylvania, and the New York Public Library, Archives and Manuscripts. The professionalism of their various staffs and the ease of the investigation process provided by these institutions were remarkable and are deeply appreciated. With some perseverance, I was able to access a surprising number of documents in their original form on the Internet. However, I discovered that the most rewarding research in original eighteenth century records came from exploring the stacks of these comprehensive collections, requesting records from patient librarians, and sore-thumbing through hard copy.

I was fortunate to be guided by an experienced and accomplished editor of American history, David E. Kane, Publisher, American History Press. The professionalism and constructive suggestions he provided could have only been offered by another historian with an exceptional comprehension of the Revolutionary War. I also extend my heartfelt thanks to "The Watchung Writers." This eclectic group of accomplished authors was founded over a decade ago by novelist Gordon

McLenithan and is currently led by Pat Rydberg. Vivian Fransen and others patiently critiqued my work, and J.R. Bale, of BaleFire Communications, provided guidance on graphics and Internet issues. These talented people, mostly fiction writers and poets, managed to stay the course in providing feedback on my early drafts while enduring my heavy doses of life in the Continental Army. Since this book was written to be enjoyed by the average person, and not only serious military historians, their genuine interest and enthusiasm may portend its appeal to future readers.

Finally, I thank my wife, Norma, for tolerating my obsession with the Revolutionary War and my virtual absences when I morphed into a time traveler and disappeared into the eighteenth century. Corporal John Allison, my muse and ancestor, was with me during all of these adventures. He served in the Continental Army for the entire eight years of the conflict that gave birth to our nation and which made possible all that followed.

Endnotes

CHAPTER ONE

1. Fernow, Berthold, The New York Line in the 3rd Continental Establishment, New York State Archives, New York in the Revolution Vol. 1, (Albany, NY, Weed, Parsons & Company, Printers, 1887, 168.

2. Heitman, Francis B. Historical Register and Dictionary of the United States Army from Its Organization, September 29, 1789, to March 2, 1903 (Washington, D.C., US Government Printing Office, 1903), 238.

3. Fitzpatrick, John C. *The Writings of Washington from the Original Manuscript Sources, 1745-1799*, return of May 22, 1781 (Washington, D.C., US Government Printing Office, 1931-39), 102.

4. Major Christopher Richardson to Major General Horatio Gates, June 15, 1783, *Horatio Gates Papers*. (Rare books and Manuscripts Division, New York Public Library), Manuscript Collection 1118, Series 1, Container 1, Reel 13.

5. Force, Peter, American Archives, 4th Series, 2:1771-77; 3:496, 501-11, 870-71.

6. By order of Congress, John Hancock, President, dated Philadelphia, June 19, 1775. This resolution of the Second Continental Congress was the beginning of the United States Army as we know it today.

7. George Washington's letter to his half-brother, John Augustine Washington, Cambridge, July 27, 1775.

8. "Aaron Wright's Revolutionary Journal," Historical Magazine of America, July 1861, 209.

9. Letter of Instructions to the Captains of the Virginia Regiments, July 29, 1759).

10. Washington to Congress, July 9, 1775, Journal, Provincial Congress of Massachusetts, 482.

11. Muster Roll, Colonel Timothy Danielson's 18th Massachusetts Regiment, October 28, 1775, Revolutionary War Rolls 1775-1783, Publication M246, Folder 41, US National Archives.

12. The Works of John Adams, Second President of the United States (Boston, MA, Little, Brown, 1854) iii., 48.

13. Fitzpatrick, John C. *The Writings of Washington from the Original Manuscript Sources, 1745-1799*, 37 Vols. (Washington, D.C., US Government Printing Office, 1931-44), Vol. 4, pp. 299-301.

CHAPTER TWO

14. Baker, Richard Lee, *Villiany and Maddness, Washington's Flying Camp* (Clearfield, PA, Clearfield Publishing, 2010).

15. Lande, Gregory, "Invalid Corps," *Military Medicine*, 173.6 (2008), 526.

16. Fitzpatrick, 2:207-09 (May 1781).

17. Fitzpatrick 4:124 (to Joseph Reed, November 25, 1775).

18. Hillard, E. B. Rev. *The Last Men of the Revolution* (Hartford, CT, N.A. and R.A. Moore, 1864), 24.

19. Ibid., 64.

20. Chastellux, Franc¸ois Jean, Marquis de, *Travels in North-America, in the Years 1780, 1781, and 1782* (London Printed for G.G.J. and J. Robinson, 1787), 23.

21. *A Complete History of the Marquis de Lafayette, Major-General in the American Army in the War of the Revolution Embracing an Account of his Tour through the United States, to the Time of his Departure, September, 1825. By an officer in the late army.* (Columbus, OH, J. & H. Miller, publishers, 1858), 371.

22. Thacher, James, M.D. *Military Journal of the American Revolution 1775-1783*, 30.

23. DeGregorio, William A. *The Complete Book of U.S. Presidents*, 7th Edition (Fort Lee, NJ: Barricade Books, 2009), 1.

24. E. James Ferguson, *The Power of the Purse* (Chapel Hill, NC, University of North Carolina Press, 1961), 35, 44. *Also* Bezanson, Anne, *Prices and Inflation During the American Revolution* (Philadelphia, PA, The University of Pennsylvania Press, 1951).

25. Judd, Jacob, ed. *The Revolutionary War Memoir and Selected Correspondence of Philip Van Cortlandt, 1748-1800*, Vol. 1:66. (repr. Tarrytown, NY, Sleepy Hollow Restorations, 1976), 72.

CHAPTER THREE

26. John Adams to Samuel Cooper May 30, 1776, *Founding Families: Digital Editions of the Papers of the Winthrops and the Adamses*, C. James Taylor, ed. (Boston, MA, Massachusetts Historical Society, 2016).
27. Bolton, Charles K., *The Private Soldier Under Washington* (New York,Y, Scribner's Son's,1902, repr., Port Washington, NY, Kennikat Press Inc. 1964)

28. *The Philip Schuyler Papers, 1684-1851*, Letters sent 1769-1804, Vol. 4, Letterbook 1, June 28, 1775-February 24, 1776, Manuscripts and Archives Division, New York Public Library.

29. The companies include Captain Daniel Denton's Company roll, dated July 22, 1775, Captain Jacobus Bruyn's Company roll, dated August 9, 1775, and Captain Elais Hasbrouck Company roll, dated August 10, 1775. Berthold Fernow, ed., *New York in the Revolution* (Albany, NY, 1887).

30. Shy, John, A People Numerous and Armed-Reflections on the Military Struggle for American Independence (New York, NY, Oxford University Press, 1976), 174.

31. Papenfuse Edward C. and Stiverson, Gregory A., "The Peacetime career of the Revolutionary War Private," William and Mary Quarterly, 3rd series, XXX (1973), 210.

32. Saxton, Thomas R. "In Reduced Circumstances: Aging and Impoverished Continental Veterans in the Young Republic" (Theses and Dissertations, paper 718, Lehigh University, 2001), 31.

33. Sellers, Charles "The Common Soldier in the American Revolution," in Stanley J. Underal, ed., *Military History of the American Revolution: Proceedings of the Sixth Military History Symposium, USAF Academy* (Washington, D.C., US Government Printing Office, 1976).

34. Lender, Mark Edward, *The Enlisted Line: The Continental Soldier of New Jersey*, Books and Pamphlets, July-Dec. 1975, Microfilm 15, Aug. 1975, 1669376 (Washington, D.C., Copyright Office, Library of Congress, 1977), 113.

CHAPTER FOUR

35. *Pennsylvania Packet*, June 12, 1775: *Virginia Gazette*, June 24, 1775. Quoted in *Diary of the American Revolution from Newspapers and Original Documents*, Moore, Frank, ed. (New York, 1858), 71.

36. *New York Gazette*, October 2, 1775.

37. Lowell, Edward, J., *The Hessians and other German Auxiliaries of Great Britain in the Revolutionary War* (New York, NY, Harper and Brothers, 1884), 104.

38. Roberts, Cokie. *Founding Mothers* (2004: New York, NY, Harper Collins), 118-130

39. Ford, Chauncey, ed., Journals of the Continental Congress, 1774-1789, Washington, Library of Congress, Government Printing Office, 1904-1937, Vol. IV, 403.

40. Gano, John, *Biographical Memoirs of the Late Rev. John Gano* (New York, NY, Printed by Southwick and Hardcastle for J. Tiebout, 1806).

41. Rogers, William, "Journal of Rev. William Rogers, D.D., chaplain of Gen. Hand's Brigade in the Sullivan Expedition, 1779." *Pennsylvania Archives*, Second Series, Vol. 15.

42. Fitzpatrick, Recruiting instructions, Excellency George Washington Headquarters, December 17, 1776.

43. Fitzpatrick, George Washington to John Banister, April 21, 1778.

44. Sellers, John R. "The Common Soldier in the American Revolution," in Underdal, S. J., *Military History of the American Revolution: Proceedings of the Sixth Military History Symposium*, USAF Academy (Washington, D.C., US Government Printing Office, 1976).

45. BLWT No. 7109-100-12, Issued to John Ellison, Pvt. New York Line, assigned to Samuel Coe, US National Archives.

46. Robert Ellison, Pension Application, S 45192/3301, Military Tract Township 15, Fabius, Lot 45, 600 acres, Bounty Land Book 4, 31, US National Archives.

47. Tate, Thad W., *Desertion from the American Revolutionary Army* (M.A. thesis, University of North Carolina, Chapel Hill, NC, 1948).

48. Lender, Mark E., *The Enlisted Line: The Continental Soldiers of New Jersey* (University Microfilms 1977), 203-234.

49. Brackenridge, Henry H., *Six political Discourses Founded on the Scriptures* (Lancaster, Printed by Frances Bailey, 1778, Library of Philadelphia), 43-44.

CHAPTER FIVE

50. Bolton, *The Private Soldier Under Washington*, 219.

51. Raphael, Ray, *A Peoples History of the American Revolution* (New York, NY, 2002, Harper Collins), 94.

52. Cruson, Daniel, *Putnam's Revolutionary War Encampment* (Charleston, SC, The History Press, 2011), 15.

53. Richard Montgomery to Robert R. Livingston, October 5, 1775, Robert R. Livingston Papers, New York Public Library.

54. Frederick von Steuben to Baron De Gaudy, 1787, in Frederick Knapp, *The Life of Frederick William von Steuben* (New York, 1859), 699.

55. Rush, Dr. Benjamin, in *Massachusetts Magazine* (1791), 284, 360.

56. "Papers of General Elias Dayton," *Proceedings of the New Jersey Historical Society*, Vol. 3 (1848-1849), 185.

57. Ewald, Johann von, Captain Field Jager Corps, *Diary of the American War, A Hessian Journal*, translated and edited by Joseph P. Tustin (New Haven and London, Yale University Press, 1979). Ewald was a Hessian officer who came to America in 1776 with the British military forces. He was a participant in many of the significant battles of the war, and was with Cornwallis at the surrender of Yorktown in 1781. He kept a diary of his experiences throughout the war, but just as importantly created numerous maps of the areas he was in, including the placement of troops and fortifications. The diary was acquired following World War II by Major Joseph P. Tustin, a historian for the United States Air Forces in Europe who came across it in his travels. He spent thirty years translating the work and verifying facts.

58. Waldo, Dr. A., "Dr. A. Waldo's Diary," *Historical Magazine*, May, 1861, 131. [-www.americanrevolution.org/soldier/soldier10.php]

59. Mayers, Robert A., *The War Man, The True Story of a Citizen-Soldier Who Fought from Quebec to Yorktown* (Yardley, PA., Westholme Publishing, 2009).

60. Aaron, Wright, Private,"Revolutionary Journal of Aaron Wright, 1775," *The Historical Magazine of America*, No. 5, July 1861, pp. 208-212. The diary spans the period from June 1775-March 1776.

61. Harrington, Hugh T. and Jordan, Jim, "The Other Mystery Shot of the American Revolution: Did Timothy Murphy Kill British Brigadier General Simon Fraser at Saratoga?" *The Journal of Military History*, Vol. 74, No. 4, October 2010, pp. 1037-1045.

62. New York State Division of Military and Naval Affairs, "Timothy Murphy: Frontier Rifleman," (Saratoga Springs, NY, Military History, 2008).

63. Revolutionary War Pension and Bounty-Land Warrant Application Files for: Richard Wallace, Vermont, dated July 24, 1832. Compiled Service Records of American Army Soldiers during the Revolutionary War 1775-1783, National Archives Microfilm Publication M881. *Also see* Dann, John C., ed. *The Revolution Remembered, Eyewitness Accounts of the War for Independence* (Chicago and London, The University of Chicago Press, 1977), 95-100.

64. Pension Application, S12630 Mass., Thomas Craige, Windsor, Vermont, November 11, 1833, US National Archives.

65. Pension Application, Samuel Woodruff, Windsor, Connecticut, June 7, 1832, US National Archives.

66. Pension Application, Edward Elley, Spotsylvania County, Virginia, July 2, 1846, US National Archives.

67. Pension Application, Thomas Haines, Louden, New Hampshire, W 323217, BL Wt 5072-160-55 September, 1833, US National Archives.

68. General Orders, Cambridge, January 1, 1776.

CHAPTER SIX

69. Muster Rolls, 3rd New York Regiment, Captain Robert Johnston's Company, roll dated August 10, 1775, Captain Daniel Denton's Company, roll dated July 22, 1775, Captain Jacobus Bruyn's Company, roll dated of August 9, 1775 and Captain Elais Hasbrouck Company, roll dated August 10, 1775. Berthold Fernow, ed., *New York in the Revolution* (Albany, NY, 1887).

70. Trussel, John B., *The Pennsylvania Line, Regimental Organization and Operations, 1775-1783*,

(Harrisburg, PA, Pennsylvania Historical and Museum Commission, 1993), 244.

71. Papenfuse, Edward C. and Gregory A. Stiverson. "General Smallwood's Recruits: The Peacetime Career of the Revolutionary War Private." *William and Mary Quarterly* 3rd Series, Vol. 30, No. 1 (January, 1973), 211.

72. Johann Döhla, *A Hessian Diary of the American Revolution* (Norman and London: University of Oklahoma Press, 1913), 23.

73. Taylor, Peter K., *Indentured to Liberty: Peasant Life and the Hessian Military State, 1688-1818* (Ithaca, NY, Cornell University Press, 1994), x.

74. Sellers, Charles J., *The Common Soldier in the American Revolution*, Underdal, Stanley, ed. (Honolulu, Hawaii, Proceedings of the 6th Military History Symposium, USAF Academy October 10-11, 1974), 151.

75. Bridges, Myrtle, *A Descriptive List of Men of Bladen County, North Carolina* (North Carolina State Archives, 1998).

76. Lender, Mark E., *The Enlisted Line: The Continental Soldiers of New Jersey,* Ph.D. dissertation, Rutgers University, 1975 (University microfilms, 1977).

77. Ewald, Johann; Tustin, Joseph P. trans., ed., *Diary of the American War: A Hessian Journal.* (New Haven, CT, Yale University Press, 1979), 340-341.

78. Drymple, John, *Considerations Upon the different Modes of Finding Recruits* (London, T. Cadell, 1775, Gale ECCO Print Edition June, 2006), 18.

79. Serle, Ambrose, Secretary to British General William Howe, New York, September 2, 1776, in *The American Journal of Ambrose Searle* (San Marino, CA, Huntington Library, 1940), 75.

80. Crevecoeur, Compte Jean-Francois-Louis, *Connecticut 1781,* An Excerpt From the Journal of De Clermont-Crevecoeur, Lieutenant of the Auxonne Regiment (Columbiad Club, reprinted with the permission of *The American Campaigns of Rochambeau's Army*, 1973).

81. Revolutionary War Pension and Bounty-Land Warrant Application Files for John Hudson, S38848 Vermont, dated March 18, 1818 Compiled Service Records of American Army Soldiers during the Revolutionary War 1775-1783, National Archives Microfilm Publication M881.

82. Neimeyer, Charles P, *America Goes To War: A Social History of the Continental Army* (New York and London, University Press, 1996), 20.

83. Inspection reports of Rochambeau's units (except Lauzun's Legion) on November 10-11, 1781 (one month after Yorktown).

84.Pension Application, Obadiah Benge, R 743 North Carolina, US National Archives

85. Cox, Caroline, *Boy Soldiers: Lessons from the American Revolution* (Stockton, CA, University of the Pacific, Society for the History of Children and Youth, 2007).

86. Pension Applications, Cyrus Allen, W8094; Elijah Lacy, W10189; Moses Piper, S33474; Joshua Davis, S38656, US National Archives.

87. Muster roll of Robert Johnson's Company, 3rd New York Regiment, under command of Col. James Clinton October 3, 1775, Camp at Ticonderoga.

88. Land Records, Harford County Circuit Courthouse, Bel Air, Maryland.

89. Papenfuse, Edward C., and Stiverson, Gregory A., "General Smallwood's Recruits: the Peacetime Career of the Revolutionary War Private," *William and Mary Quarterly*, Series 3, 1973, 32.

90. Service records, Isaac Wheeler, 5th Connecticut Regiment, 1775, US National Archives.

91. The Nathan Futrell Bible (printed 1816) and copied April 1999 by Charleen Peel, Rancho Cucamonga, CA, [www.westernkyhistory.org/trigg/bible/futrell/record.html]

92. Broughton-Mainwaring, Rowland, *Historical record of the Royal Welsh Fusillliers, Late the Twenty-Third Foot* (London, Hatchards-Piccadilly, 1889), 100.

93. (Marker No. 994) County: Trigg, Location: Six miles south of Golden Pond, off US Route 68.

CHAPTER SEVEN

94. Recruiting Poster, Philadelphia, 1776, *Evans Collection of Early American Imprints*, No. 151639 (Washington D.C., Georgetown University Library).

95. Mayers, Robert A., *The War Man-The True Story of a Citizen-Soldier who Fought from Quebec to Yorktown* (Yardley, PA, Westholme Publishing, 2009), 14-15.

96. Royster, Charles, *A Revolutionary People at War* (New York, W.W. Norton & Co., 1981), 25.

97. Mayers, *The War Man,* 14, 15.

98. Force, Peter, *American Archives*, Correspondence and Proceedings, July 6, 1775, 1592.

99. Martin, Joseph Plumb, and Sheer, George E., *Private Yankee Doodle: Being a Narrative of the Adventures, Dangers and Sufferings of a Revolutionary War Soldier* (1962; reprint Boston, MA, Little, Brown, 2006), 16-17.

100. New York Provincial Congress, June 1775, in Roberts, James A. *New York in the Revolution as Colony and State* (1897; reprint Baltimore, MD, Genealogical Publishing Co. 1996), 104.

101. Greene, George Washington, *The Life of Nathanael Greene: Major-General in the Army of the Revolution,* Vol. 1. (1867; reprint Hong Kong, Forgotten Books, 2013), 220-221.

102. The terms *regiment* and *battalion* were interchangeable at that time, since nearly every Continental Army regiment consisted of a single battalion.

103. Recruiting Instructions, *Virginia Gazette, Williamsburg, January 3, 1777*, printed by Dixon and Hunter (No. 1326).

104. Fitzpatrick, *Writings of Washington*, X, 366.

105. Acomb, Evelyn M., ed., *Revolutionary War Journal of Baron Ludwig von Closen 1780-1783* (Chapel Hill, NC, University of North Carolina Press, 1958), 203.

106. Fitzpatrick, *Writings of Washington,* XI, 98-99.

107. Ingaro, Charles W., *The Hessian Mercenary State: Ideas, Institutions and Reform Under Frederick II* (Cambridge and New York, Cambridge University Press, 2003), 160.

108. Armstrong, David A., "Steubens Contribution to the Patriotic Cause," *Military Review* 56(6) 1976, 58-68.

109. Von Zemensky, Edith, ed., *The Papers of General Friedrich Wilhelm von Steuben* (Millwood, NY, Kraus International Publications, 1982).

110. Steuben to the Continental Congress, Henry Laurens and George Washington, December 6, 1777, *The Papers of General Friedrick von Steuben*, 1:15-17.

111. Lockhard, Paul, *The Drillmaster of Valley Forge: The Baron de Steuben and the Making of the American Army* (New York, Harper Collins, 2008).

112. John Laurens to Henry Laurens, May 7, 1778, in *The Papers of Henry Laurens*, Hamar, Philip M. et. al., eds. (Columbia, SC, University of South Carolina Press, 1968).

113. von Steuben, Baron. *Baron von Steuben's Revolutionary War Drill Manual* (1779) (reprint, Mineola, NY, Dover Publications, Inc., 1985).

114. Shrader, Frederick Franklin, *Germans in the Making of America.* (Boston, MA, Stratford Co. 1924).

115. Rosengarten, J.G., *German Soldiers in the Wars of the United States* (Philadelphia, PA, J.B. Lippincott Co. 1886).

116. Palmer, John McAuley, *General von Steuben.* (New Haven, CT, Yale University Press, 1937).

CHAPTER EIGHT

117. "Construction of Tent Dimensions, January 1, 1781," Miscellaneous Numbered Records (The Manuscript File) in the War Department Collection of Revolutionary War Records 1775-1790s, No. 31492, 1971 (US National Archives, Microfilm Publication M859, reel 111).

118. Boatner, Mark M., *Encyclopedia of the American Revolution: Library of Military History*, 2nd Edition, Vol. 2 (New York, NY, Charles Scribners & Sons, 2006), 1068-1069.

119. Friedrich von Steuben Papers, Manuscript Collections, New York Historical Society.

120. Heath, William, *Memoirs of Major General William Heath,* Abbatt, William, ed. (New York, NY, W. Abbatt, 1901)

121. Demsey, Janet, *Washington's Last Cantonment-High Time for Peace* (Monroe, NY, Library Research Associates, 1987).

122. General Orders, 28 June 1779, Orderly book of Col. Oliver Spencer's Regt., June 1779-24 July 1779, *Early American Orderly Books 1748-1817*, Collection of the New York Historical Society.

123. Benedict Arnold's Regimental Memorandum Book, June 14, 1775. In South Carolina seines were provided for the Continental troops that were detailed to fish. *Also* Captain B. Elliott's Diary, in *Charleston Year Book 1889*, 231.

124. Freedman, Russell. *Washington at Valley Forge.* (New York, NY, Holiday House, 2008), 30.

125. Samuel Talmadge and James Barr, *Orderly Books of the 4th New York Regiment 1778-1780* (Albany, NY, University of the State of New York, 1932),General Orders, January 30, 1780, Headquarters, Morristown, New Jersey.

126. Whiting, John, *Revolutionary Orders of General Washington: Issued During The Years 1778, 1780, 1781, And 1782* (1844; reprint, Whitefish, MT, Kessinger Publishing, 2010), 75.

127. Gano, John, *Reverend. John Gano's Biographical Memoirs* (New York, Historical Magazine, 1806), Vol. 5, 332.

128. Van Cortlandt, Philip "Autobiography of Philip Van Cortlandt," *Magazine of American History*, May, 1878, 296.

129. Ford *Washington's Writings*, Vol. 5, 495.

130. Bolton, *The Private Soldier Under Washington*, 85.

131. Ford, *Washington's Writings*, Vol. 3, 195.

132. Pickering, Timothy, "*Regulations for the Government of Sutlers,*" (US National Archives, September 8, 1782, Numbered Record Books, Vol. 84,) 96-97.

133. Albigence Waldo, "Diary of Surgeon Albigence Waldo, of the Connecticut Line Valley Forge, 1777-1778," (Philadelphia, PA, Historical Society of Pennsylvania, *Pennsylvania Magazine of History and Biography*, Vol. 21, No. 3, 1897), 299-323.

134. Risch, Erna, *Supplying Washington's Army* (Washington, D.C., Center of Military History, United States Army, 1981), 193.

135. Fitzpatrick, *Writings of Washington*, March 24, 1783.

136. Fitzpatrick, *Writings of Washington*, General Orders, July 5, 1777.

137. *The 1777 Continental Army Diary Of Sergeant John Smith, First Rhode Island Regiment*, Collection of the American Antiquarian Society, Worcester, Massachusetts.

138. Senter, Isaac, *The Journal of Isaac Senter* (Philadelphia, PA, Historic Society of Pennsylvania, 1846).

139. Martin, *Private Yankee Doodle*, 141.

140. Aimone, Alan and Aimone, Barbara, ed., *The Siege of Yorktown Made a Lasting Impression On a Young Soldier's Mind* (*American History Illustrated*, Vol. 16, 1981):18-23. Originally published as "Narrative of John Hudson: A Revolutionary soldier and now resident of Cincinnati," in *Cist's Cincinnati Advertiser*, Jan. 28-Apr. 22, 1846, Vol. 3.

141. Fitzpatrick, *Writings of Washington*, 26, 222.

142. Mayers, *The War Man*, 189.

143. Cox, Caroline. *A Proper Sense of Honor: Service & Sacrifice in George Washington's Army*. (Chapel Hill, NC, University of North Carolina Press, 2004).

CHAPTER NINE

144. Angell, Israel, *The Diary of Colonel Israel Angell Commanding Officer, 2nd Rhode Island Regiment, Continental Army*, transcribed from the original manuscript by Edward Field and Norman Desmarais. (Providence, R I, Preston and Rounds Company, 1899).

145. Ford, Chauncey, ed. *The Writings of George Washington*, 14 Volumes (New York and London, G.P. Putnam's Sons, 1889), Vol. 10, 153.

146. General Orders, Headquarters, Cambridge, Massachusetts, January 1, 1776.

147. Journals of the Continental Congress, Ford, ed., III, 323.

148. Major General Enoch Poor to Governor George Clinton, February 16, 1778, in *Valley Forge Guide and Handbook* by James W. Riddle (Philadelphia, PA, J. B. Lippincott, 1910).

149. Idzerda, Stanley J., ed., *Lafayette in the Age of the American Revolution: Selected Letters and Papers, 1776-1790* (Ithaca, NY, Cornell University Press, 1977), 199-201.

CHAPTER TEN

150. Tomlinson, Abraham, *The Military Journal of Two Private soldiers, 1758-1775* (Poughkeepsie, NY, Published by Alan Tomlinson, at the Museum, 1855), 77.

151. Service Record, Pride, James, W 26939, New York, US National Archives.

152. Orderly Book of Colonel William Henshaw, April 20 to September 26, 1775 (Boston, MA, James Wilson and Son, 1877), 219.

153. Fisher, Elijah. *Journal While in the War for Independence, 1775-1784* (Augusta, ME, Badger and Manley, 1880).

154. Fitzpatrick, *Writings of George Washington*, Head Quarters at the Gulph, December 17, 1777.

155. Journals of Congress, September 12, 1777, 99.

156. Fisher, *Military Journal*, 186.

157. Loammi Baldwin to his wife, June 17, 1776, (*Baldwin Papers*, Harvard College Library, as quoted in *Rebels and Redcoats*, George F. Sheer and Hugh F. Rankin (New York, NY De Capo Press, 1957,) 146.

158. Martin, *Private Yankee Doodle*, 123.

159. Selig, Robert A. "A German Soldier in America, 1780-1783: The Journal of Georg Daniel Flohr," (*The William and Mary Quarterly*, No. 3, July 1993,) Selig describes a recently-discovered 1787 manuscript-journal of an enlisted fusilier of the Royal Deux-Ponts Regiment who was in Rochambeau's Expedition. The German text, written in 1787, was found in Strasbourg in the 1970s.

160. Bangs, Edward ed. *Journal of Lieutenant Isaac Bangs, April 1 to July 29, 1776* (New York, NY, John Wilson and Son, 1890), 12.

161. Tudor, William "Memoir of Hon. William Tudor," (*Collections of the Massachusetts Historical Society*, Second Series, Vol. VIII. Boston: 1819), 285-325.

162. Peter Muhlenberg, Brigade Orders, Sept. 5, 1777, Orderly Book of General John Gabriel Peter Muhlenberg March 26 to Dec. 20, 1777.

163. Tiffany, Osmond, *A Sketch of the Life and Services of Otho Holland Williams*. (Baltimore, MD, J. Murphy & Co., 1851).

164. Robert Steele to William Sumner, July 10, 1825, in *Samuel Swett Papers on Bunker Hill*, New York Historical Society.

165. General Orders issued by General Greene, Long Island, August 6, in Orderly book of Colonel William Henshaw, 219.

166. General Orders, Newburgh, May 16, 1782.

CHAPTER ELEVEN

167. Lamb, Roger, Sergeant in the Royal Welsh Fuzileers. *An Original and Authentic Journal of the Occurences during the Late American War from its commencement to the year 1783* (Dublin, Ireland, 1809), 361.

168. Fitzpatrick, *Writings of Washington*, Vol. V, 361.

169. Cooper, Robert, Rev. *Courage in a Good Cause, Or The Lawful and Courageous Use of the* Sword: A Sermon, Preached Near Shippensburgh, Pa. August 31, 1775 (Lancaster, PA. Francis Bailey, 1775), 24-25.

170. American Archives, V, Vol. 3, Col. 602.

171. *Regulations for the Order and Discipline of the Troops of the United States*, by Baron von Steuben. Boston, 1794, Chapter 21 (reprinted by Dover Publications, NY, 1985).

172. Brown, G. I. *The Big Bang: A History of Explosives* (Gloucester, UK Sutton Publishing, 1998), 97.

173. Franklin, Benjamin. *The Life of Benjamin Franklin*. (Philadelphia, PA, J.B. Lippincott, 1874), Vol. 6, 2.

174. Flayderman, Norm *Flayderman's Guide to Antique Firearms and Their Values* 7th Edition (Iola, WI, Krause Publications, 1998).

175. Wright, John W., *The Rifle in the American Revolution*, *American Historical Review*, January 1924; Vol. 29, No.2, 293-299.

176. *Timothy Murphy: Frontier Rifleman*. New York State Military Museum and Veterans Research Center (New York, NY, Random House Publishing Group), 46.

177. Cline, Walter M., *The Muzzle Loading Rifle* (Huntington, WVA, Standard Printing and Publishing Co., 1942.)

178. Harrower, John, "Diary of John Harrower, 1773-1776," *The American Historical Review*, Volume: 6. October 1, 1900, 100.

179. Willis, Chuck, *Weaponry: an Illustrated History*,(New York, Hylas Publishing, 2006), 90-91.

180. Dillin, John, *The Kentucky Rifle*. (York, PA, George Shumway, 1967), XI.

181. Ward, Christopher, *The War of the Revolution*. (New York, NY, MacMillan, 1952), 216.

182. Town, Ithiel _ *A detail of some particular services performed in America during the years 1776, 1777, 1778 and 1779, Compiled from Journals and Original Papers. . .taken from the Journal Kept on Board of the Ship"Rainbow' Commanded By Sir George Collier* (New York, NY, Printed for Ithiel Town, 1835).

183. Brooks, Noah, *Henry Knox, A Soldier of the Revolution, General in the Continental Army, Washington's Chief of Artillery, First Secretary of War Under the Constitution, Founder of the Society of Cincinnat,;1750-1806.*(New York, NY, G.P. Putnam's Sons, 1900).

184. Joseph Plumb Martin, *A Narrative of a Revolutionary Soldier: Some of the Adventures, Dangers, and Sufferings of Joseph Plumb Martin* (1830; reprint, New York, NY, Signet Classic, 2001), 280.

CHAPTER TWELVE

185. Raphael, Ray, *A People's History of the American Revolution: How Common People Shaped the Fight for Independence* (New York, NY, Perennial, 2002), 311, 355. Raphael estimates that at the time of the American Revolution there were about 430,000 slaves in the Southern colonies and 50,000 in the North.

186. De Crèvecoeur, J. Hector St. John, *Letters from an American Farmer and Sketches of Eighteenth-Century America* (New York, NY, Penguin Classics, 1981).

187. Lanning, Michael, *African Americans in the Revolutionary War*. (New York, NY, Kensington Publishing, 2000).

188. Raymond, Marcus, D., *Colonel Christopher Greene of Rhode Island*, read before the Rhode Island Historical Society, April 26, 1902. (Tarrytown, NY, Published by the author, 1902).

189. Prince, Mason, M, *Slavery and Politics in the Early American Republic* (Chapel Hill, NC, University of North Carolina Press, 2006), 12.

190. Quarles, Benjamin. *The Negro in the American Revolution* (Chapel Hill, University of North Carolina Press, 1961).

191. Clinton Proclamation, *Clinton Papers*, June 30, 1779 (*Royal Gazette*, July 3, 1779 to September 1779), William L. Clements Library.

192. Froner, Philip. *Blacks in the American Revolution* (Westport, CT, Greenwood Press, 1976), 44.

193. The service of African-American soldiers alongside their white partners is vividly shown in an August 24, 1778 "Return of the Negroes in the Army," which lists 755 black soldiers in fifteen brigades of General George Washington's main army at White Plains, New York.

194. Rhode Island State Archives: *Records of the State of Rhode Island, December 1777-October 1779*, 10:4.

195. Raymond, Marcus D. *Colonel Christopher Greene of Rhode Island.*

196. Acomb, Evelyn M., ed., *The Revolutionary Journal of Baron Ludwig von Closen, 1780-1783* (Chapel Hill, NC, University of North Carolina Press, 1958), 90, 92.

197. Ray W. Pettengill, ed. and trans., Letters from America 1776 1779: Being Letters of Brunswick, Hessian, and Waldeck Officers with the British Armies during the Revolution (Port Washington, NY, Kennikat Press, 1964), 119.

198. Pybus, Cansandra, *Epic Journeys of Freedom, Runaway Slaves of the American Revolution and their Global Quest for Liberty* (Boston, MA, Beacon Press, 2006). Pybus describes *The Book of Negroes*, a list drawn up by the British authorities between May and November in 1783, in which they recorded the personal details of some 3,000 African-Americans evacuated from New York. The great majority of these people were originally enslaved workers who had defected to the British. Although they were now leaving America as free people, they were soon re-enslaved when they reached their destination. The most significant fact about *The Book of Negroes* is that most people are recorded with surnames that allow them to be tracked through the archives.

CHAPTER THIRTEEN

199. Thomas Jefferson to John Page, August 5, 1776 in *Papers of Thomas Jefferson*, Julian C. Boyd, ed. (Princeton, NJ, Princeton University Press, 1950), 4:622-24.

200. Fitzpatrick, *Writings of George Washington*, Vol. 15, 171-173, Washington to Major General John Sullivan, Headquarters, Middlebrook, May 28 and 31, 1779.

201. Bruce G. Trigger, ed., *Handbook of North American Indians, Volume 15: Northeast* (Washington, DC, The Smithsonian Institution, 1988).

202. Pell, Joshua, *Diary of Joshua Pell, Junior: An Officer of the British Army in America, 1776-1777*, J. L. Onderdonk, ed., *Magazine of American History*, 2 (1878), 43-47, 107-112.

203. Moody, T. W., Vaughan, W. E., *A New History of Ireland: Eighteenth Century Ireland, 1698-1800* (Oxford, Clarendon Press, 1986), 4:214-15.

204. Leyburn, James G., *The Scotch-Irish: A Social History* (Chapel Hill, NC, University of North Carolina Press, 1962), 180.

205. *Timothy Murphy: Frontier Rifleman*, New York State Military Museum and Veterans Research Center (New York, NY, Random House Publishing Group), 46.

206. Stoudt, John B. "The German Press in Pennsylvania and the American Revolution," *Pennsylvania Magazine of History and Biography*, 59 (1938): 74-90.

207. Burgoyne, Bruce E., *A Hessian Report on the People, the Land, the War: The American Revolutionary War as Recorded by the Hessian Participants* (Berwyn Heights, MD, Heritage Books, 2004).

208. Cronau, Rudolf, Drei Jahrhunderte deutschen Lebens in Amerika (Hamburg: Severus Verlag. 2010).

209. Lowenthal, Larry, ed., *Days of Siege, A Journal of the Siege of Ft. Stanwix in 1777. Journal attributed to Lt. William Colbrath of the 3d New York Regiment* (Jamestown, VA., Eastern Acorn Press, 1983).

210. Documents of the Assembly of the State of New York, One Hundred and Twentieth Session, Vol. 6, No. 17-26 (Albany and New York, Wynkoop, Hollenbeck, Crawford Co., State Printers, 1897), 38.

211. Kennett, Lee B. *The French Forces in America, 1780-1783* (Westport, CT, Greenwood Press, 1977), 22-23.

CHAPTER FOURTEEN

212. Bolton, Charles, *The Private Soldier*, 220.

213. White, Todd J. and Lesser, Charles H., ed. *Fighters for Independence* (Chicago, IL, The University of Chicago Press, 1977) 64. This compendium of 538 diaries of Revolutionary War Military personnel

lists other principle sources: Mathews, William, *American Diaries Written prior to the year 1961* (Berkeley and Los Angeles, CA, University of California Press, 1945) and American *Diaries in Manuscript, 1580 to 1954* (Athens, GA, University of Georgia press, 1974). MacDonald, Bob, *Index of Continental Army Enlisted Men's Diaries,* [www. RevWar75.com] contains sixty noteworthy diaries of enlisted men.

214. Fischer, Elijah, *Elijah Fisher's Journal, 1775-1784* (Augusta, ME, Press of Badger and Manley, 1880).

215. Talmadge, Orderly Book, 4th New York Regiment, 191.

216. Fitzpatrick, *Writings of George Washington*, 4:387.

217. Lossing, Benson John, *The pictorial field-book of the revolution; or, Illustrations, by pen and pencil, of the history, biography, scenery, relics, and traditions of the war for independence* (New York, NY, Harper & Brothers, 1860)Vol. I, XXIV, 565.

218. Fischer, Elijah, *Elijah Fisher's Journal, 1775-1784.*

219. Greenman, Jeremiah**,** *Diary of a Common Soldier in the American Revolution, 1775-1783; An Annotated Edition of the Military Journal of Jeremiah Greenman*, Robert C.Bray and Paul E. Bushnell, eds., (DeKalb, Illinois, 1978, 333 pages, Orig. manuscript within private in private possession. [www.revolutionarywararchives.org], Pension Documents, Jeremiah Greenman, W 24305 BLWt. 28, 580-160-55, US National Archives.

220. Rau, Louise, ed., "Sergeant John Smith's Diary of 1776," *Mississippi Valley Historical Review*, No. 20, 1933, 247-270. Manuscript within the collections of the American Antiquarian Society, Worcester, MA.

221. *The Narrative of Ebenezer Fletcher, A Soldier of the Revolution, Written by Himself,* Charles L. Busnell, ed. (New York, NY, Privately printed, 1866).

222. Revolutionary War Pension and Bounty-Land Warrant Application Files for Joseph P. Guerney, S 17435, Massachusetts, dated March 7, 1832 and Whitcomb Pratt, S 22429, Massachusetts, dated August 11, 1832, Compiled Service Records of American Army Soldiers during the Revolutionary War 1775-1783, US National Archives Microfilm Publication M881.

223. *Journal of Solomon Nash, A Soldier of the Revolution, 1776-1777*, Charles L. Bushnell, ed. (New York, NY, 1861) 41 pages.

224. *Diary Of David How, a Private in Colonel Paul Dudley Sargent's Regiment of the Massachusetts Line, in the Army of the American Revolution* ,George W. Chase and Henry B. Dawson, eds., (Morrisania, NY, H.G. Houghton, 1865).

225. Martin, Joseph Plumb, *Private Yankee Doodle, Being a Narrative of Some of the Adventures, Dangers and Sufferings of a Revolutionary Soldier,* George F. Scheer, ed. (Boston, MA Brown & Co., 1962). Many reprints under alternative titles are available.

CHAPTER FIFTEEN

226. Lincoln, Abraham, The Perpetuation of Our Political Institutions: Address Before the Young Men's Lyceum of Springfield, Illinois, January 27, 1838, [www.abrahamlincolnonline.org/lincoln/speeches/lyceum.htm]

227. Shy, John, *A People Numerous and Armed: Reflections on the Military Struggle for American Independence* (New York, NY, Oxford University Press, 1976), 21.

228. Letter from George Washington to the President of Congress, *On Recruiting and Maintaining an Army,* September 24, 1776.

229. Nathanael Greene to Jacob Greene, in *Nathanael Greene: A Biography of the American Revolution,* Carbone, Gerald M. (New York, NY, Palgrave Macmillan, 2008), 41.

230. Thomas Paine, "The American Crisis," December 23, 1776. [www.ushistory.org/paine/crisis/]

231. Martin, Joseph Plumb, *Private Yankee Doodle, Being a Narrative of some of the Adventures, Dangers and Sufferings of a Revolutionary Soldier* (New York, NY, Eastern Acorn Press, 1962), 283.

232. Alexander Hamilton (publishing under the pseudonym *Publius*), Federalist Paper No.25, December 21, 1787.

CHAPTER SIXTEEN

233. Fitzpatrick, *Writings of Washington*, vol. 8 (1933), 181. General orders, June 4, 1777, vol. 8 (1933), 181.

234. Ibid., Washington to the Superintendent of Finance, January 29, 1783, Vol. 26 (1938), 78-79.

235. John U. Rees' articles include "The Multitude of Women: An Examination of the Numbers of female Camp Followers with the Continental Army," *The Brigade Dispatch* Vol. 23 No. 4 (Autumn 1992), 5-17; Vol. 24 No. 1 (Winter 1993), 6-16; No. 2 (Spring 1993), 2-6; "The Number of Rations issued to Women in Camp: New Material Concerning Female Followers With Continental Regiments." "The Proportion of Women which ought to be allowed: Female Camp Followers with the Continental Army." *The Continental Soldier. Journal of the Continental Line* Vol. 8, No. 3 (Spring 1995), 51-58.

236. Pension and Bounty Land Warrant Application Files, Patrick Cronkite, Fifer, 1st New York Regiment, 1777-1783, W16932, contains supplementary depositions of Maria Cronkite (*nee* Humphrey), US National Archives.

237. Lesser, Charles H., ed., in a "Return of the Negroes in the Army, 24 August 1778," *The Brigade Dispatch*, Vol. XXVIII, No. 1 (Spring 1998), 9.

238. Regimental orders, September 30, October 7, 1778, Orderly Book of the 2nd Pennsylvania Regiment, 1778, Regimental orders, August 14, 1782, Orderly Book of the Tenth Mass. Regt., 1782, Daughters of the American Revolution Museum.

239. Regimental Orders, 4th New York Regiment, Headquarters, Highlands, June 28, 1780.

240. Blumenthal, Walter H., *Women Camp Followers of the American Revolution* (Philadelphia. PA, George S. MacManus Company, 1952), 65-66.

241. North, Louise V. *In the Words of Women: The Revolutionary War and the Birth of the Nation, 1765-1799*, (Lexington Books, 2011)

242. Martin, Joseph P., *Private Yankee Doodle.* Martin quotes an officer observing a column of camp followers on the way to Tappan, New York in 1780, 197.

243. General Orders, August 23, 1777, George Washington, Headquarters, Stanton near Germantown.

244. Freeman, Lucy and Bond, Alma, *America's First Woman Warrior: the Courage of Deborah Sampson.* (New York, NY, Paragon House, 1992).

245. Rockwell, Anne, *They Called Her Molly Pitcher* (New York, NY, Alfred A. Knopf, 2002).

246. Virginia Legislature, February 6, 1808, Approval of Special Pension Application with award of One Hundred Dollars per annum to Anna Maria Lane.

247. Pension Application, Sarah Osborn, Record Group 15, US National Archives, Washington, D.C.

248. Abigail Adams to John Adams March, 31, 1776.

CHAPTER SEVENTEEN

249. Fitzpatrick, *Writings of Washington*, Washington to Colonel Goose Van Schaick, October 27, 1778; Washington to Brig. Gen. Samuel Holden Parsons, April 25, 1777; Washington to Brigadier General George Clinton, May 5, 1777.

250. Cox, Caroline A., *Proper Sense of Honor: Service & Sacrifice in George Washington's Army* (Chapel Hill, NC, University of North Carolina Press, 2004), 94-98.

251. Cox, Caroline, *A Proper Sense of Honor* (Surrey Hills, AU, Accessible Publishing Systems, PTY, Ltd. 2008), 180.

252. Thacher, James, *Military Journal*, 196.

253. Martin, *Private Yankee Doodle*, 47, 48.

254. Oman, Charles. *Wellington's Army, 1809-1814* (London, Greenhill, 1913 (1993)), 107.

255. General Orders, September 20, 1776, October 1, 1776, December 22, 1777; June 11, 1780, November 19, 1782, Washington to President of Congress, February 3, 1781; General Orders, September 20, 1776, October 1, 1776, December 22, 1777; June 11, 1780, November 19, 1782.

256. Winthorp, William, Col., *Military Law and Precedents*, War Department Document 1001, 1886 (Washington, D.C., US Government Printing Office, 1920), 110.

257. General Orders, June 27, 1776; Washington to President of Congress.

258. Ibid.; Thacher, *Military Journal*, 252.

259. Thacher, *Military Journal*, 196.

260. Bowman, Allen, *The Morale of the American Revolutionary Army* (Washington, D.C. American Council On Public Affairs, 1943.) 88, 92.

261. General Orders, October 26, October 30, November1, 1777, May 6, 1778, July 4, 1779.

262. Wild, Ebenezer, *Journal of Ebenezer Wild*, 1779 (Boston, MA, *Proceedings of the Massachusetts Historical Society*, 2nd series, Vol. VI, 1891), David Library of the American Revolution Collection, 79-160.

263. Rees, John U., "The Music of the Army," *The Brigade Dispatch*, Vol. XXIV, No. 4, Autumn 1993, 2-8.

264. Thacher, *Military Journal*, January 1, 1780, 186.

265. General Orders, September 16, 1775.February 8, 1778; March 14, 1778; Janurary 5, 1778; May 11, 1783.

266. General Orders, May 10, 1776, May 14, 1776, January 3, 1780.

267. General Orders, November 15, 1776, May 12, 1776, February 21, 1777, September 11, 1776.

268. General Orders, February 8, 1778, March 14, 1778, January 5, 1778; May 11, 1783, September 16, 1775.

269. *Deseret News and Telegram*, Salt Lake City, UT, April 9, 1962.

270. General Orders Headquarters, Middle-Brook, June 10, 1777.

271. General Orders, September 16, 1775, January 5, 1778, February 8, 1778, March 14, 1778, May 11, 1783.

272. General Orders, January 1, 1776, June 10, 1777.

CHAPTER EIGHTEEN

273. Charles Cushing, in *American Archives V*, Vol. I, Cols. 128-132.

274. Butterfield, L.H., ed., *Adams Family Correspondence*, Vol. 2 (Cambridge, MA, Belknap Press of Harvard University Press, 1963).

275. Lossing, Benson, *The life and Times of Philip Schuyler*, Schuyler to Congress, November 20, 1775 Vol. I (New York, NY, Mason Brothers, 1860), 466.

276. Henshaw, William, Colonel William Henshaw's Orderly Book, April 20-September 26, 1775, *Proceedings of the Massachusetts Historic Society*, for October, 1876 (Boston, MA, Press of John Wilson, 1877), 75.

277. Waldo Albigence, Dr., "Diary of Surgeon, Continental Army, Valley Forge 1777-1778," *Historical Magazine*, May, 1861 (New York, NY, Charles B. Richardson and Co., 1861), 105.

278. Washington's Orderly Book, May 26, 1778; Orderly Book of the Northern Army at Ticonderoga, 126.

279. Becker, Ann M., *Smallpox in Washington's Army: Strategic Implications of the Disease During the American Revolutionary War, The Journal of Military History*, Vol. 68, No. 2, April, 2004, 381-430.

280. Saxton, Thomas R., *In Reduced Circumstances: Aging an Impoverished Continental Veterans in the Young Republic* (Lehigh University Preserve, Theses and Dissertations, Paper 718. 2001), 37.

281. George Washington to John Augustine Washington, May 31-June 4, 1777, *The Papers of George Washington*, Revolutionary War Series, Vol. 4, 1 April 1776?–?15 June 1776, Philander D. Chase, ed., Charlottesville, VA, University Press of Virginia, 1991) 411–414.

282. Abrams, Jeanne E., Revolutionary Medicine:The Founding Fathers and Mothers in Sickness and in Health (New York, NY, New York University Press, 2013), 55-57.

283. Eichner, L. G., M.D., "The Military Practice of Medicine During the Revolutionary War," *Tredyffrin Easttown Historical Society History Quarterly*, 41.1 (Winter 2004): 25-32.

284. Pension Application, William Hutchinson, 1836, US National Archives.

285. American Archives V., Vol. 3, Col. 1031.

286. von Steuben, "Regulations for the Order and Discipline of the Troops of the United States," 1778-1779, Of Treatment of the Sick, Chapter XXIV, 65.

287. Greene to Congress December 28, 1780, *The Papers of General Nathanael Greene* (Chapel Hill, NC, University of North Carolina Press), William L. Clements Library.

288. The Committee for Foreign Affairs to the American Commissioners, May, 2 1777, Two LS: American Philosophical Society; three copies: National Archives.

298. Jefferson, Thomas, *The Writings of Thomas Jefferson from Original Manuscripts* (New York, NY, Riker, Thorne & Co., 1854), 304.

290. *Virginia Gazette*, Williamsburg VA, June 15, 1776.

291. Gill, Howard B., "Colonial Germ Warfare", *Colonial Williamsburg Journal*, Spring 2004.

292. Donkin, Robert *Military Collections and Remarks* (New York 1777, reprint by Gale ECCO, Print Editions, May 28, 2010).

293. Fenn, Elizabeth A., *Pox Americana-The Great Smallpox Epidemic of 1775-1782* (New York, NY, Hill and Wang, 2001), 132.

294. US National Archives, R & PO War Department, returned to files May 16, 1898.

CHAPTER NINETEEN

295. *Treaties and other International Acts of the United States of America*, Hunter Miller, ed., Vol 2, Documents 1-40 (1776-1818) (Washington, DC, US Government Printing Office, 1931).

296. General Orders, Newburgh, April 18, 1783.

297. General Orders, February 28, 1783

298. The Paris Peace Treaty of September 30, 1783, Article 7.

299. *G Washington,* Headquarters, Newburgh, New York, no date [June 1783]. Countersigned by Jonathan Trumbull, Jr.

300. Fitzpatrick, *The Writing of George Washington*, 27:10.

301. George Washington to the Continental Army, Farewell Orders, November 2, 1783, Rock Hill near Princeton. George Washington Papers at the Library of Congress, 1741-1799: Series 4, General Correspondence, 1697-17.

302. Fisher, *Military Journal*, April 10, 1783.

303. Sellers, John R., Stanley J. Underal, ed. "The Common Soldier in the American Revolution," in *Proceedings of the Sixth Military History Symposium*, October, 1974, USAF Academy (Washington, D.C., US Government Printing Office).

304. Heath, William, *Memoirs of Major William Heath, By Himself* (Boston, MA, I. Thomas and E.T. Andrews, 1798), archived at the Massachusetts Historical Society.

CHAPTER TWENTY

305. Martin, *Private Yankee Doodle*, 283-289.

306. Peckham, Howard, *The Toll of Independence* (Chicago, IL, University of Chicago Press, 1974).

307. James Starr, Pension Application R10, 079, US National Archives.

308. Leroy Starling, Pension Application S 40515, US National Archives.

309. Isaac Lewis, Pension Application, S 42835, US National Archives.

310. Sellers, John R., *The Common Soldier in the American Revolution* (Proceedings of the Military History Symposium, Air Force Academy, Colorado, October 10-11, 1974).

311. Papenfuse, Edward C., Stiverson, Gregory A., "General Smallwood's Recruits: the Peacetime Career of the Revolutionary War Private," *William and Mary Quarterly*, January 1973, Vol. 30, No 1.

312. The decision to award pensions represented a significant political shift in the treatment of the veterans of the Revolutionary War. *See also* Charles Royster, *A Revolutionary People at War: The Continental Army and American Character, 1775-1783* (Chapel Hill, NC, The University of North Carolina Press, 1979), *and* E. Wayne Carp, *To Starve the Army at Pleasure: Continental Army Administration and American Political Culture 1775-1783* (Chapel Hill, NC, The University of North Carolina Press, 1984).

313. John Allison Pension Certificate, 1657-100, May 29, 1821, District of New York, Orange County, Publication 804, US National Archives.

314. Martin, *Private Yankee Doodle*, 292-93.

CHAPTER TWENTY-ONE

315. Mayers, Robert A., *The War Man* (Yardley, PA, Westholme Publishing, 2009).

316. De Witt, Sutherland, ed., "Journal of Henry Pawling," *Olde Ulster*, Vols. 1 and 2 (1905-1906): 335-8; 361-5; 18-25.

317. Mayers, *The War Man*, 90.

318. Mc Dougall, Alexander, "General McDougall's Report into the loss of Forts Clinton and Montgomery, April 5, 1778," *Alexander McDougall Papers*, New York Historical Society, 1942, Vol. 3.

319. Dewitt, *Journal of Henry Pawling*, 338

320. Ibid.,

321. Mayers, *The War Man*, 100

322. Ibid.

323. Mayers, *The War Man*, 103.

CHAPTER TWENTY-TWO

324. A four-volume set by Virgil D. White is useful in locating information from these files: *Genealogical Abstracts of Revolutionary War Pension Files* (Waynesboro, TN, National Historical Publishing Co., 1990-92). Also helpful are the compilations by Murtie J. Clark, including *The Pension Lists of 1792–95*; *Revolutionary War Pension Records* (Baltimore, MD, The Genealogical Publishing Co., 1991 (1996)) and *The National Genealogical Society's Special Publication No. 40* [Arlington, VA, National Genealogical Society, 1976).

325. Hatcher, Patricia Law. *Abstract of Graves of Revolutionary Patriots,* Four Volumes (Dallas, TX, Pioneer Heritage Press, 1987-88).

326. Bockstruck, Lloyd D., *Revolutionary War Bounty Land Grants: Awarded by State Governments* (Baltimore, MD, Genealogical Publishing Co., 2006).

327. Neagles, James C., *U.S. Military Records: A Guide to Federal and State Sources, Colonial America to the Present* (Salt Lake City, UT: Ancestry, Inc., 1994).

328. *Rejected or Suspended Applications for Revolutionary War Pensions* (Washington, D.C., US Department of Interior, 1852, reprint Clearfield Co., Inc. Baltimore, MD 2003), also *Pensioners of the Revolutionary War-Struck Off the Rolls* (Washington, D.C., US War Department, 1836, reprint Clearfield Co., Baltimore, MD, 2003).

329. Prechtel-Kluskens, Claire, "Tracking Revolutionary War Army Pension Payments" *Prologue Magazine,* Winter 2008, Vol. 40, No. 4.

330. Saxton Thomas, R. "In Reduced Circumstances-Aging and Impoverished veterans in the New Republic," M.A. thesis (Bethelem, PA, Lehigh University, 2001), 30.

331. Glasson, William Henry, *Federal Military Pensions in the United States* (New York, Oxford University Press, 1918).

332. States that issued bounty land warrants were: Connecticut, Georgia, Maryland, Massachusetts, New York, North Carolina, Pennsylvania, South Carolina, and Virginia.

333. Bockstruck, Lloyd Dewitt. *Revolutionary War Bounty Land Grants: Awarded by State Governments* (Baltimore, MD, Genealogical Publishing Co., 1996).

Appendices

Appendix A

INFANTRY REGIMENT 1781

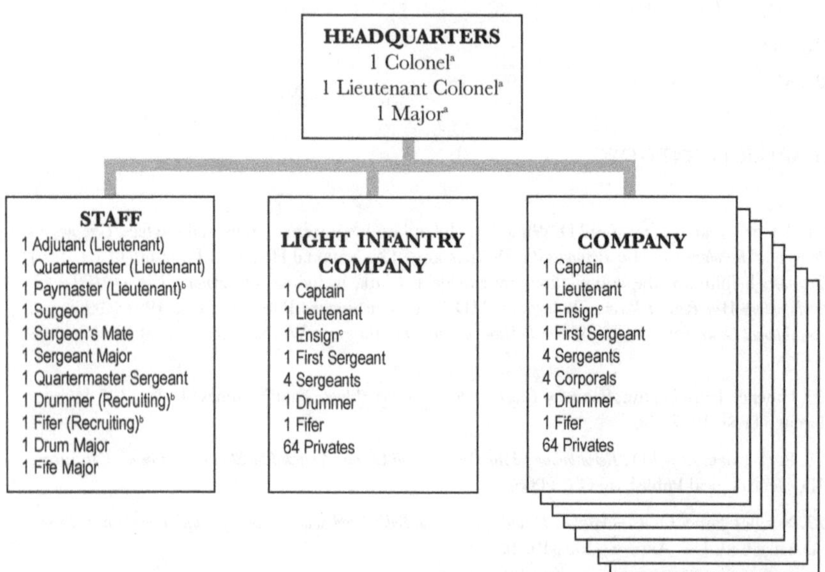

[a] When regiment was commanded by a lieutenant colonel commandant, two majors were authorized.

[b] One lieutenant and a fifer and a drummer were permanently on duty in the regiment's home state as a recruiting party.

[c] Initially the temporary retention of a lieutenant in the ensign's position was authorized.

The reorganization of the Continental Army, effective January 1, 1781, continued the basic regimental alignment of one light and eight line companies, all equal in size. A regiment engaging in combat at full strength could deploy 544 rank and file, 40 sergeants, 24 company officers, and 3 field officers. It was substantially better organized and more efficient than the typical British regiment. (Courtesy *The Continental Army*, Robert K. Wright, Jr., Center of Military History United States Army, Washington, D.C., 1983).

Appendix B

DISTRIBUTION OF REGIMENTS BY STATE 1777

State	Estimated 1775 Population (in thousands)	Infantry Regiment Quota September 17, 1776	Actual Regiments Raised Under Quota	Additional Regiments (Infantry)	Extra Regiments (Infantry)	Artillery Regiments	Light Dragoon Regiments	TOTALS
New Hampshire	100	3	3	0	0	0	0	**3**
Massachusetts	350	15	15	3	0	1	0	**19**
Rhode Island	58	2	2	1/2	0	0	0	**2 1/2**
Connecticut	200	8	8	1 1/2	0	1/2	1	**11**
New York	200	4	5	1/2	0	1/2	0	**6**
New Jersey	130	4	4	2	0	0	0	**6**
Pennsylvania	300	12	139	2 1/2	1/2	1	1	**18**
Delaware	30	1	1	0	0	0	0	**1**
Maryland	250	8	7	0	1	0	0	**8**
Virginia	400	15	15	3	0	1	2	**21**
North Carolina	200	9	9	1	0	0	0	**10**
South Carolina	200	6	5	0	0	1	0	**6**
Georgia	25	1	5	0	0	0	0	**5**
Other	0	0	0	0	31	0	0	**3**
TOTAL	**2,443**	**88**	**92**	**14**	**32 1/2**	**5**	**4**	**119 1/2**

(From Wright, Robert K. Jr, *The Continental Army*, Lineage Series, Center of Military History, United States Army, Washington, D.C. 1983)

Appendix C

ENLISTED MEN'S DIARIES - Continental Army

This index lists diaries that were written by enlisted men on active duty who served in the regiments of Washington's Continental Army. It does not include journals composed by officers or militia members of any rank. Any memoirs, pension applications---and other records not written in the field such are not included. Therefore, this select index represents only a small number of the all journals written by Revolutionary War soldiers.

The entries included here are courtesy of Bob McDonald's *Index of Continental Army Enlisted Men's Diaries* (www.RevWar75.com/library/bob [accessed April, 2016]). McDonald lists sixty diaries, identifies repositories of original manuscripts, alternate sources and references: *Fighters for Independence,* compiled by Todd J. White, and Charles H. Lesser (Chicago, The University of Chicago Press, 1977), an index of 538 Revolutionary War Military diaries.

[Anonymous]: Independent Pennsylvania Rifle Company.
Diary spans July - December 1776.
Service at Manhattan, in Westchester County, on New Jersey retreat, and at Trenton.
Published as "Journal of a Pennsylvania Soldier, July - December, 1776" in *The Historical Magazine of America,* Vol. 7 (New York, NY, 1863), pp. 367-369. Also published in *Bulletin of the New York Public Library,* Vol. 8 (New York, NY, 1904), pp. 547-549.

Daniel Allen: Private, Bradley's Connecticut State Regiment (in Continental service).
Diary spans July - October 1778.
Service at Manhattan, captured at Fort Washington.
Published in *A History Of Cornwall, Connecticut, A Typical New England Town,* Edward C. Starr (Tuttle, Morehouse, and Taylor, New Haven, CT, 1926), pp. 252-254.

Josiah Atkins: Private, Light Infantry Company, 5th Connecticut Regiment.
Diary spans April - October 1781. (Died of disease.)
Service in Hudson Highlands, March to Virginia, in Lafayette's campaign of summer 1781.
Published as "The Journal of Josiah Atkins of Waterbury, Farmington Society In Ye State Of Connecticut N. England 1781", *The Mattatuck Historical Society* (Waterbury, CT, Occasional Publications), New Series, No. 21, October 1954, 16 pages.
Manuscript in the collections of the New Haven Colony Historical Society.

Aaron Barlow: Sergeant, 5th Connecticut Regiment (Waterbury's.)
Diary spans June - December 1775.
Service at Fort Ticonderoga and St. John's.
Extracts published as "The March To Montreal And Quebec, 1775," edited by Charles B. Todd, in *The American Historical Register*, No. 7 (March, 1895), pp. 641-649.

Enos Barnes: Sergeant, 5th Connecticut Regiment.
Diary spans ? - 1778.
Service at the Battle of Monmouth.
Transcription of unpublished manuscript in private possession.

Henry Bedinger: Sergeant, Stephenson's Independent Company of Virginia Riflemen.
Diary spans July 1775 - June 1776.
Service at Boston.
Published in *Historic Shepherdstown*, Danske Dandridge (Charlottesville, VA 1910), pp. 97-144.

Samuel Bixby: Private, Learned's Massachusetts Regiment.
Diary spans May 1775 - January 1776.
Service at Boston.
Published as "Diary of Samuel Bixby," in *Proceedings of the Massachusetts Historical Society*, Vol. 14 (Boston, MA, March, 1876), pp. 285-298.

Thomas Boynton: Sergeant, Frye's Massachusetts Regiment.
Diary spans April - August 1775.
Service in Boston.
Extracts published as "Thomas Boynton's Journal" in *Proceedings of the Massachusetts Historical Society*, No. 15 (Boston, MA, 1876-77), pp. 321-322.
Manuscript in the collections of the Massachusetts Historical Society.

Leonard Broome: Sergeant, 4th Continental Artillery Regiment.
Diary spans February - April 1781.
Note: This volume is a mixture of orderly book entries, company returns, and limited, but nonetheless interesting, diary entries.
Service at the North Redoubt, Eastern-shore Hudson Highlands.
Manuscript at the United States Military Academy Library, West Point, NY.
Unpublished. Transcribed. Not microfilmed.

Obediah Brown: Private, 16th Continental Regiment (Sargent's.)
Diary spans January 1776 - January 1777.
Service at Boston, Manhattan, in Westchester County.
Published as "Military Journal, January, 1776 - January, 1777, around Boston and New York" in *Quarterly Bulletin of the Westchester County Historical Society*, No. 4 (Elmsford, NY, 1928), pp. 67-72; No. 5, 1929, pp. 10-20.
Published article Microfilmed. Manuscript in the collections of the Westchester County Historical Society.

William Chapman: Private, 6th Connecticut Regiment (Parsons'.)
Diary spans July - December 1775.
Service at Boston.
Manuscript within the collections of the Connecticut Historical Society, Hartford, CT.
Unpublished. Microfilmed.

Samuel Chase: Private, New Hampshire Regiment.
----------(1) Diary spans August - October 1779. Service in Sullivan's Expedition.
----------(2) Diary spans July 1781 - January 1782. Service at unknown location.
----------(3) Diary spans May 1782 - April 1787 Service at unknown location.
Manuscript (71 pp.) in the compiled pension application files, US National Archives.
Unpublished. Microfilmed.

Elihu Clark: Private, 2nd Connecticut Regiment (Wyllys').
Diary spans April - December 1775.
Service at Boston.
Manuscript in the collections of the Connecticut Historical Society, Hartford, CT.
Unpublished. Microfilmed. Copy may be found within the Force Transcripts, Library of Congress.

Ichabod Corbett: Private, Massachusetts Regiment
----------(1) Diary spans December 1776 - March 1777.
Service in the Hudson Highlands.
----------(2) Diary spans January - April 1778.
Service in Rhode Island.
Published as "Diary of a Revolutionary Soldier," in *Proceedings of the Worcester Society of Antiquity*, No. 19 (Worcester, MA, 1903), pp. 171-186.

John Dewey: Private, 3rd Continental Regiment (Learned's.)
Diary spans April 1776 - February 1777.
Service at Boston, Manhattan, the New Jersey retreat, and Trenton, Princeton, and Morristown.
Published in *Life of George Dewey, Rear Admiral, U.S.N., and Dewey Family History*, edited by Adelbert M. Dewey (Westfield, MA, 1898), pp. 278-281.

Russel Dewey: Fife Major, 15th Continental Regiment (Cady's, late Paterson's.)
Diary spans January - March 1776.
Service at Fort Ticonderoga, Quebec.
Published in *Life of George Dewey, Rear Admiral, U. S. N., and Dewey Family History*, edited by Adelbert M. Dewey (Westfield, MA, 1898), pp. 266-271.

George Ewing: Private/Ensign, 2nd New Jersey Regiment, 3rd New Jersey Regiment.
Diary spans November 1775 - June 1778.
Service at Forts Stanwix, Schuyler, Herkimer, and Ticonderoga, in Philadelphia Campaign, winter quarters Valley Forge.
Published as *The Military Journal of George Ewing (1754 - 1824), a Soldier of Valley Forge* (Yonkers, NY, 1928). Also published as "Journal of George Ewing, a Revolutionary Soldier, of Greenwich, New Jersey" in *The American Monthly Magazine* (D.A.R.), Vol. 37, No. 6, 1910, pp. 471-473; Vol. 38, No. 7, 1911, pp. 5-8, 50–53.

Amos Farnsworth: Corporal/Ensign, Prescott's Massachusetts Regiment, 13th Continental Regiment (Read's), 2nd Massachusetts Regiment (?).
Diary spans April 1775 - December 1776 (with several pages missing from manuscript and publication.)
Service on Lexington Alarm, at Boston, and at Bunker Hill (wounded) as enlisted man, at Fort Ticonderoga in 1776 as ensign, Massachusetts militia.
Published as *Diary Kept By Lieut. Amos Farnsworth Of Groton, Mass., During Part of the Revolutionary War, April, 1775 - May, 1779*, edited by Samuel A. Green (Cambridge, MA, 1898). Also published in *Proceedings of the Massachusetts Historical Society*, Second Series, Vol. 12, 1899, pp. 74-107.

Moses Fellows:Sergeant, 3rd New Hampshire Regiment.
Diary spans June - September 1779.
Service in Sullivan's Expedition.
Published in *Journals of the Military Expedition of Major General John Sullivan.*, Frederick Cook (Auburn, NY, 1887), pp. 86-91.

Elijah Fisher:
Diary spans May 1775 - April 1781.
Many service locations.
Published as *Elijah Fisher's Journal While in the War for Independence* (Augusta, ME, 1880).

John Flanders: Private (unit unknown.)
Diary spans January - April 1776.
Service at Quebec, and prisoner.
Published in *The History of Boscawen and Webster* [New Hampshire] *from 1773 to 1878*, by Charles C. Coffin (Concord, NH, 1878), pp. 250-251.

Thomas Foster: Private, 7th Massachusetts Regiment.
Diary spans May 1782 - June 1783.
Service at West Point, Verplancks Point, New Windsor Cantonment.
Manuscript in the collections of The Huntington Library, San Marino, CA

Simon Giffen, Sgt. Major Webbs, additional Continental Regt.
Diary spans May 1777 - September 1779.
Service at West Point, White Plains, Newport.
Manuscript in the collections of the Beineke Library, Yale University, New Haven, CT. Unpublished. Microfilmed.

Benjamin Gilbert: Sergeant-Major, 5th Massachusetts Regiment.
Diary spans January 1778 - January 1780.
Service in Connecticut and the Eastern Shore, Hudson Highlands.
Published as *A Citizen-Soldier In The American Revolution: The Diary of Benjamin Gilbert in Massachusetts and New York*, edited by Rebecca D. Symmes (Cooperstown, NY, 1980), 93 pages.
Manuscript in the collections of the New York State Historical Association, Cooperstown, NY. Microfilmed.

George Grant: Sergeant Major, 3rd New Jersey Regiment.
Diary spans May - December 1779.
Service in Sullivan's Expedition.
Published in *Journals of the Military Expedition of Major General John Sullivan*, by Frederick Cook (Auburn, NY, 1887), pp. 107-114.

Jeremiah Greenman: Sergeant/Adjutant, 2nd Rhode Island Regiment.
Diary spans September 1775 - December 1783.
Many service locations
Published as *Diary of a Common Soldier in the American Revolution, 1775 - 1783; an Annotated Edition of the Military Journal of Jeremiah Greenman*, edited by Robert C. Bray and Paul E. Bushnell (DeKalb, IL, 1978), 333 pages.
Manuscript in private possession.

Caleb Haskell: Fifer, Little's Massachusetts Regiment, 12th Continental Regiment
Diary spans May 1775 - May 1776.
Service at Boston and Quebec.
Published as *Caleb Haskell's Diary* (pamphlet), edited by Lothrop Withington (Newburyport, MA, 1861). Also published in *March to Quebec*, by Kenneth Roberts (New York, NY, 1938), pp. 455-499.

John Hawkins: Sergeant-Major, 2nd Canadian (Congress' Own) Regiment.
Diary spans September 1777 - December 1782 (though not continuously).
Service locations numerous and diverse.
Manuscript within the collections of the Historical Society of Pennsylvania (Philadelphia, PA). Unpublished. Microfilmed.

Samuel Haws: Private, Read's Massachusetts Regiment.
Diary spans April 1775 - February 1776.
Service at Boston.
Published as "A Journal for 1775," in *The Military Journals of Two Private Soldiers, 1758 - 1775*, edited by Abraham Tomlinson (Poughkeepsie, NY, 1855), pp. 49-90.

David How: Private, Sargent's Massachusetts Regiment, 16th Continental Regiment (Sargent's.)
Diary spans December 1775 - December 1776.
Service at Boston, Manhattan, in New Jersey retreat, and at Trenton.
Published as *Diary of David How, a Private in Colonel Paul Dudley Sargent's Regiment of the Massachusetts Line, in the Army of the American Revolution*, edited by George W.Chase and Henry B. Dawson (Morrisania, NY, 1865), 51 pages.

Phineas Ingalls: Private, Frye's Massachusetts Regiment. (1776 unit??)
Diary spans April 1775 - December 1775; July - November 1776.
Service in Lexington alarm, at Boston and Fort Ticonderoga.
Published as *"Revolutionary War Journal, Kept by Phineas Ingalls of Andover, Mass., April 19, 1775 - December 8, 1776"*, Vol. 53, edited by M. V. B. Perley (Salem, MA, 1917), pp. 81-92.
In the collections of the Essex Institute Historical Collections.

Joseph Joslin, Jr.: Teamster in Continental service.
Diary spans March 1777 - August 1778.
Service in Connecticut and the Hudson Highlands.
Published as *"Journal of Joseph Joslin, Jr., of South Killingly, a Teamster in the Continental Service, March 1777 - August 1778"* in the *Connecticut Historical Society Collections*, No. 7 (Hartford, CT, 1899), pp. 299-369.
Manuscript in the collections of the Connecticut Historical Society. Microfilmed.

Andrew Kettell: Sergeant, Jackson's Additional Regiment (16th Massachusetts), 9th Massachusetts
Regiment.
Diary spans April 1780 - May 1781.
Service at West Point, in Northern New Jersey and at West Point.
Manuscript (66 pages) within the compiled pension application files, US National Archives. Unpublished. Microfilmed.

Enoch Long: Private, (?) New Hampshire Regiment.
Diary spans July 1779 - December 1780.
Service in Sullivan's Expedition, winter quarters Danbury, in northern New Jersey, winter quarters New Hampshire Village (north of Peekskill).
Manuscript (30 pages) within the compiled pension application files, US National Archives. Unpublished. Microfilmed.

Simeon Lyman: Private, Connecticut Regiment.
Diary spans August - December 1775.
Service on Connecticut coast and at Boston.
Published as "Journal of Simeon Lyman of Sharon, Aug. 10 to Dec. 28, 1775" in *Collections of the Connecticut Historical Society*, No. 7 (Hartford, CT, 1899), pp. 98, 111-134.
Manuscript in the collections of the Connecticut Historical Society. Microfilmed.

Thomas McCarty: Sergeant, 8th Virginia Regiment.
Diary spans August - September 1776; November 1776 - February 1777.
Service at Fort Lee, on New Jersey retreat, at Trenton and Morristown.
Published as "The Revolutionary War Journal of Sergeant Thomas McCarty," edited by Jared C. Lobdell, in *Proceedings of the New Jersey Historical Society*, Vol. 82, No.1 (Newark, NJ, January, 1964), pp. 29-46.
Manuscript in the William Croghan Papers, Draper Collection, State Historical Society of Wisconsin.

Daniel McCurtin: Private, Cresap's 1st Company of Maryland Rifles.
Diary spans July 1775 - May 1776.
Service at Boston and Manhattan.

Published as "Journal of the Times at the Siege of Boston since our Arrival at Cambridge, Near Boston", edited by Thomas Balch, in *Papers Relating Chiefly to the Maryland Line During the Revolution, within Publications of the Seventy-Six Society*, No. 4 (Philadelphia, PA, 1857), pp. 11-41.

James McMichael: Sergeant/Lieutenant, Miles' Pennsylvania Rifle Regiment, 13th Pennsylvania Regiment.
Diary spans May 1776 - May 1778.
Many service locations.
Published as "Diary of Lieutenant James McMichael, of the Pennsylvania Line, 1776-1778," *The Pennsylvania Magazine Of History And Biography*, Vol. 16 (1892), pp. 129-159. Also published in *Pennsylvania Archives*, Second Series, Vol. 15, pp. 195-218.

James Melvin: Private, 1st New Hampshire Regiment.
Diary spans September 1775 - August 1776.
Service at Quebec, and as prisoner.
Published as *The Journal of James Melvin, Private Soldier in Arnold's Expedition,Against Quebec in the Year 1775*, edited by Andrew A. Melvin (Portland, ME, 1902). Also published in *March To Quebec*, Kenneth Roberts (NY, 1938), pp. 433-454. Also published in *The Life and Times of Aaron Burr*, by James Parton, 2 Vols. (Boston, MA and New York, NY, 1900), pp. 375-390.

Solomon Nash: Matross, Knox's Regiment of Continental Artillery.
Diary spans January 1776 - January 1777.
Service at Boston, Manhattan, in Westchester County and the Hudson Highlands.
Published as *Journal of Solomon Nash, A Soldier Of The Revolution, 1776 - 1777*, edited by Charles I. Bushnell (New York, NY, 1861), 41 pages.

Nahum Parker: Private/Corporal, 15th Massachusetts Regiment.
Diary spans July - December 1780.
Service in the Hudson Highlands, northern New Jersey, at West Point.
Manuscript (30 pages) within the compiled pension application files, US National Archives. Unpublished. Microfilmed.

Ebenezer Parkman: Private, Baldwin's Artillery Artificers Regiment.
Diary spans June 1779 - June 1781.
Service at Morristown and in the Hudson Highlands.
Manuscript within the collections of the American Antiquarian Society, Worcester, MA. Unpublished. Microfilmed.

Thomas Roberts: Sergeant, Spencer's Additional Continental Regiment (5th New Jersey.)
Diary spans May - September 1779.
Service in Sullivan's Expedition.
Published in *Journals of the Military Expedition of Major General John Sullivan*, by Frederick Cook (Auburn, NY, 1887), pp. 240-245.
Manuscript in the collections of the New York Historical Society.

William Rogers: Sergeant, 2nd New York Regiment.
Diary spans April - September 1779.
Service in Sullivan's Expedition.
Published in *Journals of the Military Expedition of Major General John Sullivan*, by Frederick Cook (Auburn, NY, 1887), pp. 266.

William Slade: Private, Bradley's Connecticut State Regiment (in Continental service.)
Diary spans November 1776 - January 1777.
Service at Fort Washington, and as prisoner.
Published in *American Prisoners of the Revolution,* by Danske Dandridge (Charlottesville, VA, 1911), pp. 492-502.

John Smith: (1) Sergeant, Lippitt's Rhode Island State Regiment (in Continental service.)
Diary spans August 1776 - January 1777.
Service at Manhattan, in Westchester County, on New Jersey retreat, and at Trenton.
Published as "Sergeant John Smith's Diary of 1776", edited by Louise Rau, in *Mississippi Valley Historical Review*, No. 20 (1933), pp. 247-270.
Manuscript within the collections of the American Antiquarian Society, Worcester, MA. Manuscript contains both the original field diary and a later revision
with minor modifications. Microfilmed.
----------Also: (2) Sergeant, 1st Rhode Island Regiment.
Diary spans July 1777 - January 1778.
Service in the Hudson Highlands, at Fort Mercer, Whitemarsh, winter quarters Valley Forge.
Manuscript within the collections of the American Antiquarian Society, Worcester, MA. Unpublished. Microfilmed.

Moses Sproule: Sergeant, 3rd New Jersey Regiment.
Diary spans May - October 1779.

Service in Sullivan's Expedition.
Published as "The Western Campaign of 1779", edited by R.W.G. Vail, in the *Quarterly of the New York Historical Society*, No. 41 (New York, NY 1957), pp. 47-69.
Manuscript at the New York Historical Society.

Ephraim Squier: Sergeant, 3rd Connecticut Regiment (Fellows'.) (1777 unit? Militia?)
----------(1) Diary spans September - November 1775.
Service at Quebec.
----------(2) Diary spans September - November 1777.
Service in Saratoga Campaign.
Published as "Diary of Ephraim Squier, Sergeant In The Connecticut Line Of The Continental Army," edited by Frank Squier, in *Magazine of American History*, No.2,
part 2 (1878), pp. 685-694. Diary (1) also published in *March to Quebec*, Kenneth Roberts (New York, NY, 1938), pp. 619-628.

Benjamin Stevens: Private, Burrall's Connecticut State Regiment (in Continental service.)
Diary spans February - May 1776.
Service in Canada.
Published as "Diary of Benjamin Stevens, of Canaan, Conn.", in *Daughters of the American Revolution Magazine*, Vol. 45 (August-September, 1914), pp. 137-140.

James Stevens: Private, Frye's Massachusetts Regiment.
Diary spans April 1775 - December 1775.
Service in Lexington alarm and at Boston.
Published as "The Revolutionary Journal of James Stevens of Andover, Mass." in *The Essex Institute Historical Collections*, Vol.48 (Salem, MA, January 1912), pp. 41-71.

Abner Stocking: Private, 2nd Connecticut Regiment (Wyllys'.)
Diary spans September 1775 - September 1776.
Service at Quebec, and as prisoner.
Published in *March to Quebec*, by Kenneth Roberts (New York, NY, 1938), pp. 545-569.

Solomon Stowe: Private, 15th Massachusetts Regiment.
Diary span unknown.
Service locations unknown.
Cited in "History of Palmer (Massachusetts)", pp. 556, per listing in *New England Diaries, 1602 - 1800*, by Harriette M. Forbes, privately printed (Topsfield, MA, 1923), pp. 277.
Unpublished manuscript believed to be in private possession.

Timothy Tuttle: Private, 1st New Jersey Regiment.
Diary spans December 1775 - November 1776.
Service at Fort Ticonderoga.
Published as "The Diary of Timothy Tuttle," edited by Donald Wickman, in *New Jersey History*, Vol. 113, Nos. 3-4 (Newark, NJ, 1995) pp. 61-77.

John Twiss, Jr.: Drummer, 7th Connecticut Regiment (Webb's.).
Diary spans August - December 1775.
Service at Boston.
Photostat of manuscript within the collections of The Connecticut State Library, Hartford, CT. Unpublished. Not microfilmed.

Zebulon Vaughan: Private, 5th Massachusetts Regiment (Putnam's.)
Diary spans August 1777 – May 1780.
Service at Saratoga, West Point, and throughout east-shore Highlands.
Manuscript within the Americana Collection, National Society of the Daughters of the American Revolution. Published within the *Daughters of the American Revolution Magazine*, 113,Virginia Steele Wood, editor (1979), pp. 100-114, 256-7, 320-1, 478-487.

Joseph Ware: Private, 1st Rhode Island Regiment.
(Also erroneously attributed to Ebenezer Tolman and to Ebenezer Wild.)
Diary spans September 1775 - September 1776.
Service at Quebec, and as prisoner.
Published as "Expedition Against Quebec," in the *New England Historical & Genealogical Register*, No. 6 (Boston, MA, April 1852), pp. 129 - 147.

Nathaniel Webb: Sergeant-Major, 2nd New York Regiment.
Diary spans June - September 1779.
Service in Sullivan's Expedition.
Published in *Journals of the Military Expedition of* Major *General John Sullivan*, by Frederick Cook (Auburn, NY, 1889), pp. 285-287.

Bayze Wells: Private/Lieutenant, 4th Connecticut Regiment (Hinman's), Burrall's Connecticut
State Regiment (in Continental service), 8th Connecticut Regiment.
Diary spans May 1775 - February 1777.
Service at Fort Ticonderoga, Crown Point, in action at Valcour Bay.
Published as "Journal of Bayze Wells, of Farmington; May 1775 - February 1777, at the Northward and in Canada," in *Collections of the Connecticut Historical Society*, No. 7 (Hartford, CT, 1899), pp. 239-296.
Manuscript in the collections of the Connecticut Historical Society. Microfilmed.

Ebenezer Wild: Sergeant/Lieutenant, 6th Continental Regiment, 1st Massachusetts Regiment.
Diary spans August 1776 - December 1781.
Service locations numerous and diverse.
Published in the *Massachusetts Historical Society Proceedings*, Second Series, No. 6 (Boston, MA, 1891), pp. 78-160.
Manuscript in the collections of The Massachusetts Historical Society. Microfilmed.

Ebenezer Withington: Matross, Knox's Regiment of Continental Artillery.
Diary spans October - November 1776.
Service in Westchester County, on New Jersey retreat. (?)
Extracts published in *The Magazine of American History* (December, 1908).

Aaron Wright: Private, Thompson's Pennsylvania Rifle Battalion.
Diary spans June 1775 - March 1776.
Service at Boston.
Published as "Revolutionary Journal of Aaron Wright, 1775", in *The Historical Magazine of America*, No. 5 (July, 1861), pp. 208 - 212.

Appendix D

Muster roll taken a month after the battle at the Twin Forts shows the appalling losses in the 2nd company, 5th New York Regiment. Those listed as missing were either killed or captured. Those shown as absent had not returned after escaping when Forts Montgomery and Clinton fell on October 6, 1777.

A Muster Roll of Capt. Amos Hutchings Company of Foot of the United States of America, Regiment Commanded by Colonel Luis Debois from the first day of September to the first day of November 1777

Commissioned

November 25, 1776	Capt. Amos Hutchings	Absent.
November 25, 1776	Lieut. Patten Jackson	Missing since 6th of October
November 25, 1776	Lieut. John Furman	D'o
November 25, 1776	Ensign Edward Weaver	Absent

Serjants appointed 3 years		**Corporals appointed 3 years**	
Seth Stalker		John Allison	on gard
William Willis	Missing	John Wilson	
James Pride		Cornelius Ackerman	Missing
Francis Gains	Missing	Samuel Conklin	Missing
Jasper Allen	drum	John Vactor	fife

Privates enlisted

Samuel Langelin	on gard	George Marks	on command
Benjamin Lattimore	Missing	Abraham Cooper	absent
Samuel Babcock	Missing	Nathaniel Weeks	on command
Phillip Richards		John Allis	
John Willis		Roger Lattimore	
Peter Wells	Missing	Roger Conklin	Missing
Cornelius Rhodes	Missing	John Conklin	Missing

William Banks	Missing	Benjamin Yoemans	absent
Lawrence Bonker		Benjamin Hallack	Missing
Jacob Travis	Missing	Samuel Garrison	Missing
Danford Windston	Missing	Peter Hopper	on gard
Thomas Jones		John Ferrer	Missing
Francis sears	Missing	John Secor	
Amos Kniffen	Missing	Edward Murphy	on gard
Jacob Crum	sick absent	Ephram Adams	Missing
Isral Outhouse	sick absent	Francis Drake	Missing
John Rhode	on command	Joseph Jones	sick absent

Nov. 4, 1777 Mustered then Capt. Amos Hutchings Company as identified in the above roll—Henry Rutgers Jr., D. Hallach.

(*Extracted from the Revolutionary War Rolls, US National Archives M246*)

Appendix E

THE TWENTY-FIVE MOST DEADLY BATTLES OF THE AMERICAN REVOLUTION

Estimates of Americans killed and wounded are totaled in parentheses. British killed and wounded estimates are in brackets.

Battle of Camden, August 16, 1780 **(1,050)** [314]
British forces routed American forces.
Battle of Germantown, October 4, 1777 **(652)** [519]
Washington's 11,000 troops in divided columns did not proceed uniformly; general retreat.
Battle of Brandywine, September 11, 1777 **(600)** [581]
All day battle that ended in American retreat.
Battle of Eutaw Springs, September 8, 1781 **(513)** [382]
About 2,200 Continentals and militia attacked a camp of 2,000 British regulars and Loyalists.
Siege of Savannah, September 16-October 20, 1779 **(457)** [103]
Franco-American besieging forces launched failed attack on British fortification.
Battle of Bunker/Breeds Hill, June 17, 1775 **(411)** [1054]
British overrun American fortifications.
Battle of Flamborough Head, September 23, 1779 **(302)** [117]
John Paul Jones's famous naval battle.
USS *Randolph* vs HMS *Yarmouth*, March 6, 1778 **(301)** [16]
Randolph and four ships engage Yarmouth. Randolph blew up, killing all but four of its crew.
Battle of Paoli, September 20, 1777 **(300)** [11]
British surprise attack at night.
Battle of Freeman's Farm, September 19, 1777 **(280)** [600]
Burgoyne moved on Gates's fortified position and met hot resistance.
Battle of Monmouth, June 28, 1778 **(267)** [295]
Washington's advance division caught up with enemy, retreating American troops reformed.
Battle of Waxhaws, May 29, 1780 **(263)** [17]
Banastre Tarleton's Legion attacks Continental infantry and cavalry; surrender gone wrong.
Battle of Guilford Courthouse, March 15, 1781 **(261)** [506]
Cornwallis held battlefield, but lost a third of his army.
Battle of Wyoming, July 3, 1778 **(227)** [11]
American forces leave Forty Fort to attack invading force; close combat with Indian raiders.
Siege of Charleston, March 29-May 12, 1780 **(227)** [265]
Benjamin Lincoln surrendered town and forts after one-month siege.

Battle of Long Island, August 27, 1776 **(200)** [367]
Beginning of successful British campaign to capture New York.
Battle of Ramsour's Mill, June 20, 1780 **(170)** [170]
Outnumbered Patriot militia defeat Loyalist militia.
Battle of Rhode Island, August 29, 1778 **(167)** [248]
Franco-American forces laid siege to British in Newport, but abandoned siege.
Battle of Fort Washington, November 16, 1776 **(154)** [458]
American garrison of several thousand surrendered.
Battle of White Plains, October 28, 1776 **(150)** [229]
Howe's troops drive Washington's troops from high ground.
Battle of Forts Clinton and Montgomery, October 6, 1777 **(150)** [183]
British forces capture two American-held forts in Highlands of Hudson River Valley.
Battle of Brier Creek, March 3, 1779 **(150)** [16]
Large Patriot force attacked by surprise.
Battle of Fishing Creek, August 18, 1780 **(150)** [16]
Tarleton surprises Thomas Sumter's militia company.
Battle of Oriskany, August 6, 1777 **(147)** [93]
Loyalists and Indians ambush 800 Patriot militia and Indians.
Battle of Stono Ferry, June 20, 1779 **(147)** [119]
Rearguard of retreating British expedition hold off assault by Patriot militia.

Of these 25 battles, only Ramsour's Mill is considered a decisive American victory.

OTHER FAMOUS BATTLES OF THE AMERICAN REVOLUTION

Battle of Groton Heights, September 6, 1781 **(145)**
Battle of Bemis Heights, October 7, 1777 **(130)**
Battle of Hobkirk's Hill, April 25, 1781 **(126)**
Battles of Lexington and Concord, April 19, 1775 **(90)**
Battle of Kings Mountain, October 7, 1780 **(90)**
Siege of Yorktown, September 28-October 19, 1781 **(90)**
Battle of Cowpens, January 17, 1781 **(72)**
Battle of Springfield, June 23, 1780 **(64)**
Battle of Princeton, January 3, 1777 **(43)**
Battle of Trenton, December 26, 1777 **(12)**

The most comprehensive source of casualty numbers is Howard H. Peckham's *The Toll of Independence-Engagements and Battle Casualties of the American Revolution*, (The University of Chicago Press, 1974). This list is based on Peckham's figures of Americans killed and wounded. Based on records for 1,331 military and 218 naval engagements, Peckham concluded that 7,174 were killed and

8,241 were wounded during the eight-year war. Missing and captured could substantially increase the totals.

The Revolutionary War is second only to the Civil War in deaths relative to population. The British killed and wounded totals are from multiple primary sources collected by Todd Andrik.* Casualty figures during the Revolutionary War were often used as propaganda. They are still debated, and do not reflect on the outcome of the battle.

*Andrlik, Todd, "The 25 Deadliest Battles of the American Revolution," *Journal of the American Revolution*, May 13, 2014

Appendix F

DISTRIBUTION OF THE FORCES AT YORKTOWN, 1781

American Army: 9,150

- Continentals 350 officers and 5,500 men (return of 9/26/1781, including 411 sick) [includes Lafayette's forces and other reinforcements who joined along the march]
- Militia 3,300 officers and men

French Army: 9,300

- Rochambeau's forces 425 officers and 5,300 men (return of 11/11/1781, including 741 detached and 427 sick)
- Saint-Simon's forces 225 officers and 3,300 men (including 800 Marines)

French Navy: 28,400

- French Marines 5,200 officers and men (minus about 800 Marines at Gloucester)
- Ship crews 24,000 officers and men (18,000 under de Grasse, 6,000 under Barras)

British forces: 9,700

- 15 September 8,885 effectives, plus 840 naval personnel
- 19 October 7,247 rank and file (4,750 fit for duty), plus 840 naval personnel for a total of 8,100 rank and file at surrender. The force comprised 4,418 British troops, 1,900 German auxiliaries, and 800 Loyalists (of whom 142 from North Carolina did not surrender). The vast majority of the missing 1,600 men were casualties.

Source: The US National Park Service, The Washington-Rochambeau Revolutionary Route, Statement of National Significance, Revised Draft Report, January 30, 2003

Index

C

I

J

N

About the Author

Bob Mayers thrives on discovering facts about the American Revolution not found in the work of earlier writers. As the descendant of patriot soldier Corporal John Allison, the revolution is personal to him.

His on-site visits to battlefields, encampments and places of many critical events of the Revolutionary War shed light on revered places that have been lost or neglected by history, places where patriots fought and died but are unmarked, shrouded in mystery, distorted by mythology and unknown even to local people.

These field trips, combined with research into original documents and oral accounts passed down in his family through many generations, bring the history alive. His readers often comment that they regret that during their school days that they tuned out history as distant and dull. His writing can be enjoyed by average readers and not just hardcore history or genealogy fans.

Bob is an active member of ten historical societies and is a frequent speaker and contributor to their publications. His service as a combat officer in both the Navy and the Marine Corps provides him with a deeper perspective of the many battles depicted in his work. He is a graduate of Rutgers University and served as an adjunct professor at Seton Hall University.